WALTER BENJAMIN AND
THE IDEA OF NATURAL HISTORY

Cultural Memory | *in the Present*

Hent de Vries, Editor

WALTER BENJAMIN AND THE IDEA OF NATURAL HISTORY

Eli Friedlander

STANFORD UNIVERSITY PRESS
Stanford, California

Stanford University Press
Stanford, California

© 2024 by Eli Friedlander. All rights reserved.

Printed in the United States of America on acid-free, archival-quality paper

Library of Congress Cataloging-in-Publication Data
Names: Friedlander, Eli, author.
Title: Walter Benjamin and the idea of natural history / Eli Friedlander.
Other titles: Cultural memory in the present.
Description: Stanford, California : Stanford University Press, 2024. | Series: Cultural memory in the present | Includes bibliographical references and index.
Identifiers: LCCN 2023017359 (print) | LCCN 2023017360 (ebook) |
  ISBN 9781503636552 (cloth) | ISBN 9781503637702 (paperback) |
  ISBN 9781503637719 (epub)
Subjects: LCSH: Benjamin, Walter, 1892-1940. | Natural history—Philosophy. | Environmental psychology.
Classification: LCC B3209.B584 F755 2024 (print) | LCC B3209.B584 (ebook) |
  DDC 201/.6508—dc23/eng/20230912
LC record available at https://lccn.loc.gov/2023017359
LC ebook record available at https://lccn.loc.gov/2023017360

Cover design: Michele Wetherbee
Cover photograph: Bernd and Hilla Becher, Fördertürme, Belgien, Frankreich *(Winding Towers, Belgium, France)*, 1967–1988 gelatin silver print; nine, overall: 67 9/16 x 55 1/2 in. (171.61 x 140.97 cm) San Francisco Museum of Modern Art, The Doris and Donald Fisher Collection at the San Francisco Museum of Modern Art © Estate of Bernd and Hilla Becher

Contents

Acknowledgments ix

INTRODUCTION
The Natural in the Human 1

PART I
Nature in Language

1 God, Nature, and Man in Language 13
2 Naming Beauty 33
3 The Life and Afterlife of Words 45
4 The Life of Forms 65

PART II
Life and Fate

5 The Guilt and Innocence of Life 87
6 Fate, Redemption, and Hope in Love 101
7 Myth, Law, and Life in Common 119

PART III
Body and Corporeality

8 The Language of the Body and the Body of Language — 145

9 Acting Naturally — 164

PART IV
Primal History

10 "From the Pagan Context of Nature... into the Jewish Context of History" — 187

11 Matters of Memory — 206

12 First and Second Nature in Art — 228

PART V
The Image of the Contingent

13 Distorted Life — 251

Notes — 281

Bibliography — 311

Index — 317

Acknowledgments

Conversations with friends, colleagues, and students contributed over the years, directly and indirectly, subjectively and objectively, to the writing of this book. I taught parts of it in the philosophy department at Tel Aviv University, the School of Criticism and Theory at Cornell University, and the NYU German Department. I thank the students who participated in these seminars for their attentiveness, engagement, and patience with my often-hesitant approach to Benjamin's complex writings. Some of the chapters were presented in an early form at conferences of the research group Life and Mind: The Metamorphoses of the Kantian Moment in Philosophy. I greatly benefited from the responses of many who took regular part in the meetings of that project: James Conant, Hent de Vries, Paul Franks, Ido Geiger, Eva Geulen, Keren Gorodeisky, Johannes Haag, Arata Hamawaki, Thomas Khurana, Christoph Koenig, Christian Martin, Jean-Philippe Narboux, Benjamin Pollock, and David Wellbery. I also had many fruitful meetings with Lindsay Waters, whose commitment to the publication in English of Benjamin's writing is admirable.

For many years now I have been conducting a reading and discussion group with graduate students at Tel Aviv University. Some completed their theses and dissertations, other joined, but to my great pleasure most continued to attend our meetings every other week even after returning from doctoral studies or postdoctoral stays abroad. Among the "older generation" I single out the significant conversations on Benjamin I had with Jonathan

Soen, Yuval Kremnitzer, and Amichai Amit. I greatly benefited from discussions of many issues touching on the concerns of the book with them, as well as with Moran Godess-Ricittelli, Amir Yaretzki, Noam Melamed, and Pioter Shmugliakov. I thank Yam Weinberg, for the intelligence with which she undertook research related to the last stages of writing, as well as for her help with the often-tedious work involved in completing the manuscript. Grants from the Israel Science Foundation and the German Israeli Foundation contributed generous financial support at various stages of the writing.

Hent de Vries's interest in and involvement with my work goes far beyond his role as editor of the Stanford University Press series Cultural Memory in the Present, in which this book on Benjamin is being published. I am grateful for his generous responses and for the inspiring conversations we have had in many different settings over the years, from Tel Aviv to Baltimore, Ithaca, and New York. I thank Erica Wetter for her support and commitment to making Stanford University Press a home for this book and Caroline McKusick for her assistance in bringing it to publication. Christine Gever did a wonderful job editing the manuscript.

I cherish my friendship with Ilit Ferber, which began with our common interest in Benjamin some twenty years ago and has only deepened since. I am grateful for her advice and responsiveness as well as for many thought-provoking conversations with her and with Noa Naaman-Zauderer and Ruth Ronen, dear friends who I am happy to also have as colleagues in the philosophy department at Tel Aviv University. Zvika Schwartzman's unfailing presence and intelligent responses have been for many years, and still are, a source of insight and encouragement.

The material conditions of my work included a table, a chair, and countless cups of coffee at café Meshoulash, where most of the writing of the book took place. Natan, Naama, and Muhamad will stand for everyone I have to thank for making this place so pleasant and inviting.

Michal, Omer, and Elam, whom I love so much, are a source of joy in my life. Elam's music, Omer's writing, and the ways they make for themselves in the world are truly inspiring. I draw comfort from happy reunions with my siblings David and Michal, with whom for some years now I also share the sadness in the absence of our kind and loving mother, Hagit. The love and affection of my father, Saul, and Orna mean a great deal to me; my father's critical acuity and sensibility as a historian especially made for many significant conversations on parts of this book.

After a failed attempt to cross the border from France to Spain at Portbou, Walter Benjamin committed suicide on September 26, 1940. Two years later, on or just after September 26, 1942, my father's parents attempted to cross the border from France to Switzerland near the town of Saint-Gingolph. They were arrested, turned into the Vichy police, and deported to Auschwitz, where they perished. The name I use most of the time, Eli, is short for Elhanan, a combination of Elli and Hans (Jan), the proper names of the grandparents I never met. I dedicate this book to their memory.

WALTER BENJAMIN AND
THE IDEA OF NATURAL HISTORY

INTRODUCTION

The Natural in the Human

We are, for sure, but *how* are we, natural beings? What does it mean that we, humans, belong to living nature? How does nature permeate, and how is it transformed by, human existence? And how far does the rule of natural life extend? In seeking answers to these questions, reflection avails itself of oppositions such as nature and spirit, rationality and animality, body and mind, natural life and history. These oppositions are often the source of simplifications in our conception of the natural in the human.[1]

Human beings are animals that belong to nature. And we might begin an investigation of what is animal in us by seeking something common to us human and other living beings. Yet this attempt to begin with the common almost inevitably distorts the natural dimension in human existence. The natural would be identified as an independent, self-contained aspect of our being, even if it is not narrowly understood in reductive naturalistic or scientific terms. And since we humans also have features distinguishing us from other creatures, these would be attributed to something over and above that common nature—say, to our reason. We would then seek ways to think how the two come together by asking how reason can assist us with the satisfaction of our natural side or how it can thwart natural inclinations for the sake of higher ends—as though we have something in common with the animal (call it organic, biological life) and then in addition to that a distinguishing characteristic, our rational capacity, which is capable of ordering, assisting, directing, binding, or limiting the animal condition.

We might also take a different approach and start from above, as it were, seeking the specific unity of the human *form of life*. It would then become clear that there is a qualitative transformation of natural life in human existence. This natural life in us might initially become evident in considering the all too human character of stages of life in childhood or old age. It will be present in the specific character of human desire and sexuality and in what love and death are for human beings. The specific inflection of our perception might not be reducible to a conceptual synthesis of a natural sensuous given, and our human habits wouldn't be accounted for merely by referring to conventions that build on unchangeable nature. Once we recognize the specificity of the human-natural in those dimensions of our life, it might be easier also to admit that there is nature in what is uniquely human, that is, what hardly has a correlate in other life-forms—say, language, history, art, and culture. A whole range of questions would then open up: What are forms of life in language, or what is the time of the natural historical? Do human creations—for example, works of literature or artistic styles—have a life, and what would it mean to think of the surroundings that "nourish" such a life? How does the register of life inflect collective existence, and is there something like a unique human form of suffering deriving from the very character of that natural life in us?

It is with such questions and with this orientation in mind that the present work turns to the thought of Walter Benjamin. Walter Benjamin's writings on language, the work of art, the body, fate and character, the social order, love, passion and action, history, and redemption form one of the deepest, most concrete and significant, and, I would add, most urgently pertinent philosophical elaborations of the natural in the human. It is the aim of the present work to show the continuity, rigor, and inner logic of Benjamin's thought on this fundamental theme.

This book is in one sense, then, pursuing the task I set myself in writing *Walter Benjamin: A Philosophical Portrait*. The earlier book expressed a conviction that Benjamin presents us with a unique configuration of philosophy, of a force that has not been sufficiently brought out in the interpretation of his writings. This conviction has only grown in the years since that first attempt. It was on the right track but still far from expressing the depth and rigor of Benjamin's thought. Thus it is not so much a change of view that led me to return to Benjamin but rather an intensification and concentration of what I could only view from afar. But there is also a significant difference in my approach here: I propose to address the unity of Benjamin's thought by pursuing a fundamental theme that runs through his work. The problem of nature in the human constitutes a cross section of Benjamin's thought, traversing it (meaning *all* of it) from a certain perspective. Isolating an aspect of Benjamin's thought allows me not only to bring out the tenacity of his questioning but also to devote attention to many details without losing the unifying momentum. It has also proved fruitful in illuminating anew his better-known works. The fruitfulness of this approach will, I hope, be proved in the novelty of the readings I propose.

The book is divided into five parts, each consisting of several chapters: "Nature in Language," "Life and Fate," "Body and Corporeality," "Primal History," and "The Image of the Contingent." The first part of the book is also the most abstract or philosophically fundamental. The chapters revolve around the question of the actualization of natural life in meaning. The idea that guides us is that the purposiveness of natural life has its highest end not in its own sphere but rather in the actualization of its significance. This end of life in meaning is the thread that guides me in reading of "On Language as Such and on the Language of Man," "The Concept of Criticism in German Romanticism," and "The Task of the Translator," as well as Benjamin's few yet important writings on painting and color. The first part of the book will also serve to develop Benjamin's speculative metaphysics of experience, or what I will also call, after Schelling, his metaphysical empiricism by way of reading the "Epistemo-Critical Foreword" of the *Origin of the German Trauerspiel*. It is to provide the armature or scaffolding by means of which to conceive of the turn toward the historically concrete that is so characteristic of his later writings.

Benjamin's early essay "On Language as Such and on the Language of Man" serves to articulate his vision of living nature and its presence in the language of man. In language as such, God, Nature, and Man come together. A higher, created nature is revealed as its expressive power is actualized in man's language. The essay also sets the stage for thinking how nature is present and expressed in human practices and products, and in particular in works of art. I will initially consider an exemplary case of naming nature in a human artistic practice by interpreting Benjamin's early forays into the nature of color and painting.

The reciprocal bond between life and art is central to Benjamin's dissertation on the Romantic concept of art criticism. In an epilogue to the work, Benjamin sets up an opposition between the reflective "enlivening" of the literary work in the Romantics and a wholly different model of the presence of *nature* in art: Goethe's understanding of art at its highest as having the task of revealing pure contents, ideals, or archetypes of true nature. Benjamin's own concept of critique, articulated in the opening pages of his essay "Goethe's Elective Affinities," will be presented as the overcoming of the fundamental opposition he sets up between the Romantics and Goethe.

One of the more striking expressions of the life of meaning is found in the famous essay "The Task of the Translator." There life is attributed, in a "nonmetaphorical sense," to a literary work. Translation is a vital nexus that actualizes the work's significance, identifying the work's life in terms of its inner history. The reflection on this historical life of meaning, distinguished from the understanding of life in terms of soul, sensibility, or the organic, allows Benjamin to introduce the all-important register of afterlife. In the afterlife of the work afforded by its translations, a higher, more than natural life, belonging to language as such can be revealed.

The reflection on the life of a literary work can itself be extended to the question of the life of an artistic *form*. It is in this context that we are to understand Benjamin's account of the natural-historical character of such a form as the baroque *Trauerspiel*, "the metaphysical content of which must appear not merely as something lying within but as something actively working and, like blood, pulsing through the body" (O 17). What is striking in Benjamin's take on this vital context is the way it is paired with a theory of (the presentation) of ideas. Rather than dissociating the vital movement from ideal eternal contents, Benjamin shows how to think of them as belonging together. As he puts it: "The task of interpreting works of art is to concentrate creaturely life in ideas. To establish the presence of that life" (SW 1:389).

The problem of actualizing nature in meaning must be considered in relation to the fulfillment of human life. This might require that we inquire first of all about the character of unfulfilled life. It is primarily through an investigation of the inner relation between nature in the human and fate, in the second part of this book, that we will clarify Benjamin's understanding of the *guilt* of mere, or unfulfilled, life. We will begin this investigation with Benjamin's essay "Fate and Character" and its elaboration of the duality of the natural guilt and natural innocence of life as they are reflected in tragedy and comedy.

The guilt and innocence of life pertain to the character of life as a whole. We can deepen our understanding of the presence of fate in human existence by considering what most clearly bears on the form of human life as a whole, namely, love. Benjamin's essay on Goethe's *Elective Affinities* is an investigation of the ways the mythical or primal register of fate is manifest in the vicissitudes of love. The essay also allows us to reflect on a context that is often addressed in thinking of the vitality of existence—namely, the understanding of the creativity of genius as well as the affinity between the work of art and the artist's own life.

The organization of life in society through law and the violence inherent in it constitute a further dimension of Benjamin's reflection on the presence of nature in human existence. We read Benjamin's "Toward the Critique of Violence" so as to bring out the sense in which the violence of the law belongs to the order of fate—how law can be an instrument of fate. Fate is often taken to be a concept of the ancient world, belonging to an age when mythology was, as it were, a "worldview." The achievement of a written and public body of laws appears to be a victory over this conception of the world in which unwritten laws ruled human existence. Yet for Benjamin, the mythical (which should not be confused with "mythology") can permeate the space of life. Mythical violence and the law are intertwined—even, or particularly, in the modern state—precisely in order to make fate present in human life *through* law.

One of the most important and most intuitive aspects of the way we are natural beings is our having a body. Our discussion of life and nature will be extended and reconceived in the third part of this book through Benjamin's understanding of the body and corporeality. The nature of perception, the sense of space, gesture and movement, behavior, the erotic and sexuality, and character, as well as action, all will be systematically reoriented in relation to our bodily existence. A short account of Benjamin's "Outline of the Psycho-physical Problem" will serve to establish how, while rejecting the dualism of mind and body, Benjamin introduces two aspects of their identity, which can be called, respectively, the "mind-bodily" and the "spiritual-corporeal." As is the case with every aspect of Benjamin's thinking, identity is not a given but is to be actualized: It orients our bodily existence toward fulfillment. There will therefore be different yet related "vectors" of fulfillment, depending on whether we think in terms of the mind-bodily or the spiritual-corporeal.

With our consideration of the essay "On the Mimetic Faculty," we extend our discussion of corporeality and embodied existence so that it bears on and relates back to Benjamin's account of language. While still concerned with how human language can be conceived of as realizing creaturely nature, the essay also enunciates the involvement of human corporeality in meaning. Mimetic behavior brings out the role of the body in language and at the same time opens to what Benjamin calls "the body of language." The language of the body and the body of language come together in the understanding that the production of signs that make meaning visible and audible involves a mimetic identification. We do not operate with arbitrary dead signs that we then pair with objects and concepts. The production of signs must be conceived of as essential to the possibility of the recognition of significance. We do not breath life into them; they are permeated with the life we partake in.

Our analysis of body and corporeality, as well as the mimetic faculty, leads us to inquire about the place of such concepts as action, gesture, behavior, activity, and habit in Benjamin. Each should be given a distinct analysis under what I will call Benjamin's account of action. The character of the practical, of human intelligent activity, is often articulated in terms of the concepts of intention, of purpose or end, as well as the choice of means to further this or that end. Benjamin's concept of action needs to be distinguished from the account that makes purpose the ultimate determinative ground of action. We will show the different forms in which the means-end structure is avoided in Benjamin's thought, leading to an understanding of action not in relation to the representation of a purpose but to what Benjamin calls the "image." It is in the analysis of the way that an action deploys its image and unfolds in consuming it that we will extend the understanding of corporeality to the "innervation" of the collective.

In the fourth part of the book, I bring together many of the themes developed in previous parts to bear on the question of historical life. It is centered on reading the theoretical parts of the *Passagenwerk* that erect what Benjamin calls the "thin philosophical scaffolding" of the construction with the most historically concrete material content. The primary focus in this part is on convolutes K and N. This part of the book differs from the others in a further respect: it seeks to position systematically Benjamin's thought in relation to figures central to its articulation, namely, Goethe, Bergson, and to some extent Marx.

One of the interesting indications of the reformulation of the relation between the natural and the historical is Benjamin's appropriation of Goethe's method of investigation of nature. In his own concept of origin, already developed in the *Trauerspiel* book, as well as in the *Arcades Project*," Benjamin sees himself in effect as extracting the concept of "*ur*-phenomenon" from the "pagan context of nature" and bringing it into the "Jewish contexts of history." Certainly the attempt to think of the human form of life in analogy with the metamorphosis of plants raises difficult questions. In particular, does this translation of the principles of investigation of nature to the context of history distinguish history from nature? Or does it show that there is in the historical a dimension of the natural?

Even though the register of life and nature is omnipresent in Benjamin's writing, we also find a very distinct attempt to separate himself from so-called vitalist philosophy. Benjamin's relation to Bergson is, I will argue, a special case. I will follow indications that Benjamin seeks to translate Bergson's conception of memory into his own account of history as remembrance. Bergson's theory of the pure memory of the individual enables Benjamin to characterize the historical, involuntary memory of humanity. The mediating figure that will allow us to form a bridge between Benjamin and Bergson's vitalism, and to whom Benjamin relates explicitly at crucial junctures of the *Arcades Project*, is Proust.

What vitalism might lack most is an understanding of the dialectical relation of technology and nature in the production of life. Instead of setting technology and nature against each other, what is at issue in Benjamin is the possibility of incorporating technology into the natural life of human beings, of conceiving how technology opens nature anew. For Benjamin the question is always what forms of nature are revealed in the new technology: "Technology is always revealing nature from a new perspective" (A 392 [K2a,1]). Our consideration of technology and its transformation will serve to bring out how an investigation of the culture, of the superstructure, expresses the economic base. It will provide indications of the tendencies in relation to which the class struggle may be organized. Our case study of this complex relation between nature and technology will be Benjamin's account of the transformation of the very idea of art in the emergence of the technology of photography and film.

With our consideration of "Paris, Capital of the Nineteenth Century," the exposés of the *Arcades Project*, we reach the most concrete part of our investigation of Benjamin's thought. It is one thing to interpret Benjamin's theory of the ordering of the contingent, factual, and transitory material for the presentation of ideas, but it is a totally different thing to make clear how in the *Arcades Project* he presents the configuration of the historical *in concreto*.

Our reading of the exposés must present as clearly and concretely as possible what Benjamin calls the "primal history" of the nineteenth century. This is tantamount to showing the presence of myth and how it is confronted in the emergence into the freedom of history. The primal or mythical, as is already evident, is not confined to the character of early human societies or primitive forms of human existence. The force of Benjamin's view of primal history lies in the understanding that the mythical is ever present, always to be overcome in the emergence into historical existence.

The resistance to treating Benjamin's corpus of writings as philosophy is both surprising and understandable. It is surprising if we reflect on the terms that come into play in his work: truth, world, nature, language, judgment, name, categories, orders, identity, existence, degrees of being, intention, extensive and intensive universality, creation, revelation, redemption, religion and metaphysics, reflection, critique, idea and ideal, form and content, pure content, archetype, symbolic knowledge, material content and truth content, beauty, character, consciousness, spirit, body, corporeality, pleasure and pain, eros and sexuality, action, habit, means and ends, history, dialectic, materialism, fate, law, force and violence, justice, image, time, memory, color, imagination, fantasy, education, tragedy and comedy, experience, commodity, and capitalism. But it is also understandable that there is some resistance to calling Benjamin a philosopher—perhaps because he wrote essays on Kafka, Brecht, Karl Kraus, Proust, and Baudelaire, but more likely because he wrote on toys, food, children's books, Mickey Mouse, and Charlie Chaplin as well as writing radio plays for children and an endless number of reviews of books published in newspapers and journals during the twenties and thirties, and of course because of the incomplete project, which contains a mass of material on fashion and collecting, on idleness and prostitution, on the streets of Paris and world exhibitions. Or maybe it is all just too much. How can a person write with depth and rigor on so many matters? Wouldn't this, by itself, be proof that he is merely skimming the surface of things? Some would go so far as to say that Benjamin's writing not only lacks the consistency of a weighty philosophical treatise but tries to make inconsistency and contradiction into a virtue.

Given such an orientation toward Benjamin's writing, the philosophical unity I aim to present would appear to be a speculative reconstruction of what can at most be called a "Benjaminian" philosophy, which, in fact, was never elaborated in that way in the corpus of his writings. No doubt my sense of the unity of Benjamin's thought is informed by other work I have done, primarily on Wittgenstein and Schelling. Yet here I rarely stray from Benjamin's texts. I do not take myself to be "filling in the blanks," as it were, with ideas of my own. Every insight, every advance of understanding, is the result of a close and patient reading of Benjamin. I think of the chapters of this book as a series of commentaries: commentary need not forego new insight, and I hope that what follows is a transformation, even a radical revision, of received views of Benjamin. I will deny only that such insights are the result of inventive readings.

My method can be further explained by considering another familiar problem in writing on Benjamin: call it the temptation to quote. Benjamin methodically uses quotations "without quotation marks." For us the problem might very well be how to *avoid* quoting. Quoting that parades as explanation can only lead to repeating formulas rather than reaching any deeper understanding. We need to overcome the tendency to hold to Benjamin's words and formulations as though they constitute an explanatory ground level that merely needs to be mentioned to gain assent. Consider Benjamin's references to the passing character of the dialectical image. We can take it as needing no more explanation when someone says that he has spotted a rare bird that flew over the field and disappeared. But is there *anything* clear in just repeating that an image of history fleets by never to be seen again? Or should we just affirm, without further ado, that Benjamin seeks to explode the temporal continuum, as though it is clear at all what that could mean? We surely have various pictures in mind when hearing such things, but these are mostly obstacles to understanding and can only lead to wide-eyed fascination, to using Benjamin's words as incantations and remaining with the *frisson* of the enigmatic. This is why, while not foregoing quotation, I will generally try to translate Benjamin's often highly concentrated language in the most analytical and precise way of which I am capable.

PART I

Nature in Language

ONE

God, Nature, and Man in Language

The beginning of our investigation of the natural in the human is not the easiest entry point into Benjamin's thought, but it is the most fundamental. We will open with language and ask how nature is in language. The best way to initially raise this question is through Benjamin's early and difficult essay "On Language as Such and on the Language of Man." In discussing this essay, commentators sometimes avail themselves of Benjamin's reading of the opening chapters of Genesis offered in it. It is therefore all the more important, given the orientation of this book, to show how a philosophically rigorous conception of language is articulated, even in broad outlines, while foregoing, for the most part, the scriptural "crutches." Only in the last part of the chapter will we consider how its themes are echoed in Benjamin's reading of Genesis.

The three traditional domains of metaphysics are world (nature), that is, rational cosmology; man, or rational psychology; and God, or rational theology. There are different variations on the ordering of these realms: we could articulate the relation of God to nature through the concept of creation or, with Spinoza, deny the createdness of the world ex nihilo and identify God and nature, positioning human beings as a mode of the one substance, God or nature; or we might, with Kant, think of the three as regulative ideas and limit knowledge to phenomenal nature.

In order to recognize how Benjamin's thought bears on these considerations, we must then ask ourselves what is his way of establishing the separateness of these three dimensions, as well as his understanding of the coming together of world, man, and God. The title of the essay suggests the central role of language in regard to these three. Recognizing how language is the *medium* in which they come together requires an elaborate explanation, and it is the purpose of the present chapter to lay it out. But at the outset we should stress that language is not conceived of as one particular field of human activity. Indeed, the peculiar title of the essay suggests an initial distinction between "the language of man" and "language as such," so that properly recognizing what is at issue requires first articulating the nature of language as such and then understanding how human activity in and with language partakes in it.

What is language if it is to be a medium in which God, man, and world meet? Clearly these are not merely *represented* in human language. An initial, somewhat simplistic formulation that might nevertheless provide some orientation would be that if language as such is that medium of convergence, then it must be present, albeit in different ways, in God, in nature, and in man. The Word is that by which God is said to create the world; it is also the medium through which nature is expressive of this origin, and it is that through which man actualizes the expression of nature and thus partakes in creation. There will be different aspects of language, depending on whether we take it as the medium of creation, of expression, or of actualization. Let us define "language as such" as that which encompasses these three aspects. It follows that the convergence of God, nature, and man in language is not a given but rather involves a task of man. There is no given external or internal relation between the three registers; instead we must think of their coming together as a problem, a task of actualization of meaning.[1] In other words, it is necessary just as much to insist that neither dimension is reducible to the other(s) as it is to understand how only through language do they come together in the actualization of meaning.

Even this cursory formulation allows us to see that the proper understanding of language as medium suggests that it has an inherent temporality: not a temporal relation represented in language but a time of Being coming to itself in language. Think once more of the theological model. The origin, or the dimension of the past, is what we have called creation. The full actualization of that original character can be called the Now of revelation. But it is accessible only through that actualization of the expressive character of nature by man, in the language of man. It is a *task* that establishes the form of the future as redeeming nature by way of man's actualization of it.[2] Temporality that belongs to Being as such is not captured by our common representation of past, present, and future. We might wish to speak of primal time (or "ages," as Schelling calls these dimensions): the primal past, or creation; the primal present, or revelation; and the primal future, or redemption.

Language as Communication and Medium

In order to find an entry point and a direction for addressing the complexities of the essay, we will follow the transformation of the notion of communication in its opening paragraphs. Our intuitive understanding of communication (*Mitteilung*) usually involves a threefold structure in which we distinguish the one who communicates, the content communicated, and the one to whom the communication is addressed. The opening of the essay is in many ways an attempt to recast these presuppositions and thus establish a new concept of communication that will best express the idea of the mediality of language, presenting language as a self-communicating medium. As Benjamin puts it: "All language communicates itself in itself; it is in the purest sense the 'medium' of the communication" (EW 253).

In order to introduce us to the idea of language as a self-communicating medium, Benjamin asks us, to start with, to consider a human practice (such as law, music, sculpture, etc.). Even ordinarily we speak of such practices as languages. This may be clearest in the case of an artistic practice, such as painting, for example. When we speak of the "language of painting," we mean something like the medium in which paintings are made; here, medium would not merely refer to the material conditions for making a painting but also the conditions of possibility of painting, such as flatness, color, depth out of the surface, and so forth.

Or take the field of law, another example mentioned by Benjamin of a human practice that involves the use of language. It engages people in characteristic meaningful interactions: they judge, reason, justify, prosecute, defend, appeal, present evidence, consider such and such as testimony, and apportion punishment to guilt. Benjamin suggests that by considering such a field of activities, we can recognize in this multiplicity a reflection or expression of the unified or essential character of this human form of existence; think of this essential character as something like the unifying spirit or soul of the practice. Benjamin calls it "spiritual being" (*Geistige wesen*) and calls its corresponding manifestations in language the "linguistic being" (*Sprachliche wesen*).

The linguistic being, or language associated with a human practice, is not merely the sum total of various particular uses of language. There is an inner unity to this space of expression that is thereby characterized as *the* linguistic being. But initially at least we can presume that linguistic being only partly corresponds to spiritual being. Linguistic being only reflects certain aspects of the complete spiritual being; it reflects it to a degree. The different aspects of a practice, its multiple expressions, do not yield immediate insight into the deeper unity of the practice. But we might very well envision the possibility of bringing together the different uses in a way that allows us to recognize the essence of the practice in its language.

Put more generally, establishing relationships or revealing affinities between different expressions belonging to the space of linguistic being might allow us to recognize in linguistic being the reflection of spiritual unity. We would then have, as it were, a full or fulfilled presence of spiritual being *in* linguistic being. In such fulfilled expression there would be an identity of linguistic and essential being. Starting from the differentiation of spiritual being and linguistic being, the assertion of their identity can appear paradoxical (for isn't language distinct from reality itself and only refers to it?). Yet our analysis should aim to articulate the possibility of this ultimate identity by understanding how language can be ordered so as to completely reflect in itself the essence that expresses itself in it.

We have taken as our example a specific human practice and asked whether its essence can be fully reflected in its linguistic being. Presumably, we could even take a complete spoken language—say, the German language—and ask ourselves whether and how we can realize and recognize in it something of a spiritual unity—say, the German spirit. Again, this would not be reflected if we merely considered dispersed assertions and language uses without further ado. The linguistic being would not be merely the various things that can be said in German but also a form of unity that emerges in considering what is shown by bringing these ways of saying together: "The German language ... is by no means the expression of everything that we could—theoretically— express *through* it, but is the direct expression of that which communicates *itself* in it" (EW 252).[3]

This last quote provides us with some terminology that can summarize our considerations and advance our understanding:

(a) What is communicated *through* language / *in* language.

We can look at language as a means for speakers who use it to communicate factual contents to others. These contents are communicated *by means of* language. Language, then, has an instrumental status: it is a means for the purpose of communicating between speakers about the world. Those speakers communicate *through* language. But as we saw in elucidating the distinction and relation between linguistic being and spiritual being, we can also consider what is recognized *in* language—that is, by considering the language of a practice as a whole and asking about the unified manifestations in it of a spiritual being. If the specific communications in language are what we *say* through it, here we would think of what reveals or *shows itself* in it. This leads us to the following distinction.

(b) What *we* communicate by means of language / what communicates *itself* in language.

We speakers of language communicate various contents *through* it. We can choose what to say to each other; we are in control of the communication, and language is at our service. But if we consider what is revealed *in* language, then the focus is not on what *we* say. We have to recognize what expresses itself in language. The spiritual being manifests *itself* in and as a unity of language. Here we do not consider the assertions of speakers but rather must be attuned to what communicates itself in language. While we can definitely identify conscious or self-conscious intentions on the part of the speakers in the various assertions made, the same cannot be said about the linguistic being. It reveals *itself* in an ordering of assertions belonging to a field of linguistic practice. In other words, linguistic being is not attributed to a speaker of language but is the expression of what is essential, of spiritual being. If we consider communication at this fundamental level, we can begin to understand why Benjamin would claim that "there is no speaker of languages" (EW 253).

(c) *What* is communicated / The language of the communication.

This leads us to the most difficult point that Benjamin makes, which I will only be able to elucidate partially at this point. If we adopt the standpoint in which languages have no speakers, can we retain the common distinction we make between the content of a communication and the language in which it is communicated? This separation of language and content is evident if we consider the same assertion in two different languages, for example, "Pass me the salt" and "Passez moi le sel." But this distinction is problematized if we consider that spiritual being expresses itself. That expression is not something added over and above spiritual being (which is not to be understood on the model of a speaker that communicates something other than itself). Spiritual being communicates itself, meaning communication is essential to it. Language, therefore, is not a medium external to spiritual being; rather, spiritual being has the character of language. It is not as though we have on one side an extralinguistic essence, something that has nothing to do with language, and on the other its "appearance" in another place that we call its language. Instead, essence is already *essentially* communication, already language. Thus Benjamin writes: "Language communicates the linguistic being of things. The clearest manifestation of this being, however, is language itself. The answer to the question "*What* does language communicate?" is therefore: *"All language communicates itself"*" (EW 253). Language is the medium of its own communication, a self-communicating medium, a medium of communication of itself in itself.[4]

The Communication of Nature

With these last distinctions in mind, it might be easier to accept a further extension of the concept of language, central to Benjamin's essay—namely, to the communication of essential being in nature, that is, to the expressive character of nature. What would it be to think of the different domains of nature as partaking in language? Is it like attributing lawfulness to nature? Indeed, we do speak sometimes of the laws of nature as a language, but it would be strange to say that in these laws nature communicates itself. Natural phenomena may be governed by general laws, but those laws cannot be said to be the *expression* of essential being in nature. Laws hold of phenomena, but to speak of the expression of nature is to attribute to nature an inner life or tendency to make manifest its essence. Moreover, this expression does not take the form of a generalization, but rather, as an expression of essence, it has the character of an inner unity or a whole, a language.

If we take as a model our discussion of human practices, we could similarly speak of different phenomenal manifestations that pertain to a certain domain of nature and conceive of the way they can be ordered not in terms of general laws but as having an expressive unity, forming a whole; this would be the language of that domain of nature. Thus, to make things simple, we would have a language of matter, which is different from the laws of physics, and a language of the vegetal world, which presents it as an original unity expressing itself in the manifold phenomena of the vegetal world and different from a division into genera and species. Or, to take another example, there would be a language of color that is not captured, for example, by the principles of optics.

Just as we established a distinction between the specific assertions in a human practice and the language that manifests itself in gathering those assertions into a whole, we might say that with nature as well there is a need to bring together the phenomenal manifestations in order to recognize their expressive nature (as a language). We might have a variety of models to account for this kind of ordering of phenomena that is the expression of an underlying essential being. One such model, which will be described in greater detail in Chapter 10, is Goethe's scientific method.

Remaining with Benjamin's essay, however, and assuming the possibility of gathering phenomena so as to show the expression of essential being in nature, it is precisely at this point that we must raise the question of the place of human language in realizing the expression of nature. The realized form of the language of a domain of nature, its fulfilled expression, is not fully achieved by nature by itself, as it were. It is man's unique capacity to bring together phenomena into that kind of expressive unity in language.

In establishing the relation of the language of nature to the language of man, nature is not considered in Benjamin's essay in terms of how we represent it but rather in terms of how it communicates itself to man. It is not as though things speak to us, as though we have to listen to the wind and the surf; rather, as I will argue, all depends ultimately on recognizing in human language or significant human practices the linguistic being that is the expression of an essential being in nature. It might well be, for instance, that in order to recognize the spiritual essence of space we would not turn to the axioms and theorems of Euclidean geometry but to the human practices of sculpture and painting.

In sum, Benjamin's essay seeks to present human language as a medium of communication. But it is not a medium of communication of factual content from one speaker to another. Rather, in human language the languages of nature, the expression of essential nature, can be discerned and realized. In language, nature communicates itself to us. We are receptive to nature *in* our human language that is in our significant form of life. What shows itself in our being with language can be called the receptive dimension in human language. Just as Benjamin reconceives what receptivity to and in language is, he will rethink anew the spontaneity whose medium is language: it is not a matter of what we choose to say but of the actualization of what we are receptive to, of the forms of nature, in human language. Human language has the capacity to realize in words this communication and therefore, in some sense yet to be clarified, reveal fully or fulfill the tendency of essential being to communicate itself. Man partakes in the communication of living nature by giving it full expression in and through his own language. In human language, to paraphrase Goethe, "nature might finally fathom itself."

The Language of Man

Whereas the spiritual being of nature communicates itself as its language, man's essential being is to *have* language, that is, the language of words, of names and sentences. This suggests that man does not ultimately have a specific substantive essence, as it were, comparable to that of other natural beings. One might say that man's having a language is distinct from how language is attributed to essences in nature—not only because a plant is mute and man can speak but also because having language is of a different order altogether from essential being expressing itself *as* language.

One could argue that if having the language of words allows man to fulfill the communication of nature, then only in human language can we envisage the identity of spiritual being and linguistic being. Language is man's defining characteristic and his essential being is therefore a linguistic one. More precisely, man's spiritual being is language because in it he can actualize the communication of nature. Only in human language can language as such fully be a medium of communication of itself, communicate itself without residue.

If the expression of nature is fully realized in the language of man, then, conversely, we could say that man answers his calling by giving expression to nature, by realizing in his language the identity of the spiritual being and linguistic being of nature. This identity is not expressed in acts of judgment but rather in naming. Naming, Benjamin writes, is "not only the ultimate exclamation [*Ausruf*], but also the true calling [*Anruf*] of language" (EW 256; translation modified). In other words, man's calling is to name nature, and in naming it, he both realizes the communication of nature and expresses his own true being: "Thus, in the name appears the essential law of language, according to which to express [*aussprechen*] oneself and to address [*ansprechen*] all else is the same" (EW 256).

The radical claim implied by this relation between man and nature, between the self-fulfillment of man and the emergence of a significant world in naming, must be explicated gradually. To start with, we can ask what is it that is "added" to the languages of nature by the human expressive capacity to name nature? Surely the difference cannot be captured in terms of additional facts or objects. Different forms in nature are not merely reflected in separate domains of human language but are gathered or come together in the human form of life in language. In human language the forms of nature come together in the concrete unity of a *world*. Naming, then, would express what things are in their belonging to one's world. The realization of essences is in their belonging together in the wholeness of a significant human world.

To clarify, consider Benjamin's distinction between the extensive and the intensive universality of human language. Calling human language extensively universal reflects our capacity to represent everything in language. Calling it intensively universal means that language can sum up in itself the forms of nature and express their unity as world; intensive universality is a matter of degrees of expression. We can conceive of a scale of nature, of the different orders of matter—the vegetal and the animal—understood in terms of degrees of expression, degrees of clarity of the communication of nature as a whole in each such order: "The differences between languages," Benjamin writes, "are those of media that are distinguished, as it were, by their density—which is to say, gradually" (EW 257). This figure of gradation not only serves to identify each language with a medium of specific density but also allows us to conceive of a communication running through all of the orders of nature, each time refracted differently by the density of the medium through which it is "passing." There is no specific message that is passed; instead the "content" of the communication is, at each level, the language of that order of beings as it takes up the communication and expresses in its own language the lower orders of the hierarchy. As Benjamin puts it at the end of the essay: "The language of a being is the medium in which its spiritual essence communicates itself. The uninterrupted flow of this communication runs through the whole of nature, from the lowest form of existence to man, and from man to God.... The language of nature is comparable to a secret password that each sentry passes to the next in his own language, but the content of the password is the sentry's language itself. All higher language is translation of the lower, until in the clarity the word of God unfolds, which is the unity of this movement of language" (EW 267; translation modified).

Translation and Ontology

As may further be gleaned from this last quote, the concept of translation is introduced in "the deepest stratum of linguistic theory" (EW 261) to elucidate the idea of intensive universality. That deepest stratum relates translation and the languages of *nature*. Benjamin's famous essay "The Task of the Translator" can hardly be understood if it is not seen as continuous with the considerations of the earlier essay on language, where translation is a concept of *ontology*: "But for receptivity and spontaneity together, found uniquely bound as they are only in the linguistic realm, language has its own word.... It is the translation of the language of things into that of man" (EW 261; translation modified).

It is not as the synthesis of concepts and intuitions but as the translation of forms constituting thereby a hierarchical order that we are to articulate the unity of receptivity and spontaneity in language. In an intensive scale of languages of nature, the lower is taken up in being *translated* in the higher. A higher language is receptive to a lower language of nature by incorporating it in itself. "Translation is the carrying over of one language into another through a continuum of transformations. Translation passes through continua of transformation, not abstract regions of identity and similarity" (EW 261; translation modified). This last distinction between regions of similarity and continua of transformations is key to understanding the difference between the subsumption of lower concepts under higher concepts and a hierarchical order of forms. The higher has taken the lower into itself and conserves it, transformed or translated. The lower is expressed in the language of the higher. The lower is echoed, as it were, in the higher. Thus, take for example the language of matter: it is not merely duplicated in the language of organic nature but transformed in serving a higher order that limits it. It is this ordered and limited takeover of matter in a higher rung of nature that we can model on translation, the translation of the language of matter into the language of the organic.[5] We will return to this point in Chapter 4.

Our account of naming must be reconceived in light of this vertical sense of forms of life or in terms of the translation of nature into the human form of life. We should not take "naming nature" to be an external relation between man and nonhuman nature; rather, it must be explicated in terms of the meaningful realization of nature *in* the human form of life. Put differently, in our account, it seems, we have neglected to reflect on nature in the human. In the hierarchy through which we think of meaning fulfillment in naming, we do not have a leap from the mute languages of nonhuman nature to the word language of man. Instead, the natural in the human is that highest rung in the hierarchy of languages. In particular, we would account for the natural capacities of a human being—for instance, perceptual capacities or bodily imitation—as higher languages in which we can envisage the summation of nature.

Revelation

Revelation, while no doubt a concept of religion, also belongs to the metaphysical framework of language Benjamin develops. It is introduced through the consideration of the identity of linguistic being and spiritual being that can be actualized in the language of man: "The equation of spiritual and linguistic being is of such great metaphysical moment to linguistic theory because it leads to the concept that has again and again, as if of its own accord, elevated itself to the center of the philosophy of language and constituted its most intimate connection with the philosophy of religion. This is the concept of revelation" (EW 257; translation modified).

In other words, the identity of linguistic and spiritual being actualized in the language of man is at the same time the revelation of the highest, of the absolute, in and through man. It introduces into the account of man's task to actualize the communication of nature in his language the third dimension as well—namely, God. "Revelation" is the self-presentation of the absolute in and through man's actualization of nature. The actualization of the languages of nature in the language of man, can be equally described as the revelation of the self-identity of the absolute in concrete existence. To put it somewhat paradoxically, it is not man who cognizes nature in language but rather God who cognizes himself through man's actualization of created nature.[6]

If we think of the matter through the identity of linguistic being and spiritual being, we recognize that the highest articulation of meaning in human language can be called the (self-)revelation of the absolute. As long as this identity of spiritual being and linguistic being is not realized, there will be a sense of the unexpressed, or even inexpressible in language, as though language were not adequate to express what is highest, the ultimate spiritual being: "Within all linguistic formation a conflict is waged between what is expressed and expressible and what is inexpressible and unexpressed. On considering this conflict, one sees at the same time, from the perspective of the inexpressible, the ultimate spiritual being" (EW 257).

Note that the inexpressible is relative to linguistic formations—that is, what is inexpressible in a lower language can receive expression in a higher one. This is essential in order to recognize that Benjamin disputes the common identification of the highest with what is inexpressible, the inverse proportionality between spiritual and linguistic being. His thesis is that "the deeper (that is, the more existent and real) the spirit, the more it is expressible and expressed . . . so that the expression that is linguistically most existent (that is most fixed) is linguistically most precise and definitive—in a word, the most expressed—is at the same time the purely spiritual" (EW 257).

Put somewhat differently, the ladder of languages of nature, the gradation of linguistic being in nature, is also a gradation of spiritual being, so that the highest, the most real, is revealed by the fulfilled expression of nature in man's language. The highest reality is that which does not involve negation or nonbeing. This also means that the mysterious or the unsayable in language, which is often associated with the highest spirituality, is shown to ultimately come to nothing: "The highest spiritual region of religion is (in the concept of revelation) at the same time the only one that does not know the inexpressible" (EW 257). The significance of this claim, not only for this essay but for the "spirit" in which to read Benjamin throughout, cannot be overestimated.

The Standpoint of Identity

The consideration of the standpoint of identity can yield further insight into the coming together of God, Nature, and Man in language. Linguistic being and spiritual being are distinct in the unrealized state of man's relation to creaturely nature and can be thought of as identical precisely in and through man's naming of nature in his own language. This naming is the way man partakes in creation, the way in which we are to recognize the revelation of the absolute in the world. If, for God, knowing and known are identical, then we could say that this ground of identity is to be *actualized* in existence, in the language of man. Through man's naming, that which is unique and self-identical (God) reveals itself in the existing. Identity is not a concept or category of finite *thinking* but rather stands for the self-revelation of what is absolute in and through man's naming the world.[7] Man actualizes in his language the expression of essential being into an identity of language and essence and thereby exists in the being of divine knowledge: "To be in the being of knowledge is to know" (SW 1:96).[8]

Benjamin relates the problem of identity to the task of actualization of meaning in a fragment composed around the same time as he wrote the essay on language.[9] What concerns him is the characterization of what is in reality "a-identical" (*Aidentische*) but nevertheless potentially identical (i.e., identical if actualized). In terms of the essay we are discussing, we could say that nature is a-identical. Man can actualize the a-identical—that is, partake in the identical, in the being of divine identity by naming nature.

Certainly any attempt to formulate the concept of identity through the standpoint of judgment—that is, as a proposition communicated through language—will yield a tautology. "The relation of tautology to the problem of identity," Benjamin writes, "arises with the attempt to conceive of the identity relation as a judgment" (SW 1:75; translation modified). Indeed, the standpoint of identity, connected as it is with naming as the actualization of the language of nature in the language of man, stands beyond judgment. Identity should not be confused with the subject-predicate relation in judgments (or be thought of as a limiting case of the category of substance and accident).

Identity marks the dimension of actualization of what there is, and therefore, as Benjamin puts it: "The identity relation is not reversible" (SW 1:76). Benjamin gives an example of this by considering the expression "I myself [*ich selbst*]." This is the expression of unrealized identity, insofar as "the 'myself' is, so to speak, only the inner shadow of the 'I.'" Here the self is only an example of a structure that must serve to think the realization of nature in the language of man. (This is why Benjamin uses, as Schelling does, the schema $A = A$, rather than $I = I$, which is Fichte's first principle.) The separation of the logic of identity from that of judgment is then the basis for Benjamin's claim that "a nonreversible relation exists that is not made logically possible by any of the three categories of relation (substance, causality, or reciprocity)" (SW 1:76).[10]

The separation of identity from the system of the categories suggests that actualization is not an "achievement" of thinking. In other words, if we think of this standpoint as characterizing what is highest (truth), it is not to be understood as the truth of a synthesis achievable by thinking. This might be why Benjamin writes in a letter to Scholem: "I would deny that there can be identity in thinking.... *I dispute that any "thinking" is the correlate of truth*" (C 106; my emphasis). This is a prefiguration of a well-known theme in Benjamin—namely, the intentionless character of truth. It will be further elaborated in our discussion of the relation of truth and knowledge in Chapter 4.

On Language as Such from the Sources of Judaism

In this second half of the chapter, I want to work through the details of Benjamin's interpretation of Genesis as developing the account of language whose dimensions we started to explore. As Benjamin himself stresses, it is not to be taken as biblical exegesis. In other words, every moment that is expressed through the story of creation must be capable of receiving a rigorous philosophical formulation. The schema of creation, revelation, and redemption will direct us in the reading of the coming together in language of God, Nature, and Man in Genesis 1–3.

THE THREEFOLD ACT OF CREATION

Benjamin draws our attention to the repeated threefold rhythm in the characterization of creation: "God said and it was"/ "God saw that it was good"/ "God named." Each of these moments, and the unity of the three, brings out the radical otherness of the standpoint of the divine, the absolute.

That is to say, each of the moments problematizes a fundamental duality that belongs to the finite intellect.

Thus the expression "God said and it was" shows the distinction between thinking something and its existence not to hold in God. For finite beings, thinking gives only possibility, whereas the actuality of what exists does not follow from its mere concept. In the expression "God saw that it was good" problematizes the distinction in the finite between the theoretical and the practical, between cognition and action, or between seeing and goodness (that belongs to acting). Finally, the expression "God named" points to a form of knowledge that is intuitive, that corresponds to the singularity of seeing (of an intuition). Naming is intuitive knowledge of the singular, whereas our cognition is discursive (or assumes the use of concepts).

THE CREATION OF MAN

In the second version of the story of creation, Benjamin notes, it is said that man is created from matter, from earth into which divine breath is breathed. This means that, as opposed to the rest of creation, man is not created by the divine Word. If the divine Word is in nature that which determines essential being, it follows that man, not being created by the Word, has no natural pre-given unity of essence. It is as though, when creation is immediate from the Word, essence is posited and subordinate to language. When it is mediated by matter, strangely enough, this doesn't imply a lower kind of creation but rather a release of man from the immediacy of divine creative power into a higher task: "Man who was not created from the word is now endowed with the *gift* of language, and he is elevated above nature" (EW 258). Language is set free in man: "God did not create man from the word, and he did not name him. He did not wish to subordinate him to language, but in man God liberated language, which has served *him* as medium of creation; he freed it from himself. God rested when he left his creative power to itself in man" (EW 259).

Moreover, the creation from breath suggests for Benjamin the material dimension of language, that is, the capacity to sound it. The spiritual being of man is his capacity to give language as such a material actuality in sounding it. While this points to the question of the nature of signs and symbols in language, the elaboration of the material basis of language is not directly addressed in the essay. We will return to it in Chapter 8.

THE TASK OF MAN

"God rested when he left his creative power to itself in man. This creativity relieved of its divine actuality became knowledge" (EW 259). Note first the idea of creation "relieved of its divine actuality." In releasing language in man, the actualization of the creative power that rests in nature becomes a task of man. But second, there must therefore be a sense in which in the medium of finite knowledge there is an analogue to the divine naming that seals the threefold act of creation. As Benjamin puts it: "Man is the knower in the same language in which God is the creator. God made things knowable in their names. Man, however, names them according to knowledge" (EW 259). This is the sense in which man is created in the image of God.

The creative word makes it possible to have knowledge of nature manifest in naming. As Benjamin puts it: "The creative word in [things] is the germ of the cognizing name" (EW 261). What is for man a task does not have a prior "solution" in divine naming. Divine naming is an immediate "expression of the identity in God of the word that creates and the name that knows, not the prior solution of the task that God expressly assigns to man himself: that of naming things" (EW 261–262).

Recall further that the threefold act of creation involved a unity of knowledge and value: "And he saw it was good." The understanding of naming in the finite must similarly show that naming is itself good. Knowledge and goodness are one in naming, insofar as they fulfill the task of man to actualize the essential being of nature. The identity of knowledge and value in finite naming can be called "being in significance." What it comes to for a finite being will become clearer when it is contrasted with the knowledge of good and evil, that is, knowledge after the Fall.

THE PROPER NAME OF A PERSON

Human beings name not only nature but also others of their kind. The proper name of a person, however, does not belong to the same logical category as the name of essential being in nature.[11] God did not name man, and similarly human beings do not name their kind in the way they name nature. The naming of another is simply the dedication of that human being to God, that is, to the task of naming the world. "The proper name is the communion of man with the *creative* word of God" (EW 260).

A proper name is distinct from a general concept in being a singular term.

This singularity of the name is nevertheless not to be identified with the uniqueness of a person, understood in terms of their subjectivity or something internal to that person. Nor does the singularity of the name result from an act of baptism causally relating it to the person. Benjamin implies that self-expression is precisely the same as naming one's world. Thus, what emerges as unique, as the correlate of the proper name, is *this* world. Indeed, the world opened to us in naming is unique in being fully actualized in meaning. The highest actuality is unique. One could say, after Wittgenstein, that singularity expresses itself in the world being my world.[12]

NAMING AND JUDGMENT

As with every other aspect of the story of Genesis, Benjamin seeks to think of the Fall in terms of his understanding of language. This rests on a contrast between naming and judging, which we must first clarify in broad terms. The mediateness and abstraction associated with judgment contrast with the concreteness and singularity of naming. While we speak of naming a being (an essence) or a person, judgment relates to states of affairs or facts. Thus, we can judge *that* the table is round, *that* the sky is blue. The object of judgment is a possible state of affairs that we judge to be the case. Moreover, we judge that such and such is the case—say, that the table is round—by subsuming, in the simplest case, an object (the table) under a concept (being round). The table can be what is immediately present in perception, but the concept determines the general perspective under which it is seen. We judge according to its shape (we could equally have produced a judgment as to its color, its size, its weight, what it is made of, and so on). In that sense the judgment by means of concepts is an impoverishment of the singular totality of a thing.

There is a further important issue to note in distinguishing name and judgment. When something is up for judgment, we ask ourselves whether such and such is the case; we can judge that it is the case or that it is not the case. In other words, with concepts we open the space of the possible and the distinction between the possible and what is the case. Naming is actuality (or actualization), but judgment contains within itself the polarity of correct and incorrect.

JUDGMENT AND THE POLARITY OF GOOD AND EVIL

The Fall, as the Bible tells it, results from Adam and Eve eating from the fruit of the Tree of Knowledge. Knowledge is knowledge of good and evil.[13] The introduction of two distinct and opposed contents, good and evil, is to be contrasted with what we identified as the goodness of naming as such. The latter is tantamount to actualizing the language of nature. It is not as though the account of human language has to do with meaning and that apart from this there is another dimension of value adding to the factual judgment a division into good and evil. Rather, the way in which the human being partakes in the identity of knowledge and goodness in God is by recognizing the goodness in and through the opening of significance in naming. Meaning that is at the same time value is what we call "the significant." Being in significance is what Benjamin identifies as the Edenic blissful state of man in language.

But this means that good and evil are not meaningful categories. They are not like green and red, which would divide a space of visible objects into those that are green, those that are red, and all the others (which would be, as it were, what corresponds to value-neutral possibilities). Whenever man finds himself in this dichotomy, articulating his actions in terms of a choice he has to make between good and evil possibilities, he has already abandoned the goodness of significance. Indeed, this is precisely why Benjamin argues that good and evil cannot be named: no concreteness corresponds to them. "The knowledge to which the snake seduces, the knowledge of good and evil, is nameless. It is vain (empty, void = *nichtig*) in the deepest sense, and this very knowledge is itself the only evil known to the paradisiacal state" (EW 263). In a deep sense, taking good and evil to be substantive categories would be to introduce emptiness, the nothing, into language. In other words, the threat to our meaningful existence in language will not be the danger of speaking falsely, but rather of falling into *nonsense*: "The knowledge of things resides in the name, whereas that of good and evil is, in the profound sense in which Kierkegaard uses the term, 'empty talk,' and knows only a purification and elevation, to which the man engaging in empty talk, the sinner, was therefore subjected: Judgment" (EW 263; translation modified).

To inquire about good and evil, as if they are contents to be "learned" from outside, is sinning that subjects the questioner to judgment. Benjamin works here with a double meaning of judgment: judgment as a particular unity of sense (expressed by a proposition, in contrast to a name) and being judged as "being tried" or "sentenced." The important insight here is that it is precisely abandoning naming in favor of judgment (rather than judging falsely) that precipitates guilt.[14] "The tree of knowledge stood in the garden of God not in virtue of any enlightenment it might have provided concerning good and evil but as emblem of judgment over the questioner. This immense irony marks the mythic origin of law" (EW 264). The mythic origin of law is evident in a strange reversal: it is not eating from the tree, gaining the knowledge of good and evil, that constitutes the guilt of man; rather, it is the very approach, the questioning that seeks knowledge—that is, seeks value in the form of judgment—that already makes one guilty. Guilt is not a matter of the infringement of the law, of not heeding the prohibition. It is the very approach to the law as providing knowledge of value, as if value was something external to be discovered, that makes one guilty. It is thinking of good and evil in terms of law as determining the content of good and its negation, the content of evil, that is the problem. This fatal bind of mythical guilt and the law is a central theme of "Critique of Violence," which will be discussed in Chapter 7.

THE PLURALITY OF LANGUAGES AND TRANSLATION

Since we have a linguistic interpretation of the Fall, it is not surprising that Benjamin relates that moment to the story of the tower of Babel and the emergence of the multiplicity of languages:

After the Fall, which, in making language mediate, laid the foundation for its multiplicity, linguistic confusion could be only a step away.... The subjection of language in empty talk is followed by the subjection of things in folly almost as its inevitable consequence. In this turning away from things, which was their subjection, the plan for the Tower of Babel came into being, and with it the confusion of tongues.[15] (EW 264–265; translation modified)

It would require some work to draw the connection between judgment, the plurality of languages, and linguistic confusion. The subjection of language that manifests itself in its permeation by empty talk means precisely making language into an instrument that man masters. What is lost is the receptivity to nature that expresses itself. Thus, we subject things to what we make of them (rather than fulfill nature expressing itself in them). But what must be kept in mind is that the very multiplicity of language is not in itself the source of confusion and emptiness. Indeed, it is only by admitting the condition of multiplicity that we can recognize the significance that translation acquires for Benjamin. It is precisely translation that is key to the actualization of meaning. This is indeed in line with the way Benjamin positions translation as a central concept through which we form a hierarchy of languages of nature, all the way to man. In other words, we are to conceive of the intensive scale not only as leading to man's language but also in such a way that translation between human languages forms a further rung to the fulfillment of language as such, or as Benjamin also calls it, the "pure language." We will return to this issue in Chapters 3 and 4.

THE SADNESS OF NATURE

The fall of man from his task of naming nature is the abandonment of nature. It remains in its unfulfilled state; therefore one can speak here of a new kind of muteness of nature. Initially we spoke of nature as soundless and of the way man sounds language in abiding by the task to give expression thereby to nature. But at this stage we conceive of the muteness of nature as a betrayal of man, who abandons his task. An important indication of the bond between man and nature is the fact that Benjamin would identify sadness, the affective mood correlative with it, as the mood of nature (rather than a feeling of human beings projected onto nature). When the expression of nature is the fundamental way of being-in-the-world, the mood of sadness can be said to permeate the world as it reveals itself for us: "It is a metaphysical truth that all nature would begin to lament if it were endowed with language" (EW 265). It is as though with the Fall the world is pervaded by sadness. The residual presence of expression in language, as nature is abandoned, is the mere sensuous breath, a mere lament.[16] Nevertheless, it is still man who would give expression to this affective face of nature. Since man no longer expresses nature in language, he is reduced to merely feeling it in the mood of mourning.

TWO

Naming Beauty

In Benjamin's metaphysics, human language is the medium of actualization of the communication of created nature. Unlike nonhuman nature, the human is not an essence; rather, human beings have the gift of language. The task of actualizing nature in language defines their unique place in nature. One is liable to adopt simplistic views of the actualization of nature in naming by forgetting that human beings also belong to the intensive hierarchy of nature. It is not as though nature parades in front of man, who stands apart from it (as we might be tempted to think given the picture of Adam naming the animals). It is important not to conceive of the actualization of nature as our tending to a nonhuman nature external to us. We do not relate to the movement of creative nature from the outside; rather, as man belongs to the hierarchy of nature, naming is to be understood as a summation, transformation, and translation of nature in the human form of life. Human beings have the capacity to transform that life, that nature, which expresses itself intensively in their existence.

In other words, we are to think of the movement of revelation of nature as expressing itself in a variety of human practices, in the life of the individual as well as in the social form of life and in different configurations at different stages of history. It is this space of manifestations of the life of nature in the human world—that is, a space internal to the human form of life, that is to be actualized. We find such expressions of the higher life of nature in cognition, perception, and human love, in action and in passion, and in forms of human dwelling. In the present chapter, we will be concerned with the way this task of naming nature is taken up in art and, more specifically, in the medium of painting, viewing painting as a language that actualizes and names nature.

The Colors of Fantasy

Recall that Benjamin conceives of an active as well as a receptive dimension of language. What is it to be receptive to the communication of nature in a human activity? What would it be for an artistic practice to open for us the naming of nature? And how would we identify the dimension of receptivity that betokens the presence of created nature in the work of art? In art there is, no doubt, an activity of forming. Through forming, the dimension of perfection is present in the work. The relation between beauty and perfection is well known and is often appealed to in the interpretation of classical art, especially with respect to the role played by the human figure as the ideal of beauty. One might nevertheless raise the question whether forming can lead "all the way" to perfection. After all, perfection is not a comparative term; we do not think of it as continuous with "better" but rather in superlative terms. Thinking of perfection additively would make it relative and would presuppose a concept of the object that allows of better and worse instantiations. Thus, while forming is essential to perfection in art, this is not to say that one can achieve perfection from below, as it were, merely through forming. But what else is there in the beauty of the work apart from what forming yields? Put in terms of the essay on language, the power of the beautiful work, its beauty as well as the possibility of naming nature in it, depends on holding in balance the active forming and a higher receptivity to what is not up to us to produce.

I want to elucidate this balance of the active and the receptive and ask about the counterpart to forming by considering in some detail the context in which beauty is most often identified, namely, the visual arts, and specifically painting. Benjamin's engagement with painting belongs with his early writings on color, mostly from the same period as the essay on language, and, as I will argue, is thematically related to it.[1] The writings on color and painting will serve to elucidate in a concrete context what naming nature in a human practice comes to.

Any attempt to characterize the receptive dimension—in particular, in terms of our awareness of color—must avoid the temptation of identifying it with the mere sensuous given, which in no way can underlie the spiritual dimension in which nature is named in painting. To take a central example, receptivity to color is relegated to sensuous matter both in Kant's "Transcendental Aesthetic" and in his Third Critique aesthetics. A color, according to Kant, cannot be called beautiful in itself purely, as it were, since it is mere sensation and has no form to it. The pleasure in aesthetic judgment is reflective (rather than being just pleasure in agreeable sensations). Moreover, the movement of reflection essentially involves a purposive form, which would seem to be completely lacking in color. Kant would undoubtably not deny that colors contribute to the beauty of a painting, but this would involve an appeal to the imagination that makes something of the given color and mediates its presence in the painting.

Imagination (*Einbildungskraft* or *Vorstellungskraft*) is a power (*Kraft*), a capacity of the subject. It is productive. The production or reproduction and combination of sensuous representations in the imagination will indeed distinguish its representations from the merely sensuous given. Yet precisely for that reason, it will not do to account for pure receptivity, for the counterpart of active forming. This is why it is crucial to note that Benjamin speaks of "Phantasie" in his account of color.[2] Translating *Phantasie* into English as "imagination" is extremely misleading, for the productive dimension of imagination is wholly absent in the colors of fantasy. Fantasy is not the capacity of a subject.

The colors of fantasy are not contents of perception but rather what Benjamin calls manifestations of pure vision. To follow Kant, the judgmental structure of perception relates the unity of self-consciousness to a correlative object, the product of the active synthesis of the manifold, in which we find an object of experience posited for consciousness. To be open to the manifestations of fantasy, however, depends neither on spontaneity of understanding nor on mere sensuous receptivity. It does not take the form of "*someone seeing something.*" As Margarethe says about her color dream in Benjamin's "The Rainbow: A Conversation about Fantasy," "I was not someone seeing; I was only the seeing itself. And what I saw . . . was not things, but only colors" (EW 215).[3]

"Color seeing" in fantasy does not have the form of judgment. It is not a perceptual experience articulated in terms of the category of substance and accident, like seeing the color of something. The identity in which there is neither independent seeing nor seen is the sense of color as pure quality, not the experience of an object that has qualities but a qualitative medium, as it were, without substantive support: "Color originates in the inmost core of fantasy precisely because it is quality alone; in no respect is it substance or does it refer to substance. Hence, one can say of color only that it is quality, not that it has quality" (EW 218).[4] Colors may be sensed as "separable" from objects, so to speak, as floating over the world.

One might further characterize this receptivity to the colors of fantasy as purely visual. Even if for a moment we discount the issue of the involvement of concepts in perception, there are elements in vision that belong to the sense of space given in touch. Thus, for instance, we have a perspectival understanding (of the small as far away, etc.) that in effect is "tactile"—understanding that has to do with distance, with the movement of our body. We interpret dark and bright as depth and surface, a judgment that again presupposes solid and opaque objects. We do not have this sense of distance with transparent colors: when, for example, we have two transparent colors in juxtaposition, we cannot tell which is above and which is below, which is far and which is close.

In attempting to distance ourselves from the conceptual unity of objects and their properties, that is, remaining with pure vision and the colors of fantasy, we are faced once again with the threat of falling into mere givenness. Yet Benjamin wants to think of a higher receptivity to the colors of fantasy as having a "spiritual" unity: "Color is something spiritual, something whose clarity is spiritual" (EW 211), he writes in the opening of "A Child's View of Color." The spiritual aspect of color is not that of a unity under a concept. "Color is One [*die Farbe ist das Einzelne*]" (SW 1:50). Oneness is not a form and should in no way be identified with uniformity, nor is it a unity that is the result of a conceptual synthesis out of prior elements. The oneness of the manifestations of fantasy could better be described as a mirror image of identity. Earlier, we discussed the centrality of identity in Benjamin's conception of language, as well as the separation he makes between identity and the categories. If we want to provide a model for oneness prior to multiplicity—that is, oneness of which multiplicity is only a delimitation—it would be space as an infinite given intuition.[5] To sense that color is one would mean that different color manifestations are delimitations of the oneness of color in something like the same way that spaces are delimitations of one and the same space.

Color can appear as one intuitive whole rather than as a multiplicity of particular colors falling under different color concepts. The individuation of colors as distinct and separate attributes, each in its own right, is a by-product of conceiving of colors as properties of the surface of individual objects. Thus the oneness pertaining to the colors of fantasy may be sought, conversely, in the possibility of their dissociation from the order of experience of objects—not that the receptivity to colors is an experience of mere dispersion, unanchored by any objective unity. Colors can be felt as belonging together because color is something "single." The spiritual character of color depends on our sensing how colors have among them elementary affinities by virtue of belonging to a single intuitive whole.

Consider a pure color space, a medium of color wholly distinct from objects. All colors belong together not because they are similar (in the sense of having a common element, for what common element is there between red and green?) but rather through all belonging to the whole of pure vision; it is not a similarity of preexisting individuals but original relatedness through belonging to a unique identity. In that sense, what is primary is not the individuation of elements but rather the differential, which always already involves relatedness. Instead of having two distinct individual colors and a transition between them, we sense the difference as primary. One could say that difference is prior to individuation. Such a sense of color can be described as a world of *nuance*: "The ... color of fantasy ... is without transitions and yet plays in numberless nuances ... a medium, pure quality of no substance, many-colored and yet one-colored [*einfarbig*], a colored filling-out of the *one* Infinite through fantasy" (EW 220; translation modified).

The primacy of the whole is also evident insofar as Benjamin replaces formation (*Gestaltung*), central to the activity of the productive imagination, with what he calls deformation (*Enstaltung*): "Fantasy has nothing to do with forms or formations.... We might rather describe the manifestations of fantasy as the de-formation of what has been formed" (SW 1:280). Such deformation is not an active distortion of impressions that would only produce the "grotesque"—say, in a caricature by exaggerating certain features. Deformation can also occur of itself, as a kind of dissolution.

The highest manifestations of fantasy that occur without active involvement of the imagination are such that deformation belongs to the very tension between form and totality. Fantasy would be attuned to a tendency at the very heart of form to dissolve in the whole to which it belongs. But dissolution is not division into parts; it is the manifestation of the oneness of the whole rather than a unity of form, that is, a manifestation through deformation. This is why the sense of color as one is at the same time the attunement to its transient or passing quality. The sense of dissolution without compulsion, also without resistance, would itself be the source of the delight in the colors of fantasy. As it is "free and therefore painless, [it] gently induces feelings of delight" (SW 1:281). As opposed to destruction, "[deformation] never leads to death, but immortalizes the dissolution [*verewigt den Untergang*] it brings about in an unending series of transitions." The self-contained world of color is not "static and 'dead.'" It presents an eternity of transience, or gives a sense, as Benjamin puts it, of "the world caught up in the process of unending dissolution; and this means eternal ephemerality [*ewiger Vergängnis*]" (SW 1:281).

This sense of the world in nuance is especially characteristic of the passing manifestations known as ephemeral colors, whose paradigm is the rainbow. Ephemerality and wholeness are thus not opposed but belong to one another. When passing away derives from the character of color itself, it is not destruction (as it would be when considering an object of experience); it is instead the other side of fulfilled wholeness. Nuance, and the primacy of transition, can also be characterized as a state beyond the polarity of positive and negative that is characteristic of the space of judgment (the primacy of difference to particularity belongs to the idea of absolute identity). Moreover, in this idea of the deformations of fantasy as attuned to the passing, we also point to a zone of indifference in regard to pleasure and pain. It is a condition in which loss, which ordinarily would occasion pain, gives way to constant differentiation, in which limits that occasion disappointment and frustration of desire give way to transition in nuances. It is a state of wonder in which disappearance and manifestation are one.

The Colors in Painting

We want now to take a further step so as to understand how receptivity to the colors of fantasy inheres in painting. This is one of the central issues of "The Rainbow: Conversation on Fantasy." Indeed, Georg is a painter and identifies Margarethe's color dream through his own experience: "I know these images of fantasy. I believe they are in me when I paint. I mix colors and then I see nothing but color. I almost said: I am color." While this is very similar to Margarethe's account, it significantly serves to characterize the inspiration of the artist. Georg speaks of intoxication (*Rausch*). Yet it is a peculiar ecstasy, in identifying the colors of fantasy with the muse. One could say that the receptivity to inspiration is brought together with the colors of fantasy as that which is the purely receptive in painting.[6]

The question remains as to how the creative activity of the artist relates itself to this pure receptivity. How does fantasy come to be in painting? One possibility is immediately dismissed: namely, that the colors of fantasy are like a model that is then imitated or copied by the artist. Treating the colors of fantasy as though they are a model "objectifies" them and yields bad painting.[7] The colors of fantasy are not "painted" or reproduced; beauty inheres in these colors, but it makes no sense to speak of painting beautiful colors.

Painting is the construction of depth out of the pictorial surface. We have seen that the colors of fantasy have a peculiar relation to depth. In pure fantasy, given overlapping transparent colors we cannot say which is above and which below. Colors in a painting share this character. As opposed to the graphic line that is a sign (*Zeichen*) inscribed on a surface (or background), a mark (*Mal*) is a manifestation in a medium. Colors that are applied in a painting are paradigmatic examples of marks, whereas the graphic line, the geometrical line, and writing are paradigmatic instances of signs. A painting is constructed from marks. Yet only in the painting is the application of color a mark—that is, it would be present as a manifestation in a medium. As marks in a medium, color in a painting exists without being a property or attribute of anything else. This is why "a picture has no background. Nor is one color ever superimposed on another but at most appears in the medium of another color.... In principle it is often impossible to say in many paintings whether a color is on top or underneath" (SW 1:85).

The canon of painting encompasses the infinitely varied and different forms of producing pictorial space, that is, depth out of the surface with color marks. Space formed in this way is not geometrical space or perspectival space. Perspective is linear and does not belong essentially to the space constructed solely by means of color. Rather, construction with color marks reveals space as ensouled depth. Soul is not form, not even organic form, but the presence of life that shows itself. Painting acquires nongeometrical, spiritual depth by relating itself thereby to the wholeness of the colors of fantasy. Color comes toward us in painting; it radiates through the construction in a medium, from that depth.[8]

The right way of conceiving of the presence of the manifestations of fantasy in painting is to think of them as originating at the heart of a construction governed by form, emerging into presence as a counterweight to the forming, as the original counterpart of the activity of the artist. That is, they emerge as a center, as if the concentration of the formal activity of construction in color opens this heart of the matter. The absolutely receptive in the painting is the heart of fantasy that is made manifest in and through the concentration of forms. In that sense the most active forming and the utmost receptivity to deformation can be recognized as two aspects of a higher identity. The restfulness in the beauty of a painting is precisely this indifference.

For the artist, the colors of fantasy are radiant in the painting, without being themselves the object of construction by way of the canon. They inhere in the construction but are not produced according to the canon. "The vision [*Anschauen*] of fantasy is a gaze within the canon, not in accordance with it; it is therefore purely receptive, uncreative" (EW 226; translation modified). It is nevertheless the radiance of the colors of fantasy in the painting that gives it the "stamp" of truthfulness, vouchsafing that the expression is not of the artist's subjectivity but of original nature. This radiant revelation is not inspiration that occurs at the beginning; rather, it announces the end of the work—the "it is so."

The identity or indifference between the constructive and the receptive is the key to how original nature can be named in a painting. The relation of true nature to the work of the artist cannot be that of a model to its copy. Nature is not a model (*Vorbild*) for painting. The presence of original nature or archetypal nature in the painting is felt as what we are receptive to at the heart of the construction of form. One might say that the presence of the colors of fantasy in the painting is the warrant that the painting relates itself to true nature, to the life of nature.⁹

We rejoin here the considerations of Benjamin's essay on language and the problem of giving expression to creaturely nature in the medium of human art. The receptive—that is, the manifestations of the colors of fantasy in the painting—mark the presence of archetypal nature in the painting. In this balance achieved between the constructive and the receptive, the subject matter of the painting emerges. Only in this balance can what is external to the painting—true nature or the archetype—be named. As Benjamin puts it: "The painting can be connected with *something that it is not*—that is to say, something that is not a set of marks—and this happens by naming the picture. This relation to what the picture is named after, to what transcends the marks, is what is created by the composition" (SW 1:85). Composition is not only up to us to "compose" but rather is that state of the construction of form in which it is balanced by the emergence of the colors of fantasy.

Creation Ex Nihilo and Forming Chaos

Let us now take a step back from our focus on the context of color and painting to consider more broadly the work of art and its relation to creaturely nature. To think of these matters at the most fundamental level would be to reflect on the work of the artist in relation to the task of actualizing nature. But this would require just as much distinguishing between the creator and the artist, or put differently, distinguishing between the created and the formed work. Benjamin discusses this opposition of the work of the artist and creation in a number of places, primarily in criticizing misguided attempts to confound the two. The following difficult passage articulates the distinction and the gist of Benjamin's critique: "The artist is less the primal ground or creator than the form-giver [*Bildner*], and certainly his work is not at any price his creature but rather the formed [*Gebilde*]. To be sure, the formed, too, and not only the creature, has life. But the basis of the decisive difference between the two is this: only the life of the creature, never that of the formed [*des Gebildeten*], partakes unreservedly of the intention of redemption" (SW 1:323–324).

This distinction can also be expressed as follows: Creation is creation ex nihilo. What is formed by the artist is chaos: "[The work of art] emerges not from nothingness but from chaos" (SW 1:340). We can avoid misleading pictures of chaos as primal matter by recalling that it is not that which we start with but what reveals itself at the extreme of forming. To take our example, we recognize the chaos internal to the painterly work in the presence of the colors of fantasy in it. Chaos is not mere lack of form but rather is indicated in the work by deformation and transience at the heart of forming. In the work of art chaos can be enchanted into harmony or world.[10] Chaos enlivens form into totality, which seems to emerge out of the work. Yet the "life" internal to the work always remains dependent on indeterminacy or deformation attested by the presence of fantasy in it.[11]

The ground of form in chaos means that there is inherent indetermination in beauty, or as Benjamin sometimes puts it, a "trembling" harmony in the work. "Form is the law according to which the beautiful ties itself to perfection and totality" (SW 1:221). Form is that which determines the constructive aspect of art, but form cannot lead all the way to perfection and totality. Indeed, as we saw with the account of painting, forming opens to the deformations of fantasy at the heart of the work. Since only through the duality of forming and deformation does the work relate itself to perfection, it would, at its highest, necessarily involve semblance: "Beauty in art is tied to semblance. It is tied to the semblance of totality and perfection, and for that reason is tied by means of semblance" (SW 1:221). This is what Benjamin points to when he writes, "All form is mysterious and enigmatic because it arises from the unfathomability of beauty, where it is bound to semblance. This is why Goethe observes, 'Beauty can never obtain clarity about itself.' Form arises in the realm of unfathomability" (SW 1:221). It is as though the self-identity of the true, its oneness or totality, can be manifest only in being veiled.

The work of art opens the polarity of form and chaos. In their balance the works tends toward full, higher perceptibility.[12] Perceptibility is not to be confused with existence. "What is decisive . . . is that the act of creation is directed at the existence [persistence, *Bestehen*] of creation, the existence of the world. From the outset, the origin of the work is directed at its perceptibility" (SW 1:221; translation modified). This duality of standpoints can be compared with Schelling's philosophy of identity, in which creation has in itself the duality of ground and existence. In distinguishing art from creation, Benjamin takes its ground to be chaos, while its mirror image is higher perceptibility (and not existence). Benjamin also speaks of this extreme as "necessary perceptibility." In empirical perception, nothing is necessarily as it is in fact. Yet in the higher perceptibility afforded by the work of art we feel that all hangs together necessarily, as a totality. The sense of that totality is not systematicity or organic form but precisely sensed in the radiance of fantasy in the work.

In order to further distinguish empirical perception and a higher perceptibility, Benjamin appeals to the distinction between perception and intuition. Intuition is not the sensuous impression; rather, what is at issue is intellectual intuition, the cognition of a divine intellect, cognition of archetypal nature. Finite perception cannot occupy the standpoint of intuition; instead, perception is brought through the work of art to that concentration in which what is invisible (what belongs to creation, existence, and intellectual intuition) manifests itself through the shining forth of the deformations of fantasy, as harmony emerges from the ground of chaos.[13]

The work of art partakes in the archetypal by bringing perception to its highest concentration of form. It would then mirror its ground as harmony out of chaos. Partaking is not simple resembling; the work is not a copy of the archetype, the primal image. "For those images," Benjamin writes, "are invisible, and 'resemblance' signifies precisely the relation of what is perceptible in the highest degree to what is, in principle, only intuitable" (SW 1:180). There would nevertheless be different degrees of this higher perceptibility: "The higher the type of beauty, the higher the type of perfection and totality it appears to carry along with itself. On the lowest plane, it is the totality and perfection of sensuous reality; and on the highest plane, those of bliss" (SW 1:221). Bliss should be distinguished from pleasure as well as happiness. In Spinoza, Kant, or Schelling, bliss is the state of harmony, even identity, of virtue and happiness (recall Spinoza's "Happiness is not the reward of virtue, but virtue itself" [*Ethics* 5.42]). This suggests that the work of art opens to what Benjamin calls "moral perception." The highest perception in art would mirror the identity of nature and goodness in the creative intellect. Higher perception in art can relate itself to "the act of creation, which is good and, by virtue only of being seen as 'good' can constitute 'seeing'" (SW 1:222). Benjamin also speaks of it as "utopian perception," in which beauty is bound to the nature of creation: "The nature of creation is paradigmatic for the moral determination of utopian perception" (SW 1:222).

It remains to ask whether the work of art can reach moral perception while remaining a harmonious, beautiful totality. Isn't the perception of significance in the work always a matter of semblance? Formulated in terms of Benjamin's essay on language, the fundamental relation of man to nature must be actualized through the medium of art. Thus, while art is forming and not creation, and while it does not have an "unreserved share" in redemption, it indirectly relates to the highest life. Creaturely life inheres in works of art, and its truth can be indirectly fulfilled in it. This means that internal to the work of art there will be not only what goes beyond the forming of the artist in the deformations of fantasy but also a moment that exceeds form in the direction of the fulfillment of creaturely nature in the truth of the work. It will be the moment of critique that goes beyond the essential beauty in the work. As Benjamin puts it in a letter to Rang: "The task of interpreting [of a critique of] works of art is to concentrate creaturely life in ideas" (SW 1:387).

What in beauty is given to us over and above form—that is, in deformation—always involves, albeit to varying degrees, semblance. "Beautiful life, the essentially beautiful and semblance—like beauty these three are identical" (SW 1:350). This semblance of totality must be destroyed, the trembling harmony arrested in the emergence of the moral moment of critique. It is this interruption or arrest that Benjamin refers to as the expressionless that *truth content* is recognized. The work of art cannot escape from chaos as long as it does not forego its beauty (and inner life):

The life undulating in it must appear petrified and as if spellbound in a single moment. That which in it has being is mere beauty, mere harmony, which permeates chaos (and, in truth, only chaos and not the world) but in this permeation only seems to enliven it. What arrests this semblance, spellbinds the movement, and interrupts the harmony is the expressionless. This life grounds the mystery; this petrification grounds the content in the work. (SW 1:340; translation modified)

We will return to explicate this difficult moment in the coming chapters.

THREE

The Life and Afterlife of Words

Human language is a space of expression of essential nature. The world and its orders find their reflection in language. But this expression of essential being cannot be understood without further ado. Language as such is not present perspicuously in language in general; it is in certain formed creations of language that we come to actualize and recognize these essential contents. One of the most evident and highest forms of actualizing the flow of revelation in the human world is in art, and specifically the poetic work. The poetic work can concentrate and make present essential being in language. In that respect Benjamin inherits the view, prevalent in Romanticism and German idealism, that the work of art is one of the highest expressions of spirit. Hegel, for instance, counts art, with religion and philosophy, as belonging to what he calls "absolute spirit": "It is simply one way of bringing to our minds and expressing the *Divine*, the deepest interests of mankind, and the most comprehensive truths of the spirit."[1]

Benjamin's early writings are a sustained investigation of this decisive configuration of philosophy. What is characteristic of his orientation, it seems, is the weight he gives not only to the forming but also to the *critical* moment in art. He shows how a variety of practices of critique, translation, or commentary partake in the unfolding of this higher life of nature in human language. The present chapter will consider some of these contexts, particularly the way that the vitality of meaning, correlative with a higher nature, expresses itself in them. The first part of the chapter is devoted to clarifying a fundamental opposition in post-Kantian aesthetics, namely, that between the Romantics and Goethe. The second part will indicate how Benjamin's account of the critique of the work of art, and in particular his concept of mortification, serves to dialectically overcome this opposition. The third part will be devoted to a different model yet, the account of the afterlife of meaning in "The Task of the Translator."

Critique and Truth to Nature

ROMANTIC CRITICISM OF ART

The Romantic concept of critique that Benjamin elaborates in his dissertation can serve as an initial model of the expression of a higher life in art. Indeed, in many of his references to Romantic critique Benjamin speaks of it as enlivening its object in reflection. One might trace the internal relation between enlivening and reflection to Kant's aesthetics in terms of the intensification of the play of the mind in reflective judgment by way of which the beautiful form is presented. But it is the adoption of reflection in Fichte that is the source of the Romantics' transformation of this concept.

The first part of Benjamin's "The Concept of Criticism in German Romanticism" is devoted to relating the Romantic notion of reflection to, as well as distinguishing it from, its source in Fichte. Reflection brings to consciousness the necessary activity of intelligence in all things. Reflection is thinking that is concerned with itself, yet not merely as self-consciousness devoid of an object. Rather, in any thinking of an object, reflection reveals the subject's contribution, the transcendental form of thinking that is already implicit in the very possibility of thinking the object. In other words, any thinking of something has in addition to its content a subjective form that conditions the possibility of thinking that object. It is that subjective form which is elevated by reflection to consciousness. In that sense it is both a return of thinking to itself as well as a transformation of its object. It follows that reflection can be said to be both discursive and immediate. Its immediacy is not that of intuition modeled on the sensuous but instead depends on understanding the internal relation of the form of thinking a given content to that form itself being the new content given in reflection. Insofar as reflection is a way for thinking to recover what is most its own, its own form, one can conceive of it as immediate.

The immediacy involved in taking reflection as a method should be distinguished from the presupposition of intellectual intuition as a first principle. The Romantics would reject any appeal to intellectual intuition as an unconscious primary ground out of which the deduction of the theoretical and practical forms of consciousness proceeds. Reflection in the Romantics becomes a method of thinking that would begin in medias res from the thinking of any subject matter.

Fichte stresses the finite character of theoretical reflection, leaving the opening onto the infinite to the constitution of the practical "I." Indeed, as Benjamin points out, for Fichte an open repetition of theoretical reflection would threaten the very possibility of an actual unity of self-consciousness. The Romantics, on the contrary, embrace that infinity as the true form of the unfolding cognition of an object. They do not conceive of it as an empty regress, as merely the thinking of thinking of thinking that would gradually lose all substantial content. Rather, self-consciousness is gradually heightened by reflection's being ever more encompassing. The transformation of forms in repeated reflection is understood through the way they come to be seen as interdependent in entering into systematic relationships with other forms. Form comes to itself as forms come together ever more intensively. This intensification of relationships is, as we will see, key to revealing the necessary place of the work (its a priori necessity to exist) in the medium of the idea of art in relation to other exemplary works.[2]

And yet a peculiar aspect of the heightening of reflection should be noted, albeit at this stage only schematically. If we call the thinking of something the first level of reflection, then the second level of reflection would be the thinking of (the form) of that first thinking. Benjamin describes what happens at the third level as follows: "The thinking of thinking of thinking can be conceived and performed in two ways. If one starts from the expression 'thinking of thinking' then at the third level, it is either the object thought of, thinking of (thinking of thinking), or else the thinking subject, (thinking of thinking) of thinking. The rigorous original form of second level reflection is assailed and shaken by the ambiguity in the third level reflection" (SW 1:129). Put in this general way, it is wholly unclear what this duality in reflection comes to. I will indicate how it becomes a productive element of Romantic critique in the discussion of irony.

The Romantics recognize the field of the highest and fullest manifestation of the method of reflection in the sphere of art, not so much in poetic production but primarily in the critique of the work of art. This is the concern of the second part of Benjamin's text titled "Criticism of Art,"[3] in which he presents a rigorous reconstruction of the systematic aspirations of the Romantic theory of art. This is initially evident in his characterization of the critique of art as a form of knowledge of the work in reflection. This knowledge is not expressed in judgments about a work, determining it by way of concepts; rather, reflection unfolds in the object. It is that through which the object, the artwork, is transformed and realizes its essential character. Works of art are conceived of as germ cells, and what unfolds their inner growth is reflection itself. But it is not the reflection of an individual subject on a work; instead, "the subject of reflection is, at bottom, the artistic entity itself, and the experiment consists not in any reflecting *on* an entity, which could not essentially alter it as Romantic criticism intends, but in the unfolding of reflection—that is, for the Romantics, the unfolding of spirit—*in* an entity" (SW 1:151). It is maybe here that we can first note the proximity of these considerations to the program laid out in "On Language as Such and on the Language of Man." Indeed, the fulfillment of the work in criticism is its receiving its place in its world, that is, in the idea of art as such.

Critique is thus seen to be internal to the realization of the essential identity of the work, thereby challenging the simple separation between the creative moment and the reflective, critical moment. As Schlegel puts it: "Every great work of whatever kind, knows more than it says, and aspires to more than it knows."[4] The problematization of the distinction between genius and critic is indeed another characteristic aspect of the writings of the Romantics, also evident, for instance, in their production of fragments, which are equally small works of art, and critical reflections.[5]

We can further clarify the character of the cognition of an object in reflection by considering the place of the negative in it. A judgment about an object belongs to the same logical space as its negation. But if reflection is the realization of its object, it is essentially positive: "In it," Benjamin notes, "a necessary moment of all judgment, the negative, is completely curtailed" (SW 1:152). Thus Benjamin draws a distinction between critique that passes judgment (or evaluates a work as good or bad) and reflective critique, which realizes the intelligible necessity in the work. A bad work is not an object of criticism; criticizability is itself what testifies to the value of a work. As Benjamin puts it: "For the true critic, the actual judgment is the ultimate step—something that comes after everything else, never the basis of his activity. In the ideal case, he forgets to pass judgment" (SW 2:547). (Note here as well the way this relates to the problematization of the bipolarity of judgment in the essay on language.)

Reflection is, importantly, formal. It elevates the thinking of a content to a consciousness of the form of that thinking. An object is presented through reflection in light of the delimitations of its inner form. But, initially, the specific particularity of a work involves contingent contents. It would have what can be called an "empirical form." Its necessary, "intelligible" form only emerges gradually in the realization of the work in criticism. Critique, though immanent—that is, realizing the work out of itself—does not remain with the work in isolation. The latter's essential character is recognized as it is shown to belong with other forms. The duality internal to reflection, necessary to establish the essential identity of a work by relating it to what is other than itself, is what Benjamin identifies as objective irony. The empirical presentational form is purified of its contingency, dissolved by irony, so as to establish the essential character of the work as a moment of absolute form. As Benjamin summarizes it:

> We must introduce a double concept of form. The particular form of the individual work, which we might call the presentational form, is sacrificed to ironic dissolution. Above it, however[,] irony flings open a heaven of eternal form, the idea of forms, (which we might call the absolute form), and proves the survival of the work, which draws its indestructible subsistence from that sphere, after the empirical form, the expression of its isolated reflection, has been consumed by the absolute form. (SW 1:164–165)

The work's a priori necessity to exist, its necessary place, its true form, is revealed in its becoming a moment of the idea of art. Reflection reveals the essential form of the work when it is seen to belong to a continuum of forms. One could speak of the constitution of a medium of reflection of forms. "In this medium," Benjamin writes, "all the presentational forms hang constantly together, interpenetrate one another, and merge into the unity of the absolute art form, which is identical with the idea of art. Thus the Romantic idea of the unity of art lies in the idea of a continuum of forms. For example, tragedy . . . would continuously cohere with the sonnet" (SW 1:165).

The idea of a continuum of works and forms is suggested, Benjamin claims, in Schlegel's view of antiquity. "All poems of antiquity," Schlegel writes, "link up to one another, until the whole is formed out of continually greater masses and members. . . . And thus it is not empty metaphor to say that ancient poetry is a single, indivisible, perfected poem" (SW 1:167). Taking reflection into account, it might very well be that it is only for us, not in itself, that antiquity can be such a whole. Antiquity is not naïve, unreflective nature, as Schiller would think of it. Rather, in the words of Novalis, "nature and insight into nature arise at the same time, just as antiquity and knowledge of antiquity; for one makes a great error if one believes that the ancients exist. Only now is antiquity starting to arise" (SW 1:182).

There is a form that can include in itself the ironization of presentational forms and thus can contain within itself, in miniature as it were, the connectedness of forms: this form is the novel. It is a form that can "reflect upon itself at will, and, in ever-new considerations, can mirror back every given level of consciousness from a higher standpoint" (SW 1:172). The novel is the quintessential modern form; it also functions as the form that is not just a specific genre but rather can stand for the medium of reflection of forms. Goethe's *Wilhelm Meister's Apprenticeship Years* was for Schlegel the paradigm of these possibilities of the novel. Not only does it contain in itself a poetic critique of other works, most famously of Shakespeare's *Hamlet*, but it is also raised by critique to a higher power of itself. Schlegel expressed this wittily by titling his critique of the novel "Über Meister," meaning not just "about" but also "higher" *Meister*, as the novel is potentiated by reflection, showing thereby its self-mastery.

The importance of the novel lies, further, in its prosaic character.[6] Prose is not just a characterization of one genre among many (as opposed, say, to lyric, epic, etc.), nor can it be defined as literal or plain factual expression. It names the limit of reflection. This leads Benjamin to say that "the reflective medium of poetic forms appears in prose; for this reason prose may be called the idea of poetry. Prose is the creative ground of poetic forms, all of which are mediated in it and dissolved as though in their canonical creative ground. In prose, all metrical rhythms pass over into one another and combine into a new unity, the prosaic unity" (SW 1:174). The prosaic, the inner limit of reflection in the work, is, as Benjamin puts it, the sober light of the idea in which the plurality of works dissolves.

GOETHE AND THE ROMANTICS

After this summary exposition of the early Romantics, we are better equipped to recognize their polar opposite in Goethe's theory of art, that opposition forming the main theme of the epilogue to the dissertation. "The theory of art propounded by the early Romantics and that formulated by Goethe," Benjamin writes, "are opposed to each other in their principles.... This opposition ... signifies the critical stage of [the history of the concept of art criticism]: [in it] the pure problem of the criticism of art[] comes immediately to light" (SW 1:178). We can appreciate the stakes of this opposition by placing it in a broader philosophical context. On the one hand, with the Jena Romantics we have the infinitization, or absolutization, of the subject-activity, making critical reflection internal to the realization of the work of art, to the revelation of its essential form in placing it in a medium of forms. On the other hand, we have the submission of art to the standard of a higher nature exemplified by Goethe's position. Whereas, as we have seen, the early Romantics related themselves to Fichte's philosophy, Goethe's pantheism, indebted as it is to Spinoza, would express its antithesis; it is a higher realism, that is, a way to take art to be most itself in presenting preexisting, archetypal nature.

This schematic opposition is clarified and deepened by Benjamin through the consideration of a number of contrasting terms: criticizable and uncriticizable, idea and ideal, reflection and refraction, realization and imitation (taking part), continuum and discontinuum, medium and discreteness, as well as the a priori of form and a priori of content.[7] "The entire art philosophical project of the early Romantics can be summarized by saying that they sought to demonstrate in principle the criticizability of the work of art. Goethe's whole theory of art proceeds from the view of the uncriticizability of works" (SW 1:179). As we have seen, the Romantics take the activity of criticism to be inseparable from what the work of art essentially is, as the latter literally fulfills or realizes itself only through the former. Through criticism the work of art is to acquire its limit intelligibility, so to speak, by becoming a moment of the idea of art.

Conversely, "according to Goethe's ultimate intention, criticism of an artwork is neither possible nor necessary" (SW 1:184). This is not merely due to Goethe's tendency to keep for himself the secret of his work and thus the ultimate authority over it, refusing, as it were, to delegate the constitution of its meaning to critics. (This posture is discussed by Benjamin in his essay on "Goethe's *Elective Affinities*"; see Chapter 5.) More important, it has to do with the understanding that a work of art presents us with an ultimate measure or standard of true nature and must itself have something of the character of the standard it "imitates." A standard or measure precludes criticism, insofar as being unchangeable belongs to its very concept. It literally makes no sense to say, for example, that critique reveals that the standard meter is not yet quite what it ought to be; only in relation to the standard does rightness of measurement have a meaning. If the task of a work is to present the immutable standard of original nature, critique cannot be essential to it. A great work cannot be further transformed by criticism but would, at most, allow elucidatory commentary.

This can be further explicated through the opposition of "idea" and "ideal": "The category under which the Romantics conceive of art is the idea.... What motivates [Goethe's philosophy of art] is the question of the ideal of art" (SW 1:179; translation modified). Recall that for Kant an idea is essentially regulative; it is the focal point correlative with a method of advance. That method is identified through an activity, which for the Romantics, in the case of art, is reflection or criticism. Reflection realizes the form of the work of art by placing it in a systematic relation to other forms that emerged in the history of art. The essential a priori form of a work emerges in seeing it as internally related to, hanging together with, or continuous with other forms in the totality of the idea of art.

We can similarly trace the correlative term "ideal" to the dialectic of Kant's First Critique, where an ideal is defined as the idea realized *in concreto*, in an individual. Insofar as it is the intuitive concretization of the idea, the ideal is unique by being the highest reality, at the origin of all plurality. It is unique by being the quintessence of content. Thus, for instance, the ideal of knowledge is God as the highest actuality, the "ens realissimum." Whereas an idea is "one" as the highest *formal* unity, an ideal is an original intuition, the unique highest reality, that is, an a priori of *content*. Ideals are not concepts or ideas but rather primal images or archetypes. Put differently, a primal image is not an idea in Kant's sense but in Plato's sense of the term, the preexisting archetype of which all phenomena are copies or ectypes.

Benjamin writes that "the idea is the expression of the infinitude of art and of its unity. For the Romantics unity is an infinity" (SW 1:179). We have seen how in Romantic critique the infinity of works coalesce through reflection into the unity of a single medium. Reflection tends toward the formation of a continuum of forms. For Goethe, the ideal is a multiplicity: the ideal is presented, as Benjamin puts it, in "a limited multiplicity of pure contents into which it decomposes" (SW 1:179). It is a "limited harmonic dis-continuum of pure contents" (SW 1:179). The ideal is not an object of reflection but rather of refraction; it is refracted into a multiplicity of discrete, self-standing contents. A multiplicity that presents the ideal is not a mere plurality of particulars, nor is it the ideal's division into related "parts." Instead, each pure content would be an aspect of the one, independent of other aspects yet harmonizing with them. This difficult characterization will be discussed further in the next chapter, in reading Benjamin's "Epistemo-Critical Foreword," but I want to suggest here what it means by way of an example.

In his "Lectures on the Philosophy of Art" from around 1800, Schelling conceives of the original multiplicity of content in art as the gods of Greek mythology. In the Pantheon each deity is wholly self-standing, encompassing the world as a whole under an aspect. Their harmony is the presentation of absolute identity. Similarly, for Benjamin, "the idea of the Muses under the sovereignty of Apollo, interpreted by the philosophy of art, is the idea of the pure contents of all art" (SW 2:179). These are not the forms of art (say, the different arts) but the ultimate contents, the muse-inspired (*Musische*), meaning the harmony of the highest contents worthy of being expressed in art.

The fit of discrete pure contents is characterized through the concept of harmony. Harmony allows us to think both the inalienable separation of the pure contents and their coming together, attuned as they are "at a distance." Aspect, discontinuous multiplicity, and harmony—these terms are essential to characterize not only the ideal of art but also the character of a work of art that imitates the ideal: "Art is always wholly represented in every individual work" (O 1). Each work refracts anew the original multiplicity from its own standpoint, in a monadic, intensive presentation. A work would be the prototype of an archetype; it would not coalesce with other such works or prototypes into a unity, as is the case with Romantic reflection oriented by the idea.

To conceive of nature as an ultimate standard, as an archetype that art makes present, means that there is a mimetic character to the highest task of art. The work partakes in the ideal. "Works of art," Benjamin writes, "cannot attain to those invisible—but intuitive—archetypes. . . . They can resemble them only in a more or less high degree" (SW 1:180). A difficulty with the nature of that resemblance will lead us further into Benjamin's own concept of critique.

Life, Semblance, and Critique

To start with, one can describe Benjamin's concept of critique as overcoming the fundamental opposition between Goethe and the Romantics. Benjamin wants to secure both the presentation of the highest archetypal content (which he calls "truth content") in art as well as the necessity of a critique of the work to recognizing it. How can Goethe's higher realism make room for critique? And how is critique, the Romantic term of art, transformed in serving the presentation of the ideal?

Benjamin suggests that the problem in Goethe's theory of art can initially be put in terms of a confusion between a model (*Vorbild*) and an archetype (*Urbild*). When we conceive of true nature as a model, we assume it first to be given to us in order for us to be able to imitate, so as to make a copy (*Abbild*) of it. Yet the archetype, the *Urbild*, is not given to us but must be made perceivable in and by the work of art. Put differently, the archetype is invisible, and we can grasp it only in and through forming a work in which we recognize it to inhere. "True, intuitable, *ur*-phenomenal nature, would become visible . . . *only* in art" (SW 1:181). The making of a work is always based on forming, on the productive activity of an artist, and on principles of giving form. Only in the medium of form can we be productive. But it is only in what shines out, what appears to give itself to us, at the heart of a work that we sense the presence of pure content, of an archetype. As we saw in the previous chapter, the heart of a work, in which we sense or feel something not visible giving itself to us, is what Benjamin also thinks of as the mystery or secret inherent in beauty.

Ideals are never present to us abstractly, as the most general concepts would be, but must be recognized in the concrete. There is no higher perception without forming material content. In a great work, the idea completely permeates the inessential, the contingent and sensuous. The great work of art is thus a unity of truth content and material content, of the essential and the inessential. "The more significant the work is, the more inconspicuously and intimately its truth content is bound up with its material content" (SW 1:297). Material content and truth content are thus initially inseparable in the experience of the work. But as we saw earlier, even if the ideal shines forth in the lived experience of art, it does so as the secret, invisible core of the work; it is in no way perspicuously present, purely as truth content.

A critique of semblance is demanded for the presentation of the ideal, of truth content. It must be a form of critique that would forego the interpretive-creative activity of the subject, central to the Romantic, reflective model, and instead would depend on commentary, the fundamentally descriptive stance appropriate to the presentation of what preexists, the archetype. Importantly, the possibility of a commentary on a work is opened with time. "In the course of its duration, the concrete realities rise out before the eyes of the beholder all the more distinctly the more they die out in the world" (SW 1:297). Material content that might have remained inconspicuous for contemporaries, or even for the author, emerges in time as strange or striking and therefore as material for philology or commentary.

The material content acquires its peculiar character in time. In its material content the work is most clearly an expression of its historical times; thus one could speak here of a historical dimension that opens up by attending to the material content. But philology is not to be taken as historicizing, as attempting to reposition the work in its element of life, in that world in which it took form. On the contrary, attention to the peculiarities of the material content serves to reveal tendencies in the work that were not visible in the lifeworld in which it was formed. A philological inquiry attends to the emerging transformations of the contingent meaning-material in what Benjamin calls the afterlife of the work. Commentary is, first of all, a form of detailed, piecemeal knowledge that gradually extinguishes the semblance of wholeness in the immediate experience of the work. But in a second moment, the transformations of the material content, now released from the unity of the form, reveal for us a hidden tendency in the work—call it the vector of the actualization of its meaning—through which we are directed to the order of the truth content. Thus critique, properly understood, is inescapably wedded to commentary that, as it were, prepares the material for its reordering as a configuration of truth. "The truth content emerges," as Benjamin puts it, "as that of the material content" (SW 1:300).

It is here that we also recognize how Benjamin's concept of critique differs essentially from reflective criticism. If Romantic criticism seeks to dissolve contingent material content in irony, Benjamin's philological critique depends on attending to the emergent striking peculiarities of the material content. The infinitizing of reflection, through which the work becomes part of the medium of the idea of art, enlivens the space of meaning, but it cannot yield measured, utterly concrete truth content. Critique, intertwined as it is with philological knowledge that attends to the peculiarities of contingent content does not enliven but is a "mortification of the works. Not the intensification of consciousness in them (that is Romantic!) but their colonization by knowledge" (SW 1:389).

Translation and the Life of Language

Benjamin's concept of translation exhibits some of the central characteristics of what he understands as the non-Romantic idea of critique. In order to recognize this, we need initially to bring out his concern with the dimension of life in the literary work as it is articulated in "The Task of the Translator."

THE LIFE AND AFTERLIFE OF ART

We are to conceive of translation as a vital nexus, starting from the understanding that a literary work has an inner life of its own: "A translation issues from the original—not so much from its life as from its afterlife.... The idea of life and afterlife of works of art should be regarded," as Benjamin puts it, "with an entirely un-metaphorical objectivity" (SW 1:254). Life, as we want that term to apply to the literary work, is not to be understood in terms of organic form, nor is it a matter of enlivening reflection, and in no way is it an appeal to the sensibility or lived experience of the reader. The following passage will be pertinent to us well beyond the specific context of translation:

The concept of life is given its due only if everything that has a history of its own, and is not merely the setting for history, is credited with life. In the final analysis, the range of life must be determined by the standpoint of history rather than that of nature, least of all by such tenuous factors as sensation and soul. The philosopher's task consists in comprehending all of natural life though the more encompassing historical life. (SW 1:255; translation modified)

In considering the inner life of a work of literature, its "having a history of its own," we are not concerned with placing the work in, say, the history of art or literature. The work has an inner tendency, which expresses itself in its having its own history. This understanding of the inner life of a work is reflected in Benjamin's account of the relation between life and purposiveness. He wants to retain something of the traditional articulation of life in terms of the concept of purposiveness. But he notes that "the unfolding of a special and high form of life . . . is determined by a special high purposiveness. [It] reveals itself only if the ultimate purpose toward which all the individual purposiveness of life tends is not sought in its own sphere but in a higher one" (SW 1:255). The strivings of the living being do not partake in what is highest by way of setting a maximum or highest purpose to be realized by the purposive organization of its life; rather, it is as though these purposive strivings indirectly reinforce a vector that points to fulfillment in a higher sphere.[8] That higher fulfillment, not surprisingly perhaps, is that of the actualization of the meaning of life (or of life in meaning), the expression of its significance: "All purposeful appearances of life, just as their very purposiveness, finally are purposive not for the life but for the expression of its essence, for the presentation of its significance" (SW 1:255).

In particular, we will not recognize the highest achievement of translation if we hold to the common analogy of the work of art with an organism. What we would refer to as the terminus of the task of the translator does not lie in presenting the work as an organic totality. The revelation of a higher life in the work would require precisely the destruction of the purposive unity of the individual work. This mortifying moment is reflected in Benjamin's identification of the history of the work not with its natural life but rather with its afterlife. Moreover, the higher life of meaning revealed by the translation of the work is the life of language. Translation reveals language as such by establishing the kinship of languages: "Translation thus finally is purposive for the expression of the innermost relationship of languages to each other" (SW 1:255).

THE INTENSIVE PRESENTATION

The starting point for a reflection on translation is the unity of the original, the individual literary work. Yet the translation will use that context to present what pertains to language as such: "The intention of a translation . . .

differs from that of the literary work—namely [it is] a language as a whole, taking an individual work in an alien language as a point of departure" (SW 1:259). The point of departure is a partial and provisional linguistic context, yet it presents the harmony of languages.

Insofar as we think of the character of translation as the presentation of language as such, or as Benjamin also calls it, the "pure" language, we must hold to two extremes: on the one hand, the singular character of the work and its specific meaning nexus; on the other, the totality of the pure language expressed by the kinship between languages. The former is a specific linguistic context, the latter something that pertains to language as a whole. In translation we make the singular express that which pertains to the whole. It is this dual focus, on the particular work and through it on the presentation of language as such, that is implied by Benjamin's idea of intensive or embryonic presentation. "Translation," Benjamin writes, "cannot possibly reveal or establish [*herstellen*] this hidden relationship [between languages] itself; but it can present it in embryo, that is as intensively realized [*intensive Verwirklicht*]" (SW 1:255; translation modified). The intensive—call it monadic—presentation refracts the whole in the individual. It is an embryonic presentation insofar as it has the harmony of languages refracted in miniature by the translation of the individual work. More precisely, we can say that the translation brings out an affinity or kinship between languages, showing them thereby to belong to a higher whole, to the pure language.

This kinship is not a historical relation between languages. What Benjamin seeks through the intensive presentation is supra-historical kinship, to reveal the way languages present aspects of one and the same world: "All supra-historical kinship between languages consists in this: in every one of them as a whole, one and the same is meant. Yet this is reachable not by any single language but only by the totality of their intentions supplementing one another: the pure language" (SW 1:257).

THE FORM OF TRANSLATION

What is probably most striking in Benjamin's description of the form of translation is that it is not cued to the unity of sense. It isn't as though sense is absent from a translation, or that a translation reads as nonsense. More to the point is that the expression of sense is taken care of by the original, and what is "added" by the translation is of another order: "Translation must in large measure refrain from wanting to communicate something, from rendering the sense, and in this the original is important to it only insofar as it has already relieved the translator and his translation of the effort of assembling and expressing what is to be conveyed" (SW 1:260).

What is translation cued to, if not to the reproduction of sense? Here we need to follow the distinctions that Benjamin makes between sense, meaning, and way of meaning. Sense pertains to the judgment, or the communicated propositional content. While words in different languages can have one and the same meaning (reference), the ways of meaning it would differ. The difficulty in translation is not so much in reproducing the sense, nor does it lie with the meaning that is the same in both languages; rather, the translation seeks to echo in its own language the way of meaning of the original. Ways of meaning in different languages tend to exclude one another—indeed, this is precisely what it is for languages to be foreign to one another. Therefore we should not expect to have, ready-made and waiting in the language of the translation, a way of meaning corresponding to the way of meaning of the original.

This is why Benjamin thinks of a translator as complementing their own language by reproducing in it the way of meaning of the original. Complementing is not introducing a new way of meaning into the language of the translation; the translator does not create a new form in their language. (Ways of meaning are not up to us to invent.) Insofar as in the original a way of meaning befits precisely the presentation of the content, then in the translation there will be a lack of fit between language and content. As Benjamin puts it in a pregnant figure: "Whereas content and language form a certain unity in the original, like a fruit and its skin, the language of the translation envelops its content like a royal robe with ample folds" (SW 1:258). It follows that a translation cannot be translated. There can be no translation of a translation "because of the looseness with which sense attaches to [it]" (SW 1:262). In that respect a translation is an endpoint: "Translation transplants the original into a further, and in that respect—ironically—more definitive, linguistic realm, since it can no longer be displaced by a secondary rendering" (SW 1:258; translation modified).[9]

We can also say that what appears as a unified way of meaning in the original is "dispersed" in the translation. That is, it will not correspond to a unified context in the language of the translation. This is further expressed in the figure of the echo that Benjamin uses to distinguish the unity of intention in the original and its transformation in the translation: "The task of the translator consists in finding the particular intention toward the target language which produces in that language the echo of the original" (SW 1:258). Echo suggests dispersion, as though what is a unified context can be refracted, inflecting or modifying any and all of the words of the translation. The translator, one might say, takes advantage of all of language to echo a specific meaning context.

The poet is concerned with finding language fitting to the expression of a content, whereas the translator has language as such in view. The translator is not primarily attending to the content of the work (though of course they are not ignoring it). Rather, their concern is with their own language and how to make it reverberate (though not reproduce) the way of meaning of the original. Plainly, the poet too is concerned with language, but in a different way than the translator: "The intention of the poet is spontaneous, primary, manifest; that of the translator is derivative, ultimate, ideational. For the great motif of integrating many tongues into one true language informs his work." In this respect the task of the translator is likened to that of the philosopher: "This very language, in whose divination and description lies the only perfection for which a philosopher can hope, is concealed in concentrated fashion in translations. There is no muse of philosophy, nor is there one of translation" (SW 1:259). This alignment of the philosopher and the translator demands interpretation.

THE TRUE LANGUAGE

The translator has language as a whole in view, but not as though language is their object. We are certainly *in* language, but we must think how "language as such" can be presented in *a* language, how language as such communicates itself in and through a language.

In our life with language, we communicate contents by means of linguistic constructions. There are two sides to this communication, which we might provisionally call what is expressed and what does the expressing. At the same time as language communicates content, expresses something, that which allows such expressing in language is not itself communicated. The noncommunicable (*Nicht-Mitteilbares*) is not the inexpressible, lying beyond the limits of language (recall that revelation does not know the inexpressible). The noncommunicable is language itself insofar as it is purely a medium of communication. "In all language and linguistic constructions [*Gebilden*], there remains in addition to what is communicable, a noncommunicable; depending on the context in which it appears, it is symbolizing or is symbolized. It is symbolizing in the finite products of language; symbolized in the evolving languages themselves" (SW 1:261).

This passage expresses the duality we have considered already: in attending to the inner life of the finite construct of language (such as the literary work) we seek to reveal a harmony of the languages themselves. In the becoming of languages the "kernel of the pure language" can reveal and realize itself. Yet in particular linguistic constructions, such as literary works, language as such will be overshadowed by the content communicated: "it is weighted with a heavy, alien sense." Unquestionably, language as such is always presupposed if there is symbolization at all, as it is inherent in symbolizing. The task of the translator is "to turn the symbolizing into the symbolized itself" (SW 1:261). As the symbolizing is presented—that is, becomes the symbolized in the translation—language can be said to lose its expressive character. It communicates no more; it is no more a vehicle for the expression of intention. It is purely self-identical language: "In this pure language—which no longer means or expresses anything but is, as expressionless and creative Word, that which is meant in all languages—all information, all sense, and all intention finally encounter a stratum in which they are destined to be extinguished" (SW 1:261). We can speak of this intentionless identity as "a tensionless and even silent depository of the ultimate secrets for which all thought strives" (SW 1:259).

Benjamin further expresses the turning of the symbolizing into the symbolized, the presentation of the self-identity of language, in a cryptic formulation. "The language of truth . . . ," as he puts it, "is the true language" (SW 1:259). It is not the language in which we communicate true statements, for that would establish a distinction between the medium, between language itself, and its content. Rather, it is that wherein we recognize the principle that Benjamin articulated in the early essay on language: "All language communicates itself" (EW 253). In the next and final section of this chapter we will further establish the deep connection between the two essays.

FREEDOM AND FIDELITY IN TRANSLATION

In the opening of the essay Benjamin has dismissed the prevalent understanding of fidelity and freedom in translation. The problematic conception of fidelity would be that which takes the translation to be of service to the reader who does not speak the language of the original. It would be devoted to the original by transmitting as closely as possible what the work communicates. The problematic conception of freedom assumes that there is something incommunicable in a poetic work. The translator will be able to evoke what is "unfathomable and mysterious" in a work "only if he is also—a poet" (SW 1:253). Our previous analysis yields new concepts of fidelity and freedom, as well as a way to think translation as realizing both rather than setting them as opposites. Translation, like love in that respect, overcomes the antithesis; it is a model for the higher unity of fidelity and freedom.

Fidelity in translation does not rely on similarity but instead is characterized through the concept of supplementation. It nevertheless means attending to language in the smallest details, to the multiplicity of echoes of the way of meaning of the original. This is expressed in one of the well-known figures of the essay: "Fragments of a vessel that must be glued together must match one another in the smallest details, although they need not be like one another. In the same way a translation, instead of imitating the sense of the original, must lovingly and in detail incorporate the original's way of meaning, thus making the original and the translation recognizable as fragments of a greater language" (SW 1:260). Think of the way of meaning in the original as a "large" coherent fragment. Since it is echoed as a nonunified plurality of nuances spread over the whole field of language that the translator has at their disposal to supplement the way of meaning of the original, this echoing can be figured as very small fragments, which, while in no way similar to the large fragment, nevertheless fit it perfectly. It is this *fit*, call it harmony, that justifies recognizing both as *aspects* of the pure language.[10]

Fidelity is not judged at the sentential level, yet, as Benjamin argues, it must involve a literal rendering of the sentential *syntax* of the original. The effect will be, of course, to make evident that the reproduction of sense is secondary: "A literal rendering of the syntax casts the reproduction of sense entirely to the winds and threatens to lead directly to incomprehensibility.... It is self-evident how greatly fidelity in reproducing the form impedes the rendering of sense" (SW 1:260; translation modified). A literalness in reproducing the sentential structure (the syntax), the form, would have the effect of putting all the weight on words: "Words rather than sentences [prove to be] the primary element [*Urelement*] of the translator." Insofar as language communicates sense, or content, it communicates something other than itself. Put differently, determinacy of sense is an obstacle. In working on words, translation breaks through that obstacle to language as such appearing as a pure medium of communication of itself. This is conveyed in one of the most enigmatic figures in this difficult essay:

> A real translation is transparent; it does not cover the original, does not block its light [i.e., the light that shines on it], but allows the pure language as though reinforced by its own medium[] to shine upon the original all the more fully. This may be achieved, above all, by a literal rendering of the syntax, which proves words rather than sentences to be the primary element of the translator. For if the sentence is the wall before the language of the original, literalness is the arcade. (SW 1:260)

Let me try to convey the intuition in this image by availing myself of what belongs together with light, namely, color. Light is the pure medium of visibility, and in that sense it serves as a figure for the pure language as a medium of revelation of itself. And yet, without obstacle light cannot itself become visible. We must recover the medium out of the phenomenal manifestations that, as it were, are obstacles to it. Material objects block the passage of light while at the same time producing the manifestations of light we know as the colors of objects, thereby making those objects visible. One can speak here of the colored material object as the determinate sense, the sentential wall. To have light visible as a medium would be to have colors, yet without their being properties of material objects that block the light. It is with transparent colors that we can envisage the visibility of light as a medium (think of the rainbow). One can say, then, that a translation does not itself have the consistency of a reproduction of units of sense but rather becomes through its myriad nuances transparent coloring, thereby making the light of the pure medium shine on the original.[11]

In attempting to present language as a pure medium, the obstacle is the determinacy of sense, whose paradigmatic form is attributing a property to an object in a judgment. In making words the element of the translation, they are dissociated from the function of predication; they are like our transparent colors. Translation makes the language of the translator into a medium in which language as such, the pure medium, communicates itself. Benjamin writes that the light of the pure language shining on the original is reinforced by the transparent translation as though by its own medium.[12]

This new concept of fidelity readily suggests as well what freedom comes to. Freedom is the release of the pure language from the burden of content, releasing it to become manifest in the medium of the translation. Translation frees the pure language from the obstacles to its manifestations in finite linguistic products:

> In linguistic creations [the pure language] is weighted with a heavy, alien sense [*Sinn*]. To relieve it of this ... is the tremendous and only capacity of translation.... [The new and higher justification of free translation] does not derive from the sense of the communication, the emancipation from which is the task of fidelity. Freedom proves itself by letting the pure language act on one's own language. It is the task of the translator to release in his own language that pure language which is exiled among alien tongues, to liberate the language imprisoned in a work in his re-creation of that work. For the sake of the pure language, he breaks through decayed barriers of his own language. (SW 1:261; translation modified)

Freedom is in the manifestation of language as the medium of itself. (In that sense it is like autonomy—it is only when it is the communication of itself that language is free.) This free movement communicated in language (*Freiheit der Sprachbewegung*) is what Benjamin also calls in the essay on language "the uninterrupted flow of communication" of the Word of God. In the finite product of language, sense serves as a watershed that divides the flow of language from the flow of revelation. But "just as a tangent touches a circle lightly and at but one point ... a translation touches the original lightly and only at an infinitely small point of the sense, thereupon pursuing its own course according to the laws of fidelity in the freedom of linguistic flow" (SW 1:261; translation modified). It is in this light touch that the harmony of languages can be sensed. Hölderlin's translations of Sophocles are archetypes of that form: "In them the harmony of the languages is so profound that sense is touched by language only the way an aeolian harp is touched by the wind" (SW 1:262). Such attunement of languages is what Benjamin also calls the musical character of truth.

FOUR

The Life of Forms

We use the concept of life in conjunction with the notion of form in a variety of contexts: to refer, for instance, to the unity of that which we call a life-form, an organism. We also pair the terms in speaking of a form of life, and primarily the human form of life, where this comes to signify aspects of the communal existence of man. And there is what we may call a life of forms—say, literary forms—which will concern us in the present chapter. This chapter will tackle the notorious "Epistemo-Critical Foreword" of the *Trauerspiel* book, guided by the question as to the character of the life of forms, specifically the form of the *Trauerspiel*.

The "Epistemo-Critical Foreword" of the *Trauerspiel* book has always been for readers of Benjamin, myself included, a source of both fascination and frustration. Numerous assaults attempting to conquer this impregnable text have been thwarted by its hermeticism. At the same time, certain passages (in particular his reference to the constellation, origin, and monad) have been fetishized as key to Benjamin's thought as such. I will here attempt a technical expedient or small measure to provide a fresh start and perspective: reading the foreword backward, as it were.

The Vital Context of a Literary Form

What is the vital context of a literary form? As we saw in Chapter 3, the vital unity of a literary work is its inner history. But "the idea of a form . . . is no less a living thing than any concrete work of literature" (O 29). Indeed, "the metaphysical content of [a form] . . . must appear not merely as something lying within but as something actively working and, like blood, pulsing through the body" (O 17). What initially is puzzling in Benjamin's take on this vital context is its pairing with (the presentation of) ideas. We should be struck by the strangeness of Benjamin's claim that "the *Trauerspiel* . . . is an idea" (O 15). Would it count as one in Plato's heaven? . . .

The attempt to think together life and the idea is central to a number of thinkers in the nineteenth and early twentieth centuries. In Hegel's *Science of Logic*, the idea is the self-realization of the concept; it is identified at its fundamental level in the unity of life. In his *Lectures on Aesthetics*, Hegel conceives of the beautiful work as an ideal.[1] The ideal is the concept that has given *sensuous* reality to itself. The most *beautiful* realization of the ideal is evident in the classical configuration of art. Specifically, classical sculpture is the paradigm of the complete permeation of sensuous appearance with spirit in the representation of the human figure. The statues of the gods are a paradigm of this identity of spirit and bodily expression. The great works of art gather sensuously the spiritual configuration of their time and allow it to reach self-consciousness.

But even assuming that the individual work is what is highest in art, what would it be to present the inner form of a genre? And can that form be conceived of as an idea? These questions allow us to contrast Benjamin's method with Hegel's logic of the ideal. It is not the individual exemplary work that best reflects the genre. Inasmuch as one seeks the material content that belongs to the presentation of a form, one "might be able to recognize this exemplary character only in a scattered fragment" (O 23). It is not that the exemplary work is a fragment but rather that aspects of the genre will be dispersed among details of a great number of works. In that respect the great work is of no use in exploring the inner life of such a form: "It is precisely the important works—insofar as the genre does not appear in them for the first time, and so to speak, as an ideal—that stand outside the boundaries of genre. An important work either founds the genre or dissolves it; and in the perfect works the two functions unite" (O 23). The presentation of a literary form as an idea essentially involves material from a plurality of works, and its form is not present or fully concentrated in an ideal work, wholly permeating its content.

Benjamin therefore suggests that precisely the times in which one finds no truly great "creators," and that might therefore, from one standpoint, be conceived of as "periods of 'decline' in the arts," are where an "art-will" (*Kunstwollen*) can be made most evident. This art-will expressing itself in forms is presented through a multiplicity of works more than in unique masterpieces in the "isolated finished works." And Benjamin adds: "Only the form as such, never a well-fashioned individual work, is within reach of the art-will" (O 37). This notion of an "art-will" is drawn from Alois Riegl's work, specifically his study of the later Roman art industry. It is to be understood as a (life) force that manifests itself in the total production of an epoch, in its weak and failed works just as much as in those most praised. The genre is never evident in the unity of a "masterpiece." The idea of the *Trauerspiel* is the objectification of such an "unremitting art-will," and its unity is drawn from disparate phenomena.

Ideas and Concepts

Nevertheless, it is not obvious how by starting with a plurality of phenomena gathered from a variety of works we ever get the total unity of an idea. Here we need to take a further step in conceiving of the relationship between phenomena (material content), concepts, and ideas.

Properly understanding the relation of ideas to phenomena and to concepts reveals the shortcomings of both a simplistic inductive method that draws on contingent commonalities and an idealistic logic in which the form is the object of a speculative deduction. The inductive approach is no doubt fueled by a healthy skepticism as to the hypostasis of concepts, but it confuses concept and idea nonetheless.[2] The concept expresses what objects falling under it have in common; these common traits are never the material that serves to present an idea. Benjamin refers to the common as the average and seeks to distinguish the highest universality of the idea from the structure of classification by way of concepts.

Similarly, the idealistic attempt to ground the unity of a genre on something like an inner logic of forms will miss the mark, especially if one takes into account that the investigation is not cued to the ideal, highest instances but rather to the multiplicity of material contents that cannot be "derived." This is where the dimension of facticity, the essentially historical, that which is the object of discovery, enters in. It is the underivable existence that gives the stamp of authenticity to the presentation of a form: "In the most singular and eccentric of phenomena, in the feeblest and clumsiest attempts no less than in the overripe manifestations of a late period, discovery is capable of bringing the genuine to light" (O 26).

In the unpublished fragment "Language and Logic," Benjamin draws a distinction between a system of classification by way of concepts and the hierarchical ruling of an essence (idea) over a multiplicity of essences (ideas):[3]

> The relation between concepts—and this relation governs the sphere of knowledge—is one of subsumption. The lower concepts [*Unterbegriffe*] are contained in the higher concept [*Oberbegriff*]—that is to say, in one sense or another what is known loses its autonomy for the sake of what it is known as. In the sphere of essences, the higher does not devour the lower. Instead it rules over it. This explains why the regional separation between them, their disparateness[,] remains as irreducible as the gulf between monarch and people. (SW 1:272–273; translation modified)

Take a concept such as whale; it has sub-concepts—say, mammal and sea creature. Whatever falls under the higher concept also falls under the lower concepts coordinated with it. The lower concepts are more general than the higher concept that is specified through them. The instances of the higher concept belong to the intersection of the lower concepts (or to what Benjamin calls their "average"). What is to be known, the higher concept, is in fact subordinated to the lower concepts and thus, as Benjamin puts it, loses its autonomy "for the sake of what it is known *as*" (SW 1:273).

Now, in the presentation of an essence, an idea rather than a concept, the question arises whether it too has a multiplicity of elements, or constituent essences, belonging to it. And if so, how, if not by subsumption, would these elements belong to the higher essence? An essence has indeed, belonging to it, an "inner multiplicity" of essences. Benjamin speaks of essence-unity (*Wesenseinheit*) and essence-multiplicity (*Wesensvielheit*), meaning that in the presentation of an essence there is an aspect of unity (being one) and an aspect of multiplicity (i.e., the essences belonging to its presentation). And yet the relation of multiplicity to unity is not understood through subsumption or intersection. The multiple essences do not intersect but remain wholly distinct from one another. They do not relate by having something in common but are held together, as if ruled by a force.

This is the point of the figure of the monarch and the people. The monarch does not draw authority from representing the intersection of all individual wills or the average of the wills of the various parties.[4] The monarch embodies a force that is of another order than the sum of the wills of the plurality of subjects. But through effective sovereign rule, the subjects exist in a world in which what is essential is manifest, made evident, in the life of the community. Through sovereign rule, the existence of the people is granted an essential articulation; what is essential is manifest in existence in common (call this the presence of a destiny of the people).

How is the legitimacy of the rule of a monarch established? This is essentially a matter of descent, that is, of "origins." Referring to the hereditary character of monarchy allows Benjamin to suggest that the presentation of ideas has not only a historical dimension but a justification in relation to what is original. It might echo the idea that the divine right of kings can be traced to Adam, who is the one who names. The sovereign force at issue is expressed in naming. The essences distilled out of the plurality of the phenomenal and thereby named are precisely the multiplicity internal to the higher idea. As Benjamin puts it: "The being—distant from all phenomenality—in which alone this force inheres is that of the name" (O 13; translation modified). In presenting an idea, the myriad of particular phenomena are dissected and extracted from their empirical nexus. They are brought together in a new order, thereby making possible the release of essential contents that were all but imperceptible in empirical reality. It is the emerging essential contents that are named: "In philosophical contemplation the idea as word—as the word that claims anew its naming rights—is released from the innermost reality. In the end this stance is not Plato's but Adam's, the father of humankind regarded as father of philosophy" (O 13–14).

Multiplicity and Harmony

The essence-multiplicity held together by a force is contrasted with the pseudo-justification of the inner complexity of an overarching concept. Indeed, there is no necessary belonging of lower concepts to each other, nor is there any question of lineage. Any number of concepts can intersect in what can thereby be made into their overarching concept. Any account that purports to find necessity in the realm of concepts can only be a "pseudo-justification." In contrast there is nothing arbitrary in how the aspect of essence-unity belongs with that of essence-multiplicity.

I would like to discuss briefly a case that may illuminate these considerations and which bears directly on our discussion of translation in the previous chapter. Benjamin suggests a parallel between the considerations of essence-unity and essence-multiplicity and his thinking on the pure language and the multiplicity of languages:

> The multiplicity of languages is such an essence-multiplicity. The doctrine of the mystics concerning the degeneration of the true language stands on false ground if it bases its argument on the dissolution into many languages. That multiplicity would simply amount to the contradiction of a primordial and God-willed unity, but the multiplicity of languages is not the product of decadence any more than is the multiplicity of peoples, and indeed so far removed from any such decay that we might be justified in asserting that this multiplicity expresses their essential character. Therefore, this doctrine should not focus on the dissolution into many languages as the primary issue, but, rather, must speak of the fact that the integral power to rule becomes increasingly impotent. (SW 1:273; translation modified)

It is often assumed in reading "On Language as Such" that the very multiplicity of languages is to be considered as the expression of the Fall from a so-called pure, Edenic language. But if we follow Benjamin's analysis, the pure language would be the higher essence-unity (or idea), presented by the essence-multiplicity belonging to it. The Fall is not expressed in the multiplicity of languages but in the loss of the sense of harmony among them, that harmony being the warrant of the presence of the ruling force that is the pure language.

The sovereign ruling of the pure language is manifest as a *harmony* of languages. As I have argued, the invocation of harmony is precisely what avoids construing the kinship of languages as an external relation between them. Kinship between languages is not reducible to their having a common historical stem, a common ancestor. Nor is it based on partial similarity or analogy; rather, it belongs to the standpoint of identity. Each language is *whole and self-sufficient*. Languages are *in harmony* precisely in each being a standpoint on *one and the same* absolute totality, on the world. One can speak in this sense of a preestablished harmony of languages.[5]

The ruling of an essence-unity over an essence-multiplicity is of the latter character. There are no *relations* among the multiplicity of ideas/essences that go into the presentation of the ruling idea:

And thus the ideas admit of the law that all essentialities exist in complete independence and inviolability, not just from phenomena but above all from one another. Just as the harmony of the spheres depends on the orbiting of stars that never touch, so the existence of the *mundus intelligibilis* rests on the ineluctable distance between pure essentialities. Each idea is a sun and comports itself to its like [*verhält sich zur ihresgleichen*], as suns comport themselves to one another [*zueinander sich verhalten*]. Truth is the tonal proportionality [*tönende Verhältnis*] of such essentialities. (O 14; translation modified)

Indeed, turning to tonality is precisely the way to speak of attunement without any (external) relation between essences, so that each stands in isolation and yet all are in harmony. The multiplicity of ideas is essentially discontinuous, and harmony is precisely the characterization of their attunement "at a distance," that is, apart from any external relation. Substantive independence means that the essences do not come into contact, yet they are *in fit* harmonically (as in the harmony of the spheres). This is also what Benjamin calls a musical concept of truth: "Philosophy . . . is the only realm in which the truth becomes manifest, namely with sound like music" (SW 1:272). We will return to this peculiar idea of the musical character of truth.

Taking harmony to be the mark of kinship does not imply that *we* can so contemplate pure self-standing essences. *Sub specie aeternitatis*, there is a harmony of essences, but *we* would not sense it a such without further ado. We do not grasp languages as totalities and compare them from an external divine standpoint, as it were. Nor is the harmony between languages present for someone who happens to speak several languages. It is sensed only through a concrete occasion in a specific linguistic context, that is, in the translation of a poetic work.

There is no a priori derivation of the presentation of the pure language as a harmony of languages. Rather, through the translation of a work of literature the pure language is released or freed from the heart of the contingent. In a similar way Benjamin will argue in the foreword that "every essence [possesses] from the outset a limited—and moreover determinate—multiplicity of essences in which it manifests itself, which does not derive from the unity deductively but rather is assigned to the essence as a condition of its presentation [*Darstellung*] and unfolding [*Entfaltung*] *in the empirical*" (SW 1:273; translation modified; my emphasis).

The One and the Many

Ruling and harmony bring to mind Leibniz's monadology. This model is indeed on Benjamin's mind when he speaks of the monadological character of the presentation of the idea. "The idea is a monad—this means in short: each idea contains the image [*Bild*] of the world. For the task [*Aufgabe*] of its presentation nothing less is required than to depict this abbreviated image of the world" (O 27; translation modified). An idea (essence-unity) is presented by the harmony of the entire order of ideas (essence-multiplicity) from a certain standpoint and to varying degrees of distinctness.[6] To present the harmonious attunement of essences is tantamount to revealing their preestablished harmony: "The representation [*Repräsentation*] of phenomena rests preestablished in [the idea]."[7] Each monad mirrors the world of ideas (of essences) in its own way, to a degree dependent on how high it is in the order of being. "The higher the order of the ideas, the more perfect the representation [*Repräsentation*] within them" (O 27; translation modified). The *Trauerspiel* is in that sense a domain of investigation of a higher order, rich enough to present through the gathering of phenomena belonging to it the preestablished harmony of the whole world of ideas.

The preceding discussion provides us with a clear answer as to why we have a determinate multiplicity of essences that belongs to the presentation of each essence-idea. This is just the very multiplicity of the realm of ideas, which is thus one and the same for the presentation of any higher idea. It is also the spirit of the epigraph that Benjamin chose from Goethe's *Farbenlehre*: "Just as art is always wholly present in each individual artwork, so should science always be wholly manifest in each particular matter treated" (O 1). Benjamin similarly speaks of philosophy as the repeated "struggle for the presentation of a limited number of words, *which are always the same*—a struggle for the presentation of ideas" (O 14; my emphasis).

The world is, as Benjamin puts it, "a task, in the sense that what matters is to penetrate so deeply into everything real that an objective interpretation of the world would therein disclose itself" (O 27). The objective interpretation is not to be confused with the concept of objectivity used in the sciences. Rather, the force inherent in reality is fully objectified, actualized, and presented as the order of ideas. Note further that it is only through the utmost penetration of the *real*—that is, the empirical in all its details—that one can present the configuration of the multiplicity of essences. This penetration into minute details is precisely what Benjamin suggests in his remark about Leibniz being the founder of the infinitesimal calculus. The integration of the world of ideas in an idea-unity is a "function" of the attention to the infinitesimal, to the smallest nuances of the empirical. It is precisely through the necessity of drawing the idea-unity each time out of the singularly empirical that we have the distinct standpoints on the order of ideas. The *Trauerspiel* is an idea; this means that out of a field of historical phenomena it encompasses we can draw out, or release from the heart of reality, precisely an ordered multiplicity of essences, a schema or abbreviation of the world of ideas.

The Heart of the Contingent

Thus we should not hasten to put aside the plurality of phenomena for a supposed immediate grasp of the multiplicity of essences. Essences are not given in advance, as it were, merely intelligibly or abstractly. We cannot just hold on to those "words," for which philosophy struggles, and rest content. The words are nothing unless they are recovered from the depth of contingent reality and actualized anew every time. This is why Benjamin speaks of the revelation of origin as involving repetition and uniqueness. Origin is recognized as the same primal words are presented uniquely, that is, every time anew from out of a different contingent historical reality: "The idea as word . . . is released from the innermost reality" (O 13).

The order of essences cannot be revealed merely logically (even in the broad sense of Hegel's speculative logic or Hermann Cohen's logic of origin): "The Hegelian 'So much the worse for the facts' is well known. Fundamentally, it means that insight into essential connections is the task of the philosopher, and essential connections remain what they are even if they do not clearly leave their mark in the world of facts" (O 25). But conversely, one should not take the devotion to the factual to mean that one has given up on essentiality. In that sense we can speak here of a metaphysical empiricism that out of the existent presents its a priori order.[8]

The historical and the ideal come together in Benjamin's concept of origin, for which he gives what has become a well-known figure: "Origin is a whirlpool in the stream of becoming, and in its current it swallows the material involved in the process of generation [*Entstehung*]."⁹ Going by the figure of the whirlpool, we can say that the presentation of an origin is a reordering of material and, indeed, a reordering of material at a distance from its source—for example, from the lifeworld in which the material initially emerged (call this the context of generation). Thus we have implicitly here two moments, which can be called the destructive and the constructive. The material can be reordered only if we assume the destruction of its living unity, its detachment from the unity of the lifeworld that constitutes the context of generation. But the figure of origin presupposes a second constructive moment—namely, that through this reordering a more fundamental or higher unity of life, a higher life, is revealed. It is to point to the presence of such a higher life, concentrated in ideas, that Benjamin calls origin a category of natural history, beyond the consideration of pragmatic history or the standpoint of human works and deeds. "Its history is inward in character," he writes, ". . . not pure history, but natural history. The life of works and forms which under this protection can unfold clearly and unclouded by human life, is a natural life" (O 26; translation modified).

The Imprint and Seal of Reality

In the essay on *Elective Affinities*, Benjamin formulates the dimension of facticity through which the essential is presented and actualized in an illuminating way: "The most essential contents of existence are capable of leaving their imprint on the world of things, indeed . . . without such imprint [*Ausprägung*] they are incapable of fulfilling themselves" (SW 1:298; translation modified). In other words, it is only as a force leaves an imprint in the existing *material* content that we can further conceive of the actualization that presents the force as ruling over the essential *truth* content. This receives further elucidation by means of a distinction between imprint and seal (*Siegel*). An imprint in the empirical or contingent material content of what is in itself only force is a precondition of the complete objectification of that force in truth content. Only thereby can we recognize the truth content as the *seal* of phenomena. The figure of an imprint or seal is used after Aristotle to refer to the hylomorphic unity of form and matter. But we should note that, in Benjamin, imprint and seal are separated, as it were, and that the latter is the actualization of what was made possible by the former. The necessity of the destruction of the individual unity of phenomena in order to actualize the force in truth content further makes it clear that it is not a hylomorphic model that Benjamin has in mind.

"Truth subsists not as an intention or meaning that would find its determination through the empirical world but rather as the force that first stamps [*prägende Gewalt*] in the empirical the essence of that world" (O 12; translation modified). The force first leaves its imprint in reality (for us, however, dispersed over a variety of contingent contents); its actualization is possible in a historical investigation that brings that material into an ideal configuration presenting the essential. Imprint is initial, whereas sealing marks the form of the terminal, the completed (especially as we relate seal to sovereignty).[10] One could say that the discovered "imprint" points to the presence in the empirical reality of that which must be recognized and actualized as the "seal" of that reality. "The genuine—the seal of origin in phenomena [*Ursprungssiegel in den Phänomenen*]—is an object of discovery, a discovery bound up in a unique way with recognition [*Wiedererkennen*]" (O 25).

Put somewhat differently, truth content appears as the highest actuality, as the actualization of the force that imprinted itself in the material content. It is this actualization that is the task of the philosopher. Actualization is that through which phenomena partake in the highest reality, but conversely, that "actus purus" emerges only from the ordering of the historical-contingent material content. Since it is only through the phenomenal material content that truth content reveals itself, we can speak here of a moment of discovery, and since what is discovered is the unity of the order of ideas, it is a recognition. Historical recognition is remembering akin to "Platonic anamnesis." We will return to this relation between memory and history in Chapter 11.

But in order to properly characterize what it is that is recognized, there is a further aspect of the figure of the seal that must be developed. Especially as we think of the figure of a sovereign power, a seal is an image of sorts, say, an emblem of sovereignty. Now, an image is usually something conceived of in terms of vision or intuition. And yet Benjamin denies that the emerging order of ideas is to be recognized in a visual-like fashion: "If the weakness imparted to philosophy by every form of esotericism is painfully clear anywhere, it is in the 'vision' that all the Neoplatonic teachings of the pagan world prescribed to their adepts as philosophic comportment. The being of ideas simply cannot be conceived of as the object of an intuition—not even an intellectual intuition" (O 12).[11]

The register of intuition or vision is to be contrasted here first of all with language, that is, language as such. Indeed, truth content is named: "The idea is something linguistic" (O 13). Moreover, recall that essence-multiplicity belonging to the presentation of an idea is manifest as harmony. Harmony is heard; it is not intuition or a form of vision but the musical character of truth that is revealed in "primal hearing."[12]

What is given to be named in the language of man is ideas, which are recognized as their order is sensed in a harmonious configuration of contents: "Ideas are given, however, not so much in a primal language as in a primal hearing in which words possess the nobility of their naming power undiminished by their meaning in knowledge [*erkennende Bedeutung*]" (O 13; translation modified). The (creative) word does not appear as such in language but as always dispersed and bound to contingent content, bound to the communication of sense in human language:

> In empirical hearing, in which words have been disfigured, there attaches to them, along with their more or less hidden symbolic side, an overt profane meaning. It is the concern of the philosopher, through presentation, to reestablish in its primacy the symbolic character of the word, wherein the idea comes to a self-understanding that is the opposite of all outwardly directed communication. Since philosophy may not presume to speak in tones of revelation, this can happen only through a remembering that goes back first of all to the primal hearing. (O 13)

The "freeing" or "releasing" of the pure language from overtly profane meaning is a theme that, as we have seen, Benjamin develops in various places but perhaps most clearly in "The Task of the Translator" (see Chapter 3). Freeing provides a medium for truth as force to flow through the hierarchy of language to its highest objectification in a harmonious configuration of ideas.

Ideas as Configuration

The constellation is one of the most prevalent figures taken to be key to Benjamin's thought, and it is one of the most misinterpreted. The figure of the constellation is deployed to address the problem of the relation of the oneness of truth to the original multiplicity in the presentation of the intelligible realm of ideas or essences. An idea is presented as a configuration of thinglike elements (and not of concepts as the English translation has it). These elements are revealed by a reordering of phenomena that assumes their release from their particular *object*-unity. This release is made possible by the work of the concept through which particularity is dissected. What Benjamin calls an element is a gathering of phenomena severed from their initial life context into a new order; it is akin to what Goethe calls a primal phenomenon. "Ideas—in Goethe's parlance, ideals—are the Faustian mothers. They remain dark so long as the phenomena do not declare their allegiance and flock around them" (O 11).

Benjamin uses the term "thing" (*Ding*) rather than "object" or "particular." This word is used sparingly and specifically in the foreword: truth is said to resemble "the simple being of things" (O 12). Thus, when Benjamin writes that "ideas are to things as constellations to stars," he does not mean that ideas are so related to empirical objects or particulars but rather to the elementary "thingly" character of other ideas (essence-multiplicity) subordinate to the higher idea (essence-unity). Such subordination is precisely the holding together of the essence-multiplicity harmoniously, that is, as the expression of a force.

It is precisely in order to do away with the false unity of the object or the particular that concepts are essential. The conceptual mediates between the particular and the idea, but not because it subsumes the particulars under general laws. Rather, concepts dissect and divide the particulars so as to allow a new order in which things, or elements, emerge, released from the false unity of the particular. Phenomena are purified from their seeming independence as particulars and now form a connected space in which is recognized the element as the ground of their relationships. The element is the summation of this space of dissociated and reordered phenomena.

The elements that appear through the new order of phenomena are simply ideas presented from the standpoint of the ruling idea. The configuration of ideas that goes into the presentation of a higher idea is unique insofar as it arises from the investigation of a specific subject matter (here the German *Trauerspiel*). The *Trauerspiel* contains in itself a perspective on the world of ideas. There are as many perspectives (as many configurations) as there are genuine subject matters for philosophy.

Benjamin speaks of the gathering of the phenomenal into elements of the presentation as the establishment of extremes: "The empirical . . . is more deeply penetrated the more distinctly it is seen as an extreme" (O 11). Whereas the concept establishes the "average," the idea is presented by extremes. Extremes can only be plural, inasmuch as something is an extreme only in coexisting with other extremes (a single thing cannot be an extreme). When one thinks of ideas as presented through extremes, then not only is plurality necessary but so is the force that rules over the elements and is manifest as their preestablished harmony. One could say that in the polarization of phenomena into extremes, in the harmonious balance of extremes, negation that belongs to the order of judgment is absorbed in the positivity of the ideal as the objectification of a force in a harmonious discontinuous multiplicity of truth contents.

The notion of objectification belongs to the account of the constellation: "Phenomena are not incorporated in ideas [*einverlebt*]. They are not contained in them. Ideas are rather their objective virtual ordering [*objective virtuelle Anordnung*], their objective interpretation" (O 10; translation modified).[13] It is important not to think of objective interpretation in terms of the concept of scientific objectivity that describes the lawful reality of particulars; it is the *objectification* of force in a configuration of ideas that is at issue.[14] In other words, the idea "in itself" is not a preexisting concept that is instantiated in intuition. It is wholly virtual and is recognized objectively only through its specific actualization in and through contingent historical material.

Knowledge and Revelation

In our reading of the multiplicity of essences internal to the idea we have stressed how the essences are completely independent of each other. But there is another dimension of the problem to address: namely, their independence from the subject. It is this independence that is most challenging in elaborating what a presentation of ideas comes to. The register of the concept is that of the spontaneity of the subject. It is expressed in Benjamin's claim that knowledge in concepts takes over its object, takes possession of it through concepts; therefore the object loses all independence. But ideas are, after Plato, the highest reality, and, if anything, it is the subject instead that must "lose itself" in them in partaking in that highest actuality.

Benjamin contrasts the "having of knowledge" with the "being of truth." The possessive form of "having or acquiring" knowledge reflects the way in which knowledge involves a form of synthesis that pertains to the active engagement of the subject. It is therefore essentially distinct from the original oneness of the creative force that objectifies itself in ideas. "Whereas concepts arise out of the spontaneity of the understanding[,] ideas are given to contemplation. Ideas are preestablished [*ein Vorgegebenes*]. Thus the differentiation of truth from the context of knowing defines the idea as being. That is how the theory of ideas bears on the concept of truth" (O 5; translation modified).

To be true to an original oneness of being is to acknowledge that self-presentation is a form immanent to that being. We do not represent it; it can only present itself, give itself to our contemplation. When being as such is original, then what is at issue for us is essentially to allow it to reveal itself, to construct the medium in which it presents itself on its own terms. It is for this reason that even though the method of presentation can be called constructive, it will ultimately be in the service of a contemplative stance adequate to the self-revelation of truth.

One important criterion of the distinction between knowledge and truth is that knowledge can be articulated as an answer to a question.[15] The question, or hypothesis, is that prior setting of terms by the subject which, as it were, forces a definite answer, yes or no, from nature.[16] One can ask about an object of knowledge, but there is no question to which truth answers: "Knowledge is ascertained in questioning but truth is not" (O 5; translation modified). Truth is unquestionable. This is not meant to express the subjective sense of certainty in the face of truth but rather the inapproachability of truth. It cannot be the object of questioning or of a prefiguration in the form of a hypothesis or question. Indeed, if it is self-presenting, it cannot be forced to accommodate itself to the forms of the questioning consciousness.

One could also put the point as follows: Questioning is always plural. There is no one ultimate question—say, the riddle of existence—whose response is the ultimate unity of truth. The object of questioning, knowledge, is always partial, and therefore there is a plurality of known domains. When knowledge is thought of as a unity, this can only be by establishing a systematic connection between the different kinds of knowledge.[17] But, as Benjamin puts it: "unity is present in the essence of truth as an immediate determination." This has radical implications for a Platonic theory of ideas. The Platonic idea is one by being the highest reality, in relation to which everything partaking in it is only derivative. The Platonic idea is "one" by virtue of its own nature; it is not one as a result of a conceptual synthesis, nor is it one as a unity of consciousness. It is a unity of being and not of the concept.

Establishing the unquestionable character of truth is not in service of stressing its inherently mysterious character. That which is unquestionable is "existence." ("It must be said that philosophy in its questionings can never hit upon the unity of existence" [SW 1:109].) Existence is not a categorial unity. Recall that this highest noncategorial unity that is the ground of the sphere of knowledge is characterized through "identity" (SW 1:107). Identity, as we already saw in Chapter 1, is the order of the self-revealing. Identity cannot be attained as an object of thinking (just as God cannot be reached from below but must be recognized in revealing Himself). This introduces a difficult tension: How do we work toward actualizing that which reveals itself? It is here that we recognize the essential role of beauty.

How Can Truth Do Justice to Beauty?

It is precisely the necessity of recognizing ideas in the medium of empirical reality that shows us why presentation is an inescapable aspect of philosophical method. We do not think the multiplicity of ideas or reflect upon it. We do not have to relate them to each other to form a system. Phenomena are purified and redeemed as they are incorporated in the presentation of what preexists, that is, the ideas. This is also what Benjamin calls, after Plato, "saving the phenomena." But what does saving come to here?

We can formulate our dilemma as follows: Truth is unapproachable; we cannot just start with the chaos of phenomena and try to find something like the elements that constitute the harmony of the self-standing truth. It is not as though we work on a puzzle and try to fit the small pieces together so as to get the bigger picture. The direction must be reversed: we have to start with something like a unity, which, while truthful, is nevertheless distinct from the recognition of the objective unity of the world of ideas and in some sense therefore is a semblance of totality. It is precisely by thinking of the necessity of the orientation through a semblance of totality that we recognize the role of beauty alongside the elaboration of knowledge and truth. The primary horizon of unity is what is given to us, in art, as the beautiful. It is only in methodically destroying that beautiful semblance of unity that we get our "phenomena" in their purified form. We thus rejoin here themes developed in Chapter 3 concerning the idea of critique and the recognition of truth content through the philosophical knowledge of material content. The destructive force, which is methodical, is that of the concept and of the knowledge of material content that prepares phenomena for being incorporated and presenting the higher harmony of ideas.

This is in point of fact the main issue in the interpretation that Benjamin gives of the Socratic teaching of the *Symposium*. Benjamin argues that the teaching of the *Symposium* is one of the most fundamental statements of the doctrine of ideas, precisely because it addresses the apparent paradox of working toward the self-revelation of truth. There must be a way to characterize the manifestation of the wholeness of truth for us, and yet of distinguishing it from truth itself, whose recognition is afforded by philosophy. It is precisely this difficulty that is addressed by Benjamin's account of beauty and its relation to knowledge, desire, and truth.

Let us recall, to start with, some of the central themes of Socrates' speech, which itself relates the teachings of Diotima about eros. Eros is a daimon, conceived on Aphrodite's birthday, child of lack and excess, neither human nor divine. Owing to his lack he longs for the fullness of beauty and thereby opens the way to what is higher. Its "mediating" character is evident in a series of stages or transformations: From the love of the particular to loving the universal in the human, from loving beautiful bodies to loving beautiful souls, and ultimately attaining to the view of the beautiful as such—namely, partaking in the idea of the beautiful. This doctrine is called a mystery. Its heart is an esoteric teaching of how, through the love of beauty, we achieve a view of true being, of the realm of ideas.

Even this brief sketch raises many questions: In what way can eros be said to be true to its original longing when it "ends up" with truth? Is the beauty of things only an enticing appearance, merely seducing so as to draw us to something wholly different—namely, to essence or truth? Is beauty the external appearance of the essential truth? Or is it that the true *is* the beautiful? A first step in Benjamin's approach to these problems is to point to the relational, though not relativistic, character of beauty. Something is beautiful only *for someone*. As Benjamin puts it: "The human being is beautiful for the one who loves, though in himself, he is not." The *in-itself* is essential being, that is, truth. Thus Benjamin can assert that "eros ... does not betray his original aspiration when he directs his longing toward truth, for truth too is beautiful. It is beautiful so not so much in itself as for eros" (O 6).

Eros follows the promise of beauty as its suitor, which is at the same time described as a flight of beauty from its advances as well as from the pursuit of the understanding. One might try to explicate both the seduction and the figure of flight by pointing to the evasiveness internal to beauty, as though it belongs to beauty not only to be radiant but also to hold back, to be mysterious. The understanding seeks to question that secret and receive determinate answers, that is, knowledge. Yet the method of knowledge, namely, questioning, is inadequate to recognize the secret of beauty. Indeed, it is because beauty as such ultimately belongs to truth that it resists knowledge. It is the character of "the unity of truth ... [to] elude every form of questioning. As unity in being and not as unity in concept, truth is beyond all questioning" (O 5). Truth, the idea, is the preexisting; it is being, the highest being. As what is in itself, it is nonrelational; it cannot be conditioned by a form of the spontaneity of the understanding. It reveals itself and thus cannot be an intentional object correlative with a form of unity of consciousness.

We may have saved beauty from the understanding and even hinted at why, at the heart of the doctrine of the *Symposium*, lies a mystery, but, it seems, at the price of making truth wholly inaccessible, even to reason. Indeed, questioning seems to belong to the method of philosophy (it suffices here to think of Socrates' relentless queries). Yet, for philosophy to truly be the love of wisdom, it cannot merely remain with the negativity of the understanding. Philosophy must acknowledge its dependence on the radiant fullness of beauty, without on that account aestheticizing truth or renouncing the sober recognition of truth content. Clarifying this possibility requires us to go deeper into Benjamin's understanding of the reciprocal dependence between philosophy and art, for if there is something missing from the stages of ascent described in the *Symposium*, it is the place of the beauty of art and the problem of its critique.

Critique brings back knowledge, that is, the deadening force of the understanding. Critique is inseparable from the detailed knowledge that we identified earlier as philological work, as commentary on the material content. Its piecemeal character destroys the semblance of the harmonious wholeness of the beautiful. It brings about the arrest of the evasiveness of the beautiful. The destructive moment of critique is evident in Benjamin's account of the last stage in the ascent of eros, in which he figures beauty as attempting to save itself by fleeing to the altar of truth. An altar is both a place of sacrifice and a place of communion, such as the altar of marriage. In other words, one might presume that when the love of beauty becomes communion with the truth, eros must also be witness to the destruction of the beautiful semblance. That last stage "can be described figuratively as the flaming up of the veil as it enters the circle of ideas—a burning of the work in which its form reaches its highest radiance"[18] (O 7; translation modified). The radiant disappearance of the beautiful form in truth would do justice to it. We will return to this difficult moment in our discussion of *Elective Affinities* in Chapter 6.

PART II

Life and Fate

FIVE

The Guilt and Innocence of Life

Man not only realizes nature in language but also belongs to the hierarchy of nature. We can ask ourselves how the problem of fulfillment manifests itself, not merely in art but in human life. We must of course address not only what the realization of life comes to but also, maybe first of all, what the character of unfulfilled life is. One could say that for all natural species the unrealized is the exception, whereas for human existence it is, so to speak, the norm. The essay "Fate and Character" can provide us with an initial elaboration of this natural dimension in human existence. It is evident that "fate" is not a concept attributable to the life of plants or animals, and yet it is internally related to life, to the way life is in the human form of life.

This text of Benjamin's should be approached with the understanding that we have in it a characterization of the guilt of life (as fate) as well as of the innocence of life (as character). We have here a conception of natural guilt and innocence. In addition, Benjamin identifies two ways in which art takes up these dimensions: one is facing the guilt of life in tragedy, the other manifesting natural innocence in comedy. This already makes clear that Benjamin's first task in this essay is to break apart the spheres of fate and character, which are often linked together. Indeed, the essay begins with a critique of the modern understanding of these notions that makes fate and character interdependent.

The Modern View of Fate and Character

The modern view of the relation of the two concepts, fate and character, can be described as follows. If, on the one hand, we have knowledge of the character of someone and, on the other hand, knowledge of all the external situations that this person will find themselves in, then it would be possible to predict how they will act/react in every situation and thus to predict their fate. Character, according to this view, is a psychological category identified, say, as a stable complex of beliefs and desires. The world facing a person, considered in terms of its facts and events, is just as determined and distinct, and so the various "encounters" that someone has in the external world impinge on their inner constitution and bring about determinate reactions, reactions recognizably associated with the complex of beliefs and desires of such a person.

Fate would then be the course of that person's life, understood causally and deterministically—the expected reactions of that person to unknown and independent yet already determined future events. Whereas according to the modern worldview one might believe in the possibility of having complete knowledge of the sphere of psychology—call it the inner world—it is hopeless to seek complete knowledge of the external causal nexus that someone might be faced with in their life. It will therefore be impossible to read a person's fate, where reading someone's fate is identified, given a knowledge of their "character," with predicting future occurrences that will befall them. The predictive assessment of someone's life course, then, would merely be logically possible, but in no way is it a real possibility.

Problematizing the Distinction between Inner and Outer

According to the modern worldview, the physiognomy of a person, understood as behavior manifested in bodily gestures and experience, may be affected by their deep-seated psychology. But there is no reason to expect the lines of the hand to express someone's psychology; the practice of palm reading for the prediction of fate would therefore appear to be absurd. While Benjamin is not concerned in "Fate and Character" with providing a justification of mantic practices, he does make an important point about the general perspective from which to approach these matters. Whereas the modern picture sketched above depends on a vision of causality and determinism, fate is a nexus of meaning. Reading fate always concerns the interpretation of signs rather than the knowledge of facts: "It [fate] is never accessible except through signs, because it is situated above the immediately visible level" (SW 1:201).

Whereas the modern concept of fate rests on a causal account, the authentic understanding of that notion is one that pertains to meaning, and "a nexus of meaning can never be founded causally" (SW 1:202). It is not that we turn to reasons as opposed to causes; as will become clear, the dimension of meaning in question pertains to the fulfillment and unfulfillment of a higher life, and as such is over and above what is ruled by the principle of sufficient reason (i.e., either by causes or by reasons). Indeed, as Benjamin returns to the presentation of fate in art, in the essay "Calderon and Hebbel" he writes: "Without wishing to become involved in extensive debate about the concept of fate, we must emphasize one point above all others: fate does not involve the inescapable nexus of cause and effect as such. . . . How could art put itself in the position of supporting a hypothesis that lies at the heart of determinism? The only philosophical ideas that can enter into the structure of art are those which concern the meaning of existence" (SW 1:377).

Challenging the modern articulation of the idea of fate—that is, showing what the authentic concepts of fate and character come to—also makes clear, as Benjamin argues, that they belong to different spheres. In order to establish this separation it will initially be necessary to distinguish the notion of character from that of the psychological makeup of a person and, more generally, to reject the model of the relation between fate and character as an external relation between person and world. In other words, the concepts of both fate and character precisely challenge our ways of setting self and world apart. They are both signaling a higher standpoint indifferent to the distinction between inner and outer.

Character is not a psychological, empirical category. Character is inherently one and is logically prior to the multiplicity of desires and psychological features of a person. Character is presupposed as a ground underlying all its manifold expressions in the life of a person. Character is, of course, revealed to a person in time, as though a posteriori, through what that person does or suffers. There is no access to character through, say, introspection, since it is not to be identified with the inner world of a person. But what is thereby revealed is a primal unity rather than a complex of properties that may change with time owing to a variety of factors. It is a timeless ground that has different manifestations on various occasions over time and comes to be known through these manifestations.

A person's character may manifest itself in different ways, according to circumstances, but circumstances do not change character over time. Given different circumstances of life, the same character-type can be expressed in different ways. (To give a somewhat simplistic example, someone can be both a tyrant and a solitary recluse, but only on account of there being different occasions for manifesting the same character.) There is an intensive dimension to the manifestation of character in life: while it is unchanging, its "visible expressions" are a matter of degree. In other words, character can be more or less manifestly expressed in the life of a person. One might also say that the manifestations of character can be more or less distorted in a human life. But as we think of the fullest or highest manifestation of character, we can no longer hold to the opposition between an inner sphere and external events; rather, character and world are shown to be wholly reciprocal: "It is impossible to form an un-contradictory concept of the exterior of an active human being whose core is taken to be character" (SW 1:202; translation modified). With the expression of character comes a constancy of experience (of the world). With the full presence of character there appears an indifference between inner and outer, which one could think of as an agreement or fit with the world that is wholly different from so-called success and is achieved by the satisfaction of a person's particular desires and purposes. (This will be further developed in Chapter 8.) In other words, the person of character, the person who actively exhibits character exists in a world "of that character." One could say that a "strong" character is a mode of being in the world, of having a world of one's own.

The unchanging ground of character is correlative with a stability in the "character" of the experience of that person. Quoting Nietzsche, Benjamin remarks: "'If a man has character, he has an experience that constantly recurs.' This means: if a man has character, his fate is essentially constant. Admittedly, it also means: he has no fate—a conclusion drawn by the Stoics" (SW 1:202).

This last sentence shows how the critique of the modern worldview leads to a fundamental distinction between the spheres of fate and character. It might seem at first that if someone has a recurring experience, then they are, as it were, determined. And wouldn't that amount precisely to having a fate? As will become clear, however, in the proper understanding of fate, it is indeterminacy and ambiguity that rule. Suffering from fate is, one might say, a condition of subjection to an inexorable ambiguity in one's way of being in the world. To be precise, fate works its ways ironically, through ambiguity. Conversely, to have a constant experience, a constancy of being—in sum, to have character wholly manifest—is, as Benjamin clearly puts it, to have no fate, to be released from the orders of fate. We will return to the analysis of character later on, after clarifying the nature of fate.

Fate and Ambiguous Life

The notion of fate is often used to refer to the state of a person who suffers from an affliction that is not meted out by human hand but, as it were, through the agency of the world itself. In attempting to conceive of fate as having meaning, we might identify fate with a punishment. But in that case it would be necessary to further distinguish suffering at the hands of fate from punishment that is incurred by an infraction of the laws of a social order. Suffering human punishment for a wrongdoing punishable under law is distinct from being punished by fate, and so the character of the guilt would also be different. The common view would explain the difference by the latter's being punishment for a sin against the gods, thus making fate a category of religion.

While the notion of fate is not unrelated to the mythical register, this way of opposing an infraction of human law to a sin against the gods is skewed, in part by not realizing the place of law in the constitution of a field of fate. It is not so much that the model of punishment for an infraction of human law is translated into fate's being a punishment for an infraction of divine laws; rather, it is the guilt of life itself that is the original form of fate to contend with. Only in view of the guilt of mere life can we pose the further question of how to position law in relation to that predicament.

A clear distinction between being guilty through an action (whether it infringes upon human laws or divine laws) and the guilt associated with fate is that the latter lacks altogether a corresponding concept of innocence (and with it that of a reward opposed to the punishment of fate). A coherent characterization of the guilt of a person through their actions must also have a corresponding concept of innocence. But there is no negation of guilt that remains within that same field of fate; there is no such thing as innocence being one's fate (no innocence in the field of fate). Similarly, we cannot conceive of a reward of fate; fate knows only guilt. There is no "good" fate. We might imagine that being fortunate is the opposite of being guilty by fate while belonging to the same dimension. Yet Benjamin stresses that often having what seems like "good fortune" is precisely what tempts a person to hubris, and thus it is precisely the instrument of fate, what leads to submitting to the orders of fate in one's life. There is indeed a notion of fortune, which will be correlated with character, but it is wholly different from the possibility of being rewarded by fate. As Benjamin remarks, the highest happiness, the blissful existence of the gods, is precisely the indication of their being one with their nature, not of being subject to the ambiguity of fate.

If the standpoint of the gods signifies a realm not subject to fate, it would suggest that fate is a category of finite human existence.[1] It is intrinsically related to the nature of human life. This would mean in the first place that fate does not belong to a specific person through something or other that they do but rather that it is a condition of human life. Benjamin speaks of the guilt of life prior to any act attributable to a person. This is the sense in which we speak of fate as a form of natural guilt. Though Benjamin reflects here on the pagan rather than the Judeo-Christian tradition, the kind of guilt of life at issue can be compared to original sin. Fate is not something that belongs to an individual and differs from one individual to another; it is the character of finite human life. And only against this ground of guilty life can one speak of actions that precipitate or make visible that condition through extreme suffering that befalls that person.

Just as character has to be conceived of with respect to life as a whole and in such a way that the distinction between inner and outer is problematized, so fate should be considered through the form of being in the world. One can say that an existence ruled by fate is a form of unrealized being-in-the-world. In particular, fate need not be attributed to an individual per se but could be a mode of being in the world that can even be attributed to the life of a collective.[2]

Needless to say, we often speak of a fateful moment, an encounter, that would change the course of one's life, which in that sense would seem to make fate a personal matter—that is, one's own fate, caused or brought about by such and such a chance circumstance. But as Benjamin puts it, there are fateful moments only in bad novels. A moment can serve to precipitate the visible concentration of fate, but it is not what is to be identified as the cause or origin of fate. The moment is an occasion for bringing out what was always there. To speak of fate as a mode of human existence in the world means precisely that various moments can potentially be occasions for the visible concentration of fate. When we look at life and say, "If only this and this had not happened to me, I could have made it (my life would have been a happy one)," we are deluded concerning the workings of fate, for it is not a specific event that has a fateful character. When the world in which one exists and one's existence in it are of a certain character, there will be no lack of occasions to precipitate misfortune, the unfolding of fate.[3]

Fate and Tragedy

The nature of fate can be further elaborated in terms of one of the artistic forms that makes its presence evident dramatically or catastrophically—namely, tragedy. As will become clearer in the course of the following chapters, there is a history of the manifestation of fate, and different literary forms express the different ways in which fate is present in life. In particular, the contrast between tragedy and *Trauerspiel* will bring out how the baroque transforms our understanding of the presence of fate and the modes of its overcoming.[4] Tragedy is the ancient form of art that brings out most perspicuously what compromised existence in fate comes to, while at the same time showing how in the acceptance of sacrifice the hero (or heroine) overcomes the orders of fate. Tragedy contains the most vivid dramatic presentation of what it means to lead a life in which the ambiguity of inner and outer that is characteristic of unrealized life is brought to its extreme expression and thereby, as it were, arrested.

Ambiguity is not mere vagueness. In fact, it is utterly precise, as is made terribly evident when in the course of pursuing its unfolding to the limit, the tragic hero suffers its catastrophic precision. The inherent ambiguity in each action and assertion of the tragic hero constitutes tragic irony, of which the hero is unaware until fate closes on him. It's as though the tragic hero goes all the way, whereas weaker persons would suffer the ambiguity without ever realizing the source of that suffering. This capacity for bringing to an extreme what belongs to a form of existence would then be a sign of nobility, of heroism, and not of depravity. The tragic heroine—say, Antigone—is someone with the force to make the presence of fate evident in her life surroundings, who thus is singled out as an exemplary individual. While, as we have seen, there is something in the prevalence of fate in a form of life that recalls original sin, we should, following Nietzsche, conceive of it in tragedy, as *Promethean* original sin—precisely what only a being of titanic force is capable of precipitating to the full.[5]

This ambiguity is evident in the way that the tragic hero—Oedipus, for example—must recognize as his own, that is, as what pertains to his identity at the most fundamental level, what has appeared to be the work of forces beyond the scope of what he could intend or control. In tragedy, we come to recognize, for instance, the impossibility of clearly distinguishing between a person's inner world of intention and their life surroundings. Thus, Oedipus does not sin intentionally; rather, what appears wholly external and coincidental "catches up" with him. The movement that consciously takes the direction of escaping the prophecy is what leads to the encounter with certain "external" occasions that will fulfill the prophecy. But the arrest of ambiguity isn't yet the revelation of a new form of existence. There is no expression adequate to that moment; for this reason Benjamin characterizes the position of the tragic hero as sublime speechlesness: "The paradox of the birth of genius in moral speechlessness . . . is the sublimity of tragedy." The expressionless silence is what marks the highest individuation as a paradox. It can be seen as an extreme act of freedom, in which a person recognizes what their proper name comes to by accepting as belonging to them what befalls them from outside. The hero of tragedy is therefore not only a victim of fate, not only atoning through punishment: in him fate, in its utmost extreme unfolding, is worked through.

By gathering and concentrating fate in his person, the tragic hero reveals in a decisive light the contradiction underlying collective existence. Tragedy "concentrates" fate and "reflects" it in the person of the hero so that this very reflection is the arrest of fate's pernicious ambiguity. This arrest, even as it brings life to an end, is a release from the rule of guilt: "Guilt, which according to the ancient statutes falls upon men from without through misfortune, is taken over by a hero in the course of the tragic action and absorbed into himself. By reflecting it in his consciousness of himself, he escapes its demonic jurisdiction" (O 131).

Tragedy turns a space ruled by demonic ambiguity into one in which measures can be taken. It involves a decisive moment: "Tragedy ends with a decision—however uncertain this may be" (O 137). The state in which, through his terrible suffering, all possibilities end for the tragic hero shows in his person the paradoxical condition of existence of the community. It allows the community to envisage the order that will be raised beyond the violence of unformed life: "[The tragic sacrifice] is the representative action, in which new aspects of the life of the nation become manifest" (O 107).

The concentration of guilt in the person of the tragic hero is key to recognizing the redeeming character of tragedy, its way of addressing the "natural guilt" that is part of the very being in the field of life.[6] Benjamin refers to Hegel's understanding that "it is a point of honor of these great characters to be culpable" (O 131). The tragic hero makes contradiction visible but does not resolve it in speech. His position is characterized by silence, which, with all the suffering, has a dimension of defiance. It marks the emergence of the infinity of morality in which man senses, without being able to express in any other way than defiance, that he is "better than his god." This is the "birth of genius in moral speechlessness" (SW 1:203).

Law and Fate

After dismissing the common connection formed between fate and a sin against the gods, Benjamin seeks another sphere that is instrumental in the realization of the principles of fate, that is, the essential guilt and misfortune that belong internally to human life: "Another sphere must therefore be sought in which misfortune and guilt alone carry weight, a balance on which bliss and innocence are found too light and float upward. This balance is the scale of law. The orders [*Gesetze*] of fate—misfortune and guilt—are elevated by law [*Recht*] to measures of the person" (SW 1:203; translation modified). Note the distinction between *Gesetze* and *Recht* (reflected in my translation by using "orders" for *Gesetze*). This is not just the distinction between two kinds of laws; strictly speaking, the concept of law belongs together with the notion of judgment (be it in its logical or juridical sense). Over and above the standpoint of universality of judgment, we recognize in fate something that pertains to the failure in realizing a higher unity in human life (call it the standpoint of identity). This is why Benjamin writes that at the basis of the concept of guilt in the eyes of the law, we have the more fundamental order of fate, in which one has to speak of misfortune that belongs to the original guilt of life: "It would be false to assume that only guilt is present in a legal context; it is demonstrable that all legal guilt is nothing other than misfortune" (SW 1:203).

Fate is localized, concentrated, and its ambiguity arrested in the tragic hero. But this just means that for the vast majority of human beings, while there is suffering from that condition, there is in no way a precise and determinate visibility of that suffering. This opens up the possibility of forming, through law, an order in which there is seemingly a proportional relation between infraction and punishment, but it is an order that will ultimately serve the dictation of fate. This is what is hinted in the following passage: "It is not therefore really man who has a fate; rather, the subject of fate is indeterminable. The judge can perceive fate wherever he will; with every judgment he must blindly further fate's dictation" (SW 1:203; translation modified).

The relation between law and fate is one of the most difficult issues of this difficult essay, in part because one has to bring together the natural dimension in the account of life as a field of fate and the function of the law in society in the manifestation of fate. A full appreciation of the complexity of the relationship between law, life, and fate will involve the interpretation of Benjamin's "Critique of Violence," which I leave to the next chapter. But initially the following may be said: Law is the instrument through which fate manifests itself in the life of a person, insofar as one conceives of the ways in which fate pervades human collective existence. Law makes itself an agent of fate in the following sense: it "translates" the impersonal guilt that pertains to mere life into legal guilt that essentially pertains to a specific act of the individual that is to be punished. In this sense the workings of fate are hidden by the appearance of law and judgment, but at the same time law becomes an instrument of fate. Law does not truly give form and determinacy to the ambiguous environment of mere human life. On the contrary, it is through law that the ambiguity of the rule of myth manifests itself.

Fate and Time

Benjamin returns to the possibility of understanding mantic practices such as fortune-telling after clarifying the idea of fate in tragedy. Inquiring about that possibility, while not central to our concerns, brings out important aspects that pertain to the relation between fate and time. As we have seen, the practice of soothsaying should not be identified with the prediction of future occurrences; this is how the modern worldview distorts its meaning. What is read is what is always there, and the fortune-teller's system of signs constitutes one way among many of relating a person to this always-present dimension. The fatal character of life can also be identified as the presence of the primal or of myth in human existence.

A person can abandon themselves to life ruled by the primal, letting that guilty life in them take over. Indeed, seeking out the soothsayer is a sign of this abandonment: "The man who visits her gives way to the guilty life within himself" (SW 1:204). All that the technique of the fortune-teller can do is to couple cards, planets, or whatever gives the appearance of calculation so that they serve as signs to that hidden yet ever-present dimension of the primal.

This presence of the primal is the point of the description of the temporality of fate. Fate is a distorted temporal category. There is no past, no future, nor any inherent progression internal to fate. Fate is the dimension of the ever same, of eternal return, in human life, which seeks to insert itself into the temporal order: "Since fate, the true order of eternal recurrence, is only inauthentically—that is parasitically—to be conceived of as temporal, its manifestations seek out space-time" (O 135). We might then ask, What is the time of fate parasitical on? Is it parasitical on our ordinary sense of time? This seems doubtful, for what the time of fate is contrasted with is "the time of redemption, or of music, or of truth." In other words, we might say that the time of fate is a distortion of a higher authentic temporality. Following our earlier analysis, we can say that the mythical eternal is a distortion of the standpoint of identity.

Character

This leaves us with the question of how to articulate the innocence of life released from natural guilt, from the bond of fate. As Benjamin makes clear, natural innocence must be thought in relation to the spiritual unity of life, which is character (as opposed to, say, the connection of original guilt with sexuality and therefore the understanding of innocence through virginity, as in the Christian tradition). As Benjamin puts it in the essay on "Elective Affinities":

> To be sure, like natural guilt, there is also a natural innocence of life. The latter, however, is tied not to sexuality—not even in the mode of denial—but rather solely to its antipode, the spirit (which is equally natural). Just as the sexual life of man can become the expression of natural guilt, his spiritual life, based on the variously constituted unity of his individuality, can become the expression of natural innocence. This unity of individual spiritual life is "character." (SW 1:335)

Just as tragedy is the emergence of the person from a field of nonmoral guilt, comedy is the manifestation of the nonmoral yet spiritual innocence of character.[7] The nonmoral aspect of character becomes clear in its artistic manifestation in comedy. The "characters," as is evident in Molière, to which Benjamin refers, are often scoundrels, misanthropes, misers, and so forth, but this is never the basis of a moral judgment against them. In an extremely condensed discussion, Benjamin provides an analysis of the concept of character that can be elucidated in terms of the following headings:

The absence of (psychological) complication

We have already seen from Benjamin's critique of the modern understanding of the relation between fate and character that for him character is not a psychological notion. This becomes further evident in the complete lack of "interiority," reflection, or complex psychological motivations of comic characters: "A great comic playwright ... excludes psychological analysis from his work" (SW 1:205).

The simplicity (single trait) of character

If ambiguity is the form in which fate manifests itself, then univocity indicates character. There is an essential simplicity to character: "To attribute to a human being a complicated character can only mean, whether rightly or wrongly, to deny him character" (SW 1:335). In other words, there is no duality or inner struggle in the manifestations of strong character. This is something that is to be contrasted with the inner world that is the object of psychology. The inner world is the place of reflection, of self-consciousness, but therefore also of the possibility of being divided against oneself—that is, of a complex inner life. Character is the individual as the embodiment of a character trait.[8]

The typicality of characters

Benjamin thinks of the embodiment of a character trait as constituting individuals to be tantamount to their anonymity. Here we are not quite thinking of a unique individual but rather of the way in which a trait of character has come to be embodied and everything about the person embodying this character trait makes it evident. One can speak therefore of typicality and thus of anonymity: "The sublimity of character comedy rests on this anonymity of man and his morality, alongside the utmost development of the individual [*Entfaltung des Individuums*] through its exclusive character trait" (SW 1:205; translation modified). We do tend to connect the constitution of our unique individuality with a struggle for authenticity; it is something that can hardly be separated from our sense of the depth and complexity of one's inner world. Yet reflection and self-consciousness are also possibilities of being divided against oneself— that is, of a self-entanglement that can appear irresolvable. In such a state character appears as freedom in a unified simplicity of existence. With Benjamin we have a possibility of conceiving of spirituality in the typical.

The rigor and consistency of character

The simplicity and typicality of character makes it true that such character is always on the surface, as it were, always manifest. What is crucial is that every expression of the life of a person is deployed out of the character trait. One could say that everything is an occasion for the character to manifest itself. This is not to say that the individual of character always succeeds in achieving what they want—only that character is present regardless of success or failure. There is therefore a certain rigor or utter consistency in the life of that individual, which is why I take it that Benjamin speaks of its "affinity to logic."

The freedom in character

This consistency of character is of something that works wholly according to its simple inner law. It raises the threat of "determinism," as though everything is necessarily determined mechanically, as it were.[9] But Benjamin writes that we have here something that is the utmost expression of freedom: "The vision of character, on the other hand, is liberating in all its forms: it is linked to freedom, as cannot be shown here, by way of its affinity to logic" (SW 1:206). This depends on properly understanding the enslavement of spirit in being divided against oneself. This is not merely the opposition between inclinations and reason; rather, as we have seen, the character of existence in a field of fate is ambiguity. For this reason there is immense freedom in simplification: "While fate brings to light the immense complexity of the guilty person, the complications and bonds of his guilt, character gives this mystical enslavement of the person to the guilt context the answer of genius. Complication becomes simplicity, fate freedom. For the character of the comic figure is not the scarecrow of the determinist; it is the beacon in whose beams the freedom of his actions become visible" (SW 1:205–206).

The radiance of character

"Character," Benjamin writes, "develops [in comedy] like a sun, in the brilliance of its single trait, which allows no other to remain visible in its proximity" (SW 1:205). Character is radiant; it is fully turned outside.[10] The radiant is what lightens: it illuminates its surroundings, opens a world. Just as when the sun shines the less brilliant stars are invisible, so one might say that the presence of the person of character spreads over all who interact with them. The person of character opens meaningful surroundings tailored to their measure (making things happen at their own pace, according to the unfolding of their own logic of character). This is why the illumination (maybe one could call it coloring) of the world would be the best way of characterizing its way of being.

SIX

Fate, Redemption, and Hope in Love

The orders of fate reveal themselves in what bears on the life of a person as a whole. There is hardly a dimension of human life in which these orders are more dramatically present than that of love. Indeed, it is in "love and death" that we recognize the struggles of humanity to master elemental nature. Benjamin's essay on Goethe's *Elective Affinities* will allow us to develop this theme. In reading the essay, we will follow Benjamin's schematic plan, in which he suggests that its three parts are to be understood in terms of a dialectical schema where myth is the thesis, redemption the antithesis, and hope the synthesis. In order to achieve an understanding of the moment of hope, several further "detours" will become necessary, in particular in order to illuminate the stages of erotic ascent, the nature of the beautiful semblance and its relation to truth, as well as the character of veiling and exposure in human life and in art.

Myth

The first part of the essay is devoted to showing how myth is the hidden configuration of the material content of the novel. "The mythic is the real material content of this book," Benjamin writes. "Its content appears as a mythic shadowplay staged in the costumes of the Age of Goethe" (SW 1:309). "The mythic" is Benjamin's way to refer to a space of life that has not undergone meaningful realization, what he also calls "bare" or "mere" life

(*Blosse Leben*). The predominant characteristic of this primal configuration of life is its being ruled by the orders of fate: "The impact of nature falls not on people's actions but on their lives, which alone are subject to fate" (SW 1:398).

The logic of fate, of mythical sacrifice and its perverse relation to the "elective," to choice, is already evident in the epigram from Klopstock that Benjamin places at the opening of the first part of the essay: "Whoever chooses blindly is struck in the eyes / By the smoke of sacrifice" (SW 1:297). Apparently, the problem suggested by the verse is in choosing blindly; therefore, it seems, it could be remedied by choosing rationally, with understanding. But note the peculiar dual place of blinding, as though something of the temporal succession is reversed: whoever is struck in the eyes with smoke is blinded, but here it seems as if blinding is already at work from the outset (choosing blindly). This reversal is characteristic of the form of the mythical; recall our discussion of the logic of the Tree of Knowledge as the emblem of the mythical source of law. The guilty is not the one who infringes the law but the one who seeks knowledge that allows choice between good and evil. Accordingly, the epigram suggests that the turn to choice, rather than expressing freedom, awakens the mythical demand for sacrifice.

Let me touch briefly on some of the themes through which Benjamin establishes the presence of mythical forces in the novel. Myth is often identified with the emergence of culture from nature, wherever and whenever cultivated existence faces primal nature. As Benjamin notes, the novel is concerned throughout with cultivation of the land, yet such cultivation remains at the surface; it is only ornamental, not producing fruit (SW 1:303). This parallels the obliviousness of the characters to the forces of elemental nature, which, below their surface interactions, govern unformed human life. This is evident in the project of Eduard and Charlotte to rearrange the gravestones in the cemetery, showing no concern for what lies in the earth beneath the surface. Similarly, Benjamin speaks of water as a further element in which the character of the primal comes into play in the novel. Water draws us to the dark depths in the tempting reflection of its surface. It is not in its stormy manifestation that it brings catastrophe but rather in its misleadingly calm appearance.

The manifestation of fate in the space of the novel is amply evident in numerous "premonitions." They are a sign that the space of life has been invaded by an inexorable yet wholly ambiguous repetition. Unformed and ambiguous, life is not marked off from death, not concretized in its finite possibilities out of that ultimate limit. The characters of the novel are described as leading a somnambulistic existence, unaware of the forces that govern their actions and bring their existence to its catastrophic demise.[1]

Given the role Benjamin attributes to the proper name of a person in his essay on language, it is not surprising that he focuses on the problematic of names in the novel. We are referred to the similarity and repetition of "Ott": Eduard is Otto, the Captain is Otto, the baby is named Otto, and the combination is similarly reflected in *Ott*ilie, Charl*otte*—as though instead of individuation we have some devious logic that does not "respect" the bounds of the person. Repetition is also present in the fact that "OTTO" is a palindrome—as though containing in itself demonic mirroring. The characters' names can be seen as metamorphoses of each other—that is, they are bound by a single "primal" force (see Chapter 10).

The ambiguity inherent in mythic existence is revealed not just in the characters of *Elective Affinities* but also in Benjamin's analysis of Goethe's relation to his novel,[2] as though for Goethe the writing of the novel is itself a recognition and struggle with the mythical forces in his creative life. The mythical themes recognized in the peculiarities of the material content of the novel are reflected in Goethe's statements about his work, which must be understood "too, on the basis of the same hidden jurisdiction as the work" (SW 1:309). Goethe's summary of his own work hides more than it reveals: "For it is precisely [the] aim [of his words] to forbid access to critique." We apparently return here to the themes of the dissertation and the contrast between the ultimate criticizability of the work for the Romantics and its uncriticizability for Goethe; yet here the refusal of critique seems to Benjamin to involve self-deception.

Goethe presents the "secret" of the work as a secret of technique. He refers to a hidden unifying idea that is the foundation of the conception of the novel. And in order to retain the key to this secret, Goethe destroys the drafts of his work. And yet, Benjamin points out, this tendency to "keep secret" is a symptom of the rule of the mythical over the creative process: "All mythic meaning strives for secrecy" (SW 1:314). In his rejection of the necessity of critique, Goethe takes himself to have privileged access to the primal nature he presents in the work. He seeks to ground the complete authority of the artist over the work by means of his intuition of primal nature: "This insight into nature, with which the author believed he could always accomplish the verification of his works, completed his indifference toward criticism. There was no need of it. The nature of the *ur*-phenomena was the standard; the relation of every work to it was something one could read off it" (SW 1:315).

Criticism would be unnecessary if one could have immediate access to the truth of nature and, as it were, copy it in art. But in assuming this, Goethe introduces an ambiguity into the concept of true nature: "The *ur*-phenomena as archetype [are] too often turned into nature as model" (SW 1:315). Intuitive access to the truth of nature takes it to be a model, or *Vorbild*, of art. But if it is the *Urbild*, or archetype, that art is after, then such essential nature can be made present only in the work of art. As was argued in Chapter 3, it becomes present to us for the first time through critique. The primal phenomenon emerges in the artwork; indeed, ultimately, it requires its critique in order to be recognized: "The *ur*-phenomena do not exist before art; they subsist within it" (SW 1:315).

This distortion of the relation to primal phenomena is reflected, according to Benjamin, in the way the phenomena become for Goethe a *"chaos* of symbols,*"* an abundance with no hierarchy, which is the breeding ground of confusion and the ambiguity of fate. This amounts to an adulation of nature, such as, in Benjamin's view, Goethe expresses in an early fragment: "She has brought me here; she will lead me away. I trust myself to her. She may do as she wants with me" (SW 1:315–316). Benjamin similarly recognizes this spirit in the introduction of the *Farbenlehre*: "From the fiercest cry of passion to the gentlest word of reason, it is nature alone that speaks, revealing its existence, energy, life, and circumstances" (SW 1:315). The word of reason is one with nature, and intuition rules over sober thought.

This is further reflected in the adoption of the idea of metamorphosis, which expresses the undying life of nature. This idea, while it might be valid for plants, becomes problematic when transposed to human existence. As we saw in Benjamin's interpretation of the novel, the indistinction of life and death is a sign of the presence of the mythical realm of fate. Goethe's embrace of the chaos of nature constitutes a submission to the orders of myth: "In this world view lies chaos. To that pass at last leads the life of the myth, which, without master or boundaries, imposes itself as the sole power in the domain of existence" (SW 1:316).

This pact with the demonic (*Dämonisch*) is not without its price: "Mythic humanity pays with fear for intercourse with daemonic forces. In Goethe such fear often spoke out unmistakably." The mythical nature is eternal transformation in which nothing dies; one could say then that the fear at issue is that of facing death: "For death most threatens the formless panarchy of natural life that constitutes the spell of myth." Benjamin does not deny that the idea of immortality has a place in human existence, but it must be opened through hope. When the survival of the soul is sought in the undying life of nature, it is ultimately nothing more than "an incapacity to die," that is, the incapacity to own up to one's mortality. When the hope of immortality does not arise from the acknowledgment of finitude, then "immortality is not the journey of the soul to its homeland but rather a flight from one boundlessness into another" (SW 1:317).

The ambiguous chaos of symbols is sought in life presenting itself through "signs and oracles." With Goethe this is manifest perhaps most of all in his old age, in the attempt to find significance in any and all events of his life, in the obsessive collection of each and every moment of his life in his diaries. Those details would be precisely the material for the presentation of the *ur*-phenomenon of creativity through his own life, of his life as the *ur-phenomenon* of a poetic "life." As will become clear in the remainder of this chapter, Benjamin also conceives of the writing of *Elective Affinities* as Goethe's great struggle with the mythical ruling his creativity. This means recognizing how the novel is not an act of heroic creativity of a demigod but rather the expression of what is proper to human life.

Redemption

In the second part of the essay, Benjamin lays out the configuration of "redemption." The moment antithetical to myth is identified, strangely enough, in terms of a novella that is included within the scope of the novel, a story told to the main characters by a visiting traveler. If the catastrophic drowning of a child stands at the center of the novel, in the novella a decisive rescue from the element occurs. Benjamin shows how every one of the novella's details has its parallel in the novel: "The mythic themes of the novel correspond to those of the novella as themes of redemption" (SW 1:333). These correspondences are not a further instance of the mythical repetition of fate, nor is the structure of incorporation a device of *mise en abyme* that provokes endless reflection between the overarching frame of the novel and the novella in it. Rather, we must ask how the incorporation of the novella in the novel gives us an orientation by which to recognize the redemptive overcoming of myth.

Benjamin notes that *Elective Affinities* was planned initially as a novella inserted into the novel *Wilhelm Meister's Apprenticeship*. Despite having eventually developed into a novel, it retains a relation to its original conception, through the incorporation of a novella in it. The conflict between the novella form and the novel form is "subdued" by incorporating the former in the latter: "[Goethe] ennobles (so to speak) the form of the novel through that of the novella" (SW 1:330). Describing the novella as ennobling the novel construes it as a higher realization of the content of the novel; in other words, one could almost say that the novella is the novel fulfilled.

Benjamin suggests this peculiar "sameness" between the two in the following: "In this way, despite its breadth, *Elective Affinities* has remained novella-like. In its effectiveness of expression, it is not superior to the actual novella contained in it" (SW 1:330). Having the same "effectiveness of expression" means that the novel does not add anything essential to the content of the novella or, conversely, that the novella is something like the quintessence of the content of the novel. It is as though the same essential content that appears dispersed in the novel is concentrated in the novella. Construing the novella as having the same essential content serves to characterize what the emergence of truth content out of contingent material content comes to. This concretization of truth is also evident in the way Benjamin writes that "the novella is more prosaic than the novel. It confronts the novel in prose of a higher degree" (SW 1:331).[3]

"In [*Elective Affinities*] a boundary form [*Grenzform*] has been created" (SW 1:330). This could certainly be understood as referring to a new form in between novel and novella, but it would be more interesting to think of it as referring to the possibility of reaching an inner limit or boundary inside the novel, where everything is sharply delimited: "But in the novella a brilliant light holds sway. From the outset everything, sharply contoured, is at a peak. It is a day of decision shining into the dusk-filled Hades of the novel" (SW 1:331). An inner limit is reached through concentration, which makes content decisively present and thus transforms the ambiguity of the mythical into the clarity of the novella. If, as Benjamin puts it, the novel is a maelstrom into which all characters are swallowed, the concentrated center is the resting point where all that is essential holds together.

This transforms our way of thinking of "fulfillment": it is not an infinite task defined by an idea toward which one strives but a concentration, abbreviation, and tying together of what we already have.[4] Indeed, this explains why the novel is compared by Benjamin to a large cathedral that cannot be encompassed by the gaze from outside but contains in the penumbra of its interior a miniature image of itself as a whole—the novella. The correspondence thus shows how concentration and miniaturization are key to the reversal from myth to redemption. It is as though the very space that cannot be circumscribed in the life of the characters of the novel is presented in a surveyable abbreviation in the novella. Unsurveyability allows evasiveness, the presence of ambiguity that is merely the other side of fatal precision. Concentration makes recognizable the contours of the essential, thus allowing decisiveness, courage, and fidelity to play a role in life.[5]

This bears in particular on the distinction between choice, the elective (*Wahl*), which serves as the guiding concept for the formation of passionate attachment in the novel, and decision (*Entscheidung*), which is the key in the novella to the rescue of the beloved from drowning. The supposed freedom to choose one's love only serves the unfolding of fate and is to be distinguished from the decisive affirmation that is at once freedom and necessity. "Choice is natural... decision is transcendent" (SW 1:346). Choice, one could say, belongs to lived experience (*Erlebnis*); the decision is a precipitate of the unity and consistency of one's life experience (here *Erfahrung*). As the notion of concentration suggests, the inner coherence of one's experience becomes the necessary condition for there being a decisive moment at all. The rescue of the beloved in the novella would then make vivid, would dramatize, what it means to act from that unity of life, by staking one's happiness on a moment in which all is risked.

Hope

What are we to make of the fact that redemption is identified in the novella and set as the antithesis to the mythical logic of the novel? Can redemption be the final word for the characters of the novel? Can it be imagined for Ottilie, as she "lingers... in the precincts of fate," never overcoming the peculiar ambiguity of innocence and guilt characteristic of beautiful life?[6] She doesn't even struggle and lacks all the decisiveness that one would find, say, in a heroine of tragedy, or for that matter, in the love depicted in the novella. "Nothing more untragic can be conceived than this mournful end" (SW 1:337). There is no decision, Benjamin argues, even in her letting herself die: she dies by denying herself food, yet dislike of food was always natural to her. If it is, nevertheless, her beautiful life that is to be rescued, the concept of hope must be invoked as the ruling term of the synthesis in the third part of the essay.[7]

Indeed, the figure of Ottilie stands at the center of the novel as "the appearance of the beautiful." "The belief in Ottilie's beauty," Benjamin adds, "is the fundamental condition for engagement with the novel" (SW 1:338). Ottilie's beauty has a peculiar character: she is reserved (as though holding back a secret), unapproachable, unreachable, "like someone in trance," Benjamin writes. She does not have the distance of nobility but of utmost passivity. He also speaks of her presence as insubstantial. All the relations formed around her would be threatened with the same insubstantiality. In particular, this would bear on the truthfulness of any reconciliation seemingly achieved in the world of the novel, which would be only the semblance of reconciliation. What hope is there for her? This question cannot be answered without going over a number of further themes of Benjamin's essay.

THE ASCENT OF EROS

The transformation of love in relation to Ottilie's beauty in the novel allows Benjamin to characterize stages of the *ascent of eros*: in passion (*Leidenschaft*), affection (*Neigung*), and the great, shattering emotion (*Rührung*).[8]

The first configuration of the erotic is evident in the passionate attachment of Eduard and Ottilie. In passion the demonic character of eros prevails. Passion for a particular other has a superlative character: for it, the beauty of the beloved is incomparable. Benjamin does not problematize passion because of its unbridled character but rather distinguishes it from true love because it is lacking force. Despite its tumultuous character, it is not an expression of the active life but of passivity, spellbound as it is by the image of beauty. It is vision, the gaze, that governs passion, and therefore passion is to be distinguished from the wildness in the love of the novella's young woman. Because wildness can be violent, beauty is not ultimate in it. This is evident in the incident recounted in the novella where an innocent childhood game turns into a furious attack in which the young girl claws at the eyes of the boy, her neighbor. For Benjamin, this all but explicitly sets wildness against the spell of semblance that is enthralled by the vision of beauty. Yet wildness can also be a healing manifestation of the natural when further contrasted with the problematic cultivation of the characters of the novel. Their tolerance is not a sign of true grace and nobility but is at one with the passivity of passion. Wildness, in contrast, is essential to the struggle, to the force of love, or to love having force. Because it can manifest itself in life as enmity, revenge, or envy, or even internally as lament, shame, or despair (SW 1:343), it is all the more important for Benjamin to point out how Ottilie is not touched by such violent emotions. Passivity colors her passionate attachment just as much as her muted sadness.

Passion is ultimately solitary. It is unable to establish a true bond to another, and its chaotic side must destructively break through any attempt to ground fidelity solely on it. The cultivation of the characters of the novel might very well allow them to pacify the turmoil of passion, which is revealed primarily in the transformation of eros into affection, bringing together the friends as Ottilie renounces the fulfillment of her passionate attachment to Eduard. But just like passion, in that circle of existence affection is only the semblance of love; it does not lack feeling but rather any truly redeeming character. Affection is "helpless." "Sounder than passion yet not more helpful," Benjamin writes, "affection likewise only brings about the ruin of those who renounce passion. But it does not drive the lonely ones to ruin like them. It tenaciously escorts the lovers in their descent; they reach the end conciliated" (SW 1:348). Benjamin carefully distinguishes conciliation (*Aussöhnung*) from reconciliation (*Versöhnung*). Whatever else reconciliation might involve, it presupposes giving up the semblance that there is always something further that is lacking, as though beyond the task of making concrete, more real, what one has. In reconciliation, the quietist agreement with what is truly one's own presupposes precisely a sense of the unity of one's life, of what it ultimately comes to. As we saw earlier, the recognition of this coherence or unity is tantamount to decisiveness: the capacity of the individual to stake all, risk life for what truly matters, proving thereby that they are worthy of being given life back, albeit transformed by that decisiveness. Such is the solitary moment in reconciliation, which remains at the heart of fidelity to another in love.

Reconciliation is contrasted by Benjamin with "conciliation," which puts pacifying others first. Affection can pacify, can placate, but it cannot serve the perfection of love. To remain with affection would be to despair of decisively concretizing existence with another in love. It would be, as Benjamin puts it, the admission that this human being cannot truly love: "Into all loving that human nature alone determines, affection enters as the real work of *Eros thanatos*" (SW 1:345). It would be the gentle passing away rather than the woeful demise of passion. But it still delineates a trajectory of decline, a way for death to hold sway in life.

We have seen how beauty involves an outgoing manifestation, a radiance, as well as an inwardly turned moment, the secret inherent in beauty. It both shines forth and veils the essential. Benjamin calls these two aspects the "triumphant" and the "declining" semblance. Their tense coexistence makes for the height of beauty in certain works of art (Benjamin mentions in passing the *Mona Lisa*). In the novel the two aspects are separated and assigned to different characters. The "wide sunny circle" of Luciane, whose "radiance . . . shines painfully" (as is suggested by the association of her name with Lucifer), is contrasted with the nocturnal beauty of Ottilie, to her "secret lunar environment," to her mild light, that is a "consolation for the eyes" and "the hearth of all semblance." Ottilie's decline is true to the character of her semblance. It is as though the sadness of transience belongs to her beauty. Referring to Goethe's "Trilogy of Passion," Benjamin notes how the sentimental or lyrical mood associated with loss, which fills the eyes with tears, is both the dimming of the gaze that ruled passion but also the most authentic veil, the highest intensification of the semblance that dawns most powerfully as it is on the verge of disappearing.

This is, once more, to be contrasted with the young woman in the novella. Her lover undresses her, for the first time, not with the gaze of passion but rather to save her life after she has drowned. Only Ottilie's death opens to a further transformation of love, from the sweet sadness of affection that "delights in itself" to shattering emotion (*Rührung*). The sad veil of tears becomes lament: "The lament full of tears: that is emotion. And as with the tearless cry of woe, the space of Dionysian shock gives it resonance" (SW 1:349; translation modified). Just as a concussion to a concentrated solution will precipitate crystallization, so the shock of a great emotion has a petrifying effect, as it were, raising meaning to a different consistency. Emotion is not a final moment but "a transition from the confused premonition . . . to the uniquely objective correlative of shock, to the sublime" (SW 1:349).[9] As the reference to the sublime suggests, that transition is something of a break, a heightening or raising of meaning to another order altogether. Benjamin's reference to the space of Dionysian shock suggests the register of tragedy. This is puzzling, since he also stresses that *Elective Affinities* is no tragedy and Ottilie no tragic heroine. Clarifying what is at issue demands us to go deeper in interpreting the character of beauty in general and of Ottilie's beauty in particular.

SEMBLANCE, NAKEDNESS, AND CONJURATION

We have followed the transformation of the love for Ottilie and raised the question of the possibility of the truthfulness of love in view of her beauty. Benjamin pairs this theme of the novel with his reflections on beauty, truth, and the nature of critique. Returning at the beginning of the third part of his essay to questions with which he opened it, he offers a parable of the relation between art and philosophy:

> Let us suppose that one makes the acquaintance of a person who is beautiful and attractive but impenetrable, because he carries a secret with him. It would be reprehensible to want to pry. Still, it would surely be permissible to inquire whether he has any siblings and whether their nature could not perhaps explain somewhat the enigmatic character of the stranger. In just this way critique seeks to discover siblings of the work of art. And all genuine works have their siblings in the realm of philosophy. (SW 1:333; translation modified)

We can understand the problem of critique when faced by enigmatic and impenetrable beauty by recalling issues discussed in earlier chapters. Benjamin takes truth to be unquestionable, and that which is unquestionable is "existence": "It must be said that philosophy in its questionings can never hit upon the unity of existence" (SW 1:109). Existence is not a categorial unity; the highest noncategorial unity that is the ground of the orders of knowledge is "identity" (SW 1:107). Philosophy cannot pose an ultimate question whose answer is the oneness of identity, that is, the ideal or highest reality. Yet there is, as Benjamin puts it, a "non-existent question, which asks for the unity of philosophy" (SW 1:334; translation modified). With this paradoxical formulation, Benjamin wishes to suggest that there is in another sphere something akin to this question that is absent from philosophy: "There are nevertheless constructions which, without being questions, have the deepest affinity with the ideal of the problem. These are works of art" (SW 1:334). The work of art does not have the form of a question, but it presents itself as mysterious, as withholding or harboring a secret. "Never yet has a true work of art been grasped," he writes, "other than where it ineluctably presented itself as a secret" (SW 1:351). The work relates itself to truth by way of its secret, enigmatic core.

The pursuit of truth must forego the questioning of understanding and orient itself to the highest unity shining forth as the secret heart of the work of art. But just as philosophy needs the work of art, the latter needs its kin in philosophy. "Beauty can never become lucid about itself." Philosophy thus becomes critique, and the concrete truth content of the work emerges in the eradication of the beautiful semblance. In other words, philosophy needs beauty when it comes to relating to what is highest for it, the unquestionable character of truth. Yet precisely because truth inheres in beauty as a secret, veiled core, it calls for philosophy to vouchsafe that it is indeed truth that inheres in it and not mere semblance.[10] But can truth do justice to beauty?

Beauty is truth veiled. This is not to be conceived of in terms of a simple, undialectical opposition between essence (truth) and appearance (veil). Appearance, we say, is a very partial reflection of truth, an appearance of, at most, part of the true. The veil, on the other hand is what allows for the *wholeness* of the truth to be manifest. Veiling allows that which the understanding cannot grasp, the self-identity internal to the true, to manifest itself. Critique cannot be figured simply as the "lifting" of the veil (for then we would again be assuming the simplistic model of separation of essence from appearance). Critique must work through the inessential rather than try to separate out the essential. As Benjamin argues, it is inseparable from detailed, piecemeal philological knowledge of the peculiar transformation of material content in time. Engaging these transformations of the inessential is both a "meticulous" destruction of the semblance of totality in the work as well as the concretization of a fragment of the "true world." Critique is mortifying, not enlivening.

Veiling pertains to beauty both in nature and in art, but it is in human beings that the polarity of veiling and nakedness is most extreme. For a human being to be raised above semblant life, the truth content of their life must be exposed and recognized. We can gain an understanding of what such nakedness of the true means by referring to Benjamin's interpretation of the first chapters of Genesis. Indeed, nakedness here does not signify the state prior to the Fall but rather the exposure that destroys the guilt and shame of mere life governed by myth. Nakedness does not show the beautiful body to arouse passion but instead signifies the solitude of the corporeal substance, the human being in the face of exposure to the divine gaze, life seen "*sub specie aeternitatis*": "In veil-less nakedness the essentially beautiful has withdrawn, and in the naked body of the human being are attained a being beyond all beauty—the sublime—and a work beyond all creations—that of the creator" (SW 1:351; translation modified).

The moment of recognition of truth over and above the self-veiled evasiveness of life itself is the counterpurposive moment of the sublime, in which the human being is raised above the purposive unity of life. In *Elective Affinities*, such a moment is suggested in the novella, in the decision of the youth to risk his life to save his beloved: The unveiling of the beloved, the exposure of her naked body, is not for the sake of passion but to save a life. The beyond of beauty, the sublimity of the naked truth, is what Benjamin calls "the expressionless." This term has been the subject of numerous misinterpretations. To start with, the expressionless is not the inexpressible; on the contrary, the expressionless is a moment in which the secret, ungraspable core inherent in the beautiful semblance is destroyed. Indeed, to the extent that we speak here of a moment of revelation, we ought to follow Benjamin's identification of the highest with what does not know the inexpressible (see Chapter 1). Note further that the expressionless is not to be taken as a characterization of the state of a person or of a moment in the work or even of the work itself. Viewed in relation to the purposive unities of meaning in the work, the expressionless involves a counterpurposive moment, a caesura, where "every expression simultaneously comes to a standstill." But this is only "in order to give space to an expressionless force" of another order altogether (SW 1:341).

What is expressionless is not the work but a *force freed* to reveal itself in the medium of art. We have encountered this logic a number of times in Benjamin's writings. But perhaps most clearly it corresponds to the account of the freedom of translation developed in Chapter 3—namely, it is the *freeing* of the pure language from the burden of communicating content.[11] Freeing is letting it become manifest as a *force* in the medium of the translation.

Translation frees the pure language from the obstacles to its manifestations in the finite linguistic product. Significantly, the term "expressionless" is also used in that context: "In this pure language—which no longer means or expresses anything but is, as expressionless and creative Word, that which is meant in all languages—all information, all sense, and all intention finally encounter a stratum in which they are destined to be extinguished" (SW 1:261).[12]

Benjamin identifies the counterpurposive moment of the expressionless with what Hölderlin calls in his writings on tragedy the "caesura." Tragedy is indeed something of a paradigm of this arrest of the ambiguities of living meaning in which the truth of life is recognized.[13] But this reference to tragedy only makes clearer the problem of seeking a parallel in *Elective Affinities*, that is, in relation to the beauty of Ottilie. We have already seen that Benjamin rejects the idea that Ottilie is a tragic heroine. No decisive moment is identifiable in her passive existence. This is reflected also in the particular character of her beauty, or of the way Goethe evokes it. There is in Ottilie's presence—that is, in the mode in which Goethe makes her beauty palpable—something that doesn't belong to the novelistic form. Benjamin calls her beauty painterly and says that it "lies outside of the sphere of epic material" (SW 1:338). More important, her presence is as though *conjured* rather than truly formed.

Conjuration is contrasted both with creation and with forming in art. "Conjuration intends to be the negative counterpart of creation. It, too, claims to bring forth a world from nothingness" (SW 1:340). The conjured is, like creation, "ex nihilo," but it has no immediate or mediate share in truth. Contrary to both creation and the forming of chaos in art, conjuration is identified as *mere semblance*. It is beauty that frees itself from the dimension of form or perfection, beauty whose semblance is merely intensifying, merely enlivening. Benjamin refers to it as *demonic* semblance. It does away with what holds together beauty and truth. It is, as it were, mere seduction: "A beauty whose appearance ceases to tie itself to totality and perfection, and which remains free by intensifying its beauty, is no longer artistic beauty but demonic beauty. The seductive nature of beauty is based on the shamelessness, the nakedness of the semblance that arms it" (SW 1:221). *This* nakedness is not the overcoming of shame in truth but rather "shameless" seductiveness.

It is then all the more surprising when Benjamin writes that "in *Elective Affinities*, however, the daemonic principle of conjuration irrupts into the very center of the poetic composition. For what is conjured is always only a semblance" (SW 1:339). A work of art must open onto a moment beyond its appearance of life, to the mortification of critique; otherwise it belongs to the magically conjured: "Therefore no work of art may seem wholly alive, wholly unbound [*gänzlich ungebannt*] without thereby becoming mere semblance and ceasing to be a work of art." In other words, in order for what is formed to partake in the life of the created, it must involve the moment of arrest of the ambiguous life of meaning, as if spellbound; as Benjamin puts it: "The life undulating in it must appear petrified and as if spellbound in a single moment" (SW 1:340; translation modified).

Yet the novel, unlike tragedy and even unlike Hölderlin's hymnic poetry, does not contain in itself the sublime break of the expressionless in which exposure reveals truth content. It leads to a limit in another direction: "In Goethe it is the beautiful that comes forth to the limit of what can be grasped in the work of art. What stirs beyond that limit is, in one direction, the offspring of madness, and in the other, the conjured appearance" (SW 1:341). What would it be to draw truth content out of what borders on mere semblance, on the conjured?

This is very clear in the way Benjamin treats the theme of nakedness in relation to Ottilie. In contrast to other figures of beauty in Goethe, such as Mignon in *Wilhem Meister's Apprenticeship* and Helena in *Faust II*, Ottilie does not give up the semblance inherent in life: "In contrast to these ... the veil of Ottilie remains as her living body" (SW 1:353). "Let me seem until I am"—this line of Mignon's that Benjamin quotes could stand for the problem of transition from veiled beauty to true Being. Ottilie cannot renounce semblance, since it is so much one with her life. But it is not clear that she is released by death. Even lying in her open casket she does not lose any of her beauty. Is there something beyond death in which to recognize the concretization of truth of that life? The exposure necessary for Ottilie's rescue belongs to the afterlife, to the corpse, as Benjamin disturbingly puts it.[14] But what would that mean if we do not conceive simplistically of a divine "Last Judgment"?

THE EVENING STAR IS THE MORNING STAR

We had an inkling of Benjamin's concern with the unity of form and content in his discussion of the transformative concentration that rules the relation of novel to novella. Benjamin has already indicated the importance and necessity of theorizing form in his discussion of Goethe's theory of art in the epilogue to "The Concept of Criticism." Insofar as Goethe's aesthetics of the ideal is based on the primacy of content, there is lacking in it a philosophical account of form, so central to Romantic aesthetics. Through his reading of *Elective Affinities*, Benjamin schematically derives a theory of literary form suited to the presentation of the ideal. Form, in a great work of art such as *Elective Affinities*, would be precisely that through which we conceive of the stages in the ascent of eros. A ladder of forms in the novel allows the ascent or approach to pure truth content, to what it ultimately is in itself. Thus we get the following description of the hierarchy of forms and the corresponding order of material content: "The novel's epic basis in the mythic, its lyrical breadth in passion and affection, is joined by its dramatic crowning, in the mystery of hope" (SW 1:355).

Beauty as such is not identified with any specific order in the hierarchy. As he puts it: "Neither the language of humor nor of tragedy can grasp beauty" (SW 1:348). Even if devotion to the beautiful determines the traversal of the hierarchy of forms, the fulfillment of the ascent of love is identified with the musical only to immediately problematize its presence in the world of the novel:[15] "If music encloses genuine mysteries, this world of course remains a mute world, from which music will never ring out. Yet, to what is it dedicated if not redemption, to which it promises more than conciliation?" (SW 1:355). Music, the promise of reconciliation, will not resound in the world of the novel, devoid as it is of hope. What good is its promise if it can only be heard in another world?

The final pages of Benjamin's essay are devoted to elucidating how holding to semblance beyond all unity of form is indeed the key to opening the dimension of hope, to a reconciliation belonging not to life but to the afterlife. This theme is developed through a series of references to the starry heavens that befit Ottilie's nocturnal beauty. The falling star, a well-known figure for a wish or the hope of its fulfillment, is introduced by the narrator in the novel in recounting the last embrace of the lovers, Ottilie and Eduard, by way of an abrupt phrase that Benjamin identifies as the caesura in that work: "Hope shot above their heads like a falling star" (SW 1:354). There is something strikingly cruel, indeed arresting, in this phrase, as it signifies so evidently that the lovers are doomed and their fate sealed. Fate manifests itself in repetition, and we recognize its workings in the juxtaposition of the embrace and the shooting star, which is the repetition of an earlier moment, namely, Eduard's lavishly planned celebration of Ottilie's birthday, interrupted by the drowning of a child. Eduard insists on proceeding with the planned fireworks, even though all the guests disperse and he remains with Ottilie alone to witness the lights in the night sky. True to the logic of fate, the shooting star marks the embrace of the lovers on the shores of the same lake as the prelude to a new incident of drowning. It throws Ottilie into confusion, and her rush to return home, carrying the baby she is in charge of, is the immediate cause of its drowning. One cannot say more clearly that there is no hope in that circle of existence.

Is the shooting star then merely another element of the astrological canon of myth? There might be no possibilities for redemption in that world, and yet there is hope *for* that world from outside it, from another-worldly standpoint, as it were. There would thus be a duality in the space of hope, a separation of the one who hopes from the one *for whom* there is hope. "Only for the sake of the hopeless have we been given hope" (SW 1:356), Benjamin famously writes. But here we face a dilemma: a world in which there is no room for hope cannot share the same possibilities with that world from which we hope for the hopeless. In what sense, then, can the world to come fulfill what belongs to the world that was doomed? What kind of mediation can be established between the two worlds? Benjamin proposes a powerful figure to address this difficulty: "That most paradoxical, most fleeting hope finally emerges from the semblance of reconciliation, just as at twilight, as the sun is extinguished, rises the evening star which outlasts the night. Its glimmer of course is that of Venus" (SW 1:355).

To fully unpack that figure, consider that Phosphorus, which appears at one time of the year in the eastern sky toward dawn, is the very same star as Hesperus, which appears in a different season in the evening sky of the west. The duality of worlds that belongs to the structure of hope is figured by the duality of the morning star and evening star.[16] Their ultimate identity means that the dawning of new possibilities really belongs to the mournful world, even as their horizons are as different as east and west. Yet establishing that identity requires us to further recognize that both aspects belong to that star we call Venus. What beauty holds in itself, what love seeks in its insubstantial shimmer, offers the "bridge" between worlds. Reconciliation demands the mediation of semblance and its peculiar transformation in the night of meaning—that is, without the support of any form. This suggests to Benjamin that "Plato's tenet that it is absurd to desire the semblance of the good suffers its only exception. For one is permitted to desire the semblance of reconciliation—indeed, it must be desired: it alone is the house of the most extreme hope" (SW 1:355).

But what is it to hold to the semblance of reconciliation even beyond life? Who is to attend to the fulfillment of meaning in the afterlife? Love, Benjamin remarks, returns to beauty, that is, holds to it in memory. Recollection, to use another Platonic term, is the medium of the final transformation of semblance as living beauty dies away from the world. This makes evident the metaphysical function of the standpoint of the narrator, who has figured hope as the shooting star. The narrator takes up, literally assumes into himself, the meaning of the event: "It is he alone who, in the feeling of hope, can fulfill the meaning of the event" (SW 1:355). It would further explain Benjamin's characterization of the mystery of hope as the dramatic par excellence. Indeed, drama would show, would present, the mystery, yet its articulation belongs to a higher language, unavailable in the world of the novel. The narrator outside that world is all but identified explicitly with Goethe himself as Benjamin relates an account of how, journeying in a carriage at night, the rising stars steer the thoughts of the elderly Goethe back to his love for Ottilie's beauty. Ultimately, if in the standpoint of the narrator we find the expression of Goethe's "love" of the beautiful, his holding in memory to the figure of beauty he created, it is because, as Benjamin understands it, in writing that novel Goethe rebelled against the demonic power of myth that was the source of his creativity as well as exacting a sacrifice for it; such struggles should not be given heroic contours. Reconciliation must be sought not in the stance of the hero but in terms of what is fundamental to a human life. To liberate Goethe from the form that his fame had taken, providing an authentic afterlife to his work, would ultimately demand the standpoint of the philosophical rescuing critique—that is, of Benjamin's essay itself.

SEVEN

Myth, Law, and Life in Common

The problems we have discussed in bringing together fate and individual life need now to be raised in relation to our life in common. In particular, we want to take up what was initially only hinted at in "Fate and Character," namely, the relation between the order of fate and the law. Law is a form of ordering of life in common. If we conceive, say, of Hegel's understanding of ethical life, there is an internal connection between the full realization of the human will and life under law in the state. Benjamin attempts to provide us with a different vision of the function of law in historical life and initially does so through an investigation of the concept of legal violence.

What has most fascinated readers of "Toward the Critique of Violence" is the relation developed in the essay between legal violence and two other forms of violence that Benjamin calls "mythical" and "divine violence."[1] The nature of these latter forms as well as the implications they have for our understanding of legal violence have been the object of numerous interpretations and disagreements. If the fate of Niobe served to figure the first, mythical, violence, the destruction of Korah and his clan is the epitome of the second, divine, violence. It is crucial to recognize the role and force of these examples, as well as which aspects to include and which to ignore; otherwise, it will be difficult to show how these exemplars from antiquity bear on the modern form of life and cohere with Benjamin's historical materialism.

The Antinomy of Law

The essay "Toward the Critique of Violence" (*Zur Kritik der Gewalt*) must be read in relation to Benjamin's understanding of critique, extending it from such contexts as Kant's critical philosophy and the critique of a literary work to the political critique of the state. The standpoint of critique can initially be framed in the spirit of Kantian critique, as *an* antinomy in the thinking of means and ends. The problem of violence arises from the consideration of means in an ethical or legal context. It is articulated in terms of the familiar opposition between natural and positive law. One side asserts the existence of natural ends and justifies the means based on how they further those ends; the other side asserts that ends are justified only to the extent that they are pursued through the right means. What is common to both positions is the inner relation formed between ends and means in law: just ends justify means as opposed to justified means determine the justness of ends. This presupposition is what serves Benjamin to present these two positions not merely as an opposition but as an antinomy. To overcome it would depend on showing the falsity of the presupposition common to both views. Thus Benjamin asks what if "justified means on the one hand, and just ends, on the other, were in irreconcilable conflict?" (CV 40).

It is difficult at this point to fathom why there would be such a conflict or what the dissociation of just ends from justified means would come to. But the framing of the problem suggests that in our reading we should pay attention to moments in the essay in which Benjamin prepares this dissociation, for instance, in the consideration of what is purely a sphere of means (without ends), as well as in the possibility of articulating pure means as a sphere of nonviolence. We will also have to consider forms of immediate (i.e., unmediated, without means) violence.

Natural law conceives of ends as essential contents of the nature of man that are to be protected by the legal system. For natural law theory, then, there appears to be a simple solution to the problem of the violence of means: violence is justified as means insofar as it serves to establish and protect natural ends. Natural law, with its focus on ends, is therefore unable to distinguish among the different forms of violence that belong to the sphere of means. It would be blind to any more exact distinction between kinds of violence within the realm of means. Initially, therefore, the essay will be following the perverted state of law arising from the antinomic situation by focusing on the side of positive law, articulated in formal terms.

The Monopoly on Violence

Positive law has an inherently historical dimension, that is, it seeks to ground the legitimacy of violence in relation to the historical process through which legal arrangements are justified. But initially at least, even within positive law, we could distinguish between those justified means that establish legal ends and what is still left outside the purview of legal authority, what can be called natural ends (as opposed to historical-legal ends). There is a sphere of the use of force by individuals that does not fall under any legal jurisdiction. Benjamin points to the family and the education of children in the family as a sphere in which some uses of force (e.g., punishment) stand outside the law.

But this very example, as Benjamin argues, serves to illuminate a certain tendency within modern legal systems—namely, the tendency of making any natural ends remaining in the hands of individuals into a matter for legislation (or turning them into legal ends): "This means: in all areas where the ends of individual persons could be purposively pursued with violence, this legal order insists on erecting legal ends that only legal authority can realize" (CV 42; translation modified).

It is possible to identify this as a tendency of the legal system to monopolize violence, that is, to strive not to leave any use of force to individuals unregulated by law. This phenomenon needs to be analyzed; it points to something problematic in the relation of law to violence, yet it is not clear at this point what the problem is. Benjamin clarifies the tendency to monopolize violence by way of two cases in which, apparently at least, the state leaves out of the scope of legal violence certain ends of individuals or groups.

One important example is the right of workers to strike. The strike, even though in a sense a nonaction, is nevertheless a use of force for an end, namely, the transformation of working conditions. And yet this "patience" of the state in granting the right to strike—that is, the use of force—to an individual group within the state has very clear limits that become apparent in the proletarian general strike. Benjamin speaks of the proletarian strike as a contradiction in the legal system that emerges in a particular situation (even if, on the face of it, it is not a contradiction in the law in the abstract). Every workers union has the right to strike, but this does not lead to the right for all to strike together. This situation is a contradiction that precipitates the violent opposition of the state.

The proletarian general strike brings out the counterviolence of the state precisely because it seeks not merely local gains but a transformation of the legal system as such or the creation of a new order of law: "The strike shows . . . that it is capable of grounding and modifying legal situations, however offended the feeling of justice may thereby find itself" (CV 44). In other words, the violence that emerges in this situation has a certain characteristic: it is what Benjamin calls law-positing violence. This law-positing violence is what the state seeks to keep for itself. The state then cannot allow for violence that can become law-positing to be held by individuals or groups within the state. We will eventually have to inquire what it is about the law-positing character of violence that is disturbing and why exactly the state "reserves" it to itself. But let us first consider a further example of this kind of situation in the modern state.

The use of force by the military for natural ends (e.g., to protect lives) is sanctioned by the state. But there are situations—for example, an all-out war—where the use of violence becomes massively present outside the legal system. This situation, in which it is the right of the military to deploy violence, is similar to the general strike in being something of a contradiction. In this case, without doubt, the military violence outside the law is not opposed by violence of the state but rather is reincorporated into the legal order through its transformation. It is retroactively made or turned into legal violence by way of a peace treaty. In a peace treaty, what resulted from violence outside the law is the basis of a new law, which the state gives "equally" to itself and to the vanquished party. In other words, "if a conclusion may be drawn from considering military violence, as an original and archetypal form of all violence, it would be that there inheres a law-positing character in all violence used for natural ends" (CV 45).

Both the general proletarian strike and war are exceptions with respect to the legal system, and yet they reveal something about the law that is scarcely visible in its day-to-day application—namely, the tendency internal to the legal system to monopolize all law-positing violence.

The Duality of Law-Positing Violence

According to Benjamin, law-positing violence is inherently ambiguous. Force is internal to establishing a specific law. Such force is manifest, for instance, in determining new restrictions on the actions of those who fall under its jurisdiction; thus, a law that establishes taxation for something like travel from one place to another would be in that sense an expression of the violence of law. But, while this law-positing violence might be fully justifiable in terms of the doctrine of positive law, Benjamin suggests that a duality is at play (clearly visible only in certain extreme circumstances, such as the general strike)—namely, that there is a force that is associated with the law as such. It is as though behind the violence in positing a specific law, the law as such appears in its violent self-positing.

Benjamin gives further examples of that ambiguity in considering the structure of punishment in a legal system. In particular, he rejects the idea of punishment as something like a deterrent (the utilitarian notion that knowing that the offense might involve a punishment proportional to it might serve as a deterrent). Instead, Benjamin describes the essence of punishment in terms of the ambiguity of threat. Threat does not involve any calculation or proportionality; its force depends precisely on not knowing exactly what would unleash it, as well as the utter disproportion of the punishment to the offense. The threat of punishment is not correlative with the specific offense but with the very affirmation of the absolute force of law. This, according to Benjamin, becomes clear when one considers capital punishment and in particular its place in ancient systems of law, where it could be incurred for "such offenses as property misdemeanors, to which it seems entirely out of 'proportion'" (CV 47).

This duality in the manifestation of the force of law is also hinted at in Benjamin's short discussion of the decline of parliaments. One could take the work of parliaments to be solely concerned with the specific legislation at issue. And yet, as Benjamin notes, the life of the political body depends on such legislation expressing something like the condition of the instauration of law as such. The disappearance of that original force is manifest in how specific legislation is overtaken by compromise: "If the consciousness of the latent presence of violence in a legal institution disappears, the institution falls into decay. In current times, parliaments constitute an example of this:

they offer a well-known, woeful spectacle because they have not remained conscious of the revolutionary forces to which they owe their existence" (CV 49).

To put the duality at issue in relation to a somewhat similar situation in social contract theories, consider that in such theories we find two moments: the first is the acceptance of law as such (which is unconditional and unanimous, as Rousseau understands it) and which does violence to nature in emerging out of it. The second is expressed in the "life" of the body politic through constant legislation. One might nevertheless wonder whether the force establishing the very existence of the social order (call it revolutionary force) has to be, even if implicitly, present in the specific legislation enacted in the state. It's as if the original, mythical moment of arising out of nature must always be present in the legislation that ensures the continuance of the state. The legislator, as Rousseau conceives it, must see himself as transforming human nature.[2]

Now, one could say, in the context of social contract theory, that revolutionary force is inherent in the original contract to form a society out of nature.[3] For Benjamin, this is tantamount to asking about the relation between the natural condition of man and society under law. As we saw in discussing "Fate and Character," this is precisely the relation of law to the rule of fate over man. Whereas social contract theorists attempt to justify the legal order and the basic institutions of society through the idea of an agreement out of nature, Benjamin seeks to diagnose the perverse character of legal institutions and the state through precisely the same question of the relation of the law to bare life. It is for that reason that he seeks within the scope of specific legal arrangements and situations the manifestation of the "mythic origin of law." Before turning to the problem of the relation between mythic violence and law, let me elaborate a few other moments of Benjamin's analysis.

The Perverse Ambiguity of Law-Preserving Violence

Benjamin's analysis has brought out the peculiar character of law-positing violence in the state. There is a further manifestation of force that needs to be considered, namely, law-preserving force. Is the monopoly of violence by the state also evident in law-preserving violence? On the face of it, law-preserving violence is that violence which is necessary for maintaining the law in the space of social existence. Just as Benjamin brings out the peculiar ambiguity of law-positing violence, he points to a perversity of law-preserving violence, primarily through a discussion of the police.

The function of the police is apparently to enforce the law; one might also speak here of "applying" the law. And yet there is an inherent gap between the abstract general law and the particular situations of its enforcement. It is for the police to "fill" this gap—that is, extend the law—so that it applies, and in so doing they mix law-preserving with lawmaking. Just as with the analysis of law-positing violence, Benjamin diagnoses an ambiguity (he calls it "a kind of spectral mixture") that is manifest in the character of law-preserving violence. This is not so much the unity of the executive and the legislative, where the police are merely the tool of absolute power—of, say, the dictates of a monarch. Rather, the police take upon themselves to extend law-positing violence so that no domain is free of the law. One could say that through such an institution as the police, what appears is precisely the extension of the monopoly of violence by the state to every aspect of life. Benjamin describes it as "shapeless, like its nowhere-tangible, all-pervasive, ghostly appearance in the life of civilized states" (CV 48). Indeed, the absolute monopoly of violence appears in a more perverse form in democracies than in so-called absolute monarchies: "There can ultimately be no denying that its spirit is less devastating in absolute monarchies, where it represents the ruler's power, in which there is a unity of full legislative and executive power, than in democracies, where its existence, elevated by no such relation . . . bears witness to the greatest conceivable degeneration of violence" (CV 48; translation modified).

The Nonviolent Resolution of Conflicts

As we have seen, Benjamin dismisses the idea that parliaments are a sphere of nonviolent resolution of conflicts. Indeed, violence can be present in the form of extortion, when deliberation takes the form of each party's trying to bend the other's will, ultimately making the decision a sad as well as violent compromise. If violence belongs to the relation between means and ends, then, Benjamin suggests that nonviolence is a matter of pure means—namely, remaining solely within the means.

This is further characterized as the sphere of indirect solutions, outside the law. Avoiding the violence inherent in law would mean reaching a resolution of conflict in which no side is said to be victorious and no side loses. Since it is the establishment of a new law that makes plain that the conflict is determined by a drive for the monopoly of law as such, no contract would be involved in this kind of resolution (i.e., there would be nothing like a resulting agreement that implicitly refers to the violence that would be involved in breaching it). Rather, the clearest instance of nonviolent means would be making the conflict disappear without deciding it.

Not only does the activity of pure means not achieve anything for itself, but the nonviolent resolution of conflict also means that no side can be seen as victorious. Victory on one side would be violence on the other. The nonviolence of pure means can only be a dissolution of conflict. In other words, there is form of completeness correlated with pure means: the complete disappearance of the conflict. This is not a solution, as it does not lead to an agreement or a contract between the parties. Moreover the dissolution of conflict is, importantly, not a matter of doing justice; in fact, it is such as to not involve the legal system at all.

A motive that might lead people in that direction would be "the fear of the mutual disadvantages" in sustaining the conflict or even in engaging in a legal process to decide it "whatever the outcome might be." This, as Benjamin notes, is often the case with conflicts of private persons over "objects," goods, rather than what pertains to persons. The virtues of "moderation" (politeness, sympathy, peaceableness, trust) are subjective preconditions of those who deploy the technique of dissolution of conflict; in the case of states this would be the technique of diplomacy. Yet Benjamin is rather skeptical of the possibility of nonviolent resolution of conflicts between states: "When classes and nations come into conflict . . . the higher orders that threaten to overwhelm victor and vanquished alike are hidden from the feelings of most, and the insight of almost all" (CV 51).

In considering the very possibility of a sphere of pure, nonviolent means, Benjamin returns to an issue that he discussed earlier in the essay, namely, the proletarian general strike. It is indeed one thing to say that the state is driven to violence in that situation and quite another to ask whether the general strike itself is violent. Recall that there is in "local" strikes an element of force, even if the strike involves a cessation of action (and thus in a sense is not actively violent). The violence is inherent in the demand for new conditions for the workers. The general proletarian strike does not demand anything less than the dissolution of the existing order. Benjamin argues that if partial strikes are forms of extortion, then the general strike is indeed a form of nonviolence (though it is not clear whether it can in any way lead to the dissolution of the order of law, since that would provoke the violence of the law in order to establish itself as having a monopoly on power). This moment of the essay has received much attention, even to the extent of making it Benjamin's resolution of the problem of law and violence, but this is doubtful since the question of the relation between law and fate or the problem of mythical violence has not even been broached.

Mythic Violence and Law

Law-positing violence and law-preserving violence express the monopolizing of violence by the law in different ways. But what is the ground of this tendency in the law? What is it that becomes visible in the violence of law as such? With this question we broach the possibility of a violence that is not conceived of as a means to an end or, more generally, a violence considered apart from the means-end structure. What is violence that is not a means to an end? Is it merely gratuitous violence? Benjamin suggests that what is at issue is an immediate manifestation of violence. One example from the sphere of the individual is an outburst of anger: we would conceive of this outburst as violent, but it is not violence that serves a purpose; it is merely the manifestation of anger, its immediate expression (expressing that there is anger, that it exists). Benjamin takes the paradigm of this immediate manifestation of violence from mythology, specifically from the story of Niobe, and calls it mythical violence. Yet, what features of the story does Benjamin make use of to think about the violence of law? If we identify the features of mythical violence too closely with the myth of Apollo and Artemis killing the children of Niobe as punishment for her arrogance, we will be unable to find a clear parallel to modern existence under law. For this reason, Benjamin reads it in ways that appear to conflict with the common narrative: the violence of the gods is not a punishment or even something "willed" (for some end) but is rather a manifestation of their existence. Existence is beyond any "What?" or "Why?," and therefore such violence does not belong to the domain of motives.[4]

In seeking to further assess the character of mythic violence, we should note that, while it is not a response to the infringement of a law, it is nevertheless the ground of lawmaking violence. It does not *aim* to establish law (it is not a means for establishing law); rather, the very manifestation of violence establishes law. Benjamin makes this clear in recounting the legend of Niobe: "To be sure, it could appear as though the action of Apollo and Artemis were only a punishment. But their violence establishes a law far more than it punishes the transgression of an existing one" (CV 55). As we have seen, tragedy is an expression of humanity's struggle with this perverse reversal of violence and law in myth. It is not the infraction of law that leads to its terrible violence but the violence that demands atonement and establishes law. Yet the struggle of the tragic hero opens up the possibility of a new delimitation of the relationship between humans and the gods. This is the way in which Benjamin understands the legend of Prometheus, who "challenges fate with dignified courage, combats it with changing fortunes, and is not left by the legend without the hope of one day bringing a new law to human beings" (CV 55).

In further clarifying the precise nature of the law-positing character of mythic violence as well as the relation it bears to legal violence, it is important to note the shift that Benjamin makes from force (*Gewalt*) to power (*Macht*) in expressing the relation between law and myth:

> This connection promises to shed more light on fate underlying legal violence in all cases. . . . For the function of violence in law-positing is twofold, in the following sense: the positing of law uses violence as its means to establish as law its end, but at the moment of instating as law the end at which it aims, it does not dismiss violence; rather, in a strict sense and indeed immediately, it makes it law-positing, by establishing not an end that would be free of and independent from violence but, on the contrary, an end that under the name of power is necessarily and intimately bound up with it. Law-positing is power-positing [*Machtsetzung* = assumption of power] and in that respect an act of immediate manifestation of violence. . . . Power [is] the principle of all mythic law-positing. (CV 56; translation modified)

The many instances of the use of force or violence in the legal system, can be traced to the manifestation of undivided power. Power is one and unlimited. The assumption of power by the legal system is reflected in the ambiguous character of violence as a means to legal ends: it is at one and the same time an expression of the tendency of that system to monopolize violence. The latter is precisely how the assumption of power is manifest in the legal order. In other words, through the analysis of mythic violence, we come to understand what underlies law-positing violence—namely, the very existence, the self-assertion, of power. Power is of another order than effective force; it is omnipresent and thus, on occasion, immediately manifests itself even if it appears as effective violence for some end or other.

To clarify this distinction, let us make use of a different context. Consider the relation Schopenhauer establishes between the causal laws of nature, the effective force at work under such and such conditions, and power that makes manifest the omnipresence of world as will. Schopenhauer raises a strange question: Why is it that laws of nature hold in every place in space and at every time. Why is it that, always and everywhere, when these conditions are present, then that other thing happens? As long as we think here in terms of external causal relations between different states or of real processes happening in space and time, we are at a loss to address this matter satisfactorily. Our perplexity disappears as soon as we recognize that what is at issue is not a relation between different events that always and everywhere follow the same law but rather a unity of omnipresent being. Something being just what it is raises no question, nor does it require any reason or explanation. But it is exactly what is at issue when we recognize the dependence of laws of phenomena on the expression of the oneness of will, its "power." That power is not a doing but the expression of being, apart from the extension of space and the succession of time. The multitude of particular occurrences falling under a law of nature, which everywhere and always is the same, are just refractions in space and time of a oneness of being: "Our astonishment over the law-like and precise operations of the forces of nature, over the perfect uniformity of all their millions of appearances, over the infallibility of their emergence, can be compared to the astonishment of a child or a savage who sees a flower through a many-faceted glass for the first time and wonders over the perfect uniformity of the countless flowers that he sees, counting the leaves of each one separately."[5] The mirrors of the kaleidoscope are space and time, and the will is refracted in them whenever and wherever there is an "occasion" for its manifestation, forming a perfect pattern and giving the appearances their orderly and lawful character.

Thus, if we think for a moment of power in nature (as opposed to causal efficacy), we can say that power is not something that belongs to the order of law but rather is omnipresent and unlimited; it manifests itself, makes its existence manifest, through occasions for the unleashing of force. Mythically speaking, there are powers—call them the gods—that are omnipresent and unlimited, and on various occasions their existence is manifested as violence. Such manifestations may be articulated as a "specific law" that is in force; nevertheless, these omnipresent and unlimited powers take ontological precedence over the manifestation of the force of the law. The way in which power is omnipresent yet only occasionally expressed in the immediate unleashing of violence can be related to the fact that in ancient times laws were not "written": power has something like the character of what is implicit and pervasive, yet it is never formulated as law, and so the knowledge of what occasions its unleashing is never available:

> Established and circumscribed boundaries remain, at least in primeval times, unwritten laws. A human being can transgress them unawares and be thereby doomed to atonement. Each intervention of law that is provoked by the violation of the unwritten and unknown law is called "atonement" [*Sühne*] in contradistinction to "punishment" [*Strafe*]. But whatever the misfortune through which it comes to befall its unsuspecting victim, its occurrence is, in the sense of the law, not an accident but rather fate presenting itself once again in its systematic ambiguity. (CV 56; my translation)

An echo of that ambiguity in the legal system is to be found, as I have suggested, in the ambiguity of law-positing and law-monopolizing, in the indeterminate mixture of law-positing and law-preserving violence, as well as in the understanding of punishment as essentially threat. For the disproportion of threat is precisely the lack of knowledge of what can unleash the violence of fate. These features of the law are reflections of the fundamental ambiguity that is the essence of fate; in other words, we can begin to see how the realm of law is what takes up the occasions for the manifestation of the power of fate. Viewed in these terms, we can recognize the following progression in the essay: law-preserving force is bastardized by taking upon itself law-positing force; law-positing force is perverse in seeking a monopoly of violence by the legal system. This tendency itself shows that law is an instrument of mythical power (the power manifesting itself as fate). As Benjamin puts it: "Fate [is] underlying legal violence in all cases" (CV 55). Law is the instrument through which fate rules collective existence. Thus, Benjamin writes: "Far from opening up a purer sphere, the mythic manifestation of immediate violence reveals itself to be at the deepest level identical with all legal violence" (CV 57). There then remains a further question whether mythical power is not itself a distorted manifestation of a higher force.

Divine Violence

What would it mean to destroy the hold of myth (fate) as it expresses itself through the violence of law? And in what sense would that be a political task? Initially, it seems that Benjamin takes a step away from understanding this as a human task, by contrasting mythical violence with divine violence. And yet, by the end of the essay it becomes clear that partaking in divine force is possible and indeed intimately tied to the possibility of revolutionary force in the realm of the political: "If the existence of violence outside the law, as pure immediate violence, is secured, this proves that, and how, revolutionary violence, which is the name reserved for the highest manifestation of pure violence through human beings, is possible" (CV 60). Since the struggle with myth is, as will become clear, one of the features of history, we might conjecture that divine violence is also internal to Benjamin's concept of time or of history; but in order to recognize this inner connection, it is necessary to begin with an analysis of the notion of pure immediate violence.

Divine violence, in that respect like mythic violence, is a form of immediate violence. We must not think of it in terms of the means-ends scheme. It cannot be a form of causality of the will in which God brings about destruction because of some sin or infringement of a law. The rejection of the means-ends scheme is, as I have argued, a fundamental moment of the discussion of the nature of violence. The difficulty with that scheme is formulated at the beginning of Benjamin's essay as an antinomy. The resolution of this antinomy is what Benjamin addresses when he introduces the contrast between divine violence and mythic violence as antithetical forms of immediate violence, neither of which has a means-ends structure:[6]

> This is a question that at the same time concerns the truth of the basic dogma held in common by these theories: just ends can be attained by justified means; justified means can be used for just ends. How, then, would things stand, if the kind of violence that pertains to fate, as it employs justified means, were to be in irreconcilable conflict with just ends, and if at the same time a different kind of violence is conceivable, a kind of violence that definitely could *not* be either a justified or unjustified means to those ends, and would instead not relate to them as means at all but somehow differently. (CV 54; translation modified)

There is no "explanation" or "justification" for divine violence. We cannot think of it on the model of means and ends, as being of a hypothetical form, which is to say that it belongs to the dimension of the unconditioned or absolute. We are used to thinking of an unconditioned deed, as, say, Kant understands it, in terms of acting from the moral law. But this way of thinking law and the unconditioned is precisely what Benjamin criticizes. Law is not only essentially conditioned, it is essentially perverted by its dependence on the order of the immediate violence of myth. What would it be to think of the unconditioned apart from law?

It is tempting to introduce the hypothetical form into divine violence when Benjamin recounts the story of Korach and his clan as an example of its revelation, for isn't it the case that because Korach challenged Moses's leadership, God unleashed violence? But recall that what likewise appears as a will that punishes in the story of Niobe is only the manifestation of the existence of a power. Manifestation is manifestation of existence, not something that has the form of purposive behavior.[7]

There are nevertheless fundamental differences between the two forms of immediate violence, which are expressed in the following important passage:

> Just as God is opposed to myth in all spheres, so divine violence designates in all respects an antithesis to mythic violence. If mythic violence is law-positing, divine violence is law-annihilating; if the former establishes boundaries, the latter boundlessly annihilates them; if mythic violence inculpates and expiates at the same time, divine violence expiates; if the former threatens, the latter strikes; if the former is bloody, the latter is lethal in a bloodless manner. (CV 57; translation modified)

Recall that mythic violence was the source of the threatening character of law. Myth is threatening not because it warns that infringement of law leads to punishment, for warning would introduce a condition: "I warn you! If you do . . . , you will suffer." Mythical violence is immediate rather than conditional. The character of threat belongs to the mythical ambiguity that underlies the laws. Similarly, divine violence is without warning, but, as opposed to mythic violence, it is without threat because it lacks any ambiguity. And it lacks ambiguity because it is unconditioned destruction.

Divine violence is neither determined by law nor does it establish law. This latter is what distinguishes divine violence from mythical violence and shows it to be of another order, for while mythical violence is not the result of infringing a preexisting law, it establishes law. By way of the myth of Niobe, Benjamin suggests that mythical violence leaves traces of the suffering it inflicted; what remains is internal to the character of the law that was established. Indeed, the traces of suffering are precisely the threatening ambiguity of the law. Divine violence establishes no law, thus leaves no trace. In the story of the clan of Korach, those struck by divine violence are swallowed up by the earth. Destruction, one might say, is not "mixed" with the order of life.

While the outline of the distinction between mythical and divine violence becomes more evident, it is still not clear what unconditioned destruction might mean at all, and why it would be identified with the divine. Consider the traditional idea of the divine as the highest actuality, the *actus purus*. God does not *realize* anything through divine force, since that would imply a lesser actuality. In that sense, every account of divine violence in which it is said to bring about something is mistaken. This has already been made clear in the claim that such violence cannot be related the emergence of law. As Benjamin puts it: "What is at issue here is not the 'realization' of divine force. On the one hand, this process is the supreme reality; on the other, divine force contains its reality in itself" (SW 1:227; translation modified). Put differently, the highest actuality cannot reveal itself in something like a recognizable unity that governs human experience. There cannot be positive revelation of divine force, neither in miracles nor in "punishment." In the fragment "World and Time" Benjamin says: "In the revelation of the divine, the world—the theater of history—is subjected to a great process of decomposition" (SW 1:226). Insofar as we can speak of the revelation of divine violence, it can only be recognized in and through that decomposition. And a bit further on, Benjamin strengthens that intuition in arguing: "The guiding principle here is: authentic divine force [*Gewalt*] can manifest itself *other than destructively* only in the world to come (the world of fulfillment)" (SW 1:226; translation modified).[8]

The idea of the divine as the highest actuality (which can manifest itself in this world only destructively) can further explicate for us the problem with the assumption of "power" (*Macht*) so central to myth. Power as inexorably retaining potentiality is precisely the polar opposite of pure actuality.[9] Mythical violence is the arrogation of power, whereas divine violence is the manifestation of pure or highest actuality in the finite. Mythical violence cannot be truly unconditioned; the only way it has the semblance of being so is in retaining destructive force in the form of threatening power. It arrogates the force of the unconditioned to itself not as pure actuality but rather as perverse power. Its power asserts itself in misfortune, suffering, and sacrifice of the living.

Divine violence does not will or cause destruction in the world; it is not done for a reason. Rather, one should say that it is only by assuming destruction in a redemptive scheme (what Benjamin also calls "accepting sacrifice") that it will be possible to recognize the presence of that highest force in history. If anything, then, the problem must be understood in terms of what it means for human beings to partake in that divine actuality. Since it cannot be a matter of partaking in a unity of experience, it must be understood as turning the destruction wrought in time into a revelation of the highest actuality in the present. Partaking in divine violence is the actualization of that scene of destruction, which is the past, in a transformed present, the "Now." Only viewed in relation to this task can we understand both the nature of divine violence, its manifestation in relation to the historical process, and what it means for human beings to partake in it.

Mythic and Divine Temporalities

Let us try to approach the distinction between mythical and divine violence in terms of two opposite forms of temporality. Mythic temporality is primarily the temporality of impatience. Indeed, consider again Benjamin's example of the outburst of anger. The rhythm of exploding in anger is one in which there is no show of anger until suddenly all hell breaks loose. It occurs with someone in whom anger has been simmering and who has perhaps been in some sense "sending signals" but not explicitly expressing that anger. These signals would seem to be mixed until the anger explodes, and then it would seem as though the threat had been constant from the outset. Rage as the rhythm of impatience can take time to explode; indeed, what is manifest is the very existence of that anger, which can be triggered by something very small and insignificant. Furthermore, it is clear how such an explosion of anger determines boundaries not to be crossed and fills the environment with the space of threat (you do not know what will cause that person to lose it). Such a person has power precisely as the constant possibility or potential of exploding.

Consider further the connection between mythic violence and retribution. Retribution too has a particular temporal form. The temporal dimension of mythic violence leaves its mark in the structure of punishment in the legal system, as is evident in the law's having a statute of limitations. Benjamin speaks of that limitation as thirty years, roughly corresponding to the span of a generation. He also suggests that this limitation is the result of fear, as it were, or is defensive in relation to something that underlies punishment, namely, the unlimited time of mythical violence: "as if it were afraid to exceed the span of a human life" (SW 1:286). Exceeding this span would show the law to be actually expressing the endlessness that belongs to mythical forces and is without a temporal limit: "Yet we know from older forms of law that the power of retribution was able to extend its sway to succeeding, increasingly distant generations. Retribution is fundamentally indifferent to the passage of time, since it remains in force for centuries without dilution" (SW 1:286). This is suggested, for instance, in the structure of ancient tragedy (which is an attempt to address the burden of myth). Fate as guilt manifests itself in a curse that hangs over a whole royal family and extends from generation to generation: from Atreus to Agamemnon and Clytemnestra, and from them to Electra and Orestes; from Labdacus to Laius to Oedipus to Antigone.

Thus there is a strange mixture of endlessness and impatience in the rhythm of mythic violence. How then are we to characterize the temporality of divine violence? First of all, divine violence is terminating, even if it does not complete or fulfill any end. The "state" of completion is not the emergence of a new law (which always retains the bond to power and violence) but rather the complete eradication of any traces of the guilt of life. Second, there is a distinction to be made between the endless demonic inability to die and the temporality of an afterlife. One might confuse the two (e.g., in the case of *Hamlet*, the ghost of Hamlet's father supposedly precipitates the demand for retribution in the next generation). This can even lead to a conception of the Last Judgment that rests on the idea of retribution, as though in the Last Judgment something would finally put an end to the postponement and retribution would be allowed free rein. As Benjamin notes, this would be an inauthentic, "pagan" picture of the Last Judgment.

Assuming Sacrifice

We are now in a position to interpret one of the most difficult passages contrasting mythic and divine violence:

> The unleashing [*Auslösung*] of legal violence can be traced back [*geht an . . . zurück*] . . . to the incurring of guilt [inculpation] of mere natural life, which delivers the living, innocent, and unfortunate [*Unglücklich*] to atonement [*Sühne*] that "expiates" [*sühnt*] the guilt incurred—and doubtless also the guilty come to be expiated [*entsühnt*], not of guilt, however, but of law. For with [the cessation] of mere life, the domination of law over the living ceases. Mythic violence is blood violence over mere life for its own sake; divine violence is pure violence over all life for the sake of the living. The former demands sacrifice; the latter assumes it.[10] (CV 57; my translation)

Note, first, the distinction between the nonpersonal guilt of "mere life" and "the guilty" (i.e., the individuals who suffer this impersonal guilt). As we saw in the analysis of "Fate and Character," mere life is the bearer of natural guilt (just as character is natural innocence). It is guilt that is not an infraction of the law, even if the very nature of law is closely connected to its perpetuation. Law, as became clear in our account, is the instrument of the violence of fate. Law "makes guilty" the living who are misfortunate by virtue of the guilt of mere life. To return to a phrase already quoted in our discussion of "Fate and Character," "It would be false to assume that only guilt is present in a legal context; it is demonstrable that all legal guilt is nothing other than misfortune" (SW 1:203). This is why such suffering that is supposedly retribution is only called "expiation" in a manner of speaking. In effect it serves to perpetuate the condition that calls for further suffering. In fact, those deemed guilty do come to expiate—that is, be purified from—not their guilt but the law. This can be recognized only if we introduce how divine violence relates to this condition of life.

Benjamin distinguishes "mere life," "all life," and "the living." Consider the distinction between "mere life" and "all life." Mere life is life that is ruled by fate.[11] But it does not exhaust the span of life, for life is not only natural life; there is life in the human being that "identically underlies earthly life, death, and afterlife" (CV 59; translation modified). All life transcends natural life when it is conceived of from the standpoint of history, as Benjamin puts it in "The Task of the Translator," and includes what he calls afterlife.

For the sake of the living, that is, the individual living beings, pure violence exceeds the span of natural life and is a force recognizable only in history. We cannot yet offer an explanation as to why this pure violence is for the sake of the living, but it will clearly have to relate the redemptive character of history to its destructive vector.

Educative Violence

The destructive character of divine violence, especially as it is paired with a catastrophic vision of history, seems not to be something encountered in ordinary human existence. Nevertheless, Benjamin identifies one of the manifestations of divine violence as educative violence in its highest form. This is a peculiar and surprising moment in the essay, the first occasion on which Benjamin asks us to think of the human being partaking in divine violence, not in extreme circumstances but in the very midst of ordinary life. It raises the question as to what extent education is to be conceived of not merely as constructive (i.e., forming) but also as destructive.

Early on in his discussion of the monopoly of force in the state, Benjamin considered the way punishment in education is taken out of the hands of individuals and brought into the sphere of law. At this later point in the essay, it becomes clear that the aforementioned was not a mere example and that education "stands in its completed form outside the law" (CV 58). This is not because individuals have a right to, say, raise and punish their children without interference. Instead, we must ask, What is the destructive force in education (indeed, its annihilating character)? It is not directed at personality as such (the soul of the living), but rather at that which seeks to arrogate for itself the unlimited in the person—more precisely, at the unlimited will that asserts itself by retaining itself as power. In particular, it consists in the ways in which the ego arrogates for itself a form of absoluteness that can only be truly revealed in partaking in a higher, nonindividual life. It is in this spirit that I understand the following fragment:

Every unlimited condition of the will leads to evil. Ambition and lust are unlimited expressions of will. As the theologians have always perceived, the natural totality of the will must be destroyed. The will must shatter into a thousand pieces. The elements of the will that have proliferated so greatly limit one another. (SW 1:114)

One may conceive here of a moment of divine violence in education; indeed, the destruction of the will that seeks infinity for itself is a moment of education. What has to be destroyed is that which can lead the self to attribute to itself an unlimited potential or power. (One might think here of various forms of arrogance and fanaticism as such arrogation of the unlimited to one's own self.)

The Commandment and the Law

Benjamin's short discussion of the character of the commandment "Thou shalt not kill" follows upon the recognition of the presence of destructive violence in education. It can further clarify for us the manner in which human beings can relate their existence to divine violence, an issue of great importance as the essay draws to a close. Initially, however, we are presented with an apparent contradiction: Since divine violence is law-destroying, we cannot identify a commandment such as "Thou shalt not kill" with a general law. But how is a universal commandment (*Gebote*) not a law? How can we identify the divine commandment with release from the rule (*Herrschaft*) of law as such?

Isn't there a law that prohibits the killing of another human being?[12] What more fundamental law could there be for the constitution of a human society? A law is universal, and its application to particular cases is an act of judgment. Yet Benjamin writes: "No judgment of the deed follows from the commandment" (CV 58). In other words, it is not the case that, were I to consider a maxim to determine whether killing another in a certain situation is justified, I would make my judgment by way of a universalization procedure such as that implied, for instance, by the application of Kant's categorical imperative. Instead, the situation in which this question can arise for me is always singular or unique, and the struggle with it is not a matter of judgment and choice but rather of decisiveness in the face of an incomparable situation. It is the uniqueness of one's own existence that is put on the line in the struggle to act decisively. We have encountered this notion of decisiveness in thinking about the redemptive dimension of *Elective Affinities*. Law belongs together with choice (whether to apply it to a certain case or not). Only decisiveness puts an end to the ambiguity inherent in the dimension of choice and, psychologically speaking, to doubt and inner uncertainty. Such decisiveness involves the person in the dimension Benjamin calls "existence."[13]

This is why Benjamin writes that the "commandment blocks the deed, just as God was standing in front of its happening [*Dieses Gebot steht vor der Tat wie Gott "davor sei" das sie geschehe*]" (CV 58; translation modified). One is tested in one's faith in the condition where such a deed is at issue. It is therefore a solitary moment: "[The commandment] exists not as a standard [*Maßstab*] of judgment, but as a guideline [*Richtschnur*] for the agent or communities that have to confront it in solitude and, in terrible cases, take on the responsibility of ignoring it" (CV 58).[14]

Put differently, we recognize in the commandment what belongs to the dimension of justice. Indeed, Benjamin characterizes justice precisely through the idea of nongeneralizable universality. God decides on just ends:

> This is an insight that is uncommon only because a stubborn habit prevails of conceiving of just ends as ends of a possible law, that is, not only as universally valid [i.e., valid for all people] (which follows analytically from the character of justice), but also capable of generalization [i.e., generalizable to similar situations], which, as can be shown, contradicts the character of justice. For ends that for one situation are just, universally recognized, and in this sense valid universally are so for no other, even if in other respects the situation is ever so similar. (CV 54; translation modified)

Justice is a state of the world; its uniqueness is tantamount to its being the highest reality: "Virtue can be demanded; justice in the final analysis can only be as a state of the world or as a state of God." Indeed, the highest universality is not a matter of the demand of the law, but of the existing (which is not the real): "Justice does not appear to refer to the good will of the subject, but, instead, constitutes a state [*Zustand*] of the world. Justice designates the ethical category of the existent, virtue the ethical category of the demanded."[15]

The contrast formed between mere life and existence is further explicated in Benjamin's dismissal of the attempt to base the forbidding of killing on a principle of the sanctity of life as such. Mere life is, as was already claimed, natural life, guilty by being entangled in fate. It is life fraught with ambiguity, prey to demonic forces, and therefore has no sanctity to it. Existence, in contrast, is the "irreducible total state of man" (*die unverrückbaren Aggregatzustand*). As our discussion of the distinction between commandment and law explains, in decisiveness the person determines their life unambiguously. Such decisive existence, as Benjamin makes clear in his essay on Goethe's *Elective Affinities*, is reconciled with God in solitude in the face of death, the abode of the ultimate danger.

But the purifying capacity of divine violence is for those who have not been capable of such reconciliation. It is such as to assume guilt as well as the hope one should have for the hopeless, for a "morally unimproved humanity" (SW 1:226). Indeed, it is significant that the term that serves Benjamin to characterize the relation of the divine to sacrifice—that it does not demand it but rather assumes it (*Annehmen*)—is related to the term Benjamin uses in speaking of the way that Goethe assumes (*Aufnehmen*) into himself the hopelessness and destruction inherent in the world of the novel. If we are to speak of this dimension of existence in terms of the life of man, it would essentially involve "that life in him which identically underlies earthly life, death, and afterlife" (CV 59; translation modified). Existence that encompasses earthly life, death, and afterlife (of meaning) is in fact history. It is only by considering history as the actualization of meaning in the afterlife of what befalls human beings that it will be possible to recognize their life from the standpoint of existence, or what comes to the same thing, to recognize the redeeming presence of divine violence in the world.

Divine Violence and History

Approaching the end of the essay in this way, we can better understand Benjamin's identification of the critique of violence with the "philosophy of its history—the 'philosophy' of this history because only the idea of what it comes to [*Ausgang*], makes possible a critical, discriminating [*Scheidende*], and decisive attitude toward its temporal data" (CV 59; translation modified). It is from this standpoint that Benjamin describes the problematic nature of the interpenetration of the law-preserving and law-instating forces as having the character of an oscillation: "A gaze directed only at what is closest at hand can at most become aware of a dialectical back and forth in the law-positing and law-preserving formations of violence" (CV 60; translation modified). We have encountered various "oscillations" throughout the essay, correlative with problematic ways of establishing authority: the ambiguous or spectral character of the police, as well as the threatening demonic duality of the excessive precision of meaning in fate. Speaking of a dialectical movement of rising and falling as oscillation characterizes it as a movement that runs in circles. Dialectics, in that case, is no more than the manifestation of ambiguity and does not contain any overcoming or *Aufhebung*. The cycle, or oscillation, is "maintained by the mythic forms of law"; it is the mythical manifesting itself in time, as eternal return, through the perverse character of law.

To establish that there is a cycle or eternal return at play here, we must understand in what sense mythic violence "needs" legal violence in order to manifest itself. Not only is there in law-positing an arrogation of mythical violence, but the violence of law is that through which mythical violence is given to manifest itself as well. The arrogation of power by law-positing violence is indeed hubris, and it leads, out of its own dynamics, to the demise of law and the triumphant manifestation of mythic violence. This is the proper standpoint from which to assess the relation of law-positing and law-preserving violence. For now, that spectral ambiguity of law-preserving violence is itself blind to the demonic character of law and becomes the agent of the unfolding of fate. Benjamin writes that "the law of its oscillation rests on this: a law-preserving violence, in its duration, indirectly, through its suppression of hostile counterforces, weakens law-positing violence" (CV 60; translation modified). The "forces" at issue, whether new or reemerging, are supervenient on the violence of myth. Law-preserving violence is what sets in motion the unfolding of fate, leading to the victory of a new order but at the same time to the triumphant manifestation of mythic violence over the arrogation of violence by the legal order, thus inaugurating a new law-positing moment, which is destined to decay in its turn. It is the task of history to "arrest" this mythical repetition.[16]

PART III

Body and Corporeality

EIGHT

The Language of the Body and the Body of Language

Does the essay "On the Mimetic Faculty" signal a shift in Benjamin's thought from the theologically oriented to an anthropological conception of language? In what follows I will argue that it is essentially an extension and unfolding of the vision of man's actualization of nature in language. Indeed, the concept of a "mimetic faculty" is only thematized in the 1934 essay of that name, but it is clear that the problem of similarity central to it is of the deepest concern to Benjamin throughout. Its role in the epilogue to the dissertation on Romantic critique in the essay on translation, as well as in various discussions of affinity ("Two Poems by Friedrich Hölderlin," "Analogy and Relationship," and "Goethe's Elective Affinities"), is fundamental. This raises the question of what is added in considering the mimetic power to make oneself similar. The initial answer is that it is the role of the body that is brought to the fore, how corporeality belongs to meaning. This would mean both how our body is inserted into language and how language itself can be conceived of as corporeal, as a body of meaning.

Body, Corporeal Substance, and Nature

In order to provide necessary background to our interpretation of "On the Mimetic Faculty," we will look first at central themes of Benjamin's essay "Outline of the Psychophysical Problem."[1] Benjamin is no dualist; he conceives of body and spirit from the standpoint of identity. But it is just as important to recognize that there are two aspects of that identity, which can be called, respectively, the mind-bodily and the spiritual-corporeal. We need to carefully separate these two aspects of man's embodied existence, that which pertains to body (*Leib*) and that which belongs to corporeal substance (*Körper*). Benjamin uses the term *Geist* in both cases, yet we should not assume that the form of the mind as we conceive of the mind-bodily aspect is the same as the spiritual in the pair spirit-corporeality. To mark this difference in English, I will use "mind" when paired with body and "spirit" when paired with corporeal substance. As we have seen, the standpoint of identity is not a given; it is to be actualized. There would therefore be different "vectors" of actualization pertaining, respectively, to the mind-bodily and the spiritual-corporeal.

The shape of the mind-bodily is characterized in formal and relational terms. We might, for instance, conceive of the form of perception or the form of action in the mind-bodily existence of man. Such forms that establish our relation to the world are deep and fundamental. They are not individual but pertain to humanity and yet are transformed over the ages. The spiritual-bodily form of humanity, unlike the generic in nonhuman nature, would have a historical index. We are then speaking of a relational nexus that gives its character to the form of life of an endless number of individuals in history.

Benjamin marks the relational or functional form of the mind-bodily by speaking of it in terms of the relational structure of "being in" the historical. In contrast to that, the corporeal substance "is one of the realities that stands in itself in the historical process" (SW 1:394; translation modified). Being "a reality" does not mean that corporeal substance (the corporeal-spiritual) is just a particular instantiation of the form of the mind-bodily. It is not a relational structure but rather "stands in itself." The corporeal indicates a substance rather than a form.

The form(s) that identify a certain historical relational configuration of the mind (the forms of reality) are not an existent in the historical process. The concrete individual substance ultimately has to be understood in terms of the dimension of existence, and existence is not the same as reality. The corporeal is an indication of the existing as such: "Spirit and the corporeal to which it belongs are grounded not on a relation but on existence as such [*auf Dasein schlechthin*]" (SW 1:394).

A form is a condition of that which it constitutes. The formal characterization of the mind-bodily shows it to be essentially conditioned, limited; we therefore associate form and limitation in the body. This holds for all relational characteristics, specifically those of perception in the human being: "It follows that the sensibly perceived particular existence of man is the perception of a relation in which he finds himself; it is not, however, the perception of a substratum or of his own substance, as corporeality would present itself sensuously" (SW 1:394; my translation).

The body, even that body which I call mine, as it is represented in perception (when I, for instance, look at my hand), is grasped as an object determined by the conditions of experience, as conditioned, limited. But there is also another way of sensing one's corporeal existence, from within, as it were, as what is my own. There is a uniqueness that I attribute to my corporeal existence that cannot be accounted for in terms of form. For that reason, this dimension is characterized by Benjamin as without limits (i.e., as not having limits defined by way of a form), even if it pertains to a finite being, a person.

What would it be to sense (rather than perceive) the corporeal as uniquely my own, as an existence in itself, as substance, or as unlimited? What is this sense of corporeal substance from within? The two aspects of the body (referred to here as the mind-bodily and the spiritual-corporeal) might remind us of a similar distinction that arises, for example, in Schopenhauer: The body is not just given to us through the aspect of representation (subject to the condition or limitation of the principle of sufficient reason) but also in itself as will—indeed, as our access to the world as will. For Benjamin, just as for Schopenhauer, the access to this dimension that Benjamin calls corporeal substance hinges on distinguishing pleasure and pain from perceptual representation: "[Corporeal substance] manifests itself... in its specific twofold polarity: as pleasure and pain" (SW 1:394; translation modified).

Pleasure and pain are the indicators of existence, of corporeal substance. This is not to deny that pleasure and pain can be associated with the realization of bodily capacities, that is, their realization in terms of an end fitting their functional form; these are then called satisfaction and dissatisfaction and are conditioned by the aim one wants to achieve. But what is crucial is that pain and pleasure can also be sensed apart from the functional nexus. They allow one immediate access to corporeal substance apart from the mediation of the structure of desire, which assumes the representation of an end. Moreover, one might ask whether aspects of experience oriented by pleasure and pain can extend our account of the corporeal and its unlimited presence. In other words, pain and pleasure are not simple qualities or indicators separate from our existence in the world; rather, they allow us to sense in experience the involvement of corporeal substance, or they are that through which we receive "directions" in regard to the fulfillment of corporeal existence.

Consider an example in the context of perception. There is a clear dependence of perception on the body; in particular, my body is the perspective from which I represent objects to myself. Thus there is an aspect of perception that is to be understood formally and relationally as pertaining to the body. But underlying this relation of perception to its object one can recognize a ground in the corporeal. Indeed, if we think of something like a primal history of perception, then it is crucial to introduce into our understanding of it the significance of dimensions such as up and down, vertical and horizontal, near and distant. These are not represented but rather belong to one's sense of one's own corporeality.[2] They show how significance opens from our belonging to the world. This is underscored by Benjamin's considering this primal history to be given in myth: "The history of perception goes along with the elements of the transformations of nature and the transformation of the body, but it only receives its spiritual meaning and crowning (mastering, synthesis) in myth.[3] In it the great dispositions of perception, which determine how body and nature relate to one another, slowly build and change: right, left—up, down—front, back" ("Wahrnehmung und Leib," GS 6:67; my translation).[4]

Body and corporeal substance have different meanings in relation to human nature. A term such as "human nature" is liable to awaken various associations. One should recall that, strictly speaking, there is no human nature, at least if we understand nature to be an essential form, by analogy to, say, the form of plants or animals. In terms of Benjamin's early essay on language, man does not have an essential nature, in the same way as various species have an essence or nature, but is given the task to give expression to nature, to name nature. We attempt to extend this insight here by conceiving of the role of human corporeality in expressing nature.

We do not articulate what is natural in human beings as what every individual body has and shares with all others (e.g., their all having the same organs and capacities). This might be how we conceive of nature in terms of the functional form of the body. But the inherence of nature in corporeal substance is of a completely different character. In particular, what we seek is how the corporeal substance relates to the force of nature "as one," in terms of the standpoint of identity:

> Nature is not something that belongs especially to every individual corporeal substance. Rather, it relates to the singularity of the corporeal as the different currents that flow into the sea relate to single drops of water. Countless such drops are carried along by the same current. In like fashion, nature is the same, not indeed in all human beings but in a great many of them. Moreover, this nature is not just alike; it is in the full sense identical, one and the same. (SW 1:395; translation modified)

What Benjamin refers to in terms of "flow" and as one and the same is precisely the intensive dimension of the manifestation of the creative through the orders of nature (what he also calls the flow of revelation). Corporeal substance belongs to the hierarchy of the intensive manifestation of nature that culminates in its manifestation in and through man. In other words, through our corporeal existence, we sense and bind the vitality of nature, and its fulfillment is wholly distinct from the satisfaction of "natural" desires and purposes that human beings seek to pursue.

Given that we think here of the current of nature in terms of what demands intensive actualization in man, it is necessary also to recall what unactualized nature in the human comes to. As we saw in the reading of the essay "Fate and Character," this is the rule of fate over bare life: "Nature itself is a totality, and the movement into the inscrutable depths of total vitality is fate" (SW 1:396). It is through this connection of the vital with fate that one has to begin exploring the idea of nature that belongs to the human and to recognize the character of its possible corporeal realization.

The binding of the total vitality of nature is precisely that through which that life's essential (eternal) contents are recognized. Benjamin uses the figure of stamping, and not forming, to articulate the binding of nature in corporeal existence. As we saw in our discussion of the "Epistemo-Critical Foreword," stamping makes possible the actualization that is not defined by a purpose. It marks the emergence of eternal contents in and through the contingent material content of the life of that existing person: "The content of a life depends on the extent to which the living [*Lebenden*] succeeds in giving a stamp [*auszuspägen*] to its nature corporeally" (SW 1:396; translation modified). Benjamin immediately adds that a specific kind of suffering is associated with failing to give one's life this character. One can think of it as the anxiety that emerges with the presentiment of the rule of primal nature. The less the possibility of binding the corporeal, the more we are susceptible to this anxiety. Anxiety will be, for the person, one of the only remaining indications of this task that he fails to realize: "In the utter decay of the corporeal, such as we are witnessing in the West at the present time, the last instrument of its renewal is the anguish of nature which can no longer be contained in life and flows out in wild torrents over corporeal substance." At the extreme, the surrender to total vitality is madness: "The presentation [*Darstellung*] of total vitality in life lets fate flow into madness" (SW 1:396; translation modified).

Corporeal substance is that through which the current of vitality is sensed in one's existence and that through which it can be ordered. Corporeality is as it were our "instrument" for establishing such order. The direction and orientation by which we order our life must be related to how we "sense" the corporeal substance, which is, as we have seen, primarily through pleasure and pain: "For all living reactivity is bound up with differentiation, whose preeminent instrument is the corporeal substance" (SW 1:396; translation modified). Such corporeal differentiation is most evident in the two vital poles, sexuality and spirit: "Sexuality and spirit are the two vital poles of this natural life that flows into our corporeal substance and differentiates itself in it" (SW 1:396; translation modified).

All differentiation in vitality, including psychical animation, is achieved through the sensing of our corporeality: "The corporeal substance is the differentiation instrument of vital reaction, and only it is similarly that which allows us to grasp its psychical animation" (SW 1:396; translation modified). The presence of nature through the differentiation of vitality sensed in the corporeal substance suggests that one can sense as one's own what belongs to total vitality (or nature as one). It would be through corporeal substance that we partake in that oneness of nature. In other words, corporeal substance, while sensed as one's own, is at the same time what opens to total vitality. The body places one in a universal formal context, but it is the corporeal wherein we can sense in ourselves, as in the microcosm, the unity of the macrocosm: "All psychic activity can be localized in the differentiation [by way] of corporeal substance, just as the old anthroposophy attempted this in drawing the analogy between the corporeal substance and the macrocosm" (SW 1:396; translation modified).

One could think of differentiation as the becoming specific and concrete of the creative force of nature in our corporeal existence. Indeed, it is through that specificity (call it the material content of a life) that we are assessing tendencies of nature. We do not respond to vitality as an "objective" phenomenon that we merely observe in the third person but only as belonging to us, that is, present in a distinct way in our life. The corporeal substance is in that sense the microcosm through which is manifest nature as a totality, the dimension of world, that is, the macrocosm. It is because of this internal relation to totality that Benjamin conceives of the sense of our corporeal substance as something of a moral compass: "Corporeal substance is a moral instrument. It was created to fulfill the Commandments. It was fashioned accordingly at creation. Even its perceptions indicate how far they draw corporeal substance away from its duty or draw it to it" (SW 1:396; translation modified).

Mimetic Behavior

At this point I would like to turn to the essay "On the Mimetic Faculty" and show how our understanding of corporeality is at play in it. Although Benjamin does not use the distinction between body and corporeality in that essay and speaks mostly of body (*Leib*), in my view the distinction is reflected in and indeed essential to understanding the importance of the mimetic faculty.

As Benjamin makes clear from the very opening of the essay, we are not considering merely the recognition of similarity but at the same time a capacity realized in the production of similarity. It might appear that this productive aspect is left behind, as the discussion focuses on language and what Benjamin calls midway through the essay "nonsensuous similarities," as though we are to discover similarities already archived in language itself. Yet it is important to realize that in language we recognize an extension of mimetic behavior, or as Benjamin thinks of it, a transformation of the mimetic faculty itself. Thus the productive element that is so clear in the consideration of bodily mimetism will itself have to be recognized in the full-fledged use of language, in speaking, understanding, reading, and writing, just as it is evident in dances and play. Put differently, whereas in abstract reflection on similarity as it pertains to language we might be concerned with establishing the character of similarity between signifier and signified, what Benjamin is primarily concerned with is our recognition of significance as arising from the productive capacity to partake in language, which retains the form of the most basic mimetic behavior.

The examples of mimetism with which Benjamin opens his essay are those of mimetic behavior: "the once powerful compulsion to become similar and to behave mimetically" (SW 2:720). The compulsion is evident mainly in "early" stages of human existence, understood both ontogenetically and philogenetically. It is evident in the play of a child as well as in ritual practices of primitive societies. Thus Benjamin speaks of children imitating not only other persons, such as "a shopkeeper or teacher," but also objects such as "a windmill and a train." The play of a child is a particularly succinct example to employ. And one often takes it as a full-fledged manifestation of the mimetic faculty, as though the play of a child is the paradigmatic example of the use of this faculty. Yet one should pay attention to the way Benjamin speaks of play as the "schooling of the mimetic faculty," and as a form of training. What is it a training for?

Mimetic behavior brings out the fundamental role of the body, the role of one's own body in the production of similarities. One might think that there are various modes of imitation—for instance, by drawing something or by "playacting." This makes it sound as though the body is only one of several instruments through which we deploy the capacity to produce resemblance, as though it is a special case where the "means" to produce a representation are not, say, marks on paper but rather one's hands. In copying or imitating there is the producing and the produced, the playing and what is played, but as one considers the body, mimetic behavior, the two are moments of one and the same activity. Contrast this with the case of drawing, say, a cat on paper. This is a case of producing a copy of reality. Here we would distinguish the activity and means of drawing from the result (the representation of the cat); it is only the latter that we would consider to be "similar" to the object copied. But when we conceive of imitation and mimetic behavior, the activity of the body in producing the imitation simply *is* the imitation of the object.

Consideration of the body belongs with the very origin of the mimetic faculty, that is, with the very nature of that capacity; the body is not merely an instrument of that capacity. And inasmuch as such activities as drawing (copying) that produce similarities are to be accounted for at the fundamental level, they will be seen to retain something essential to that dimension of bodily mimetism. Initially we might say that mimetic behavior relates itself to the form of what is imitated: "All form, every outline that man perceives," Benjamin writes, "corresponds to something in him that enables him to reproduce it. The body itself imitates in the form of dance, the hand imitates and appropriates it through drawing" (SW 1:442; translation modified).[5] Put differently, from the perspective of our earlier discussion, the imitation of form as establishing a relation to an object belongs, at least initially, to the order of the body rather than of corporeality.

In mimetic behavior, the body becomes a locus of meaning. We usually think of meaning in the body in terms of expressions or gestures that externalize and make visible inner states of the person; for instance, pain is expressed in a distorted grimace. But we might wish to distinguish such expressions from mimetism, for they originate immediately from inside, whereas mimetism would seem first of all to be directed at an external object that is to be imitated. And yet the key to mimetic behavior is to see that it involves a sense of the world "from the inside." Mimetism is not a mere copying of what is external to us, nor is it the mere expression of an inner mental state. Rather, in its developed form, such as it appears, say, in rituals, it is the production of similarity to an object that lets us, through that bodily act, sense corporeal existence, a primordial belonging of man to the world. In mimetism we do not merely establish a new external relation to an object; rather, through the production of form, we are receptive to that dimension which underlies significance. It is only because I share with things this ground that imitation can acquire significance.

I can relate to external objects and reproduce them in certain movements of my body. But in doing so, I truly imitate only to the extent that I sense through that activity my own corporeal substance. It is at this level of the belonging together of corporeality and world that one must consider the significance of mimetic behavior. The body, one's own body, is to be considered here insofar as through its gestures it can copy. But these gestures are not merely the representation of an external object; they also make possible receptivity to a ground of belonging to the world through corporeality.[6] Throughout this account of the mimetic faculty we should keep in mind our discussion of the fundamental character of corporeality as an instrument for sensing the inner force, or what Benjamin calls the currents of nature.

This idea of mimetism as belonging to a primal dimension of significance allows us to speak of an immediacy that is at the origin of ritual or magical behavior, with which the mimetic faculty is often associated. Indeed, magic is immediate (the magical is opposed to the form of acting defined by means), and that immediacy can only be understood by partaking (through imitation) in the oneness of nature (call it world-will or world-soul). Through gestures, the object of ritual that is imitated becomes a locus in which is concentrated our being in the world as such. In other words, mimetism reveals corporeal substance as the microcosm, which in mimetic behavior magically or immediately reflects the macrocosm. This relation of microcosm to macrocosm is what Benjamin identifies as one formulation of what the mimetic faculty comes to: "As is known, the sphere of life that formerly seemed to be governed by the law of similarity was comprehensive; it ruled both microcosm and macrocosm" (SW 2:720; translation modified). This formulation is a bit misleading, however: the microcosm and the macrocosm are not two separate realms; the very meaning of microcosm is that it reflects in miniature the (macro)cosmos.

Reading the Real

Remaining with the ritual context of significance, we can move to contexts of production of resemblances in which the involvement of the mimetic faculty seems less pronounced. Even though in these cases we are tempted to think in terms of copying a model, it is nevertheless crucial to refer the external relations of representation back to that mimetic relation opening inner identification. This is suggested, for instance, as Benjamin explains how bodily mimetism is involved in the magical character of cave painting:

The knowledge that the first material on which the mimetic faculty tested itself was the human body should be used more fruitfully than hitherto to throw light on the primal history [*Urgeschichte*] of the arts. We should ask whether the earliest mimesis of objects through dance and sculpture was not largely based on imitations of the performances through which primitive man established relations with these objects. Perhaps Stone Age man produced such incomparable drawings of the elk only because the hand guiding the implement still remembered the bow with which it had felled the beast. (SW 3:253)

Plainly, the form of drawing is not identified with the form of "drawing" the string of the bow; rather, what is crucial is to recognize the way in which the production of an external representation depends on the inner sense of corporeality, showing itself in and through bodily action (in the hunt). It is only out of that sense of corporeality that the production of the representation bears witness to how man and elk belong to one and the same community of life. It is only through this relation between the bodily gestures of painting and the corporeal substance sensed in the hunt that the elk drawing acquires both its ritual or cult value and its haunting beauty. The drawing has, then, the unity of a symbol, not of a representation. The representing is merely the active form that opens the sense of the corporeal through which we are receptive to belonging to a totality that is the world.[7]

Now consider the case of a less dramatic hunt, in the context of the mimetic behavior of a child, described in the butterfly hunt in Benjamin's "Berlin Childhood." It shows how the surrounding world is absorbed receptively by the child, by way of mimetic identification with the object: "Between us, now," Benjamin writes, "the old law of the hunt took hold: the more I strove to conform, in all the fibers of my being, to the animal—the more the butterfly itself, in everything it did, took on the color of human volition; and in the end, it was as if its capture was the price I had to pay to regain my human existence" (SW 3:351). Not only does the metamorphic creature par excellence become the object of the mimetic transformation of the child, but that identification itself is the support for a deeper, formless—that is, corporeal—absorbing of the surroundings. The flight of the butterflies is governed by "the conspiring elements—winds and scents, foliage and sun" (SW 3:350). The term "conspiring" suggests that the elements come together through some secret plan, put in motion by the mimetic identification with the butterfly. The ephemeral creature can become a gathering point for those diverse intangible dimensions, and the imitation of its flight allows the child to absorb them.

Returning to the essay, consider the ritual context of reading the real in practices of soothsaying, which seems less obviously "mimetic" in character. It would be a mistake to ignore the dimension of bodily mimetic behavior and think of such reading merely on the model of decoding a representation: if one finds such and such in the entrails of the animal, say, then it means so and so about the future. But is reading not a form for activating the mimetic faculty? Reading is an activity that fundamentally involves a productive dimension, akin to mimetic behavior, through which the augur feels themselves (through their identification with the object) part of the order of world.

This becomes evident in the description Benjamin gives of reading the future in the stars:

> [The fundamental duality of activity and receptivity] exerts its effects in all reading.... At this deep level access opens to a peculiar ambiguity of the word "reading," in both its profane and magical senses. The schoolboy reads his ABC book, and the astrologer reads the future in the stars. In the first clause, reading is not separated out into its two components. Quite the opposite in the second, though, which clarifies the process at both its levels: the astrologer reads the constellation from the stars in the sky; simultaneously, he reads the future or fate from it. (SW 2:697)

The first moment of reading the constellation from the stars is, strictly speaking, the productive side of mimetic identification. And through this productive opening, the corporeal involvement of the person in the "currents of nature" is sensed and thereby fate "read," as it were, receptively.

If we return to the example of the schoolboy's reading and seek in it the separation into the two components of reading, we might say that the schoolboy in the first state must mimetically produce a configuration of signs, in recognizing what is meant by them. Think of the way in which a child must say aloud the sounds when reading.[8] This is not only external recognition but active production of similarity in the medium of the letters. It is this fundamental structure that is also at the basis of Benjamin's understanding of reading as a "profane illumination," akin to telepathic identification (see SW 2:216). In telepathic phenomena, one person reads, as it were, the mind of another as if they were "entering" it. But ultimately reading as such involves both the productive and the receptive, in which significance is sensing the world from within. The productive character of reading opens to the significant.

Indeed, it is crucial not to conceive of "reading the real" as a figurative displacement of what we think reading is but instead the other way around. It is the primal phenomenon of reading the real that, precisely through the involvement of the mimetic faculty, is at the origin of reading (or understanding) as we know it. In reading the entrails, the stars, and so forth, we have the magical origin in mimetic identification of the phenomenon of significance.

The Mimetic Faculty and Language

Benjamin began his essay by stressing that mimetic phenomena are characteristic of children and primitive people and their ritual-magical practices. We might then doubt whether they are relevant for a consideration of meaning and human existence that has emerged from this infantile or primitive state. Wouldn't such mimetic capacity gradually disappear, maybe together with the disappearance of enchantment from our existence? "This direction could, at first sight, lie solely in the increasing fragility of this mimetic faculty. For clearly the *Merkwelt* of modern man contains only minimal residues of the magical correspondences and analogies that were familiar to ancient peoples. The question is whether we are concerned with the decay of this faculty or with its transformation" (SW 2:721).

Note Benjamin's use of the term *Merkwelt*. The term is associated with the work of the zoologist Jakob von Uexküll in the early twentieth century. It is meant to characterize the environment that belongs together with an animal's sensory capacity. It is not quite the "perceptual world" as this term is translated into English; it serves to underscore the original unity of living being and its surrounding world (*Umwelt*).[9] In other words, the animal is not characterized only through its purposive form as an independent, self-contained organism but at the same time through the environment specific to it, that is, the environment to which its capacities are responsive, its own *Merkwelt*. Thus we have a further indication that the consideration of the mimetic faculty is articulated in relation to the primordial form of sensing the unity of the surroundings of life.

Benjamin suggests that the mimetic faculty is just as present, yet transformed in language: "Language can be seen as the highest level of mimetic behavior and the most complete archive of nonsensuous similarity: a medium into which the earlier powers of mimetic production and comprehension have passed without residue, to the point where they have liquidated those of magic" (SW 2:722). Language is not merely where we find a residue of mimetic behavior; it is the highest and most complete realization of the mimetic faculty. Benjamin also suggests, however, that language is the medium through which the magical aspect of primal mimetism can be overcome.

Even before our consideration of the mimetic faculty, it was clear that Benjamin takes language to be the medium through which we partake in the unity of world. The speaking subject does not "use" language or "identify" themselves with language as a means to communicate factual contents to another speaker. Language is precisely that medium through which a world exists for the speaking subject, a world in which they partake. As Benjamin puts it: "Language [is] the medium in which objects encounter and come into relation with one another... in their essences, their most transient and delicate substances, even in their aromas" (SW 2:697–698). In the language of man, objects belong together in a world. If we hold to the idea of partaking in the world as fundamental to the account of the mimetic dimension of existence, then the radical claim that Benjamin advances is that it is language through which this fundamental identity of subject and world is made possible as well as realized. It is, moreover, by way of this original identity that we recognize how "objects come into relation with one another." In man's language, essences belong to a world (come together). It is only thereby that they can be named according to their inner essence.

From Onomatopoeia to Nonsensuous Similarity

In order to bring these general considerations in line with the account of the mimetic faculty, Benjamin goes through a series of stages. One simplistic option that Benjamin suggests for recognizing the mimetic in language is to consider onomatopoeic language, where the sound of the word is similar to sounds associated with that to which it refers. But the onomatopoeic mode of explanation must be "developed and adapted to improved understanding. 'Every word—and the whole of language,' it has been asserted, is onomatopoeic.' It is difficult to conceive in any detail the program that might be implied by this proposition. But the concept of non-sensuous similarity is of some relevance" (SW 2:721). Onomatopoeic language is based on sensuous similarity of sound. But the extension of the "onomatopoeic thesis" to language as a whole requires us to develop the concept of nonsensuous similarity.

Similarity can be understood as an objective relation in which part of a complex is "identical" with part of another complex and therefore we call these two complexes similar. Thus a red ball is similar to a blue ball insofar as we think of that aspect of both which is their being round, though they are not similar with respect to another aspect, namely, their color. Similarity would be tantamount to a partial identity of attributes. This is to be distinguished from analogy, in which we can already speak of a kind of similarity between different orders, such as the particular and the abstract. Analogy concerns the two sharing a common relation between parts: "a" is to "b" like "c" is to "d." The relation that holds between parts of the particular on the one side is identical to the relation of parts on the other side. But it is only the relation, not the relata, that must be found in the object of the analogy. This would allow the sensuous concrete particular to represent (by analogy) something that itself cannot be perceived, that is nonsensuous. In this case, there is an active moment in analogy: the identity of relations is recognized by being produced (in the mind). It is this displaced activity that is the basis of analogy. This active moment already suggests that for the analogy to be experienced, it must involve a dimension of "mimetic behavior."

But it is necessary to go a step further to understand nonsensuous similarity that itself is neither partial identity nor identity of relation. Nonsensuous similarity is grounded neither on a common sensuous element nor on an analogy. We can speak of nonsensuous similarity as kinship or affinity (*Verwandschaft*). To be precise, the belonging together in nonsensuous similarity presupposes that both sides are akin or belong together by belonging to the same higher whole. Things are related not directly, neither materially nor formally, but by each belonging to the identical higher totality. It is only with this concept that we can introduce what I have called the "receptive" dimension opened by mimetic identification.

Consider the example that Benjamin gives in order to clarify the concept of nonsensuous similarity: "For if words meaning the same thing in different languages are arranged about that signified as their center, we have to inquire how they all—while often possessing not the slightest similarity to one another—are similar to the signified at their center" (SW 2:721). The nonsensuous similarity is not that between the word and the signified but between the words, by way of their being of the same world. The claim here must be understood against the argument of "The Task of the Translator." Recall first that this essay involves a critique of the concept of similarity and an attempt to elucidate what the "relationship" or "kinship" between languages comes to. One language is akin to another if both, while having nothing in common or any analogy between them, are each partaking in what is higher, namely, language as such.[10] In other words, it is only by partaking in the totality that we establish nonsensuous similarity. Conversely, showing nonsensuous similarity between two languages through translation is how we make manifest the unity of world (the flow of revelation) in pure language.

Words in different languages can have the same meaning, even if there is no similarity at all in the ways they mean that same thing. But their kinship is shown nonsensuously by the possibility of refracting the way of meaning of the original in the translation. This is precisely what is manifest in taking language as a whole, as that wherein the way of meaning of the original is refracted in the translation. In other words, ultimately it is through the unity of language as a whole that a nonsensuous similarity is established between the words in the two language. Whereas the intention on the one side has an inner unity to it, what is needed on the other side to supplement it avails itself of the whole field of language. No simple idea of similarity or analogy can account for this nonsensuous similarity.

An important conclusion can be drawn from this discussion: it illuminates how the magical character of the mimetic faculty is realized and overcome through its incorporation in language. In the example of translation we see that nonsensuous similarity is established by "spreading" or echoing what was concentrated in a way of meaning over a large expanse of meaning that does not belong to a unity of intention. It thereby both realizes and does away with mimetic identification. Indeed, magical identification through a word would avail itself of the way of meaning, the intention toward the object. This is what one can actively imitate. Yet the way of meaning draws its power to mean from language as such. It appears to us concentrated, as it were, in a specific place, in the sign.[11] In translation this concentration is returned to its original home, to the whole. The word is "echoed" over the whole expanse of language in such a way that we can no more identify with it, so that the translation would be an actualization and a disappearance of the magical-mimetic in nonsensuous similarity.

The Body of Language

We started by considering mimetic behavior in relation to the gestures of the body. But we are led to consider language itself as something of a body through which we can actualize significance at the same time as we do away with the magical character of meaning. Our active use of language opens to a sense of language as belonging to our corporeal existence. To partake in meaning is, as we have seen, to have access to it as one's own, as involving. One may call this involving dimension of meaning "significance." Significance cannot be a matter of "projection" upon the world. It is an original phenomenon of meaning: I can only recognize significance by being already receptive to what "speaks to me."

As noted earlier, the distinction between body and corporeal substance, as well as the "involving character of pleasure and pain," can be traced to Schopenhauer. We can say that the world is my representation and that the world is my will. But we can also see how representation, insofar as it is significant, is grounded in the world as will. In the opening of the second part of *The World as Will and Representation*, Schopenhauer proposes the extension of what is immediately involving from the paradigm of pain and the body to phenomena in general. He presents the space of representation as in a way accountable for knowledge and yet lacking in *significance*, as presenting itself as something of a riddle—that is, as having a deeper significance, which cannot be gleaned from the represented phenomena: "We will be particularly interested in discovering the true meaning of intuitive representations; we have only ever *felt* this meaning before, but this has ensured that the images do not pass by us strange and meaningless as they would otherwise necessarily have done; rather they speak and are immediately understood and have interest that engages our entire being" (Schopenhauer, *World as Will and Representation*, 1:121). Language is not a neutral system of arbitrary signs that are interpreted and assessed as to whether what they mean is valuable or not for our purposes. Language originally involves us, things are significant for us, as they appear to us through language. Indeed, there is a call of language, and involvement in a significant world is precisely what being in language and actualizing it in human existence comes to.

The Temporal Order of Similarity

We usually think of similarity in terms of the visual register, that is, in relation to spatial features. This face is similar to that one; they are of the same family. But we can also raise the question whether there is a time of similarity. The idea that the recognition of similarity is related to astrology or practices of soothsaying already suggests that it involves a temporal order. In Chapter 5 we encountered the idea that fate, "the true order of eternal recurrence, is only inauthentically—that is parasitically— to be conceived as temporal[;] its manifestations seek out space-time" (O 135). One could then say that the establishment of similarities, for instance in astrology, between the moment of birth and the constellation of the stars is a way of "seeking out" space and time—that is, seizing on a certain temporal-spatial configuration so as to make present another time, the time of fate in the life of a person.

In attempting to further spell out this temporality of similarity we should first note that Benjamin thinks of it not as a twofold but a threefold relation: "It is like the addition of a third element—the astrologer—to the conjunction of two stars" (SW 2:696). Similarity is usually conceived of as a twofold relation in which one term is similar to another; someone who recognizes similarity is on that view a passive observer of what already holds there, in things. But once we introduce mimetic behavior into the recognition of similarity, we assume a third term. Benjamin's account makes clear that someone who reads is involved in producing the space of similarities. And only given that active mimetic identification can one be receptive to the third term, to the higher whole through which the two terms are found to be nonsensuously similar.

Reading, even in its profane form, involves mimetic identification. Sign and symbol (the semiotic element) are not determinately related already, as though objectively. The mimetic identification by way of the sign to the symbolic register of meaning is an activity of the reader, but its significance is not in relating the reader to a specific sense. Rather, as we have seen, it allows the reader to partake in a higher totality of significance. If reading is understood as mimetic behavior, two terms, sign and symbol, have an affinity by way of a third that can only be absorbed receptively. It is the presence of the whole in which one partakes in reading that one cannot hold on to and can be said to *flash up*:

> So tempo, that swiftness in reading or writing which can scarcely be separated from this process, would then become, as it were, the effort, or gift, or mind to participate in that measure of time in which similarities flash up fleetingly out of the stream of things only in order to sink down once more. Thus, even profane reading, if it is not to forsake understanding altogether, shares this with magical reading: that it is subject to a necessary tempo, or rather a critical moment, which the reader must not forget at any cost lest he go away empty-handed. (SW 2:698)

Only on the threefold model does the recognition of similarity acquire a temporal dimension of its own. As long as similarity is conceived of only in terms of two sides that resemble each other, there will be nothing fleeting to it. (Indeed, why wouldn't it be possible to hold on to the relation between the moment of birth and the configuration of the stars at that moment?) Moreover, swiftness in reading is not advising that one go through a text at breakneck speed; it is not like running so as not to miss one's train. Rhythm must be understood as the gradual and intensive concentration or accumulation of nonsensuous similarity.[12] Through the accumulation of similarities reading is brought to a critical state, in which one is raised to the higher unity of the text. The flashing up is a moment *internal* to this accumulation of meaning. It marks the emergence of that which we cannot hold on to but can only be absorbed receptively.

This characterization of the fleeting nature of similarity may serve as an initial model that will enable us to think of a related characteristic of the dialectical image: "The true image of the past flits by. The past can be seized only as an image that flashes up at the moment of its recognizability and is seen again" (SW 4:390). We will return to this difficult issue in Chapters 9 and 11.

NINE

Acting Naturally

The character of intelligent human activity is often articulated in terms of the concepts of intention, purpose, and the choice of the best means to further this or that end.[1] The will in action would be, to use Kant's terms, causality from concepts.[2] A first step in articulating the specificity of Benjamin's account of action will be to forego the appeal to purpose as the ultimate determining ground of action.

The problematization of such notions as purpose and choice takes different forms in Benjamin's writings. One could point, for instance, to the supervenience of the conscious setting of purpose on the ground of character, which itself cannot be chosen, or focus on everyday habits and the way in which they reveal to us behavior that is not a matter of conscious choice (though they cannot simply be called unconscious). Or one could ask what it would be to forego the means-ends structure by remaining only with means (without ends) and what value that would have. One could focus on how certain activities are dependent on repetitive exercise or even on introducing rest into acting, not as a further means but to detach action altogether from the economy of means and ends. Or one could dwell on the way in which intention is, ironically, so often the instrument of the unfolding of fate and recognize the self-deception involved in thinking one can direct one's life to what is highest, acting according to a rational plan. One could be taken by the immense exertion that is necessary to achieve the smallest change that really matters in one's existence and with it the utterly empty character of certain forms of seeking success in acting. Or one could be struck by the way fortune depends on recognizing an occasion, thus being open to it. It might even be possible to dissociate what counts as success in achieving an end from fitting with the world in a way that may be consistent with constant failure.

This chapter will take up these issues, first by interpreting Benjamin's "Ibizan Sequence," then by considering a theme from his essay on Kafka, and finally by making a brief foray into the essay on surrealism.

On Fit without Purpose

THE WIND ROSE OF FORTUNE

Will, desire, and choice in particular cases presuppose an underlying unity of life that we call the character of the person. Actions are among the different expressions of character.[3] Character is the ultimate ground on which we recognize how our actions relate to one another and thus identify not what they aim at but what they express; it is the ground of which these actions are manifestations. This does not mean that such ground is given to oneself or to an external observer in advance of acting.[4] The individual can reflect on the different expressions of character in time and gather thereby a posteriori the prior ground of all action. In relation to the ground of character, what becomes important are not so much the purposes we set in advance but rather the occasions for its clear and distinct manifestation.

Character underlies everything, but one may be acting in such a way that it only appears stifled and hidden. It speaks above our will but in distorted and often unrecognizable ways. When the character of a person is fully apparent, it shows in a constancy of being. One can speak of such a person as wholly living in accordance with their character, expressing it unequivocally in their life. This would be what Benjamin refers to in "Fate and Character" as the innocence of character. As we have seen, there is in such character an indifference between inner and outer, as well as a constancy and rigor of behavior. We can establish different models of that constancy of being by simplifying to the extreme the conditions of the problem. These will be models of "fortunate characters" that exhibit fit with the world. Fortunate fit must be distinguished from achievement. Achievement is the fulfillment of the end of an action, the satisfaction of the will, whereas fortunate fit with the world foregoes the benefits of achievement. Fit with the world is the counterpart to constancy of character. It must be indifferent to choices based on the many beliefs, opinions, or specific convictions that as it were determine us at certain junctures. If anything, it will be evident equally in adopting all convictions or none.

This is the theme of the "thought picture" that Benjamin titles "The Wind Rose of Fortune." Each of the figures mentioned in it can serve as a model of fortunate fit that is not achievement but a deeper agreement with the world. Fortune, one would say, manifests itself when one is not partial, when attunement is to the world as such. Benjamin charts the four directions of this wind rose of fortune along two axes—success and conviction—each capable of taking an all-or-nothing value. One can either seek to adopt all convictions or have none; one either always succeeds or always fails. Each of the four possible combinations defines a simple unity of one's world and provides a model of fortunate existence.[5]

The directions of the wind rose of fortune, of "winds, favorable and unfavorable, that play their games with human existence," are given by various figures of scoundrels or fools (one more way to recognize how these considerations of character exclude moral judgment). Not surprisingly, given our discussion of character in Chapter 5, they are all comic figures. We find there Schweik (always succeeds without any conviction), Lucky Hans (always succeeds while adopting all convictions), Bouvard and Pécuchet (always fail in adopting all convictions), and Charlie Chaplin (always fails without any conviction).[6]

Apart from the four directions marked by the four types of fools, there is also the center of coordinates, the point of absolute indifference: "The site of the complete identity of success and failure. At this center we find Don Quixote *the man with a single conviction*, whose story teaches us that in this, the best or worst of all conceivable worlds (except that his world is inconceivable), the conviction that stories of chivalry are true can make a whipped fool happy, if it is his only conviction" (SW 2:590). A world that is both the best and the worst would presumably relieve Leibniz's God of the task of choosing. Indeed, it is not a possible, conceivable world. Does this mean that it doesn't exist? Or is it precisely the uniquely existing, the world that cannot be the object of thought, in which no possibility is left but the affirmation of utter actuality? And what does it mean that our access to absolute actuality, to existence, depends on making stories true? We will return to this point.

POLITENESS

Another way to problematize notions of success and achievement associated with the means-ends structure would be to consider Benjamin's reflections on existence purely through means. The sphere of pure means is that of the indirect, for when action is directed, means are for some end and thus not pure means.[7] Yet one should not confuse remaining in means with inactivity. There is a way in which this can be precisely the most intense and restless activity. As might be gleaned from Benjamin's writings on Kafka, it is the activity of "assistants," never the action that is to achieve something for oneself, but nevertheless it involves a form of mastery.

As we saw in discussing the "Critique of Violence" in Chapter 7, pure means are invoked in raising the possibility of a nonviolent resolution of conflicts between individuals. Benjamin refers to some subjective virtues that assist in this nonviolent resolution of conflicts, among them politeness, to which he returns in the "Ibizan Sequence." Politeness is more a matter of mores than of morality; in many cases, we might tend to think of polite behavior as inimical to true morality, as being a mere façade. This is mostly so when we emphasize authenticity, that is, something that pertains to the recognition of the true self. But the fantasy of finally doing away with all conventions in the name of one's authenticity is mostly the expression of the destructive fury of the self. The arrogant self is very much like a mythical agency that seeks to make evident its existence in unleashing destructive violence, making the one who undergoes it a testimony to its power.

The role of politeness in dissolving conflict is, strangely enough, conceived of through the way it extends conflict or makes it unlimited. This might sound at first paradoxical, for how could the extension of the conflict to more and more areas be conceived of as an indirect solution to it? To deal with the conflict directly is to address another subject face-to-face (think of it in terms of Hegel's model of the life-and-death struggle and the rule of honor that belongs to this moment). Instead of the frozen, uncompromising posture of the I, as the sole stake of the conflict, politeness serves to multiply conflict, but it extends it by emptying the rigid self over the whole realm of objects. An intensive conflict that always involves the dueling posture of two subjects must be "emptied out" into the extensive realm of objects. The symbolic conventions of the jousting arena of honor must be loosened by extending the conflict to being only over goods.[8] What appeared to be uniquely significant, a matter of "one's name" worth "dying for," is broken into as many small pieces as possible, making each in itself no big deal, not intrinsically significant.

HABIT AND ATTENTIVENESS

We have distinguished fortunate fit with the world from success. Usually we think of fortune as a matter of the special, exceptional occasion, yet the figures of the wind rose of fortune all exhibit a constancy of existence. This raises the question of the relation between the occasion and the everyday or habitual. Habitual behavior in the broadest sense of the term is to be understood as permeating, even constituting, ordinary conditions of life. It belongs to our understanding of the everyday. The everyday and the fortunate occasion seem to be polar opposites. While an occasion is nothing without the presence of mind to make something out of it, one could say that the habitual is precisely what one does not need to attend to.

In the thought-pictures titled "Habit and Attentiveness" Benjamin addresses our intuitive opposition between the two terms. We assume that what is done by habit is not done attentively. The formation of habit would involve mindless repetition, which we distinguish from mindful, concentrated attention. Habitual activity can be repeatedly performed without devoting thought to it, in distraction, as it were. There is nevertheless an illumination of the habitual in which it becomes striking—namely, what happens in a dream: "For what comes to us when we dream is a new and unprecedented attentiveness that struggles to emerge from the womb of habit" (SW 2:592). Unprecedented attentiveness belonging to the *habitual* is, so to speak, the wonder brought about by the mediation of sleep.

This mediation of sleep in attending to habit might not be very relevant to our wakeful activity, unless, of course, there were a way to illuminate the everyday and thereby make of it a field of opportunities for attentiveness to awaken. This means recognizing in the space of life itself the dream character of our everyday life. We will explore this point further below in the account of surrealism, as well as in Chapter 11, which is devoted to the dream character of the past in Benjamin's *Arcades Project*. The intelligence that belongs to acting in distraction will be further developed in our discussion of "The Work of Art" essay in Chapter 12.

PRACTICE

Let us reflect further on the overcoming of the sphere of purposive action by turning to practice and exercise, through which the most singular feat can be sunk into the nonconscious activity of the body.[9] Practice should be distinguished from practical reason on the basis of purpose and choice. Exercise with its attendant notion of "practice" suggests a form of "work" that establishes habits of the body, not a schema for actions directed toward the realization of ends. Exercise as training would remain endlessly, so to speak, within the sphere of means. Practice might indirectly relate to a goal, but in itself it is solely concerned with rehearsing a series of steps—for example, an accomplished musician doesn't practice by playing a whole piece over and over but by repeating phrases. Exercise looks to the partial, to the small, never to the whole articulated by an end.

This repetition of the partial bears on our concept of mastery and its relation to the will determined by ends. Such mastery must be distinguished from "having power over someone or something." The master juggler Rastelli who is mentioned in the thought-figure "Practice" does not control the ball—or his hand, for that matter. Indeed, to be precise, exercise releases the hand and the ball to "reach an understanding behind his back." As the end of the thought-picture suggests, true mastery lets the unconscious or involuntary intelligence of the body take over.

Mastery is not to be understood here as control based on the force of the conscious will. Practice would ultimately enable the hand and the ball to harmonize, without either of them taking over or being subordinate. Benjamin suggests that it is the organ, the hand, rather than the whole body that harmonizes with the ball. Obviously, the hand is not severed from the body, but there is a suggestion that it does not merely serve a purpose of the body conceived through the unifying power of the will. When we conceive of an organ in terms of various functions it can perform, we think of it as subordinate to the unity of the will and desire. Practice releases the organ to perform an independent mindful activity dissociated from the centralized functionality of the body.

Another moment is implied by exercise, namely, the exertion in taking exercise to the limit: "To weary the master to the point of exhaustion through diligence and hard work, so that at long last his body [*Körper*] and each of his limbs can act in accordance with their own reason [*Vernunft*]" (SW 2:591).

The exhaustion resulting from taking exercise to its limit calls for rest. Rest would not be, as we might intuitively conceive of it, the mere opposite of the effort of exercise; rather, it enables the fulfillment of exercise in the unprecedented performance.

This is also why the thought-picture "Practice" begins with sleep. More generally, the question is how to recognize the place of a pause in realizing the full force of practice. It is as though sleep is a state in which organs can acquire and express their independence. Sleep dissociates corporeality from the "central control" of the conscious will. Through sleep the organ is released to a deeper fit with the object, a fit that cannot be the result of conscious intention. That is, exercise opens to occasions for the mindfulness of corporeality, for the mind to be present in the body. The occasionalist God may be the warrant of the fit between the corporeal substance and the thinking substance, but we finite beings cannot assume parallelism without further ado. Mind and body are one *sub specie aeternitatis*, but their harmony *for us* is a matter of practice that opens to occasions in which it is expressed.

DO NOT FORGET THE BEST

In the background of our thinking about action is time. Certain things should be done at certain times if one wants to achieve certain ends. The dissociation from the sphere of action based on ends can thus be closely related to a shift in one's timing. We have seen something like that in the virtue of waiting or the importance of the pause. But it can equally be seen in the constant disruption of timing. This is the theme of the thought-picture "Do not forget the best."

Purposes and the calculation of means can give us what is comparatively good. But can we act toward the superlative or the best? Can it be achieved by better calculating means to ends? Do we need to be well organized to "reach" the best? What would it be "not to forget the best" if not to keep in mind that highest end? The best cannot belong to the succession of time; since the unity of time is essential to the successive means-end structure of action, not to forget the best would be to practice living with time out of joint, not being on time.

As Benjamin says of an acquaintance of his: "[He] was at his most well-organized at the unhappiest period in his life. He forgot nothing . . . he was punctuality itself. His life's way seemed to have been smoothly paved, and there was not even the smallest crack for time to run out of control" (SW 2:591). Living with time out of joint, in turn, must be diligently practiced: "It began with his getting rid of his watch. He practiced arriving late, and if the person he was going to meet had already left, he sat down to wait." One's timing can be affected not only in relation to people: "If he had to do something with an object close at hand, he managed to mislay it, and if he was supposed to clear something up somewhere, the confusion elsewhere increased" (SW 2:591). But it is precisely through the practice of nonpunctuality that the matters that pertain to fortune worked as in a dream: "Friends visited him when he least expected them but needed them most, and the gifts he sent, which were not sumptuous, arrived as punctually as if he had the paths of heaven in his hands."

The injunction "Do not forget the best" suggests that in fact we are prone to forget the best. It is when someone is at their "most organized" that in one sense they forget nothing—except, of course, the best. Conversely, it is out of the forgotten that we relate to the best. As Benjamin writes in the essay on Kafka: "But forgetting always involves the best, for it involves the possibility of redemption" (SW 2:813). Redemption belongs to another time from the one that is characterized by the form of conscious directedness. The forgotten is precisely what opens to that other time.

MINDFUL INNERVATION

The opening to fortune, its relation to corporeality, and the dissociation of activity from conscious choice and purpose come together in Benjamin's discussion of bodily innervation, in particular in his discussion of the gambler. Benjamin asserts that "the structure of success is basically the structure of gambling" (SW 2:146). Success here is not achievement but depends on "understanding the language in which luck makes it arrangements with us." This is a language one needs to relearn and whose grammar must be clearly distinguished from the external standpoint on the contingency in chance articulated, say, through the prism of probability and statistics: "In the grammar of success, chance plays the same role that irregular verbs do in ordinary grammar: It is the surviving trace of primeval energy" (SW 2:146). The gambler is one who is open to irregularity in the verb, in what expresses action, open to this kind of "energizing" from the primal, that is, to their corporeal existence.

Wanting to win belongs to gambling, of course, and yet the happiness associated with it has an aspect free of purpose or interest. It cannot even be called the fulfillment of "a 'wish' in the strict sense of the word" (SW 2:145). The placing of bets is not a means to winning. The gambler does not seek wealth by gambling but opens their life to chance, to luck, that out of which the win is handed. It is the victorious happiness of being graced by fortune. The gambler does not get what they deserve; indeed, undeserved success is the best sign of the presence of luck. Benjamin speaks of "the winner's highly remarkable feeling of elation, of being rewarded by fate, of having seized control of destiny" (SW 2:298). What is crucial is not the amount of gain but the way in which it came to the winner, in "the fact that money and riches, otherwise the most massive and burdensome things in the world, come to him from the fates like a joyous embrace returned to the full." And just as the gambler's utmost pleasure is not the actual gain, the factor of danger "that threatens the gambler lies in the fateful category of arriving 'too late,' of having 'missed the opportunity'" (SW 2:298)—that is, of missing the encounter with chance.

The gambler's embodied mindfulness described by Benjamin is utterly distinct from behavior directed by consciousness. It is not the power to act but innervation, which is released as an involuntary discharge in a moment of crisis. Benjamin gives as an example of such energetic discharge the way in which the true gambler places their bets at the very last moment, thereby showing presence of mind at the moment of danger, of potentially missing one's opportunity. "What is decisive," Benjamin writes, "is the level of motor innervation, and the more emancipated it is from optical perception, the more decisive it is" (SW 2:147). Moreover, Benjamin seeks both to distance mind from the primacy of self-consciousness that governs the will and to release motor reaction or reflex action from its "behavioristic" moorings (understood deterministically through the structure of stimulus-response). The psychophysiology that belongs to the character type of the gambler is summed up in Benjamin's use of the term "presence of mind." But presence of mind is not explained in terms of having a certain mental capacity, so to speak; rather, it is mind being present in the body: "The question is not whether mind is present," Benjamin writes, "or what form it takes, but only where it is. . . . Only the body can generate presence of mind" (SW 2:147).

Wishing Not to Wish

It is a commonplace that Kafka shows us at every turn the radical difficulty of action's achieving its aim, the unimaginable obstacles in acting to make even the smallest significant difference in the world. The opening parable of Benjamin's essay on Kafka about Shuvalkin the obliging clerk shows the ironic yet fated failure of the one who tries, through determined "no-nonsense" activity, ignoring obstacles, to achieve something. The difficulty is not just in our attempt to be active but pertains equally to our passivity. Kafka's parable "Before the Law" shows how passivity and patience are just as problematized as impatience and rushing to action. Considering the impasse of activity and passivity dialectically, it would be necessary to both act and do nothing at the same time.

To begin our inquiry into what this would come to, let us consider Benjamin's reference to Kafka's "Wish to Be a Red Indian": "The ardent 'wish to be a Red Indian' may have consumed this great sadness at some point: 'If one were only an Indian, instantly alert, and on a galloping horse, leaning into the wind, kept on quivering briefly over the quivering ground, until one shed one's spurs, for there were no spurs, threw away the reins, for there were no reins, and barely saw the land before one as a smoothly mown plain, with the horse's neck and head already gone'" (SW 2:800). Note the two possible readings of "consuming" in this context: the consuming sadness expresses itself in the image of a wish, while the image consumes the sadness in unfolding the wish. In expressing the wish the spurs, reins, and horse's neck and head disappear as the image is articulated.

The unfolding of the wish, that is, its articulation, is also its disappearance, consumed by the image it projects. The peculiar fulfillment in the vanishing of the wish is also the point of Benjamin's Hasidic parable in the same essay:

In a Hasidic village, so the story goes, Jews were sitting together in a shabby inn one Sabbath evening. They were all local people, with the exception of one person no one knew, a very poor, ragged man who was squatting in a dark corner at the back of the room. All sorts of things were discussed, and then it was suggested that everyone should tell what wish he would make if one were granted him. One man wanted money; another wished for a son-in-law; a third dreamed of a new carpenter's bench; and so everyone spoke in turn. After they had finished, only the beggar in his dark corner was left. Reluctantly and hesitantly he answered the question. "I wish I were a powerful king reigning over a big country. Then, some night while I was asleep in my palace, an enemy would invade my country, and by dawn his horsemen would penetrate to my castle and meet with no resistance. Roused from my sleep, I wouldn't have time even to dress and I would have to flee in my shirt. Rushing over hill and dale and through forests day and night, I would finally arrive safely right here at the bench in this corner. This is my wish." The others exchanged uncomprehending glances. "And what good would this wish have done you?" someone asked. "I'd have a shirt," was the answer. (SW 2:812)

The fulfilled dispossession of the beggar brings out how much "activity" there is in foregoing the wish so as to remain with the infinitely small change to true actuality. Such activity requires breathtaking speed in order to go through the space of the wish in order to consume it in the unfolding of its image and remain with the ground under your feet. Kafka's parable about Sancho Panza belongs to this same logic: he sends his demon, Don Quixote, ahead to perform his fictional exploits and lives by following and consuming them without attempting to achieve anything himself. This is not the figure of someone who is disconnected from reality and engrossed in stories; rather, it is true to the logic of the wish, the form of affirming actuality. The way "Sancho Panza sends his rider on ahead" (SW 2:816) corresponds to the idea of the action that puts forth its image and articulates itself by consuming that image. This also explains why Benjamin places Don Quixote at the center of the wind rose of fortune: the stories of chivalry consumed are what leaves him with the world, the best and the worst, yet inconceivable because it is the uniquely existing.

The swiftness of activity that asks only to "achieve" nothing can also be identified, as Benjamin points out, in the presence of mind of an actor: "actors have to catch their cues in a flash." The utmost intensity can be internal to playacting, which achieves nothing: "This is what Kafka was after with his desire 'to hammer a table together with painstaking craftsmanship and, at the same time, to do nothing—not in such a way that someone could say "Hammering is nothing to him," but "To him, hammering is real hammering and at the same time nothing," which would have made the hammering even bolder, more determined, more real, and, if you like, more insane'" (SW 2:814). The acting of actors is aligned with the intense activity of assistants and fools that comes to nothing. It is described, significantly, as what threatens to disappear in a "flash" and yet yield what is "more real" than reality.

We could object that the actor only playacts, or "imitates" action, and only for that reason does not seriously pursue a purpose, and moreover, that the actor plays a fictional character, whereas we have to act in the world. These are valid objections unless there is a possibility of playacting in the space of life itself. This is often understood as putting on an act, that is, presenting oneself as different than one really is, and therefore as a form of deception. But what about the possibility of playing *oneself*? What would be the difference between the person who acts seriously (so as to achieve a purpose effectively) and someone who seriously plays himself acting thus? Put differently, what is the kind of separation at the heart of identity that is expressed as "playing oneself"? Benjamin refers to technologies of reproduction that open a space between the actor and their image as allowing one to play oneself. In "The Work of Art in the Age of Its Technological Reproducibility," playing oneself is one of the peculiar possibilities opened by the photographic image. We will return to this in Chapter 12.

Action, Body, and Image

FREEDOM AND INTOXICATION

For us to begin to translate to the register of the collective the themes we discussed in relation to individual action, the essay on surrealism is important. The central problem that emerges toward the end of that essay is how to bring together the freedom expressed in dream-intoxication with a concept of action that is adequate to historical materialism. How can surrealism seek to "win the energies of intoxication for the revolution" (SW 2:215)? In attempting to solve this problem, Benjamin is faced with a number of dialectical oppositions that we have discussed in related contexts earlier in the chapter.

Benjamin conceives of surrealist practice as the expression of radical freedom with no bound or law. Radical freedom is anarchic freedom—not only freedom dissociated from any end and from calculations how to achieve it but freedom without bounds. And yet, for the surrealists, it is the freedom of dream and intoxication. We are of course familiar with a variety of attempts to think of the ecstatic state as freeing one from the limitation of consciousness. But here we must pay attention to a deep tension in coupling this freedom to historical materialism: "Are they successful in welding this experience of freedom to the other revolutionary experience, which we must acknowledge because it has been ours—the constructive, dictatorial side of revolution? In short, have they bound revolt to revolution?" (SW 2:215). When we speak of intoxication, this is usually understood as what pertains to a unique "illuminated" state of mind or attitude, but historical materialism has to do with the transformation of the material conditions of existence of the masses at their most ordinary.

As we saw in our discussion of the thought-picture habit and attentiveness, it is possible to conceive of an attentiveness to the ordinary in the dream, as well as a dream-illumination of the everyday, a dream present at the heart of the ordinary: "The true creative overcoming of religious illumination certainly does not lie in narcotics. It resides in a profane illumination, a materialistic anthropological inspiration to which hashish, opium, or whatever else can give an introductory lesson" (SW 2:216). Profane illumination is the dialectical overcoming of the intuitive opposition between the everyday, the habitual, on the one hand, and the unique extraordinary or ecstatic illumination (be it mystical, magnetic, or drug induced), on the other. It is an illumination in and of the everyday: "We penetrate the mystery only to the degree that we recognize it in the everyday world, by virtue of a dialectical optic that perceives the everyday as impenetrable and the impenetrable as everyday" (SW 2:216). Profane illumination would be the transformation of the space of ordinary life, the space of habit, one could say, to which belong reading, thinking, walking, waiting, and being alone with oneself.

Not only habits but also things acquire this illumination, and so does their environment, the city: "At the center of this world of things stands the most dreamed about of all their objects: the city of Paris itself" (SW 2:211). The illumination of ordinary things and surroundings is made possible by a dislocation of time characteristic of the outdated. In being outmoded the most everyday things acquire a dream-character: "[Breton] can boast an extraordinary discovery: he was the first to perceive the revolutionary energies that appear in the 'outmoded'—in the first iron constructions, the first factory buildings, the earliest photos, object that have begun to be extinct. . . . Not one before these visionaries and augurs perceived how destitution—not only social but architectonic, the poverty of interiors, enslaved and enslaving objects—can be suddenly transformed into revolutionary nihilism" (SW 2:210).

PESSIMISM, METAPHOR, AND IMAGE

The problematization of the sphere of ends and with it the intuitive opposition of achievement and failure is characteristic of the way Benjamin thinks of the concept of political action in surrealism. Indeed, the essay culminates with what we might think of as a "fit with the world" in the face of all but inevitable failure. This is what Benjamin also refers to as "the organization of pessimism." If optimism is to be associated with the bourgeois belief in progress and its achievements, then what is crucial in rejecting it is, from the start and without any compromise, affirming pessimism. "Pessimism all along the line" (SW 2:216) might be an expression of distrust of the institutions of society or foregoing hope in a transformation of society through the gradual reform of those institutions of power. But here the important question is what it means to *organize* pessimism.

Surprisingly, Benjamin brings to bear on this political matter the distinction between image space and metaphor: "For to organize pessimism means nothing other than to expel moral metaphor from politics and to discover in the space of political action the one hundred percent image space" (SW 2:217). This reference to aesthetic terms such as "metaphor" and "image" might be understandable in an essay on surrealism. But how exactly does an insight found in Louis Aragon's *Treatise of Style* bear on the political, and how does it have anything to do with the organization of pessimism? Why is it that "nowhere do these two—metaphor and image—collide so drastically and so irreconcilably as in politics" (SW 2:217)?

There is of course a sense in which we can take the attack on metaphor to be the expression of a form of disenchanted sobriety or realism. Benjamin quotes a parenthetical expression Rimbaud added to his poem "Barbarian": "In the margin, beside the passage 'on the silk of the seas and the arctic flowers,' he later wrote, 'There's no such thing'" (SW 2:208). But to remain merely with the rejection of the figurative would not explain the place of image. How would we account for reality's acquiring its surrealist face? Is there a way to echo how "stories of chivalry" bound to fail are key to the affirmation of the highest actuality?

At its simplest, metaphor is analogy. Through analogy what is opened is a view of the distant, and we are given, as it were, a mode of advance toward it. Through the "as if" of metaphor, we can identify with what we do not have and relate to it as aspiration. This is why the space of metaphor is related to optimism: "The socialist sees the 'finer future of our children and grandchildren' in a society which all act 'as if they were angels' and everyone has as much 'as if he were rich' and everyone lives 'as if he were free'" (SW 2:216). Through the "as if" of metaphor, says Benjamin, a line of progress is drawn in advance, and we install ourselves in the hallway, as he puts it. This is the best way to disarm the revolutionary spirit of its energies: "Once the classless society had been defined as an infinite task, the empty and homogeneous time was transformed into an anteroom [hallway], so to speak, in which one could wait for the emergence of the revolutionary situation with more or less equanimity" (SW 4:402).

One can also think of projection by way of metaphor as raising the problem of identification and empathy.[10] The sentimentalist identifies with others in feeling through an analogical transposition and thereby foregoes acting. Indeed, sentimentalism closely related to empathy is evidence of helplessness. Some of the practices of the surrealist are clearly directed toward eradicating sentimentality. This is the role of the cult of evil and cruelty in their writings: "Only in contrast to the helpless compromises of 'sentiment' can certain central features of Surrealism, indeed of the Surrealist tradition, be understood. . . . One finds the cult of evil as a political device, however romantic—a device that can be used to disinfect and isolate against all moralizing dilettantism" (SW 2:214).

IMAGE SPACE

While it might be clear what the problematic extension of moral metaphor to the political comes to and why it is rejected by Benjamin, it is far less evident what the alternative would be—namely, what image space is. First we should note that metaphor is not a "space"; there is only image space. We can find the precursor to this opposition between metaphor and image space in Benjamin's work as early as his essay "Two Poems by Friedrich Hölderlin," where he makes a distinction between the "mythological" and the "mythic." Metaphor (the figuration of the gods) is opposed to the image space that arises from the poetic concentration of relationships that tie everything together (and thereby open the poetic world). In the intensification of relationships an image space emerges that is not a figure of anything. Image space is opened by bringing everything together through relationships (yet without any similarity or analogy). Thus, it is only by expelling any means of "identification" through metaphorical transposition that the work of forming a space of relationship is rigorously adhered to.

If indeed image space arises through the concentration of relationships, there still remains a question as to what this space has to do with the surrealist image, the dream intoxication. This connection is established in effect in the essay "On the Image of Proust," written at about the same time as the essay on surrealism. There, Benjamin conceives of concentrating the space of memory through relationships and refers to it as being "distorted by similarity." This distortion is the dream face of the everyday. It is not a dream character based on metaphor or metonymy of particular contents but rather the dream character of the whole space of memory, the everyday bound by relationship in memory; as Benjamin puts it, Proust found the bridge from the everyday to the dream. This peculiar crossroads in which Proust and surrealism meet is a model for many of the formulations of the function of the image. Indeed, "surrealism" and "image" both come up in Benjamin's description of the deep yearning at the heart of Proust's writing: "He lay on his bed racked with homesickness, homesick for the world distorted in the state of resemblance, a state in which the true surrealist face of existence breaks through. To this world belongs what happened in Proust, and the deliberate and fastidious way in which it appears. It is never isolated, rhetorical, or visionary; carefully heralded and securely supported, it bears a fragile, precious reality: the image" (SW 2:240). We will return to this issue in Chapter 11.

CONSUMING THE IMAGE

Consider the following further characterization of image space: "For in the joke, too, in invective, in misunderstanding, in all cases where an action puts forth its own image and exists, absorbing and consuming it, where nearness looks with its own eyes, the long-sought image space is opened" (SW 2:217). The first thing to note is the difference between an action that puts forth its image and putting forth a purpose for action. The purpose that is set is realized by means of the action, but the image is not a representation of the aim of an action. One could say that in putting forth its dream image, the action unfolds by "consuming" itself. One could call it surrealist freedom, a way of acting for action's sake.

Action, as it is usually conceived of, produces its actual occurrence out of the representation of a state. But here actuality is just the consummation of the dream—one awakens to actuality. The joke (e.g., pun, wit) exemplifies a speech act that puts forth its image and consumes itself in its unfolding. There is in wit something like a self-destructive aspect that makes meaning brilliantly come to nothing. Think of the flashing explosion of wit in Romantic fragments: it is completely self-enclosed and gratuitously consumes itself; there is nothing to communicate as content but the very brilliance of the self-destruction and collapse of language. ("Language seemed itself only where sound and image, image and sound, interpenetrated with automatic precision and such felicity that no chink was left for the penny-in-the-slot called 'meaning'" [SW 2:208].) A joke, in this respect like a tautology, does not establish a possibility but, as it were, consumes itself in the making. Our discussion of the wish image that consumes itself so as to leave one in the same place yet transformed can be taken as a paradigm of this peculiar idea of image.[11]

Why is this a space in which "nearness looks with its own eyes"? Nearness is the everyday. It is precisely what we do not attend to with our eyes, contemplatively, but which is near through habits. Nearness is what recedes into the background belonging to our habitual actions; it is the unremarkable everyday. The illumination of the everyday makes it a space in which nearness looks with its own eyes. This dwelling place has a peculiar character precisely because nothing in it is isolated as the "best"; what produces the dream character is no element but only the concentration of relationships. We might say that the "best room," the parlor, which is not really used for everyday living, is missing; there is no room reserved for "special occasions" but only the transformation of the everyday space of living.

IMAGE, NEARNESS, AND CORPOREALITY

"This image space, however, can no longer be measured out by contemplation" (SW 2:217).[12] In seeking an alternative to the contemplative, it might also be helpful to refer to the distinction between the contemplative, on the one hand, and the tactile ruled by habit, on the other, as it is formulated in the essay "The Work of Art in the Age of Its Technological Reproduction": "For the tasks which face the human apparatus of perception at historical turning points cannot be performed solely by optical means—that is, by way of contemplation. They are mastered gradually—taking their cue from tactile reception—through habit" (SW 3:120). To master a task through the tactile rather than the optical is to make it habitual. Conversely, it is through the illumination of the habitual that we reside in image space. In other words, there is a close connection between Benjamin's call for the illumination of the everyday and the necessity to measure image space in bodily, tactile, rather than contemplative, terms.

Nearness, understood noncontemplatively, is a space one dwells in bodily. Benjamin speaks of image space as "the space, in a word, in which political materialism and physical creatureliness share the inner man, the psyche the individual, or whatever else we wish to throw to them, with dialectical justice, so that no limb remains untorn" (SW 2:217). Benjamin opposes the surrealist turn to the body to an idealistic conception, which gives primacy to the "inner man," the "psyche," or the isolated individual. But what is further significant in this quotation is that through tearing apart the unity of the body ruled by consciousness the space of the unconscious, bodily image arises. This tearing of limbs from the unity of the body ruled by the "inner man," the psyche, or the unified consciousness is to be developed in relation to the idea of the possibilities opened to the organ dissociated from the functional unity of the body.[13] We have seen that exercise can release the organ to an activity of its own. Is there something parallel for the collective—call it the exercise or training of the collective? We will see in Chapter 12 how film can become such a training ground for the collective.

The organs of the collective are identified by Benjamin with the technology that organizes nature (*physis*). In "Outline of the Psychophysical Problem," Benjamin similarly writes of the "technology in which the unity of [humanity's] life is formed. Ultimately, everything that subserves humanity's happiness may be counted part of its limbs" (SW 1:395). We may say then, in the language of the essay on the psychophysical problem, that in tearing apart functional unity we reveal corporeality.[14] The dissociation from the functional allows technology to be incorporated differently into the space of life. Far from being only the subjection of existence to the technological control of the social apparatus, what this discussion suggests is that technology can come to permeate the space of life so as to revolutionize it.

As it stands, the collective body organized through technology is a body of habits and automatisms that are subject to the social apparatus. Thus, we should reflect on the form of training, practice, and exercise that allows the transformation of the collective's relation to the apparatus, what Benjamin expresses by the idea of the interpenetration of body space and image space.[15] The body space of the collective encompasses technology and its way of organizing life. It is not the instrumental use of technology that is at issue but rather opening the occasion for bodily "innervation" (which we considered in its individual context in the discussion of gambling):

> The collective is a body, too. And the *physis* that is being organized for it in technology can, through all its political and factual reality, be produced only in that image space to which profane illumination initiates us. Only when in technology body and image space so interpenetrate that all revolutionary tension becomes bodily collective innervation, and all the bodily innervations of the collective become revolutionary discharge, has reality transcended itself to the extent demanded by the Communist Manifesto. (SW 2:217–218)

AWAKENING AND ACTION

One can think of innervation as a form of awakened presence of mind. Awakening is not a contemplative category but one that must be conceived of in terms of the transformed activity of the collective permeated by technology. The new intelligence of the corporeal is not to be modeled on the unity of spirit and body in the classical ideal of the human figure. This other form of the human that has incorporated technology is expressed in a surrealist fragment with which Benjamin closes his essay: "[The surrealists] exchange, to a man, the play of human features for the face of an alarm clock that in each minute rings for sixty seconds" (SW 2:218). Isn't this a metaphor?

If we were to remain with the analogy between the face of a human being and the face of a clock and use this similarity to signify the necessity of waking up to action, this expression would indeed be a (bad) metaphor. But a proper understanding would take into account that the body of the collective "has its organs in the new technology" in a nonmetaphorical sense. One might say that in a metaphorical sense we conceive of the alarm clock as a means for awakening the human being, whereas what is called for is the mutual permeation of the human and the technological.

Consider further that the alarm clock rings for sixty seconds each minute. This should not be taken as a description of someone who stays asleep despite the ringing of the alarm. The image can be unpacked in different ways: so, for instance, we could oppose the everyday to the urgency of the exceptional. The alarm signals an emergency, which requires decisive action; but the alarm clock is an everyday object, and if it rings constantly, then something about the relation between the everyday and the urgency of the exception is reversed. It is the everyday itself that is the locus of that emergency. As Benjamin puts it in "On the Concept of History": "The "state of emergency" in which we live is not the exception but the rule" (SW 4:392). There is something self-consuming in this last pun: the alarm ringing for sixty seconds each minute is no longer an alarm clock. The very image set forth is consumed by unfolding it.[16] It opens to another time.

PART IV

Primal History

TEN

"From the Pagan Context of Nature... into the Jewish Context of History"

Benjamin's involvement with Goethe is prevalent throughout his writings. It might nevertheless be surprising to find that in convolute N of the *Arcades Project* Benjamin relates his approach to history to Goethe's framework for the investigation of nature:

> My concept of origin in the *Trauerspiel* book is a rigorous and decisive transposition of the basic Goethean concept from the domain of nature to that of history. Origin—it is, in effect, the concept of *Ur*-phenomenon extracted from the pagan context of nature and brought into the Jewish contexts of history. Now, in my work on the arcades I am equally concerned with fathoming an origin. To be specific, I pursue the origin of the forms and mutations of the arcades from their beginning to their decline, and I locate this origin in the economic facts. Seen from the standpoint of causality, however, (and that means considered as causes), these facts would not be primal phenomena; they become so only insofar as in their own individual development—"unfolding" might be a better term—they give rise to the whole series of the arcades concrete historical forms, just as the leaf unfolds from itself all the riches of the empirical world of plants. (A 462 [N2a,4])

The central issue to be addressed in this chapter is the very possibility and character of this translation of Goethe's principles of the investigation of nature, in particular the idea of the revelation of *ur*-phenomenal nature, into the domain of history. Of course, this should not be taken to mean that nature is left behind when Benjamin turns to history. A method is not just a tool that can be used equally in this or some other domain. Specifically, Goethe's method is not related to the idea of nature accidentally; it is the method for the presentation of the forms of "living nature," of primal nature. Thus, insofar as we seek to incorporate Goethe's work on nature into Benjamin's investigation of history, this would imply that for Benjamin himself history contains a dimension of the primal or can be a field in which living nature manifests itself.

Indeed, if we think back to the *Trauerspiel* book and the idea of origin, it is clear that Benjamin seeks such a dimension of the natural within history: "*Ur*-phenomenon," he writes, "... not a pure history, but natural history. The life of the works and forms which need such protection in order to unfold clearly and unclouded by human life, is a natural life" (O 47). In viewing history as a primal phenomenon, we assume in it a dimension of natural history. A tension arises, then, as Benjamin seeks, on the one hand, to think history in relation to original or primal nature, while on the other hand aiming to overcome the pagan context of nature in the Jewish context of history. This tension is resolved in showing how authentic historical time emerges only out of and against primal history, out of the natural in human historical existence.

Goethe's method is elaborated in terms of a number of central concepts, such as intuitive understanding, archetype, morphology or physiognomic understanding, polarity, and metamorphosis. Thus, if Benjamin claims to inherit Goethe's notion of origin, we must further be able to show how these various related terms come into play in his vision of history. The structure of this chapter is therefore as follows: I will go over a number of central concepts in Goethe's theory of nature, and for each I will follow the exposition of Goethe's conception with an analysis of how it is appropriated for history in Benjamin's *Arcades Project*. Then I will complicate the picture and show that there is nevertheless an important sense in which we have in Benjamin a translation of these ideas from the pagan space of nature to the Jewish space of history.

It should be noted that Benjamin's work is in no way an isolated attempt to extend the method of Goethe from nature to culture and history. There were other such endeavors in the first decades of the twentieth century: Goethe was central to such thinkers as Spengler, Klages, and Simmel, as well

The Pagan Context of Nature into the Jewish Context of History 189

as Warburg and Cassirer. What is nevertheless unique to Benjamin's appropriation of Goethe, as we will see, is how he relates him to Marx.

Benjamin and Goethe—Elementary Affinities
EXPRESSION

Goethe seeks the expression of living nature in a field of phenomena (e.g., the vegetal realm or color). Nature is not subsumed under general laws but rather is unified as the expression of a primal origin. In exploring this idea of expression, we must pay attention to two interconnected dimensions. On the one hand, we need to gather a plurality of phenomena that are not subsumed under a concept or a general lawfulness; on the other hand, such plurality must be ordered so that we recognize through them an intensive unity of expression.

Taking seriously the need to gather the diversity of phenomena for the expression of origin means that no phenomenon is privileged (there is no crucial experiment): the observer must be "like the sun which draws forth every plant and shines on all." It is only by attending to the similarities among the diverse phenomena belonging, for instance, to the plant world that we can order them as a space or surroundings of life in which we recognize a physiognomy of living nature. To construct an environment of phenomena is not to replace phenomena in their life environment; for example, we would not seek to relate a plant to the animal that eats it. Goethe does not offer a system of external teleology. Rather, we would place phenomena in a new order whose unity is precisely the expression of the higher life of nature in that field of phenomena. Each domain of nature (colors, plants, etc.) can be presented so that through the ordering of the various phenomena belonging to that domain we make present the expression of original nature in that domain. In this sense, nature in its entirety is expressed intensively in each such domain properly presented.

Consider, for example, color: Goethe's *Farbenlehre* is divided into an account of physiological colors, physical colors, and chemical colors. These are also characterized by Goethe as entirely ephemeral colors, transient colors that linger for a time, and colors that hold constant over a long time—that is, we distinguish between color manifestations that belong to the organ or the body (e.g., afterimages), those that belong to the refraction of light in transparent and turbid media (e.g., the rainbow), and those that belong to colors that are produced through characteristics of matter (e.g., oxidation). But conversely, that means that these domains of nature themselves can be presented in color space, that is, by the different "grammars" of color peculiar to each. We recognize the character of matter through the unity of chemical color manifestations, of the body through the specific unity of physiological colors, and of light through the ordering of the phenomena of physical colors. At a further remove, the plant world is recognized through its color character, the animal realm is revealed in color, and even the human is refracted through what Goethe calls the sensory-moral effects of color. The different dimensions of a world are revealed in and through the field of color when color phenomena are ordered as the expression of primal life. One may call this aspect of the presentation of the primal a monadological and intensive presentation of nature.

In beginning to translate this understanding to the standpoint of history, we note that human beings produce the surroundings of their lives; in turn, in these surroundings we can perceive over time the expression of their life in common. As Marx puts it in *The German Ideology*: "[Men] themselves begin to distinguish themselves from animals as soon as they begin to *produce* their means of subsistence.... This mode of production... is a definite form of activity of these individuals, a definite form of expressing their life, a definite *mode of life* on their part. As individuals express their life, so they are."[1]

It is only when "form of life" is used broadly as the term that encompasses the production of life as human surroundings that we can conceive of historical products, such as architecture, fashion, and advertisement, as expressions of a unity of life. These are not to be taken merely as so many isolated expressions: brought together they reveal the unity in the form of life of the collective. We may call this idea of an expressive unity a physiognomic articulation of culture: "To write history means giving dates their physiognomy" (A 476 [N11,2]).

In a Goethean vein, we may say that in gathering phenomena as expressive manifestations of one and the same form of life, we recognize them as the unfolding of primal nature, as partaking in the unity of an *ur*-phenomenon. The challenge Benjamin faces is to relate this register of expression belonging to Goethe's method of investigating nature not only to the life of culture but, more precisely, to Marx's materialism. This is in fact Benjamin's aim when he brings the two together in the following remark: "Marx lays bare the causal connection between economy and culture. For us, what matters is the thread of expression. It is not the economic origins of culture that will be presented, but the expression of the economy in its culture. At issue, in other words, is the attempt to grasp an economic process as perceptible *ur*-phenomenon, from out of which proceed all manifestations of life in the arcades (and, accordingly, in the nineteenth century)" (A 460 [N1a,6]; my emphasis).

An implication of the distinction that Benjamin makes between following the thread of causality and following that of expression is that, whereas cause is distinct from effect, the essence from its partial reflection in appearance, that which expresses itself can be actualized, even if it is in and through its presence in the culture. Moreover, recognizing the economy as origin does not mean that we will be able to delimit a well-defined and distinct economic process "behind" the distinct cultural manifestations.

As Goethe puts it: "One must not look for anything behind the phenomena; they are themselves the doctrine." To be precise, the *ur*-phenomenon cannot be grasped in isolation; it is present in the gathering of phenomena that are then revealed as its expressions, as the unfolding of its inner life. Thus it is the very presentation of the historical material as *ur*-phenomenon that will make manifest what economy *is* as it is expressed in the sphere of culture. "The dialectic of [the] conditions of production is evident in the superstructure, no less than in the economy" (SW 4:252). Economy, the production of life, will be recognized in the culture.

There is no shortage of references in Benjamin's writings to the connection between the intensive expression and the monadological standpoint. The epigraph he chooses for his book on the baroque, *Trauerspiel*, is from Goethe's *Farbenlehre* and suggests such a standpoint: "Just as art is always wholly present in each individual artwork, so should science always be wholly manifest in each particular matter treated" (O 1). If nature as a whole expresses itself in each field of phenomena properly ordered, then we must say similarly that in the intensive presentation of history we must recognize history as a whole (which is not the same as all of what happened). The expression of the entelechy of the monad, its intensive expression of a unity of life, depends just as much on giving up on extensive universality as it does on recognizing the appeal to a multiplicity of phenomena. This is probably most

192 Chapter Ten

dramatically manifest in Benjamin's writing when he sets himself the task of expressing in terms of the seemingly endless materials of the Paris arcades, as it were in miniature, the essential character of the nineteenth century and thereby the fundamental dimensions of history as a whole.

In other words, the restriction of the investigation of history to the arcades is correlative with an intensified expressive power, as they come to reflect in their details, in an abbreviated form, the essential dimensions of history. Through the ordering of phenomena pertaining to the arcades of Paris, we can recognize the forces of primal history as such. In the intensive presentation a wide range of phenomena are ordered around a center, as it were—call it an origin—and can thus be recognized as the unfolding of that higher life in history. The more we can bring the extensive periphery together through affinities or relationships as manifestations of a single center, the more the presentation will bring out what Benjamin also calls forces or tendencies in history. In the constructed historical object, "all the forces and interests of history enter on a reduced scale" (A 475 [N10,3]).

POLARIZATION AND INTENSIFICATION

But how, exactly, are we to avoid the extensive vision of history while at the same time incorporating material that would belong far beyond the range of the epoch under consideration in the presentation? In order to clarify this point we must understand the relation between the intensive in Goethe (which he also calls the superlative) and polarization. Polarization and intensification are that through which we recognize the belonging of phenomena to an origin: a first formulation of the work of the two principles is given in the following:

Whatever appears in the world must divide if it is to appear at all. What has been divided seeks itself again, can return to itself and reunite. This happens in a lower sense when it merely intermingles with its opposite, combines with it: here the phenomenon is nullified or at least neutralized. However, the union may occur in a higher sense if what has been divided is first intensified; then in the union of the intensified halves it will produce a third thing, something new, higher, unexpected.[2]

Let me offer a concrete example, namely, the derivation of the basic colors of the spectrum—yellow, blue, red, and green—in phenomena of refraction, which Goethe calls "dioptric colors of the first class." All such colors, Goethe insists against Newton, must involve the duality of light and shadow, the presence as well as the privation of light. The illumination of a turbid medium against a dark background yields blue; light seen through a darkened turbid medium yields yellow. These two colors can be combined so that they neutralize each other and yield green. But they can also be intensified in such a way that a more opaque medium yields orange on the side of yellow, whereas thinner air, say, yields purple on the side of blue. The intensified poles unite in crimson red.

Importantly, the appearance of red through intensification is also what completes the schema of basic colors. It is therefore also the appearance of a whole, a form, of which the different colors polarized are now mutually exclusive parts. Polarization and intensification thus appear as key to the unity of constituent parts belonging to a higher whole in which nature as creative force expresses itself. For Goethe, then, polarization is essential to the idea of diversifying by intensification.

In a complete presentation of a primal phenomenon, the whole space of phenomena is, as it were, unfolded from out of its origin and actualized. This means that the abstract opposition between reality and its negation (i.e., the merely possible) is incorporated into the full positivity of a space where we recognize excluding poles that belong together. Polarity is not a formal abstract (or logical) negation; rather, it is a reciprocal exclusion of contents. Polarity is the form of the negative, and intensification is what affirmation comes to. The latter raises the opposition of polarity to a new, higher level. Polarity and intensification are principles of primal expression, which bear some similarity to the dialectic—not a dialectic of the concept, however, but, as we will come to think of it with Benjamin, a dialectic of the image.

But what would be the polarization of historical material? Polarization in nature is atemporal. In the context of history, polarization will have a temporal index. Benjamin uses the term "polarization" when he refers to a specific division of time revealed in the presentation of the object. The poles of the historical object are its fore- and after-history: "The fore- and after-history of a historical phenomenon [*Tatbestandes*] show up in the phenomenon itself on the strength of its dialectical presentation. What is more: every dialectically presented historical state of things [*Sachverhalt*] polarizes itself and become a force field in which the confrontation between its fore-history and after-history is played out" (A 470 [N7a,1]; translation modified).

Fore- and after-history should be distinguished from the successive temporality of "what comes before" and "what comes after" a specified moment in history. It is not a matter of succession in time (as though what we would be interested is what led up to a certain point and what followed it) or a matter of relying on causal connections in history, nor is it merely enough to speak of teleological development and decline. The polarization in question concerns the presentation of the significance of the historical object and belongs to its presentation as origin. Moreover, fore- and after-history are internal to the presentation of the object; as such, it is misleading to call them the fore- and after-history *of* the object, which would suggest that the object is identified in time apart from its polarized presentation. The polarization as it were reveals time that is internal to the object: "The nourishing fruit of what is historically understood contains time in its interior as a precious but tasteless seed" (SW 4:396).

The notions of fore- and after-history already appear in *Origin of the German Trauerspiel*, Benjamin's book on the baroque. Indeed, they are essential to characterize the presentation of the historical as the expression of the natural historical, as the recognition of the internal life of the original. In characterizing the historical presentation of an origin in that book, Benjamin writes that "its history is inward in character and is not to be understood as something boundless, but as something related to essential being, and it can therefore be described as the fore- and after-history [*Vor- und Nachgeschichte*] of this being. The past and subsequent history of such essences is . . . not a pure history, but natural history. The life of the works and forms which need such protection in order to unfold clearly and unclouded by human life, is a natural life" (O 26).

The fore- and after-history of the object investigated delimit a vital unity, expressing the inner higher life in the object. Natural history is cued to the internal life that can be gathered from products, works, or what we may call historical material. Insofar as materials are brought together as an order of natural history, this would serve the presentation of essential being in its life or unfolding in the phenomenal; it is in that sense that Benjamin contrasts natural history with pragmatic history. A different way of putting the matter would be to say that phenomena are extracted from the order of succession in order to be gathered in terms of another temporal order. Such phenomena would be taken out of the causal nexus, or the order of causally related succession, and considered only insofar as they contribute, or take part in, the expression of the inner life of essential being. It is in this sense that natural history is virtual rather than real.[3]

From our preceding analysis, it might seem that the fore- and after-history can be revealed in any object under consideration at any period we choose to investigate. But we would be forgetting that essential time can only be revealed "from within." The revelation of a life involves the one who can recognize it. Therefore, we must include the present in gathering the facts into a field of tensions between fore- and after-history; there is no polarity, no force field, unless the historical object is made one's own in the present, or more precisely, belongs to the possibility of transformation of one's present: "Every dialectically presented historical circumstance polarizes itself and becomes a force field in which the confrontation between its fore-history and after-history is played out. It becomes such a field insofar as the present interpenetrates it. And thus the historical evidence polarizes into fore- and after-history always anew, never in the same way" (A 470 [N7a,1]). The polarization of the historical object into fore- and after-history is inseparable from its actualization in and for the present: "It is the present that polarizes the event into fore- and after-history" (A 471 [N7a,8]). The historical "subject" is determined in terms of the polarization of the past into a field of tensions, a moment of danger and an opportunity; it does not appear in relation to an inert expanse of past facts. Through the polarization of the past we reveal the "Now," the transformed present, as the actualization of that virtual life in the object. This will be discussed further in Chapter 11.

ARCHETYPE AND IMAGE

For Goethe, the primal is archetypal nature. What characterizes the archetype as a form of unity is its nondiscursive character. It has the unity of an image. We tend to associate image with representation and therefore with ideal productions of the mind, as well as with a certain understanding of the imagination.

The Marxist suspicion as to the ideological character of a history of "ideas" would encourage turning to hard natural science to account for the dynamics of social forms in history. It has led to various internal debates within Marxism—for instance, between those who find in Marx's early writings a key to a humanistic materialism and those who see them as a remnant of Hegelian idealism and seek to overcome them by means of a form of scientific Marxism. The approach Benjamin takes to this problematic crux assumes that one must not seek the proper grounding of the critical dimension in history in the unity that subjectivity and its internal norms provide us with but in the attention to the material dimension of historical life. And yet it is just as problematic to model the materialist method on a vulgar naturalism drawn from the sciences. There is a danger that lurks in the identification of natural science as the antidote to the problematic, ideological forms of history. What needs to be challenged is "the attempted positivistic and undialectical separation between the natural sciences and the humanities" (SW 3:266).

An alternative conception of the science of nature that allows us both to hold to the most concretely contingent material and to recognize the expressive character unifying that material is given to us by Goethe, in his notion that we can conceive of a higher intuitability in the recognition of the primal phenomenon. The primal phenomenon is the higher synthesis of the phenomenal that proceeds by the arrangement and ordering of individual phenomena. Goethe, as we have seen, aims to make present an original unity in phenomena over and above the multiplicity of facts, yet without resorting to abstraction and general laws. One of the crucial points of contact between Goethe's investigation of nature and Benjamin's account of history lies in this intuitive concreteness, not only of the material content but also of the configuration that is presented through its ordering. Such an ordering is not a system but what Benjamin calls an image. Benjamin stands by his "refusal to renounce anything that would demonstrate the materialist presentation of history as imagistic [*Bildhaft*] in a higher sense than the traditional presentation" (A 463 [N3,3]). And he similarly asks himself, regarding the method of historical materialism: "In what way is it possible to conjoin a heightened intuitability [of history] to the realization of the Marxist method?" (A 461 [N2,6]; translation modified). The expression "heightened intuitability" is particularly significant in thinking of the place of intuitive knowledge in Goethe's scientific method.

The ordering of the multiplicity of phenomena serves to present an image, the *ur*-phenomenal archetype. In the book on the *Trauerspiel*, Benjamin refers to the quasi-pictorial character of the presentation through the figure of the constellation. In the *Arcades Project*, the dimension of the image is evident as the presentation of a dialectical image: "The dialectical image is that form of the historical object which satisfies Goethe's requirement for the object of analysis: to exhibit a genuine synthesis. It is the primal phenomenon of history" (A 474 [N9a,4]).

Thinking of the historical investigation in terms of the presentation of the archetype/image does not mean that one has any prior standard by which to recognize the formations of history (i.e., to judge what is valuable according to its approximation to that standard). Historical investigation is itself what leads to the recognition of that emergence of a standard for our present through which phenomena receive their significance, their proper measure and place. History is the object of a construction that presents the original, the preexisting, every time anew. This brings out a tension between the understanding of the primal as the preexisting archetype and the commitment to a constructive principle. The matter is not resolved merely by arguing that the construction makes us see better what is already given. There must be a more radical idea of actualization that brings together construction and the preexisting. We will return to this point.

METAMORPHOSIS

The concept of archetype in Goethe's theory of nature is closely related to the concept of metamorphosis. Initially, there would seem to be an opposition between these two concepts: the archetype is singular and an origin of all change, whereas metamorphosis is a way of characterizing "small" changes that are revealed in the details of a multiplicity of phenomena. But in effect archetype and metamorphosis belong to one another. It is by attending to metamorphosis that the phenomena are drawn together through similarities. In Goethe's conception of nature, thinking metamorphosis and primal image together allows us to avoid various models of form or teleological thinking that involve the idea of a plan or design. Contrary to Kant's understanding of teleology, which takes the idea of purposive activity as a fundamental schema for natural life, the stress on metamorphosis brings out an internal dynamism of incremental change that covers the whole field of phenomena. Metamorphosis is what can initially characterize the dynamics of material content. The unity of metamorphosis is distinct from the unity of purposive form. What is essential here is that we need not conceive of nature as if it were the product of a "plan" or a "design"; the incremental change in metamorphosis could be conceived of even as taking place in time through chance or by some mechanism.

Archetype is not plan or purpose but rather primal content unfolded by endless transformations. The archetype is the original content, the origin of all variations. It is the immutable image that can be recognized only in a perspicuous overview of the space of transformations as a whole. It is important to see that even if individual products of nature exhibit as particulars a purposive unity of form, metamorphosis cannot be contained in any form; instead it points to the continuous dynamism of life that is transformative.

Benjamin echoes the notion of metamorphosis when he speaks of the mutations of the arcades. The mutations belong to the dynamic character of the material content in time; in other words, the recognition of the dimension of metamorphosis in history is crucially related to the idea of a materialist history. Metamorphosis rules the currents of history that are not visible when one thinks in terms of the unity of causality, events, individuals, or ideas. It is the material content that undergoes mutations in its afterlife. This can be related to the way in which Benjamin sees his investigation of the reality of the nineteenth century as philological in character: it is a matter of "reading the real." Philology is the study of the transformations of material content released from their subordination to the initial context in which they were uttered, as is evident in the discussion of the relation between commentary and critique in the opening of the essay on *Elective Affinities* (see Chapter 3). It is also something that is explicitly discussed in a fragment titled "Methodical Types of History," where Benjamin argues that "philology is transformation-history (*Verwandlungsgeschichte*)" (GS 6:93). The small differentials of meaning in the material content constitute transformation-history.

This idea of mutation in historical material content can be understood as underlying Benjamin's notion of the time-differential (*Zeit-differential*). In other words, in seeking a historical parallel to the idea of metamorphosis in nature, Benjamin turns to differences—one might say "nuances"—of the transformation of content in time. Benjamin suggests that one of the important contrasts between his view and Hegel's idea of dialectic lies in the idea of the time-differential: "What matter are never the 'great' but only the dialectical contrasts, which often seem indistinguishable from nuances. It is nonetheless from them that life is always born anew" (A 459). In the time-differential we get a characterization of the relation between materials that is constituted by the slight changes and metamorphoses in time. Insofar as we seek the significance of a field of phenomena, the starting point is not the difference between given particulars; rather, in the destruction of the particular unities we recognize the primacy of difference in presenting the higher identity of the image.[4]

This is why Benjamin suggests in different places how his investigation is cued to slight deviations belonging to the afterlife of material content. This heeding of and attentiveness to small deviations is explicit in a figure that opens convolute N: "Comparisons of other people's attempts to the understanding of a sea voyage in which the ships are drawn off course by the magnetic North Pole. Discover *this* North Pole. What for others are deviations are, for me, the data which determine my course—On the differentials of time (which, for others, disturb the main lines of the inquiry), I base my reckoning" (A 456 [N1,2]). We will return to the idea that the differentials are deviations—one might also say, deformations or distortions.

CONSTRUCTION AND DESTRUCTION

The unity of the dialectical image, like that of the primal phenomenon, is not a given but rather a construction brought about by ordering phenomena anew. The myriad quotations that Benjamin takes as the material content of the presentation of an origin are taken out of their context (indeed, this is implicit in the very concept of quotation) and ordered so that they intensively present the unity of history: "It is important for the materialist historian, in the most rigorous way possible, to differentiate the construction of a historical state of affairs from what one customarily calls its 'reconstruction.'" In the presentation of history, "'construction' presupposes 'destruction'" (A 470 [N7,6]).

Destruction would be releasing phenomena from their dependence on the context in which they initially appeared. Construction is their higher ordering, an essential aspect of revealing the monadological character of the object of history. The expressive power associated with the monadic conception of history can never be revealed if one remains with the unities given in lived experience: "If the object of history is sprung out of the continuum of historical succession, that is because its monadological structure demands it" (A 475 [N10,3]). It is not a unified object that is extracted from history; instead, it is through the extracted material that the historical object is first constituted: "The destructive or critical momentum of materialist historiography is registered in that blasting of historical continuity with which the historical object first constitutes itself. In fact, an object of history cannot be targeted at all within the continuous elapse of history" (A 475 [N10a,1]).

This aspect of destruction of the individual phenomenon is in a way already inherent in the Goethean method, or more precisely, Goethe conceives of the formation of the new order of the phenomenal, the new continuity of the phenomenal, as a mode of dissolving the particular in the expression of a higher life. It is dissolved *by* relationship, or by incorporating it in a space of continuous transitions. Revealing the continuity of nature is, as Goethe puts it, "dissolving the particular without destroying the impression itself."[5]

The destruction of the particular is far more pronounced as we conceive of history. Indeed, one might argue that, whereas for Goethe what matters is expressions of life, for Benjamin history implies that death and afterlife are also taken as internal to the material content presented. This vision of destruction as internal to the highest actualization is peculiar and demands further clarification (even though we have seen versions of it in different contexts). The unity of an organism is judged in terms of the standard of its maturity; there is also a process of aging and degeneration that might be taken into account. Drawing a simplistic analogy between processes of growth and degeneration in nature and history would result in a scheme that separates periods of historical flourishing from those of decline—roughly the way in which Spengler thinks of the Goethean investigation translated to history. But with Benjamin's vision of historical life, destruction is itself internal to the presentation of the historical object—indeed, to its highest actualization. Far from associating himself with a vision of decline, Benjamin writes: "The pathos of this work: there are no periods of decline. Attempt to see the nineteenth century just as positively as I tried to see the seventeenth century, in the work on the *Trauerspiel*. No belief in periods of decline" (A 458 [N1,6]). The positivity that "declines decline" is not a denial of the destructive in history but rather the conviction that it can be assumed in a higher actuality. It is indeed key to revealing that higher actuality, the "indestructibility of the highest life in all things" (A 459 [N1a,4]).

Put somewhat differently, the forms characteristic of life are often paradigms of a hylomorphic unity. But the consideration of destruction as inherent in the presentation of history cannot retain this kind of unity of form

The Pagan Context of Nature into the Jewish Context of History

and matter. Not only is destruction the fate of everything living, but also the unity of a higher life in history is to be conceived of as redeeming, taking up or assuming the destruction of what was erected in time.

The incorporation of destruction means that a counterpurposive moment is part of the recognition of a higher life in history. The actualization of the past surpasses the scope and span of purposive life. It involves what Benjamin refers to as the afterlife (*Nachleben*) of material content. The central characterization of the idea of a higher, historical life that encompasses what we call "afterlife" is articulated, as we saw, in the essay "The Task of the Translator." It is also clear from that essay that it is only by giving up on the unity of intention in the original language that one can echo it through supplementation in the language of the translation. The connection between the form of the investigation of the historical and the problem of translation and the afterlife of meaning is brought out in the following remark in convolute K: "Historical 'understanding' is to be grasped, in principle, as an afterlife of that which is understood; and what has been recognized in the analysis of the 'afterlife of works,' in the analysis of 'fame,' is therefore to be considered the foundation of history in general" (A 460 [N2,3]).[6]

In characterizing the relation between destruction and meaning, what is to be taken into account is not just the time of the emergence of the arcades (say, the first half of the nineteenth century) or even adding to that the time of their decline; we have to conceive of their afterlife, in which their meaning material acquires its peculiar character of significance to be recognized by the present. It is through that decay that the material begins to show peculiarities that were far from apparent to those for whom the arcades were part of their lived experience—that is, the phenomena become material for knowledge with a view to recognizing in the commentary of such material content the truth content in history.

The consideration of destruction internal to the highest actualization also raises for us the question of the relation of these considerations to the idea of divine violence as it appears in the essay "Critique of Violence." It raises, in other words, the possibility of recognizing historical materialism, as Benjamin conceives of it, to be precisely the way in which we are to see ourselves as partaking in divine violence, or through our action partaking in the highest actuality. In Chapter 11 we will further elaborate the inner dependence of the historical on the political.

From Metamorphosis to the Distortions of History

Up to this point I have stressed some basic affinities between Goethe's investigation of nature and Benjamin's presentation of history. I want to put the weight on the distinction Benjamin draws between what he terms the "pagan" context of nature and the "Jewish" context of history. What does it mean for history to emerge out of primal nature? How is primal nature in the human world radically different from the primal nature of plants? And how might this bear on the attempt to think of Marxism through the Goethean model?

Through the investigation of the arcades Benjamin seeks to characterize the primal phenomenon of history. The primal in human existence is the mythical. The mythical isn't merely identified in the character of early human societies or of so-called primitive forms of human existence. The force of Benjamin's view of primal history lies in the idea that the mythical is ever present in the space of human life. His presentation of the nineteenth century as primal history brings out the form of the struggle with the mythical that shapes the image of modernity. Authentic historical time emerges in the struggle against the burden of myth. "Every ground must at some point have been made arable by reason, must have been cleared of the undergrowth of delusion and myth. This is to be accomplished here for the terrain of the nineteenth century" (A 456 [N1,4]). The struggle against the hold of the mythical is a dimension of the task of articulation of the space of meaningful fulfillment open to the present. The mythical has its hold for precisely as long as the space of the life of the past does not undergo the highest meaningful articulation. Thus the problem of emerging out of myth is ever renewed, both in the struggles of the individual life as well as for the collective. Myth is the primal ground against which uniqueness in history arises.

As the idea of metamorphosis is translated from nonhuman nature to the realm of meaningful human existence, it is manifest as mythical ambiguity.[7] Benjamin chooses as an epigraph to convolute B the following phrase from Balzac: "Nothing dies; all is transformed" (A 62). This is precisely the standpoint of nature as endlessly and continuously transformable, the standpoint of metamorphosis. But far from being a manifestation of creative vitality, in human beings this attempt to take up the plasticity of the natural into one's form of existence is a denial of mortality or finitude.[8] In other words, this unbounded vitality belongs to the demonic character of myth and is the other side of submission to the orders of fate.

Mythical life is life that has not undergone concretization or individualization; it is unactualized life, which Benjamin sometimes calls "mere life" (*Bloße Leben*). In the essay "Fate and Character," as we have seen, he thinks of such a field of life as ruled by fate. Such existence may not be conscious of the sources of its suffering, in part because of the close connection between the entanglement in myth and the form of a wishing consciousness. The entanglement in myth may be called the primal past and the utopian wish the primal future. (Benjamin speaks of "primordial passion, fears, and images of longing," of "the utopia that has left its trace in a thousand configurations of life, from enduring edifices to passing fashions" [A 5], as well as of the "alluring and threatening face of primal history" [A 393 (K2a,1)].) Primal history is the recognition of a period through the polarity of utopia and mythical dread, as wish and as guilt. Put differently, we recognize that the polarization internal to the historical object, between fore- and after-history, should be understood in terms of primal time, which has the polar character of utopia and myth. In order to recognize the highest stakes in history, we must present the historical phenomenon through such a primal polarization.

Even the notion of archetype central to Goethe and taken up in Benjamin's notion of the dialectical image has a mythical counterpart, which is discussed in the contrast that Benjamin makes between authentic and archaic images: "Only dialectical images are genuine images (that is not archaic); and the place where one encounters them is language" (A 462 [N2a,3]). In an earlier remark Benjamin speaks of the "archaic symbol-world of mythology," identifying his use of "archaic" with mythology and implicitly invoking the need for a critique of the false unity of the symbol. The notion of an archaic image is identified explicitly in Jung as having a regressive function. By recognizing clearly both the involvement of the mythical as well as the character of its overcoming in the construction of history, one can distinguish Benjamin's view from different forms of embracing the mythical.

There is a similar problem with the concept of transformation or metamorphosis. Insofar as we think of these transformations as unfolding the problematic character of the past, they may be called deformations or distortions of the material content. A hint as to the temporal character of this deformation in history can be obtained by relating deformation to the forgotten, which is a central theme of Benjamin's essay on Kafka. The forgotten is not nothing but rather has presence as distortion in the image of the past that emerges for the present: "The form which things assume in oblivion ... [is that] they are distorted" (SW 2:811). (The hunchback is a figure for such distortion; it appears in numerous writings of Benjamin's and famously in the first thesis of "On the Concept of History.") From the standpoint of the present, the distorted character of the past is the sign of the forgotten in history. It is by attending to the distortions that one takes notice of the forgotten for the image of history of the present.

Attending to deformation, to the presence of the forgotten, can potentially reveal a force or tendency to be taken up by the present. In a remark in convolute K, Benjamin explicitly relates the tendencies that are revealed in material content and ideas to the forgotten: "Every current of fashion or of worldview derives its force from what is forgotten" (A 393 [K2a,3]).

But at the same time, deformed life is revealed as cursed life, a compromised condition of humanity that needs to be rescued in history. This becomes clearer if we further relate the notion of deformation to the phantasmagorical character of what is "transmitted" to us through the life-forms and cultural products of the nineteenth century. This is something Benjamin refers to in the introduction to the 1939 exposé of the *Arcades Project*. These deeper tendencies expressing the conditions of existence of the nineteenth century initially reveal themselves to the historical gaze of the present in the illumination of the material culture of the past: "The new forms of behavior and the new economically and technologically based creations that we owe to the nineteenth century enter the universe of a phantasmagoria" (A 14).

The notion of phantasmagoria suggests how what achieves expression is precisely a compromised state of collective existence. In other words, the attention of the historical materialist to the "metamorphosis" of material products makes manifest the space of human life whose schema is the rule of myth.[9] Through the investigation of the arcades Benjamin seeks to characterize the primal phenomenon of history. The primal in human existence is the mythical. The construction that reveals most decisively the critical action demanded by history would involve presenting it through the hold of the mythical. It is strictly speaking a struggle against the burden of myth that we are to conceive of the emergence of authentic historical time.

It is at this point that we can see how Marx comes into this Goethean framework. The exploitation that characterizes capitalist modes of production is expressed in the culture; the base is expressed in the superstructure. As long as the relations of production in the base benefit the ruling class, culture is ideology and fosters forms of false consciousness and alienation. Benjamin interprets these well-known Marxist themes by arguing that the base will be reflected in the culture as distorted life. It will be, to put it in terms of Benjamin's discussion of Goethe's *Elective Affinities*, an expression of collective life as semblance, or to prefigure our analysis of historical memory in Chapter 11, the expressive character of material culture sought here is the dream configuration.

This relation of the dream configuration of collective life to Marx's conception of the ideological character of the superstructure, is explicit in the following passage:

> The superstructure is the expression of the infrastructure. The economic conditions under which society exists are expressed in the superstructure—precisely as, with the sleeper, an overfull stomach finds not its reflection but its expression in the contents of dreams, which from a causal point of view, it may be said to "condition." The collective, from the first, expresses the conditions of its life. These find their expression in the dream and their interpretation in the awakening. (A 392 [K2,5])

In Benjamin's framework, the dialectical image of history (what Goethe would call the archetype of history) is articulated as awakening from the dream. One of the epigraphs he chooses for convolute N is from a letter of Marx in which he singles out this very theme: "The reform of consciousness consists *solely* in . . . the awakening of the world from its dream about itself" (A 456). This grants importance specifically to presenting the distortion evident in the cultural materials, that is, establishing in the first place their dream character.

ELEVEN

Matters of Memory

The Critique of Vitalism

As we take up Benjamin's conception of history, it is particularly important to articulate how the past is related by a bond of *life* to the present. It is by considering history as memory that we can recognize that vital nexus: "History is not simply a science but also and not least a form of remembrance" (A 471 [N8,1]). This raises for us the question of Benjamin's relation to Bergson's writings and in particular to his *Matter and Memory*. The explicit references to that book, found in "On Some Motifs in Baudelaire," nevertheless evince most of all the distance that Benjamin wants to take from Bergson's account.

The essay begins with a statement about the transformation of experience in modernity and the challenges it poses to the poetic and philosophical attempts to draft a picture of modern experience. Benjamin holds the response of *Lebensphilosophie* to this transformation of the space of life to be reactionary: it attempts to rescue an authentic dimension of life in the face of such modern phenomena as the crowd, technology, and the metropolis. The forces of life and nature in "lived experience" are set in opposition to the effects of modernization and the denatured life of the masses in the city. Since the modern world presents such a bleak present, life-philosophy seeks refuge in returning to the primal unity of life in myth. (Benjamin recognizes this tendency primarily in Jung's archaic symbols and in Klages's opposition of soul and spirit, who, as he says, "made common cause with Fascism" [SW 4:314].)

Bergson is distinguished from this tendency in part through his engagement with the science of his time. As he describes Bergson's achievement, Benjamin shifts the question of memory from the individual to the collective and to tradition as what makes the past present in experience: "As the title [*Matter and Memory*] suggests, it regards the structure of memory [*Gedächtnis*] as decisive for the philosophical structure of experience [*Erfahrung*]. Experience is indeed a matter of tradition, in collective existence as well as private life. It is the product less of facts firmly anchored in memory [*Erinnerung*] than of accumulated and frequently unconscious data that flow together in memory [*Gedächtnis*]" (SW 4:314). Bergson understands memory as accessing the unconscious strata of the past, or more precisely, he takes the very reality of the past to be unconscious yet such as can be brought to consciousness (in something like the way there are expanses of space we are not perceiving yet that could be made present by our moving to them). His intensive conception of *durée* also provides a way to account for the accumulation of unconscious data "flowing together" in memory. But according to Benjamin, Bergson lacks an account of the dimension of tradition in experience, and tradition is always collective and historical. It is only the recognition of this dimension of collective memory that allows an approach to the problems of the relation of memory to history. Yet, as he puts it, "The historical determination of memory is not at all Bergson's intention. On the contrary he rejects any historical determination of memory" (SW 4:314).

The form in which Benjamin frames his critique is interesting in itself—not just the claim that Bergson cannot encompass in his view the experience of the masses and of large-scale industrialism but also its suggesting the unconscious rootedness of Bergson's thought in the historical. Bergson's thought develops at a specific historical juncture, as a reaction to the emergence of certain phenomena of modernity. In other words, his work belongs to its time, even as a defense against modernity's most significant and "blinding" transformations.[1]

It remains an open question whether aspects of Bergson's theory of memory can be translated from the context of the individual to that of the collective. Indeed, I will argue that some of the most important insights of Benjamin's understanding of history as remembrance constitute such a translation. In order to assess and develop this claim, it is necessary to understand Proust's role in mediating Bergson's thought for Benjamin.

The Shadow of Bergson in "The Image of Proust"

In the early parts of Benjamin's essay "On Some Motifs in Baudelaire," Proust is presented as the author who incorporated most deeply and concretely Bergson's conception of memory into his writing. Proust's *Recherche* exemplifies how literature can be the medium through which the depths of memory are probed and brought to the light of day. Nevertheless, Proust is said to challenge Bergson's supposition that consciousness can find its way to all of the strata of memory—that it is in principle possible for consciousness to descend at will to the most singular moments of the past, to recover what Bergson calls "pure memory." Proust problematizes the picture by drawing a distinction between the voluntary memory of intelligence and the involuntary memory that might be our only access to pure memory.

In Proust's own case the attempts at voluntarily conjuring his childhood in Combray always recall the same anxiety-ridden fixated image, the scene of being sent early to bed as Swann arrived for dinner. The radical problem introduced into Bergson's theory by Proust is that the condition for the recovery of one's past, the triggering of involuntary memory beyond the memory of intelligence, is left to an accidental or chance encounter. That the appropriation of the fullness of one's past is dependent on a contingent encounter brings out most dramatically the involuntary character of memory: it is awakened by what is wholly external to the mind, a material object.

While no doubt important, the concept of involuntary memory should be considered in the context of broader aspects of Bergson's theory that are taken up by Proust, which we will do at least in part by considering some themes in Benjamin's essay "On the Image of Proust." What follows is not an interpretation of this essay but instead an attempt to draw from it further ways in which Bergson's conception of memory is translated into Proust's remembrance of the past.

Consider first that the encounter with an object that awakens involuntary memory demands to be supplemented by an account of what allows the recovery not only of that singular memory but of the whole world of the past to which it belongs. This cannot be understood by invoking "association." Indeed, associationism presupposes a conception of the mind in which individual memories are laid out separate from each other and externally related through similarity or contiguity. Relying merely on association would not yield the unity of the past remembered. Recovering that unity of world presumes access to "the special stratum—the bottommost—of [the] involuntary memory, one in which materials of memory no longer appear singly, as images, but tell us about a whole, amorphously and formlessly, indefinitely and weightily, in the same way as the weight of his net tells a fisherman about his catch." In order to account for what it takes to "cast . . . nets into the sea of *temps perdu*" (SW 2:247) we need to invoke Bergson's distinction between the extensive and the intensive.

The significance of the distinction between the extensive and the intensive is elaborated chiefly in Bergson's *The Immediate Givens of Consciousness* (also translated as *Time and Free Will*). It reflects the incommensurability of the form of space (the extensive) and the unity of time (the intensive). When we conceive of particular memories as laid out separably in the archive of memory, externally related through associations, we import a spatial picture to account for the essentially temporal character of the mind.[2] Rather than conceiving of external relations between identifiable particular memories, we need to think intensively of the interpenetration of accumulated memories. The simplest form of interpenetration is what goes into the formation of habit. To take Bergson's most famous example, when learning a lesson by heart we might at first remember individual attempts to recite it, but at some point the ability to recite the lesson results from the interpenetration of these occasions, which become undistinguishable.

Yet habit is geared toward behavior or action. We might wonder whether there is an intensive permeation of the nonrepeatable memories. There are conceivably different degrees of the bearing of the accumulated past on action, but to simplify, we may conceive of two types of lives corresponding, as it were, to the following two extremes of memory: the first is that of the "reactive" person, who responds automatically to a stimulus with the behavior that incorporated the cumulative lesson of memory; the second is the dreamer, that is, someone who is wholly dissociated from the plane of action and wholly absorbed in the strata of unique memories of the past.[3]

Having the wisdom of experience resides between these two types. On the one hand, pure reactivity amounts to being something of an automaton. On the other hand, however, it is said that there is wisdom in waiting—but only to wait without ever acting is to live life as in a dream. Dreaming, as we usually conceptualize it, is a well-delimited state that arises with the neutralization of action in sleep. We usually account for dreaming based on the primacy of the waking state and then ask ourselves how this strange state, the dream, is produced. We might appeal to various constructions, projections, and distortions to produce the dreamworld out of various remains of the day. Bergson's model, however, reverses these terms: it is not that first we have the conscious state and then we must explain the peculiar condition of dreaming; on the contrary, the unconscious accumulation of the past in the mind has the character of dreaming, and out of it consciousness selects, as it were, what belongs to the necessity of action. The acting consciousness represents the impoverishment of the dream state of pure memory. The "deepest stratum of memory" that consciousness can reach when action is neutralized has the character of dreaming.[4]

Drawing on this deepest stratum of memory would not involve remembering specific events or focusing on stories involving the various persons in one's past; the more we speak of identifiable events, of what stands out in the flow of experience—that is, the more memories are separable—then the more it would be a matter of the conscious memory's recalling them. Rather, it is through what is found in the most everyday moments, what belongs to the weave of life, that one can access the intensive continuous yet singular character of experience: "Only the *actus purus* of remembrance itself, not the author or the plot, constitutes the unity of the text. One may even say that the intermittences of author and plot are only the reverse of the continuum of memory, the figure on the back side of the carpet" (SW 2:238).[5]

What would pure actuality be if remembrance does not draw memory into the "actuality" of action? To draw the whole weight of the past from the depth of pure memory toward pure actuality, the *actus purus*, Proust foregoes action. Benjamin describes how, by reversing day and night, Proust detaches himself from all exigencies of action. The more memory serves action and the less it involves the singularly significant, the deeper strata of memory, then the more it can be said to involve abstract generality. Indeed, Bergson's conception of general ideas is closely connected to his account of memory. In acting there is no need for the multitude of precise and detailed memories, just as we need not attend to the multitude of details of the given in perceiving the external world. To take a simple example, when we are terribly hungry and action is demanded, any food will be welcome; we do not distinguish between fruits and vegetables, meat and fish ... or for that matter, a "madeleine": we want *food*. We place ourselves on a plane of memory that does not differentiate between the different kinds of food we have tasted on various occasions.

The unity of the depth of pure memory is not produced by the unifying power of concepts. Benjamin's figure of the carpet suggests that we are to think of a "weave" of meaning. The weave is a peculiar form of convergence where each strand retains its independence as they all hold together. The figure suggests that the writing of memory is saturated with the crisscross of affinities. Memory does not reproduce impressions and relate them by association; it is a medium through which emerge affinities that signal the continuity of life. Memory is the medium of affinities.

Proust in effect interprets and transforms the understanding of intensive *durée* in Bergson. But a further and important implication of this account of the interpenetration of memories is that it is the source of the dream character of pure memory. Bergson characterized pure memory as dream primarily through its lack of conceptual unity and its dissociation from action. Benjamin understands Proust's weave of memory as introducing distortion through "similarity."[6] The recognition of affinities is the way to the dream in the medium of memory. "The similarity of one thing to another which we are used to, which occupies us in a wakeful state, reflects only vaguely the deeper resemblance of the dream world in which everything that happens appears not in identical [i.e., as self-identical particulars] but in similar guise, opaquely similar one to another.... [Proust] lay on his bed racked with homesickness, homesick for the world distorted in the state of similarity, a world in which the true surrealist face of existence breaks through" (SW 2:240).

For Bergson, memory is brought to bear on acting to varying degrees, but in all cases the exigencies of action make it depend on the external world—that is, memory is subordinated to the demands of the extensive. But there is also a suggestion that the accumulation of my past in the depth of pure memory can be brought to bear on the present. It is as though the deeper I go in the strata of memory, the greater the tension in holding together the mutual permeation of the past in its uniqueness and the action in the present. Memory has the power to contract time into the present. The more the past thus contracted draws the depth of pure memory to the present, the more an action is thereby singularly mine, then the more I can speak of my action as free. The deeper the plane of memory that is contracted into the present, the more I can insert myself freely into the world, independent of the demands of matter. This is not mere "indeterminism" or free choice; freedom is not the capacity to decide arbitrarily at any given point on a course of action. The key to the understanding of freedom is to conceive of it as an act that emerges from one's whole past, as the weight of the whole past comes to bear on one's action. The action would then reflect my life in its uniqueness, so that it is my action, an action that has it source in me rather than in a mere reaction to the demands of the external world on me: "In short we are free when our acts spring from our whole personality, when they express it, when they have that indefinable resemblance to it which one sometimes find between the artist and his work."[7]

For Proust, the contraction of life in writing does not serve the active life. There is nevertheless a concept of actualization that does not take memory as a means for action. Benjamin describes it as an energetic discharge associated with the actualization of the past, yet in no way through a practical orientation to one's surroundings in action. It is what he calls the moment of "rejuvenation" that is internal to Proust's concentration of a lifetime in an instant. In other words, what in Bergson was a free act that expresses the past as a whole becomes in Proust a freeing from the burden of the past left unfulfilled and weighing us down: "Proust has brought off the monstrous feat of letting the whole world age a lifetime in an instant. But this very concentration, in which things that normally just fade and slumber are consumed in a flash, is called rejuvenation" (SW 2:244). This formulation hints at Benjamin's own conception of history; indeed, the past that is one's own is recognized in what is failed and incomplete. But in the medium of memory that draws these remains together as a dream configuration, the past can acquire the character of an image that flashes up, thereby redeeming what in life was unfulfilled. To put it in terms of our earlier account of the image, the sadness of the past is consumed in a flash in the unfolding of the dream image.

And yet, almost insurmountable difficulties stand in the way of translating Proustian and Bergsonian memory to the framework of historical materialism. To start with, the preceding analysis might tempt us to say that "only a poet can be the adequate subject of such an experience" (SW 4:315). Only someone like Proust can weave by way of affinities a whole in the medium of memory. Indeed, as we have seen, Bergson turns at various junctures to aesthetic experience or creativity to suggest the character of the recovery of the inner experience of *durée*. There is, it seems, something like a correspondence between recovering the unity of the depth of experience in memory and the poetic. But need access to this ground of significant life be limited to genius? What exactly can it mean, not only for the gifted individual but for the collective, to have something like the weight of the particular past gathered in the present and actualized? Does such a past retain the form of a dream, or can memory be made into a technique of innervation that awakens the collective to its own present?

The Childhood of Our Present

We speak of different stages of human life, from birth through childhood, adolescence, youth, maturity, aging, and death. These are natural stages, while at the same time they are inflected by the specifically human form of life; they belong to the natural in the human. We do not understand such stages of life merely from the outside; they are sensed as what is our own life. In particular, the character of one's own memory of childhood—that is, one's relation to it in memory—is key to the possibility of a significant life. Put a bit differently, it is in the memory of one's childhood that one can best recognize the weight of the past to be taken up and actualized in the present.

Can we draw a parallel between these ages of life and historical life?[8] Each person has their own childhood, but would it be correct to say that for every historical present there is a past that belongs to it, as its childhood? In conceiving of history as memory, it is not the whole range of the past that is open to the historian to, as it were, pick and choose as an object of investigation. Rather, the historical object must have a bond of life to the present that returns to it.

It is important at the outset not to take Benjamin's account of collective childhood to be literally about the experience of children. It is not as though in order to writes the *Arcades Project* he had to investigate the life of children in mid-century Paris (which in fact he practically never mentions). Nor is the childhood of one's own present to be calculated in terms of such objective measures as the span of a generation, some twenty or thirty years ago (which is obviously not the case of his relation to the arcades).[9] Rather, we need to understand in historical terms what the "immature" is in relation to one's present, and it needs to receive a collective and materialist interpretation. We will return to this question later in the chapter, but in order to provide an initial orientation and avoid misleading pictures, we can point to Benjamin's concern in convolute K with technology and its products. It is the technology that produces the space of life of the past that counts as immature when it is compared to its all-pervasive presence (though not necessarily true incorporation) in the social order of the present. Take, for example, the technology of iron construction, which is already unremarkable as it is used so pervasively in Benjamin's present (say, the 1920s and 1930s). In mid-nineteenth-century Paris, the arcades are among the first constructions made with iron and glass and thus belong to the childhood configuration of Benjamin's present. It is the character of the technologically new and as yet immature social product that we need to understand as we think of the historical childhood of the present.

As we saw in discussing Proust, there is a dream character to the everyday past drawn together in memory. It is not the distinctive experiences of the person but rather the everyday shareable by all, or bearing on the collective experience, that acquires the dream character in memory. This suggests that the dream character belongs to the remembering of the deepest strata of the collective past as such: "A generation's experience of youth has much in common with the experience of dreams. Its historical configuration is a dream configuration. Every epoch has such a side turned toward dreams, the child's side" (A 388 [K1,1]). While every epoch has its childhood in earlier times, Benjamin argues, for earlier generations religious tradition was the medium for the interpretation of the dream character of their past. When, in modernity, tradition is no longer a spiritual force, collectively speaking, there remains the possibility for an individual genius to take hold of and recover that collective childhood. This is one way to describe the importance of Proust for Benjamin. But while much of Proust's elaboration of memory is retained by Benjamin, its translation into the medium of historical memory of the collective requires making it independent of the genius of the writer as well as of the contingencies of life that might awaken involuntary memory. This is implied in Benjamin's seeking a method, a technique, for interpreting the collective childhood.

"What follows here is an experiment [*Versuch*] in the technique [*Technik*] of awakening" (A 388 [K1,1]). Both "experiment" and "technique" suggest the distance Benjamin seeks from the unique achievement of genius—which includes, I might add, his own genius, which cannot be the ground for the image of the past he seeks to compose. Indeed, speaking of a technique and an experiment stresses precisely that it is repeatable and not dependent on the acute, even pathological, sensitivity of the individual. The case of Proust also makes clear that the possibility of recovering the past depends on a chance encounter with a material thing (the madeleine). Can there be a technique for the collective that opens up the possibility of material objects becoming such opportunities?

Awakening and Memory

Dreaming and awakening are the poles by which we are to elaborate the dialectic inherent in historical experience. In so doing we need first to relate not only dreaming but also awakening to memory more clearly. In Bergson, we conceive of the transition from the virtual to the actual in memory as it is brought to bear on the demands of action. Benjamin, putting weight as he does on the dream character of the past, conceives of awakening as key to the actualization of the dream. We shouldn't confuse the actualized with the effective reality of the present; the "automatic" reality of the present is not the actualized memory. Rather, in awakening we open to another present, what Benjamin calls "the Now" or "Now time" (*Jetzt-zeit*), which is not an inert present moment in a continuous conception of time, squeezed between past and future.

What is present has reality to us. But Now time is not the reality determined causally by its past and determining its future. It can only be accessed as the actualization of one's own memory. One might say that awakening to actuality, to the present as Now time, is possible only by going through the dream in memory, as an interpretation and actualization of the dream that is the past: "To pass through and carry out *what has been* in remembering the dream! [*Gewesenes in der Traumerinnerung durrchzumachen!*]" (A 389

[K1,3]). Since the past initially appears to us in historical memory as a dream configuration, the problem is how to characterize the form of memory through which the higher actuality associated with the Now is an awakening from that dream which is our own past. "Remembering and awakening are most intimately related" (A 389 [K1,3]).

Through its relation to memory, awakening becomes for Benjamin the fundamental schema of dialectical reversal. As long as we do not conceive of awakening as the turn of remembrance, dreaming and awakening will remain simply an inert opposition. As in the case of the individual, we go to sleep, we dream, and we awaken for all kinds of reasons (such as the ringing of an alarm clock); there is no internal relation between dreaming and awakening. In order to conceive of a dialectical overcoming of this opposition, we need first to think of the way in which the past, in the medium of memory, acquires a dream character, and then how awakening is only possible from the inner dynamic of remembering the dream: "The new, dialectical method of doing history presents itself as the art of experiencing the present as waking world, a world to which that dream we name the past refers in truth" (A 389 [K1,3]). It is not our present as it is already to which the dream configuration of the past refers but rather to a transformed present: the Now, which belongs to the peculiar teleology of the dream.

Dreaming, Awakening, and the Everyday

We have seen how in Proust's writing Benjamin conceives of an internal relation between the depth of memory, its dream character, and the everyday. This relation of memory to the everyday is also part of the dialectic of memory and awakening: "Indeed, awakening is the great exemplar of memory: the occasion in which it is given to remember what is closest, most banal [*Banalsten*], most obvious" (A 389 [K1,2]). What is probed in historical memory is precisely that dimension of the environment of life which accumulates unconsciously. What we are conscious of are the events, persons, and objective connections between things. Just as with Proust, as well as with Benjamin's own "Berlin Childhood," the attempt is to actualize in memory what was never an intentional object of consciousness, what belongs to the "darkness of the lived moment" (A 389 [K1,2]). The habitual, the banal, is by definition not what is striking in lived experience; it is only in being woven, in memory acquiring the character of a dream configuration, that it is first truly raised and concretized.[10]

Dreams are the vestiges and remains of those everyday surroundings of "experience." But, unlike the remains of the day in the mind that reappear as the individual sleeps that night, these remains of the collective must be understood in material terms as acquiring the dream quality in time, in the afterlife of cultural material. This transformation occurs precisely as materials become remains, left behind after the lifeworld in which they had their functional meaning has disappeared. The banal, the habitual, and the everyday are the gray exterior whose inner lining is the colorful dream.[11] The side of things that is turned toward the dream is the one that is most worn out by time and habit. This opacity of the everyday is illuminated in the dream configuration of the past.

Reality as Dream

When articulating the idea of the past as the dream of the collective, Benjamin is not speaking of a state of mind that might be collectively shared but of the character that the material of the past acquires in its afterlife, in the medium of historical memory. The dream configuration of the past is in no way a subjective state of mind that is "dreamy"; dream *is* the form that the past acquires in historical memory. We have to try as much as possible to get rid of subjective categories in accounting for the dream character of the past and work solely with the expressive character of material content. Note that for the most part Benjamin does not write about contents of consciousness. The collective dream is wholly externalized. The method of the philosophical-historical investigation of the arcades would have to show the historical material as a dream configuration. This is what Benjamin signifies by calling the nineteenth century "a spacetime [*Zeitraum*] (a dreamtime [*Zeit-traum*])" (A 389 [K1,4]). In other words, by the dream character of the past we do not mean to refer simply to the illusions of a period but to the character of the material reality of the past, which is readable (as dreams are interpretable) and hold the secret of its actualization in the Now.

It is in this sense that Benjamin speaks of reality acquiring its "true surrealist face." Benjamin seeks the dream expression of the unconscious that left its trace "in a thousand configurations of life, from enduring edifices to passing fashions" (A 5). The dream lets us remember what belonged to "the darkness of the lived moment." But this is the dream character of a reality: "Fashion, like architecture, inheres in the darkness of the lived moment, belongs to the dream consciousness of the collective" (A 393 [K2a,4]).

Benjamin contrasts the state where all parts of the body work together for practical consciousness with the dream condition, where this unity or convergence is slackened and the dream imagery is the correlate of the "expression" of the organs disengaged from the practical form of consciousness that directs the body: "The sleeper ... sets out on the macrocosmic journey through his own body, and the noises and feelings of his insides, such as blood pressure, intestinal churn, heartbeat and muscle sensation (which for the waking and salubrious individual converge in a steady surge of health) generate, in the extravagantly heightened inner awareness of the sleeper, illusion or dream imagery which translates and accounts for them" (A 389 [K1,4]).

To employ the distinction established in the "Outline of the Psychophysical Problem," in dreaming we do not give expression to the body but to corporeality, through which the deeper currents of nature are sensed. This can be transposed to the situation of the collective, where one may speak of the material basis as the corporeality, the "insides," of the collective. A fundamental distinction must be made between what one may call a functional understanding of the social body, through the primacy of the notion of social practices, and corporeality as the meaningful expressions of the form of life in a "dream-configuration." Similarly, it is not the realization of a capacity of the body that is sought; indeed, the dissociation of the organs from functionality is just what happens when a world "sinks" into the past. What was inconspicuous in the space of life shows its peculiarities when it is encountered as remains of that space of life.

The manifestation of corporeality is correlative with the slackening of the functional unity of the body—namely, when material is no more subjugated to our purposes. This happens as things become outdated and taken out of their life context. The material thereby becomes, in memory, dream imagery "in the interior of the collective": "So likewise for the dreaming collective, which, through the arcades, communes with its own insides. We must follow in its wake so as to expound the nineteenth century—in fashion and advertisement, in building and politics—as the outcome [*Folge*, succession] of its dream visions" (A 389 [K1,4]). Benjamin adds: "Of course, much that is external to the [individual] is internal to the [collective] architecture, fashion—yes, even the weather—are, in the interior of the collective, what the sensoria of organs, the feeling of sickness or health, are inside the individual" (A 389 [K1,5]).

In the corporeality of the collective the currents of (primal) nature can be sensed. The dream configuration belongs to expressions of this primal nature and thus to the dimension of life, which is ruled by the mythical, by the eternal return of the same. To speak of phenomena belonging to the dream space is to conceive of them as nature, as not yet conscious (nature is that which is nonconscious): "So long as they preserve this unconscious, amorphous dream configuration, they are as much natural processes as digestion, breathing, and the like. They stand in the cycle of the eternally selfsame, until the collective seizes upon them in politics and history emerges" (A 390 [K1,5]).

Telos, Waiting, Cunning, Opportunity

The dream character is not a subjective state; it belongs to the objective image of the past. And yet this dream-reality is one that can only be remembered and actualized by that present for which it constitutes its childhood: "The fact that we were children during this time belongs together with its objective image. It had to be this way in order to produce this generation" (A 390 [K1a,2]). In other words, the objective image of the past in memory is internally connected to that past being the childhood of our historical present. Our memory of childhood is the dream that affords us the opportunity for awakening in the present (i.e., transforming the merely inert present into a Now for us). We recognize in the very material of the past, as it is brought together by the historian, distortions that point or signal to a higher measure, to that which "sets them right."[12] To say that time must pass in order for something to become history may sound tautological, but as we have seen, the character of the dream in Bergson, as well as in Proust, is closely related to not acting. Not to act is not mere passivity; rather, Benjamin thinks of it as the dialectical moment of waiting.

We recognize in the dream configuration of the material of the past what we can initially call an inner "telos," or destiny, reserved for the dream. As

Benjamin puts it: "We seek a teleological moment in the context of dreams. Which is the moment of waiting. The dream waits secretly for the awakening" (A 390 [K1a,2]). It is as though that past was waiting for our present (expecting us, as Benjamin puts it in "On the Concept of History"). This formulation raises a question: How is waiting to be understood as a teleological moment? When waiting is for something, it may be possible to conceive of a telos internal to the state of waiting. Yet if it is the past that is waiting for us, so to speak, there is no clear conception of what the waiting is for. If anything, it is only upon awakening and its reversal that we recognize what the past has waited for.

The moment of waiting can be justified by the fact that it is only in the afterlife of the material content that the meaning of the past reveals itself. The time of waiting is the time in which the material content dissociated from the form of life to which it belongs acquires its peculiar, readable character. The relation between waiting and this notion of afterlife is emphasized by Benjamin's referring to this waiting as "playing dead" ("The sleeper surrenders himself to death"). The "afterlife" of meaning and the kind of destruction of living unities that belonged to the functional collective body are essential to the recognition of the inner telos of the dream; for this reason, we cannot strictly speak of a purpose that gives form to the time of waiting.

Surrendering to death so as to escape it is a form of cunning. The idea of cunning in history, which can already be found in Kant and Hegel, may be understood as the recognition of a tendency that is distinct from the purposive directedness that the historical agents take themselves to be advancing (which, as it were, uses the purposive dynamics to advance and reveal another vector), as though ultimately reason in history cannot be advanced directly but only actualized indirectly. And the space of the indirect is, precisely, opened in waiting, for it is only through the distortions of the material of the past in its afterlife that another tendency, another vector pointing to awakening, is sensed. The register of waiting as cunning is made evident by Benjamin: "The coming [*kommenden*] awakening is poised, like the wooden horse of the Greeks, in the Troy of dreams" (A 392 [K2,4]; translation modified).

The notions of waiting, the indirect, and cunning are further related to the concept of opportunity.[13] "The dream waits secretly for the awakening; the sleeper surrenders himself to death only provisionally, waits for the second when he will cunningly wrest himself from its clutches. So, too, the dreaming collective, whose children provide the happy occasion [*Anlaß*] for its own awakening" (A 390 [K1a,2]). The occasion is prepared by the children or by childhood, but it is not taken by the children: it is our present for which that childhood which is our past prepares the opportunity for awakening. The capacity to seize an opportunity is presence of mind. But such presence of mind depends on the layering of experience. The time of "gaining" experience is the time of waiting that builds imperceptibly the capacity to recognize an opportunity. There is an internal connection between the emergence of opportunities, waiting, and indirection. As we saw in Chapter 9, the directedness of purposive action hides opportunities.

The temporal dialectic of opportunity can be understood by means of the types that Benjamin treats in the *Arcades Project*: "Rather than pass time, one must invite it in. To pass time (to kill time, expel it): the gambler. Time spills from his every pore.—To store time as a battery stores energy: the flâneur. Finally, the third type: he who waits. He takes in the time and renders it up in altered form—that of expectation" (A 107 [D3,4]). Indeed, for the gambler experience does not count; his physiological innervation is discharged in the face of the danger of missing an opportunity. The flâneur exemplifies the superposition of experience that makes him see everything as though through a veil of accumulated experiences. He who waits makes that accumulation into what opens into an opportunity to act, turns waiting into expectation, the sensing of a tendency to awaken.

Task of Childhood

How does childhood prepare the occasion for the awakening of the collective?[14] "Task of childhood: to bring the new world into symbolic space. The child, in fact, can do what the grownup absolutely cannot: re-cognize [*wiedererkennen*] the new" (A 390 [K1a,3]). The expression "to recognize the new" is peculiar. We can approach it by recalling that one of the paradigmatic forms of symbolic knowledge is associated early on by Benjamin with Goethe's presentation of primal phenomena. In other words, childhood brings the new into the space of primal nature. Thus, what the child re-cognizes in the new is primal nature. Of course, we think of the new as what wasn't there before, but we can speak of recognizing the new anew by relating it to what was never a specific past that was there before; strictly speaking, primal time does not belong to the advance of time. The recognition anew of the new is bringing the new into the space of the primal.[15]

As we saw in our discussion of Goethe, symbolic space is a space of images: "Every childhood discovers new images in order to incorporate them into the image stock [treasure chest = *schatz*] of humanity" (A 390 [K1a,3]). The main example that Benjamin uses in relating the new and the primal is technological innovations: "For us locomotives have already a symbolic character because we met with them in our childhood. Our children, however, will find this in automobiles, of which we ourselves see only the new, elegant, modern, cheeky side" (A 390 [K1a,3]). It is precisely through the symbolic character acquired by the immature technology that the struggles with primal nature open anew. "The alluring and threatening face of primal history is clearly manifest to us in the beginnings of technology. . . . It is also more intense in technology (on account of the latter's natural origin) than in other domains" (A 393 [K2a,1]).

Primal nature can be revealed in the human space of life through its products, through what might appear to be the most "artificial," namely, the newest products of technology: "Technology is always revealing nature from a new perspective" (A 393 [K2a,1]). This is also true of the social and economic order that is closely related to the emergence of the new technology: "Capitalism was a manifestation of nature [*eine Naturerscheinung*] with which a new dream-filled sleep came over Europe, and through it, a reactivation of mythic powers" (A 391 [K1a,8]; translation modified). Benjamin does not mean to say that capitalism is natural to us but rather that we should treat it as the manifestation of primal nature. It is modern humanity's way of reintroducing the mythical into our existence, a "reactivation of mythic powers."

The Copernican Revolution in History

The character of awakening as actualization is initially developed through Benjamin's appropriation for history of the famous Kantian figure of the Copernican revolution. The immediate parallel with Kant's use of the figure is laid out in the following:

The Copernican revolution in historical perception is as follows. Formerly it was thought that a fixed point had been found in "what has been" and one saw the present engaged in tentatively concentrating the forces of knowledge on this ground. Now this relation is to be overturned, and what has been is to become the dialectical reversal—the flash of awakened consciousness. Politics attains primacy over history. The facts become something that just now first happened to us, first struck us; to establish them is the affair of memory. (A 388 [K1,2])

Recall that for Kant, the Copernican revolution meant that we do not take the object as the ultimate reality that is fixed in itself and around which "orbits" the power of cognition of the subject that attempts to conform itself to the object; rather, it is through self-consciousness and its synthesizing power that the unity of the objective is constituted. A similar structure is now articulated in thinking of the relation between past and present in history. It is not to be assumed that the past, "what has been," in itself, as it were, is our fixed and fundamental measure of reality. Instead, just as with Kant, we must think of the present as internal to the full reality of the past, to the actualization of the past. This is what Benjamin conceives of as the overturning in which "politics attains primacy over history."

This statement is liable to elicit misunderstanding. Recall that the Copernican moment is the idealistic understanding that there is a primacy to the subject in the constitution of the form of the object. We thus need to think carefully how Benjamin uses the same figure to think of a materialist turn in history. But what would a materialistic Copernican revolution be? Even if we assume that there is a place for defining a historical subject in the present through which we can speak of the turn of the past around the present, this cannot be understood in terms of the idealistic constitution of the unity of the object through the forms of unity of the self-consciousness of the subject. This would risk making such a turn merely a call to marshal or use history for political ends. In other words, the reversal must be made possible through a transformation of the material basis. It is precisely what occurs in conceiving of awakening as dependent on the metamorphoses and deformations of the material content through which the dream configures itself.

Reality and Actuality

Our elaboration of the dream character of the nineteenth century depended on the distinction between reality (*Wirklichkeit*) and actuality (or as Benjamin puts it in the essay on surrealism, "the world of universal and integral actualities"). Benjamin's view of history is informed by the idea of actualization of the past. To speak of actualization is to say that the past can acquire a higher degree of reality through the present in which it is actualized. In other words, what Benjamin calls the Copernican revolution in history is not to be conceived of merely in epistemic terms, as though we can come to "know" the past better than that period understood itself. It is the reality of the past that achieves a higher actuality: "In regard to such perception, one could speak of the increasing concentration (integration) of reality, such that everything past (in its time) can acquire a higher grade of actuality than it had in the moment of its existing" (A 392 [K2,3]).

If "reality" is the term we choose to use for what belongs to the effective nexus in space and time, "virtuality" would be the term to characterize the dream configuration of the past that belongs to its higher objective image. The virtual is actualized, and its actualization determines the present as Now time. "[The] founding concept [of historical materialism] is not progress but actualization" (A 460 [N2,2]). Progress can be measured, and such measuring presupposes the continuity and homogeneity of a timeline. In Bergsonian terms, progress is a category of the spatialized model of time. Indeed, Bergson's concept of virtualities precisely seeks to replace the primacy of possibility over reality in our conception of Being; thus actualization is to be distinguished from the realization of a possibility. Moreover, realization suggests a continuity between the possible purpose and the activity that realizes it. This is not the case, however, for actualization: "In order for a part of the past to be touched by actuality [*Aktualität*], there must be no continuity between them" (A 470 [N7,7]; translation modified).

This idea of a higher actualization of the past is crucial in order to distinguish a turn of consciousness from a truly materialist conception in which "the facts become something that just now first happened to us, first struck us [*Die Fakten werden etwas, was uns soeben erst zustieß*]" (A 389 [K1,2]). The striking is not a psychological category; it marks a higher degree of concretion: what was "merely" fact is taken up into a higher actuality in which, as striking, happens to us only now, so that in speaking of the higher concretion of the past in the present, one must be very careful not to reintroduce the language of subjective "interpretation."

The past actualized is the present's own past rather than a mere collection of facts that have happened. Just as the time of one's life is one's own, just as one's life is not considered as a succession of events observed from outside, so authentic historical time is the time of one's own present. The "interest" of the present belongs to the destiny reserved for that past: "It is said that the dialectical method consists in doing justice each time to the concrete historical situation of its object. But that is not enough. For it is just as much a matter of doing justice to the concrete historical situation of the *interest* taken in the object" (A, 391 [K2,3]). But that interest is precisely not something that is consciously formulated by an independent present. That interest, our present interest, is preformed in the object of the past, which we make our own. This peculiar formulation is meant to express the way in which our highest interests must be seen as themselves developing from something unactualized in the object itself. The present does not act on its own (preexisting) interest, nor does it act disinterestedly; rather, its interest is formed in actualizing the past: "And [the concrete historical situation of the *interest* taken in the object] . . . is always so constituted that the interest is itself preformed in that object and, above all, feels this object concretized in itself and upraised from its former being into the higher concretion of now-being [*Jetztsein*] (waking being!)" (A 391[K2,3]).

Actualization does not occur on its own, as though it were a quasi-natural process. As we saw in the discussion of surrealism, there is a concept of actuality that corresponds to awakening from the dream image—namely, the concreteness revealed in the unfolding and consummation of the inner teleology of the dream. It is acting out of the signal of true historical existence to which the dream points. This is why in appropriating the Kantian figure for revolution in history, Benjamin adds, "Politics attains primacy over history."

Image, Actuality, and Action

Many of the expressions used by Benjamin, especially in convolute N, such as "exploding the homogeneous continuum" and the "arrest of time" as well as the "fleeting" character of the dialectical image, have generated the most thoughtless appropriations of Benjamin's writing. Indeed, these expressions tempt us to in effect reify time, in ways that are worse than the most "homogenizing" conception Benjamin attacks. Time is treated as an object one can break, as a movement one can stop, as something disappearing on the horizon. Benjamin deserves a much more careful reading.

The historical object is not *in* time; rather, the virtual time of contents to be actualized is internal to the construction of the historical object. "History is the object [*Gegenstand*] of a construction" (SW 4:395; translation modified). The historical object is a construction of meaning that reveals within itself a telos different from the form in which we represent to ourselves the ends in the elapsing succession of time. In that sense there is no image *of* history (it is not like a photograph cropped out of a landscape).[16]

"The true image of the past flits by. The past can be seized only as an image that, and is never seen again" (SW 4:390). The "passing" character of the dialectical image is not to be understood as something that just passes quickly before the mind's eye. It is not like the passing of a train; the dialectical image flashes up. If we recall our discussion of Proust, this flashing up is the concentration of all that is forgotten and incomplete in an instant and is internal to the actualization of memory in the Now. The dialectical image is passing insofar as the past is being actualized in it. The image passes as all that is failed and incomplete, left behind by the victorious image of the present, is annihilated in being incorporated in the Now.[17]

As we saw in discussing Bergson, we need to distinguish between drawing from memory for the sake of action and the notion of contracting life as a whole in memory in order to give it expression in an act of freedom: "In short we are free when our acts spring from our whole personality, when they express it, when they have that indefinable resemblance to it which one sometimes find between the artist and his work."[18] Similarly, in Benjamin we can conceive of the contraction of historical time in the image: "Our life, it can be said, is a muscle strong enough to contract the whole of historical time" (A 479 [N13a,1]). Through the tension of memory that contracts that historical past, the present is brought to a critical state: "The materialist presentation of history leads the past to bring the present into a critical state" (A 471 [N7a,5]). Crisis is a moment of decisiveness in the face of danger; it is possible only through the contraction of one's whole past into the present moment: The possibility of action depends on the present taking up the image of the past as its own, and thereby as what determines the emerging lines of force of the present.

Of course, we can miss the opportunity to make the past pass over into our present. We can fail to construe our position as critical, to charge it with urgency. Decisiveness is possible only as the present recognizes a simple and massive state in what may otherwise appear to be ambiguous multiplicity: "All historical knowledge can be represented in the image of balanced scales, one tray of which is weighted with what has been and the other with knowledge of what is present. Whereas on the first the facts assembled can never be too humble or too numerous, on the second there can be only a few heavy, massive weights" (A 468 [N6,5]). If decisive action is owning the past (as a whole), catastrophe is failing to do so, leaving things as they are—that is, remaining with the hellish character of one's collective life (A 473 [N9a,1]). Conversely, to be decisively involved with the historical object, to face the crisis and its attendant danger, is to conceive of actualization as rescue. The contraction and simplification of the past that makes the present into a Now of actualization constitutes the decisive rescue of the past: "An object of history is that through which knowledge is fulfilled [*vollzogen*] as the object's rescue" (A 476 [N11,4]; translation modified).

TWELVE

First and Second Nature in Art

"There is no more insipid and shabby antithesis," Benjamin writes, "than that which reactionary thinkers like Klages try to set up between the symbol-space of nature and that of technology. To each truly new configuration of nature—and, at bottom, technology is just such a configuration—there corresponds new 'images'" (A 390 [K1a,3]). What would it be to conceive of technology as a configuration of nature? How does a renewed understanding of it bear on the political and the organization of society? These dimensions of technology are far from immediately evident. Benjamin suggests that "only now are we beginning to guess what forms—and they will be determinative for our epoch—lie hidden in machines" (A 155 [F2a,5]).

In thinking about a new configuration of nature opened by technology, the consideration of art has a prominent place. Indeed, in asking about the transformation that technology brings to art, we can get a premonition of the natural forms dormant in technology. Art can delineate, as it were, the tendency through which the subjugation of man by technology can be turned into an interplay with nature inherent in the technological apparatus. In order to develop these questions, I will offer an analysis of section VI in the second version of Benjamin's famous essay "The Work of Art in the Age of Its Technological Reproducibility," which develops and unfolds the implications of the polarity between cult value and exhibition value. In the second part of the chapter, I will suggest how new forms of nature are opened by the technology of photography and film and the implications of this potential of the medium for the transformation of the political.

Cult Value and Exhibition Value

Photography "make[s] the difference between technology and magic through and through historically variable." The historical variation at issue is closely related to a shift in the balance between two poles of the work of art, which Benjamin calls "cult value" and "exhibition value." The magical dimension of art is to be understood initially in its relation to cult. Art retains this bond even in its profane forms, in the so-called cult of beauty. The characteristic feature of the pole of cult is self-occlusion, while that of the pole of exhibition is shining forth. Cult value tends toward secrecy (mystery), while exhibition value tends to full perceptibiility. The power of the (auratic) work of art demands the balance between these two poles internal to its essence. It expresses the veiled character of the shining forth of beauty: it shines forth *as* what holds something secret, or its shining forth is distinct from mere perception by emerging out of what appears to us inaccessible.

We can also formulate this polarity in terms of the concepts of distance and nearness, which provide another set of terms for the definition of the aura: the self-occluding is that which is unreachable, distant, whereas the exhibitable is that which comes toward the viewer and provides a sense of the near. In the auratic work of art, we have a balance of nearness and distance at play. The aura of the work is the unique apparition of distance, however near it may be. The shift that Benjamin characterizes through the decline of the auratic in art is correlative with the production of a new division between the two poles, or more precisely, it is primarily an intensification of the pole of nearness. Its symptomatic expression is "the desire of the present-day masses to 'get closer' to things." This quantitative intensification is the basis of a qualitative transformation of the very concept of art and its separation from inherence in the form of cult.

Benjamin's initial example of the prevalence of the cultic pole in primal forms of art is drawn from the ritual function of prehistoric cave paintings. These are located in the depth of caves and need not be exhibited in order to play a role, say, in hunt rituals. The ritual object acquires its cult value by inhering in the heart of a practice. The form of that practice can be seen as a technique, broadly conceived, that determines the production and reproduction of that value. The technique serves to generate the different aspects of cultic existence and, as it were, opens the space of significance for an object to be venerated. The technique can include, for instance, instructions that serve for the production of the cult object, formulas determining the form of service of the person toward the cult object, or the formulation of practices for using the cult object in service of the person. These should not be taken as merely inert instructions to be followed mechanically; rather, since they belong to the sphere of ritual, we must conceive of them as facilitating the mimetic identification with that object, through which it reveals its utmost significance.

One may establish very general analogies between these technologies of ritual and "practices" in the realm of traditional art, suggesting thereby how to approach the presence of ritual in the secularized cult of beauty: The production of the cult object parallels the forming of the work of art by the artist; the form of service parallels the preservation of art in tradition; and the practices of use of the object have a parallel in the form of the experience of art.

First and Second Technology

In seeking the fundamental transformations of this space through photographic or cinematic technology, Benjamin is well aware that he is operating at a highly abstract level. Indeed, how else could he bring together and place in opposition cave paintings and photography or film? Yet, as he puts it, this distance in time doesn't mean they cannot be related dialectically. It is this very fundamental dialectical opposition that is initially at issue in the distinction that Benjamin proposes between a first and a second technology. This distinction, while fundamental to understanding the transformation of art with the advent of the new media, must first be elaborated in its most general scope, as it plays a role in the organization of life. The cultic aspect of the first technology is articulated in terms of a specific character of ritual, related to the prevalence in it of the mimetic—that is, the bodily involvement of human beings in the technology: "[It makes] the maximum possible use of human beings"; conversely, "the [second technology] reduces their use to the minimum" (SW 3:107).

The significance of this opposition is traced to a disturbing and extreme context: ritual that is at the heart of first technology makes use of human beings in human sacrifice. The polar opposite is exemplified by remote-controlled aircraft that have no crew. I will not speculate on what led Benjamin to choose this latter example; what is important is that the second technology is not free from violence, even though that violence wreaked upon human beings is correlative with the disappearance of human beings from the technology. Military drones used nowadays might be one realization of this idea.[1] More to the point, one might think here of operations of mechanization inherent in modern technology that gradually do away with the presence of human beings in the work process.

This general contrast is gradually going to be translated into the character of art. While not yet ready to go into details, we should note briefly how the unified human living presence is internal to the traditional forms of art and how it tends to disappear in the age of technological reproducibility: Think, for instance, how such unified living presence is essential to the mimetic behavior of the actor and the mimetic identification of the audience in theatrical experience. Even though movies are of human beings, that unity of the bodily presence, as will become clear, disappears from the cinematic experience.

A second fundamental distinction between the two technologies is expressed as follows: "The 'Once and for all' [*einmal ist allemal*] . . . [belongs to] the first technology (it deals with irreparable [*niewidergutzumachen*] lapses [*Verfehlung* = transgression, offense] or the eternally representative sacrificial death [*den ewig stelltvertretenden Opfertod*]. The 'Once is as good as never' [*einmal ist keinmal*] . . . [belongs to] the second technology (it operates with experiments and its untiring variation of the experiment arrangement)" (SW 3:107; translation modified). The reference to the irreparable offense relates the ritual context of the "once and for all" to the space of myth, where offense and guilt can only be atoned for by sacrificial death. Benjamin identifies the "Once is as good as never" with the structure of work: "With work, 'Once is as good as never' comes into its own" (SW 2:739). What is stressed here is the consideration of work insofar as it is parceled and not an activity with an aim, with the complete product in view. It is inherently repetitive and composed of the accumulation of small gestures. This character of work will only be intensified in the development of the technologies of production, and it carries with it its own kind of violence—for example, in the extreme division of labor and the alienation that results from it.

Thinking of the parallel with art, we can identify the "Once and for all" with the prevalence of uniqueness, authenticity, and eternal value—that is, with the characteristics of the auratic work. "Once is as good as never" is the best fit for the cinematic work, which is constituted by the principle of montage, which allows endless variation in the process of "assembly." "The finished film is the exact antithesis of a work created at a single stroke," Benjamin writes. "It is assembled from a very large number of images and image sequences that offer an array of choices to the editor." Then he adds, "The film is therefore the artwork most capable of improvement" (SW 3:109). But the parallel extends even further: "It cannot be overlooked that the assembly line, which plays such a fundamental role in the process of production, is in a sense represented by the filmstrip in the process of consumption. Both came into being at roughly the same time. The social significance of the one cannot be fully understood without that of the other" (SW 3:94). The question we wish to consider is whether art can take up and transform into valuable experience what appears to be a source of alienation, say, in the assembly line.

First and Second Nature

Human development is sometimes conceived of as the constitution of a second nature out of the "material" of the first nature. Starting from his understanding of the first and second technologies, Benjamin develops a somewhat different concept of the relation between the two: "The first technology really sought the mastery [*Beherrschung*] of nature, whereas the second aims rather at an interplay [*zusammenspiel*] between nature and humanity" (SW 3:107). Mastery of nature is not to be understood here in terms of instrumental reason and its capacity to dominate nonhuman nature and use it for man's purposes. Since what is at the origin of the discussion of the first technology is ritual or cult value, we should ask in what way ritual is a form of mastery of nature, even when the technique used is at its most primitive.

First nature must be understood here as elemental nature, nature in man, or that nature which pertains as a whole to human existence. For the individual the presence of elemental nature is most evident in the struggles that determine human life as a whole, namely, in the problems of love and death.

It follows that mastery here does not in any way mean "overcoming"—for what would count as overcoming love and death in human existence? Rather, there is a renewed task of mastery associated with the ineradicable presence of primal nature. In other words, the problem of the mastery of elemental nature is humanity's struggle with myth. The mythical ground of human life emerges through the "earliest attempts" at the mastery of nature. Tragedy exemplifies these struggles to master first nature, in which the first technology, ritual, and human sacrifice come together. But these struggles are just as present in the most cultivated circles of existence—say, in the form of love, as depicted in Goethe's novel *Elective Affinities* and elsewhere.[2]

The second technology opens the field of second nature: "The origin of the second technology lies at the point where, by an unconscious ruse, human beings first began to distance themselves from nature. It lies, in other words, in play" (SW 3:107). Again, we should not understand distancing as "leaving behind": the problems of the first nature are never left behind. What is at issue is gaining some freedom from the struggle with elemental nature. Play or interplay is a form of detachment from first nature.[3] While this concept has obvious relevance for the sphere of aesthetics, here we will explore its fundamental character through its role in mimetic identification. In a footnote to the "Work of Art" essay, Benjamin formulates a duality inherent in the very idea of mimetic behavior. When we say that the mime "makes himself similar," there are really two claims being made, which differ only slightly, yet significantly, from one another: "The mime only seemingly acts what he acts [*Der Nachmachende macht, was er macht, nur scheinbar*]. . . . The mime presents his object as a semblance [*Der Nachmachende macht seine Sache scheinbar*] (SW 3:127; translation modified).

In the first formulation the emphasis is on the act: the mime doesn't really but only seemingly acts, playacts. In the second, the emphasis is on the object: what is produced has the character of semblance. This duality is almost imperceptible in the first object of the mimetic faculty, the body, one's own body, since it is both the acting and the object (compare how they are distinct, say, in drawing). The separation of the first from the second is precisely that "unconscious ruse" which detaches us from nature: "Thus we encounter the polarity informing mimesis. In mimesis, tightly interfolded like cotyledons, slumber the two aspects of art: semblance and play" (SW 3:137).

It is clear that for Benjamin semblance and play constitute a polarity closely related to that between cult value and exhibition value: "Neither the concept of semblance nor that of play is foreign to traditional aesthetics; and to the extent that the two concepts of cult value and exhibition value are latent in the other pair of concepts at issue here, they say nothing new" (SW 3:127). It is the sense of emanation of a higher totality in beauty (be it inwardness of soul or the unity of idea) that is the origin of its power. Yet beauty is essentially semblance inasmuch as its truth is one only in being veiled. This veiling internal to the truthfulness of the work is precisely the self-occluding. In other words, we have a relation between semblance and the predominance of the pole of cult value, that is, the struggle with primal nature in human existence.

"As is well known, Schiller assigned play a crucial role in his aesthetic, while Goethe's was determined by a passionate interest in semblance" (SW 3:137). Benjamin's mention of Goethe's passionate interest in semblance is a clear indication that he has in mind his reading of *Elective Affinities*—the character of the beautiful semblance as the essence of Ottilie, for example, and how it is related to the orders of myth and fate in the novel.[4] The mention of Schiller in relation to the pole of play makes sense given the way in which Schiller brings into the space of the constitution of culture Kant's idea of the play of the faculties in aesthetic judgment.

Translated into the distinction between semblance and play, the decay of the aura is understood as a withering of semblance and the correlative "huge gain in the scope for play [*Spiel-Raum*]; in film, the element of semblance has yielded its place to the element of play" (SW 3:127; translation modified). We cannot assume that we know what this play element is in the space opened by technology for the work of art (whether, for instance, it is opposed to the space of work). Indeed, later in the essay Benjamin explicitly argues that a certain traditional idea of play, which is traceable to Kant's reflective play of the imagination in aesthetic judgment, is not operative in our relation to photography and film.

Second Nature, Play, and the Political

Benjamin claims that with the transformation introduced by technological reproduction into art "the whole social function of art is revolutionized. Instead of being founded on ritual, it is based on a different practice: politics" (SW 3:106). It is this bearing of art on the practice of politics that we must clarify in terms of the various distinctions established.

The elaboration of the concepts of the first and second technologies initially makes no specific reference to the sphere of art. One can speak of technology as it is deployed in society and human life at large as well as in the organization of society. The very existence of the first and second technologies does not imply that the tasks and problems set for humanity, the mastery of nature and the interplay with nature, are in any way resolved. The technologies may function on behalf of the subjugation of human beings to distorted conditions of existence that demand constant sacrifice. Take, for instance, the discussion in "Critique of Violence," where the legal order in the state would belong to the second technology yet serves to retain the hold of mythical violence over bare life, the ritual form that constantly demands sacrifice. Similarly, the economic order of capitalism is an organization of the second nature, through the second technology, and yet Benjamin's investigation of the logic of capitalism as religion brings out its ritual character, how it is an expression of primal nature in human existence: "Capitalism was a natural phenomenon... a reactivation of mythic forces" (A 391 [K1a,8]).

"The problem of the second nature, the social and the technological ones, must be very close to resolution before those of the first—*love and death*—can be distinguished even in outline" (SW 3:134; my emphasis). The second technology can be so deployed as to hide the distorted forms in which the first technology determines our relation to elemental nature; it buries the very possibility of facing these questions. We cannot even recognize what we lack in relation to the truly vital struggles. It is only by reopening the interplay of the second technology with nature that the dominion of myth is challenged and one can begin to address those vital tasks: "For the more the collective makes the second technology its own, the more keenly individuals belonging to the collective feel how little they have received of what was due them under the dominion of the first technology" (SW 3:124).[5]

One can speak, then, of two tendencies or tasks that are interdependent and that each define an ideal of their own—Benjamin also refers to a dual utopianism. The first is the striving for happiness that is furthered by appropriating the second technology; the second is "another utopian will" that engages the first nature, that is, the struggles with "love and death" (SW 3:134).[6] It is only through the progressive assimilation of the second technology that the interplay with nature is made possible. And it is only through this interplay with social and technological forces that the problem of the mastery of elemental nature can be addressed and the horizon of the utopia of the first nature be reopened. Benjamin expresses this in a beautiful figure in a footnote: "This second technology is a system in which the mastering of elementary social forces is a precondition for the play [*das Spiel*] with natural forces. Just as a child who has learned to grasp stretches out its hand for the moon as it would for a ball, so humanity, in its efforts at innervation, sets its sights as much on currently utopian goals as on goals within reach" (SW 3:124).

Nature at the Heart of Technology

In the second part of this chapter, I want to briefly indicate the implications of the various distinctions made (cult value vs. exhibition value, first technology vs. second technology, first nature vs. second nature, semblance and play) for the interpretation of some of the more important themes of Benjamin's essay. My reading of the essay will be guided by the following questions: How does the technological work of art reveal tendencies that are submerged and distorted by the social organization of technological forces? How can these new forms indicate tendencies for the transformation of social existence? What are the possibilities offered by such art for revolutionizing the hold of the cultic character of art, the prevalence of such notions as eternal value and mystery, by transforming the interplay with the second technology? And finally, how does the prevalence of exhibition value in art bring it together with the practice of politics.

To start with, let us consider the simplest explanation of what the transformation of the respective weights of cult value and exhibition value in the unity of the work of art comes to: "With the emancipation of specific artistic practices from the service of ritual, the opportunities for exhibiting their products increase" (SW 3:106). Ritual is identified with the sense of the self-occluding, with mystery and distance. It is intimately related to the uniqueness of the object of ritual but just as much to the uniqueness of the place and time it is worshipped. To take a simple example, the statue of the god must be in the temple; it cannot be exhibited outside of it or moved around. With reproduction technologies, opportunities to "exhibit" the work are multiplied, and with that the sense of its uniqueness, of the particular way it is woven into space and time, disappears. But we might further ask, How does this transform our very sense of place and time? This is first made evident in the essay in the relation of photography to the spaces of the city.

SURROUNDINGS AND LIVING PRESENCE

Recall that the second technology is characterized in terms of how it reduces the role of human beings in the technology. This is evident in the contrast Benjamin establishes between two tendencies in early photography: on the one hand, the last glimmers of the aura, the peculiar beauty of portraits (which in part has to do with the long exposure of the subject); on the other hand, "the human being withdraws from the photographic image" (SW 3:108) in the streets empty of any human subjects in the photography of Atget (which can likewise be the result of long exposure in an environment in which human beings are constantly moving).[7] Regarding the latter, Benjamin notes that " it has justly been said that [Atget] photographed them like scenes of crimes. A crime scene, too, is deserted; it is photographed for the purpose of establishing evidence" (SW 3:108).

This comparison has a dual significance. In the first place, it indicates the way a crime scene is subject to investigation and is investigated in detail. What is investigated is "singled out," isolated as a trace from its surroundings. A landscape by Rembrandt cannot be investigated in that sense, and details that count as significant in it are so only in relation to the unity of the painting. Moreover, what is investigated in the photograph are traces of reality; only for this reason are its details "evidence." Photography is *of* the world, whereas a painting is a world of its own.[8] But there is another aspect to the comparison: a crime scene is emptied of living presence in order not to destroy the evidence, and thus the surroundings are what remains.[9] A painting of a street without human presence might be uncanny (as in the paintings of Giorgio de Chirico), but it is not experienced as remains. The viewer of a photograph belongs to another time than does the reality photographed, which is past and therefore remains. One might say with Benjamin that the photograph requires captions, since it does not have the life that gives it its face of immediate meaning. The presence of death, of course, also contributes to the force of portraits of loved ones, but in holding to the human figure, they remain, as it were, with sentimental sadness, without providing the field of brooding in which melancholy fastens on objects and matter.

"With Atget, photographic records begin to be evidence in the historical trial [*Prozess*]. This constitutes their hidden political significance" (SW 3:108). What is the guilt associated with this trial for which we seek evidence? And why is it of political significance? Wouldn't a "political trial" involve photographs of violence perpetrated on human beings? And yet those streets are empty of human presence. It might be that the guilt at issue is precisely mythical guilt, or the expression of the hold of myth on a form of life. And it will be evident, as Benjamin puts it, in the traces of "a thousand configurations of life, from enduring edifices to passing fashions" (A 5). It is not the human presence that will serve as evidence in the revelation of that dream from which the historical materialist seeks to awaken but precisely material "remains."

Of course, we will find a new presence of the human figure as well. The significant presentation of the human figure in traditional art depended on the sense the work provided of a whole and undivided unity, emanating the unity of the soul, as it were.[10] In "Experience and Poverty" Benjamin suggests how even the new art of Paul Klee signals a shift from interiority expressed in the body, preeminently the face, to an exterior that relates to an interior in the same way as an engine to the body of a car. This "engineering" quality of Klee's drawings is related to what is produced through the automatism of photography. Significantly, Benjamin speaks in this context of the rejection of "the traditional solemn, noble image of man, festooned with all the sacrificial offerings of the past" (SW 2:733). In other words, it is a transformation correlative to doing away with cult value and the deformed demands of mythical nature for human sacrifice.

The disappearance in photography of human presence as an expression of inwardness also takes place in photography and can be further developed in terms of Benjamin's contrast between the theater actor and the film actor. Playing a role in theater requires the living presence of the actor. Our sense of the value of a performance depends on that presence, on the actor's mimetically identifying with a role and projecting it as a living unity for the audience to partake in that mimetic dimension. But it is through the montage of fragments of the body and behavior that the screen presence is constituted: "The stage actor identifies himself with a role. The film actor very often is denied this opportunity. His performance is by no means a unified whole but is assembled from many individual performances" (SW 3:112). The unity of the living person disappears from our experience of film, as the camera need not respect that unity of the body in constructing a photographic image or cinematic sequence of images. The theater actor's movements onstage are immediately part of the unity of the artwork, while the filming of the actor is only material for a thoroughly mediated construction of the cinematic work. The film actor, one could say, is denied the possibility of mimetic identification (or partakes of the radical transformation of the mimetic faculty).

Finally, think of the relation between the film presence of the actor and their surroundings. The "eye" of the camera does not distinguish between animate and inanimate, person and surroundings. To take an example from Benjamin's "Little History of Photography," the wrinkles on Schelling's face are treated just like the creases of his coat. This opens the possibility of certain genres or forms of film that make manifest a fit not of action and its fulfillment but of behavior with surroundings. This fit with the world demands the indistinction of inner and outer (or an existence that is devoid of the psychology of interiority). The precision that film brings into that sense of fit is what a figure such as Charlie Chaplin brings out. Every encounter, while not a success, is precisely fitting to his character. This may be why in describing him Benjamin speaks of his mode of being in surroundings: "He was the first to inhabit the new fields of action opened up by film—the first occupant of the newly built house. This is the context in which Chaplin takes on historical significance" (SW 3:118).

TEST PERFORMANCE AND EXHIBITION VALUE

In film, the element of play becomes dominant and the beautiful semblance is on the decline. The "once is as good as never" experiment-quality of film production locates it in a space of potentially inexhaustible variation. One can also speak of an experimental approach to the construction of the cinematic presence. Not only is that presence constituted by a series of "small experiments," but each is repeatable or can be the subject of endless variation. This is initially evident to Benjamin in the increase of the use of raw materials in relation to the final product.

The notion of experiment belongs in the essay together with the idea of testing. The possibility of testing assumes the dissection of behavior into measurable parameters. The more technology structures and divides the work process, the more performance is capable of being tested and measured. Testability in the workplace goes hand in hand with the increased division of labor, and therefore it inherently goes against the possibility of exhibiting the total social character of production. The more testing is introduced into human experience, the less can experience exhibit or present its conditions of possibility in specific instances of productive activity. Now, what would it be for film to incorporate this state of production and reverse it dialectically in consumption?

The notion of quality testing is carried over from the space of work, where performance testing is central to the "screen test" of the actor, their performance for the camera. The screen test tests the performance of the actor, but more specifically it tests how the actor appears onscreen. The key to the dialectical reversal, then, is that the screen test makes the capacity to be exhibited that which itself is to be tested. "Film," Benjamin writes, "makes test performance exhibitable, by making a test of exhibitability [*Ausstellbarkeit*] itself. The film actor performs not in front of an audience but in front of an apparatus. It . . . is a test performance of the highest order" (SW 3:111; translation modified). In other words, the film actor is open to testing; they relinquish the unity of auratic, unified theatrical presence and submit to the cinematic technology. Benjamin describes this exposure to the cinematic technology as inflicting a division of the whole living presence. The actor suffers the fragmentation of their bodily presence by the camera or the editing process in ways that, structurally at least, are analogous to the alienation produced by the extreme division of labor.

But since what is tested is how the actor appears onscreen, the actor also reveals that which testing procedures in general occlude—exhibitability. The actor excels precisely by taking testing by the technology of film into themselves and reversing its significance in their radiant cinematic presence. Their excelling at being shown means that they exhibit a coherence of another order, or that they are, as it were, capable of integrating the discontinuity inflicted by the cinematic technology into a new, intense bodily presence:

"To accomplish [this test performance]," Benjamin writes, "is to preserve one's humanity in the face of the apparatus. Interest in this performance is widespread" (SW 3:111).

If one calls the second technology in its social use "the apparatus," the performance of the actor allows us to envisage their cinematic presence as a triumph over the apparatus: "The majority of city dwellers, throughout the workday in offices and factories, have to relinquish their humanity in the face of an apparatus. In the evening these same masses fill the cinemas, to witness the film actor taking revenge on their behalf not only by asserting *his* humanity (or what appears to them as such) against the apparatus, but by placing that apparatus in the service of his triumph" (SW 3:111).

Initially it may seem that Benjamin construes an opposition or simple antagonism between the human and the technological apparatus, such that the human triumphs over the technology. But the last sentence quoted above makes clear the dialectical moment, as the technological apparatus is put in the service of this triumph, so that humanity does not gain the upper hand by now using the instrument for its own ends. Rather, the dialectical reversal is to be recognized in the way technology yields new possibilities for the significant presentation of the human figure, a new field for freedom and play.[11]

EXPERTISE AND PLAYING ONESELF

Let us take another example that Benjamin discusses, namely, the presence of performance tests in sports. Here testing is initially testing one's own capacities and is therefore in some sense a testing of what belongs to nature (in the human being). Of course, we have in sports the dimension of competition and thus of winning and losing. And yet what is significant in the performance test in sports is, once more, the relation of it to its public and to the public's judgment or expertise. The sense of expertise in the sports public is prevalent to a degree that is hard to match; it hardly exists, for example, in traditional training for the appreciation of a work of art—in part because, despite the difference in levels between the athlete and the spectator, the public can recognize its own activity in that of competing sports players. One might say that the difference is a matter of degree rather than of a qualitative character.

This idea of a difference of degree rather than kind is even clearer in film, where the separation between audience and actor loses its absolute character;

indeed, one can speak here of everyone's having in principle a claim on being portrayed in film. This does not only pertain to films that do not use professional actors; rather, Benjamin suggests that the very concept of acting is transformed: "Expert observers have long recognized that, in film, 'the best effects are almost always achieved by "acting" as little as possible. . . .' The development, according to Rudolf Arnheim, . . . has been toward 'using the actor as one of the "props," chosen for his typicalness and . . . introduced in the proper context'" (SW 3:112). When Benjamin speaks here of choosing the actor "for his typicalness," it might seem to indicate a tendency of film toward the stereotypical, and yet it is precisely because the reality of the actor's body is investigated by the camera that what we have is a peculiar experience of the utterly individual in the typical. It is as though film is precisely a medium for the preeminent presentation of character (in the sense discussed in Chapter 5). We may speak here of the singular unity of the individual actor with their type, when it is understood that the actor does not project their role but rather that the "reality" recognized in the particularity of their body is made possible only through the mediation of the inquisitive technology. (In this sense the example that Benjamin gives, of Dreyer's *Jeanne d'Arc*, is indeed a reflection on the camera's assuming the role of the Inquisition. Falconetti, originally a theater actor, is more than a martyr type, not because of her theatrical acting skills but rather through the concentrated focus of the camera on her face. Similarly, the judges of the Inquisition, while no doubt being types, were each chosen for the singularity of their bodily presence for the camera, which is not a matter of playacting.)[12]

Let us say, then, that the zero degree of acting is just being oneself. Yet Benjamin claims that film opens the possibility of playing oneself. At first glance, it would hardly make sense to speak of "playing oneself." In the traditional idea of acting, one plays a role. One can be oneself or fail to do so in certain situations ("Just be yourself" is a way to encourage someone who is anxious in a job interview, for example). But it is precisely the distance introduced by the technological apparatus that opens the space of playing oneself without playing a role. Certainly, watching people be themselves in the ordinary surroundings of life is not particularly rewarding; it is precisely the technology that introduces the "estrangement" that enables us to see the ordinary in another way, without having to play a role different from it.[13]

THE NATURAL IN THE TECHNOLOGICAL

Now we can begin to determine how film technology ushers in new forms of nature, how "it is another nature which speaks to the camera as compared to the eye" (SW 4:266). Initially our analysis rehearses and develops the way in which the involvement of the technological apparatus saturates the product. Indeed, the work of art has always offered the sense of a higher reality than our ordinary experience and perception; we may speak here of the way in which art introduces new forms of perception, even a new sense of the natural in our existence. But what is radically different in film is that this presence of nature appears at the heart of the use of equipment. It is truly the technology that gives us access to the new forms of nature: "*In the film studio the apparatus has penetrated so deeply into reality that a pure view of that reality, free of the foreign body of equipment, is the result of a special procedure—namely the shooting by the specially adjusted photographic device and the assembly of that shot with others of the same kind*. The equipment-free aspect of reality has here become the height of artifice, and the vision of immediate reality the Blue Flower in the land of technology" (SW 3:115).

Indeed, an important aspect of the significance of this moment is the realization that it is the technology that allows this new experience of free nature. Our understanding of the significance of technology is itself transformed: "Hence, the presentation of reality in film is incomparably the more significant for people today, since it provides the equipment-free aspect of reality they are entitled to demand from a work of art, and does so precisely on the basis of the most intensive interpenetration of reality with equipment" (SW 3:116).[14]

THE EVERYDAY AND THE OPTICAL UNCONSCIOUS

In the broadest terms, nature conceived of as the other of consciousness is unconscious. The revelation of nature anew by photographic technology is characterized by Benjamin as the opening of our access to an optical unconscious. The Freudian unconscious is closely related to the functions of repression and defense. For Benjamin, this defensive posture of the mind is central to the transformation of experience in modernity. What constitutes a defense is consciousness itself. Consciousness is thus primarily identified as a defense mechanism whose role is to parry shock. The neutralization of shock is achieved by isolating experiences from the rest of the psychic apparatus and giving them the character of information (a time and place as well as a readily available meaning articulable in, say, a caption). One could speak in this context of existing in a "prison of consciousness" that "closes relentlessly around us," so that subjectivity, far from being the source of expressive creativity, becomes precisely what is to be overcome. The optical unconscious is then the opening of a new freedom of imagination: "Our bars and city streets, our offices and furnished rooms, our railroad stations and our factories seemed to close relentlessly around us. Then came film and exploded this prison-world with the dynamite of the split second, so that now we can set off calmly on journeys of adventure among its far flung debris" (SW 2:17; translation modified).

It is a nonsubjective unconscious that is opened by technology and is revealed in what is closest to us, in the ordinary (and, in that sense, in the space in which no one is more of an expert than another). It is the very "necessities of our lives" that are made recognizable by way of the productive alienation of the technological apparatus: "Film furthers insight into the necessities of our lives by its use of close-ups, by its accentuation of hidden details in familiar objects, and by its exploration of commonplace milieux through the ingenious guidance of the camera; . . . it manages to assure us of a vast and unsuspected field of play [*Spielraum*]" (SW 3:117; translation modified).

HABIT AND DISTRACTION

We have seen how Benjamin relates the prevalence of shock in experience to the defensive presence of consciousness that sterilizes experience for poetry. The new possibilities of film are evident in part in how shock can be incorporated into art. In such movements as Dadaism and to some extent surrealism, shock is internalized by giving art the task of shocking, of scandalizing the bourgeois audience. But these forms of art still operate with a moralistic conception of their superiority to the bourgeois mentality; they cannot make shock into a productive aspect of the experience of the masses. In film, shock is internal to the technological conditions of existence of the medium (it is released, as Benjamin puts it, from its moral wrapping). The environment of shock can be transformed in film into a training field for new perceptual habits and new forms of apperception.

Shock in film is something that Benjamin identifies with the very succession of images that allows no reflective incorporation of experience. It is thus quite similar to the diagnosis of the shock character of *Erlebnis*: "*Film is the art form corresponding to the pronounced threat to life in which people live today*. It corresponds to profound changes in the apparatus of apperception, changes that are experienced on the scale of private existence by each passerby in big-city traffic, and on the scale of world history by each fighter against the present social order" (SW 3:132). But what would it be to incorporate this mode of experience into the appreciation of art? It would demand more than anything the transformation of what appreciation comes to.

Technology is characterized by Benjamin in terms of the interplay of man and nature. Art in general and more particularly film has a central role as a training ground for this interplay. To recognize this demands the transformation of the traditional form of appreciation of art. The impossibility of "reflection" when confronted by the onslaught of images put together in film can lead us to relegate film to the status of thoughtless distraction. In other words, the traditional idea of appreciation is closely bound up with reflection (as in Kant's reflective judgment). Reflection demands concentration, which in effect is a form of being absorbed in and by the work of art.

Concentration and distraction form, as Benjamin puts it, a dialectical contrast to be overcome if we are to conceive a radically new way of critically appreciating film. The first step in thinking through such an overcoming is to formulate the difference between the absorption of the single viewer in a work of art (entering it, as though it becomes one's world) and the way in which Benjamin speaks of the masses absorbing film into them. This is a peculiar idea, both because it articulates the experience from the start as that of a mass rather than that of an individual, and because of the way in which the effect of film is compared to the influence that our surroundings have on us.

The absorption of the environment should not be thought of as the experience of an intentional object of consciousness.[15] In that regard, it is not surprising that Benjamin turns to architecture as the archetype of such an absorption of art into mass existence. Architecture is not conceived of here as something to contemplate (as a tourist) but rather something one absorbs through "use." Benjamin speaks here of the distinction between the visual and the tactile, that is, what is understood, broadly speaking, through bodily behavior (in use). But even more important, it is an understanding achieved through habit—habit here not as characterizing that which lacks understanding but rather as a form of understanding, even extremely discerning understanding, that is evinced even in distraction. It is not concentration and attentiveness that are central to habit; even a distracted person can acquire habits. We may even say that a precondition for a behavior's becoming habit is precisely the capacity to perform it in a distracted state of mind.

The dramatic transformation of the environment of life associated with modernity brings up anew the task of adaptation of the forms of apperception to the social apparatus. Benjamin makes clear that such a task can only be faced through the formation of habits: "For the tasks which face the human apparatus of perception at historical turning points cannot be performed solely by optical means—that is, by way of contemplation. They are mastered gradually—taking their cue from tactile reception—through habit" (SW 4:268). How are we to develop such habits, and what is the role of art in fostering the kind of distraction productive of habits? Here Benjamin adopts and transforms Schiller's idea of the aesthetic education of mankind. This does not refer to the form of reflective play through which Kant conceives of the mediating character of art; instead, it is an idea of training, in line with other instances of expertise, tests, and so forth: "Reception in distraction—the sort of reception which is increasingly noticeable in all areas of art and is a symptom of profound changes in apperception—finds in film its true training ground" (SW 4:269).

After this analysis it becomes clear that even though distraction is invoked for characterizing the way the masses absorb film, this in no way contradicts the progressive relation they can have to film. In fact, "At the movies, the evaluating attitude requires no attention. The audience is an examiner, but a distracted one" (SW 4:269).

AESTHETICS, TECHNOLOGY, AND WAR

While the tendencies Benjamin identifies for the actualization of technology show what a noninstrumental relation of man to nature can come to, it is also important to recognize that technology can have a massive presence without its being given the opportunity to realize this new nature. We may then speak of an unnatural use of the technology, which becomes evident when technological production is intensified while social relations are not in any way transformed.

It is this that characterizes in general the capitalist mode of production, which seeks to maximize the use of technology while retaining the class structure and the ownership of the means of production. But Benjamin points to something further in considering how this situation is reflected in the relation of fascism to the masses: "Fascism attempts to organize the newly proletarianized masses while leaving intact the property relations which they strive to abolish. It sees its salvation in granting expression to the masses—but on no account granting them rights" (SW 4:269). The idea of granting the masses satisfaction, as it were, through the ideological sphere of art is a theme touched upon earlier in the essay and is widespread, including such different approaches as Clement Greenberg's "Avant-Garde and Kitsch" and Adorno's idea of the culture industry. But what becomes evident with fascism is that film has a different kind of relation to the political: it incorporates the masses while at the same time intensifying the cult value of the work of art. Earlier in the essay Benjamin points to how, "instead of being founded on ritual," through its technology "is based on a different practice: politics." But film also opens the possibility that politics and ritual value reinforce each other. Benjamin calls it a violation of the apparatus that draws the masses to a new mode of cult value in art: "The violation of the masses, whom fascism, with its *Führer* cult, forces to their knees, has its counterpart in the violation of an apparatus which is pressed into serving the production of ritual values" (SW 4:269). Take this reversal as the initial characterization of the "aestheticization of the political."[16]

Such a use of the cinematic technology is not merely a propagandistic attempt to bolster the image of the leader. Recall that cult value is developed in relation to the mastery of first nature and that the social apparatus often hides how much the problems of the first nature are left unaddressed. The distorted relation to the first nature is the introduction of the primal, that is, of the mythical and fate, into the field opened by the technology. It becomes evident as we follow Benjamin's account that in fascism the technology opens to a new form of human sacrifice—as though the distorted use of technology denies it the proper outlet and leads to its deployment in ways that make human sacrifice necessary. The violence that is opened through technology may be called, in line with our understanding of "Critique of Violence," mythical violence. It is that violence which brings ever anew the primal and fate into the form of social existence: "If the natural use of productive forces is impeded by the property system, then the increase in technological means, in speed, in sources of energy will press toward an unnatural use." This is further expressed by positing war as the extreme and necessary realization of this tendency: "All efforts to aestheticize politics culminate in one point. That one point is war. War, and only war, makes it possible to set a goal for mass movements on the grandest scale while preserving traditional property relations. That is how the situation presents itself in political terms. In technological terms it can be formulated as follows: only war makes it possible to mobilize all of today's technological resources while maintaining property relations" (SW 3:121).

It is indeed the case that war can mobilize the economy and accelerate production. But Benjamin wishes to assert the converse as well: that the acceleration of the use of technology without social transformation cannot but culminate in war. One could speak of a new form of fate: "Society was not mature enough to make technology its organ[;] . . . technology was not sufficiently developed to master the *elemental* forces of society" (SW 3:121; my emphasis). The mythical contours of this state are evident in the following description: "The most horrifying features of imperialist war are determined by the discrepancy between the enormous means of production and their inadequate use in the process of production (in other words, by unemployment and the lack of markets). *Imperialist war is an uprising on the part of technology, which demands repayment in 'human material' for the natural material society has denied it*" (SW 3:121). The repayment in "human material" is precisely the sacrificial aspect internal to myth. Technology, in the service of capital, has become the newest manifestation of fate in human existence.

One may wonder why this unnatural use of technology must culminate in war as long as it is not coupled with the transformation of society and the abolition of class domination. And, given that capitalism nowadays thrives on the use of technology without the transformation of social relations, what would be the parallel in our present? I would suggest that Benjamin's apocalyptic vision finds its reflection in the tendency of present-day humanity toward self-annihilation, which becomes more and more apparent in the climate crisis.

PART V

The Image of the Contingent

THIRTEEN

Distorted Life

What would it take to present a form of life in all its concreteness as a dream configuration? We have discussed on a number of occasions how Benjamin conceives of the gathering and ordering of contingent, factual, and time-bound material for the presentation of ideas, or what he terms truth content. But what would a concrete instance of that method look like? In what follows, we will attempt to answer this question, at least in part by drawing a picture of distorted life as it is thematized in the two versions of the exposé of the *Arcades Project* titled "Paris, Capital of the Nineteenth Century." The greatest challenge of this endeavor is holding together and not losing sight of the two poles: the most contingent and particular, on the one hand, and the most fundamental dimensions of human existence, on the other.

The contingent material includes such phenomena as the arcades, the panoramas, the world exhibitions, the bourgeois interior, and the streets of Paris, as well as the boulevards and barricades. The exposé treats of individuals such as Fourier, Grandville, Louis Philippe, Baudelaire, Haussmann, and Blanqui. It presents types such as the flâneur, the collector, the detective, and the "étuis-man," as well as the conspirator and the whore. Following the lead of our earlier discussion of Benjamin's Goethean conception of history, this material content must be presented so that every moment receives its significance from its relatedness to others. Only in this way will we be able to recognize in it the distortions of the dream image, its being distorted by similarity. Such distortion takes a polar form: of dreams and wishes for happiness, on the one hand, and of the burden and fatal character of myth, on the other. A dialectical presentation of this material must further suggest how these two aspects are inseparable.[1]

In approaching the material, we should note that the terms that appear in the discussion of the sections of the exposés include very broad and fundamental categories of human existence: means and ends, the new and the primal, utopia and myth, time and space, organic and inorganic, artifice and nature, inner and outer, dispersion and concentration, movement and petrification, life and the inanimate, human being and machine, universal and particular, construction and destruction, work and distraction, individuality and typicality, solitude and community, repetition and uniqueness. This list is only a set of guideposts to help us recognize the monadological armature in Benjamin's project—his ambition to refract the dimensions of a total form of existence, an abbreviation of the world of ideas—in the surroundings of the nineteenth-century Paris arcades.

The opening of the 1939 exposé formulates the subject matter of the work as following the implications of an antinomy of historical consciousness: the sense of progress in history, on the one hand, and a view of its repetitive character, on the other. This latter is exemplified by a view Benjamin attributes to Schopenhauer, according to which it is sufficient to compare Herodotus and the morning newspaper to have all the meaning one could draw from history. Viewed from the standpoint of the world-will, human actions in history are merely shifting configurations of the same basic tonality. All the intervening events are nothing but tedious repetitions. The opposite vision of universal history isolates the "achievements" of humanity, its great moments, so to speak, thereby providing us with a measure of progress. Benjamin calls such a view, best represented in the history of civilizations, "the treasure trove" of the present.

The two horns of the antinomy properly formulated in fact feed on one another and belong to one another. It becomes evident how the directionality of progress in the reified vision of the past is ideology. It rests on "a constant toil of society" (A 14), and progress is revealed as repetition. Yet the repetition of the historical drama in Schopenhauer's schema is only an inkling of how eternal return rules life, not in its great moments but in all and every detail, as the ever-present rule of myth. The antinomy so formulated reflects deeper tendencies that express the contradictory conditions of existence of the nineteenth century. They reveal themselves to the historical gaze of the present through the illumination of the material content of the past: "The new forms of behavior and the new economically and technologically based creations that we owe to the nineteenth century enter the universe of a phantasmagoria" (A 14).[2] The "strangely altered" contents, its distortions, give the material its dream character.[3] This illumination is not produced "theoretically" but is, as Benjamin puts it, perceptibly present or can be made so in gathering the material. Historical materialism is cued to the "metamorphosis" of material products that expresses the distorted life whose schema is the rule of myth.

Means, Movement, and Machines (Fourier, or the Arcades)

The core phenomenon of Benjamin's project, the Paris arcades, is paired with the utopia of Fourier. The deformation, in which the material content takes on the character of utopian wish images, is the expression of the still-immature incorporation of new technological developments into social life. This is evident primarily in the introduction of a new "element" or material—namely, iron—into construction. The arcades are glass-covered streets, whose possibility depends on the thin construction of the iron framework on which the glass is laid.

With the cast iron elements, something appears on the horizon whose significance will be gradually revealed and which Benjamin calls the "constructive principle." "Construction" is intimately related to the emergence of the "prefabricated," that is, of the reproduction procedures of the formed elements. Iron rails for locomotives constitute an early instance of the endlessly reproduced prefabricated elements of cast iron. Just as was evident in Benjamin's analysis of photographic reproduction, the new techniques of reproduction in iron construction utterly transform our understanding of means and ends. The dialectic of the material content discussed in this section represents the transformation of the fundamental dimension of ends and means in human existence.

The dialectic of means and ends can initially be recognized in a more overt political opposition regarding the role of the state. The tension between the state as empire and the bourgeois vision of the state as organized for the sake of capitalism is reflected as an opposition that characterizes the general spirit of the architecture of the period: the monumental "Empire Style" models itself on Hellenistic and Roman architecture, representing the idea of the state as an *end* in itself. At the same time, an alternative conception of the state as a means in service of the economy, as an instrument of domination by the bourgeoisie, itself finds a dialectical counterpart to Empire-style architecture, by opposing the monumental to the transitional.

The "architectural" image of means is expressed in the collective imagination by relegating the use of prefabricated iron to places of *transition and movement*, which are only means by which to reach one's destination. Thus, even before recognizing the functional potential of the new material, the collective limits its use to the construction of passageways, places of movement and transition: "Iron is avoided in home construction but used in arcades, exhibition halls, train stations—buildings that serve transitory purposes" (A 16).

It is with this image of the significance of the arcades that Benjamin turns to Fourier's utopia. Fourier's vision, one might say, intensifies to the point of "humorous" annihilation the bourgeois conception of the state as a means in service of the capitalist economy. It is a utopia of endless transition, of pure means, that does away with the ends of economic calculation. Fourier's utopia establishes the fantasy of a social space of constant "movement" by making passageways the schema of the entire city. The phalanstery is a city of "passages"; the center of existence in the home is shifted instead to transitory meeting places. What is initially expressed as the relegation of iron construction to secondary transitional purposes is introduced as the heart of dwelling by transforming the form and dynamics of human existence by making places of transition into what is essential to it.

Although there is in this section, as in others, an individual who did in fact put in writing a vision of utopia, the coupling of this vision with the arcades is meant to make us realize how much this constitutes not only an individual's imagination of a distant future of humanity but also something that grows out of and is recognizable in the phantasmagorical character of the arcades (in how their ordinariness can undergo illumination). The Fourierist utopia is closely linked to the ultimate development of means, that is, the emergence of machine technology: "The secret cue of Fourierist utopia is the 'advent of machines'" (A 16). The depth of the interpenetration of the technological and life that transforms the very idea of technology is evident inasmuch as Benjamin does not stress the uses of machines by human beings but rather the utopian conception of the human that has adapted itself to the machine. The organization of the phalanstery, the coordination of life in it, is based on the model of the machine, on what Fourier calls the interlocking wheels (*engrenage*) of passions. It is, one might say, a vision of humanity that has incorporated machines and thereby transformed the opposition between the machine as means and human life as end.[4] The rejection of moral motivation in the organization of society in favor of its smooth functioning as a "machine" is not the expression of a cynical conception of humanity, as though humans need to be manipulated in order to bring about a stable order; this latter would be in line with Kant's sense that one could construct a stable society even for a race of devils. Indeed, it is completely compatible with Fourier's "colossal conception of man." Fourier precedes Marx in being suspicious of appeals to morality, rights, and duties to order society and avoids this register in envisaging utopian possibilities for humanity.

Fourier presents us with a fantasy, a vision of utopia, that arises from the struggle to come to terms with the entry of the machine into the human form of life. This does not refer to the use of technology as the means for a variety of ends (the bourgeois conception); rather, Fourier points to a far deeper transformation of humanity that incorporates technology into its corporeal existence. The incorporation of technology transforms the image of man and of man's relation to nature. For Fourier, technology, the machine, would not be the means for achieving the most efficient exploitation of nature but instead "the spark that ignites the powder of nature."[5] The "propagation of the phalanstery by explosion" does not follow the means-ends understanding of nature, its teleological order; Benjamin describes it as "the cracking open of natural teleology" (A 631 [W7,4]). Technology and the new forms of cooperative labor belonging to it "will give birth to the creations lying dormant in [nature's] womb" (SW 4:394).[6]

The vision of a harmonious clockwork mechanism is a vision of the organization of human society, but it is an organization without end. Harmony lies in its transition speed and movement.[7] In the 1935 version of the exposé, Benjamin also mentions in this context Paul Scheerbart, whose novel *Lesabendio*, which Benjamin admired, lays out a fantasy of endless movement without obstacle. Here we should recall that arcades are not just iron but also glass; it is the fantasy of the latter element that Scheerbart unfolds, a hundred years after Fourier, in his treatise on glass architecture. Just as with Fourier's city of passageways, glass architecture shifts the weight of existence from the interior to the exterior, as well as shifting the role of both interior and exterior in constituting our ideas of subjectivity and objectivity. Glass is transformative not so much in allowing us to see into the interior of the house but by bringing the exterior in to bear on the dwelling: "Glass architecture . . . lets in the light of the sun, the moon, and the stars, not merely through a few windows, but through every possible wall. . . . The new environment, which we thus create, must bring us a new culture."[8]

The Commodity Fetish and the World-Soul (Grandville, or the World Exhibitions)

Just as in the first section, fantasy is prevalent in much of the section devoted to Grandville and the world exhibitions. Indeed, the saying quoted from a parodic play from 1832 includes lines such as "it will snow wine, it will rain chickens" (A 17). It recalls the description that Benjamin gives in "Experience and Poverty" of a Mickey Mouse world "in which everything is solved in the simplest most comfortable way, in which a car is no heavier than a straw hat and the fruit on the tree becomes round as quickly as a hot-air balloon" (SW 2:735). At the same time, what begins to appear is the demonic ambiguity of this world, steeped in primal dread or myth.

The world exhibitions were a celebration of industry and progress, "festivals of emancipation" for the masses.[9] The belief in the emancipatory character of industry is part of the Saint-Simonian creed that the development of technology, the industrialization of the earth, and the progress in the workers' conditions of existence go hand in hand. Globalization through industry was taken to be the key to the progress of humanity.

Yet the opposite pole to progress, the primal, is also at play, in the ritualistic dimension of these secular festivals, most evident in the relation formed between the crowd and the objects on display: "World-exhibitions are places of pilgrimage to the commodity fetish" (A 17). Commodity fetishism, together with its extension to cultural consumption, is a familiar idea of Marxism. But for Benjamin, Marx's analysis of this ritual dimension in terms of use value and exchange value must be further elaborated in terms of the opposition developed in the "Work of Art" essay between cult value and exhibition value. In the world exhibitions, the display of the commodity, the pole of exhibition value, serves the cult, whose ritualistic aspect has its ground in the first nature, the primal, that through which myth has a hold on humanity.

We can speak here of the image of the commodity in terms of a distortion of space and time in which it undergoes a peculiar illumination: the sphere of ritual value assumes a division of time into unique festive days and common and habitual days of work. And yet what is celebrated on the festive occasion is precisely what is mass-produced during the days of work: the commodity. Indeed, the supposed holy days promote identification with the product of work; thus ritual is ceaseless and offers no respite.[10]

Ritual value also presupposes distance. Distance signifies the ungraspable, the mysterious, that belongs to the object of worship; it is evident in the context of world exhibitions by the way in which the commodities are on display, excluded from the sphere of use. What is displayed in world exhibitions is the mass-produced as it is unavailable for the consumption of the masses. The distance between the masses and the commodity is expressed, as Benjamin notes, by the prohibition "Do not touch the items on display."

The impossibility in the world exhibition of appropriating the commodity as an object of use is the basis for its mimetic identification with the unique and the distant. Since use value is wholly absent, there can only be an identification with the exchange value of the commodity, which is determined through the universal comparability that money affords. The commodity loses its specificity and acquires an abstract equivalence to others that is characteristic of its price. This process hides the true basis for value—namely, the value that is associated with labor and use—and makes possible the surplus value of capital. This suggests how Benjamin conceives of capitalism as a religion in which fate and guilt rule existence (SW 2:288). The double meaning of the term *Schuld* as both debt and guilt points the way to the fatal character of the space of life of capitalism.[11] The logic of capitalism is such that the masses cannot but exist in debt (guilty), although such debt (guilt) is not traceable to any action of the individual (the breaking of a law) but to the dissociation between the sphere of exchange value and that of labor, together with the ritual identification of the masses with the former.

In other words, the world exhibitions are precisely the celebration of the alienation inherent in the commodity: "World exhibitions glorify the exchange value of the commodity. They create a framework in which its use value becomes secondary. They are a school in which the crowds, forcibly excluded from consumption, are permeated by [*se penetrent de*] the exchange value of commodities to the point of identifying with it" (A 18; translation modified). The schooling of the mimetic faculty, one might say, has taken a peculiar turn. The "world-soul" of which one partakes in venerating the object of ritual has become in the world exhibitions a "global" mimetic identification with the universal character of exchange value.

In the world exhibitions, the most universal and abstract exchangeability (exchange value) wears the appearance of uniqueness and singularity. These two poles introduce another form of ambiguity into the cult of the commodity: the entanglement of the unique and the utterly abstract and exchangeable is evident in Benjamin's claim that the crowd is penetrated by the exchange value of the commodity to the point of identifying with it. At the same time, the perception or experience of the crowd is that it is being given the unique (without which there is no cult value). Benjamin speaks of the "enthronement" of the commodity (there is only one king), as well as the theological niceties of the commodity (the divinity is one). This sense of uniqueness of the eminently exchangeable is epitomized in the *spécialité*: "The concrete expression of [the theological niceties] of the commodity is clearly found in the *specialité*—a category of goods which appears at this time in the luxuries industry" (A 18).

World exhibitions further foster the appearance of a distinction between the space of work and festive days by including distractions (*divertissements*). The development of amusement parks coincides with the advent of world exhibitions. Far from constituting respite from identification with the commodity, however, these distractions in fact contribute to it, only in this case another aspect of "abstract" identification comes to the fore. "Equivalence" becomes a matter of the crowd that attends those places rather than that of the exchange value of products. The entertainment in which individuals participate, bodily, makes them part of the body of the compact mass.[12] Distraction in such amusement parks has the character of the lived experience (the "thrill"), a unique excitement, as it were. But uniqueness is here measured solely by the intensity of lived experience, which, lacking the dimension of significance, is precisely what in the subjective world corresponds to the abstractness of exchange value. No thrill can be inherently differentiated from another—each is as good as any other.

We should note a further peculiarity in the examples of the attractions listed by Benjamin: their names are associated with nature—mountains (*montagnes russes*), twisters (*tête a queue* in the original), and caterpillars (*chenilles*). This hints at another motif in Benjamin's presentation: the ambiguous presence of nature in the world of commodities.

The world exhibitions collect in one place singular exemplars of what is produced all over the world: "World exhibitions construct a universe of *specialités*. The fantasies of Grandville achieve the same thing" (A 18). In Grandville's *Un autre monde* (Another world) this logic is inverted: the commodity character invades the whole world. The fantasy of globalization through industry that is at the heart of world exhibitions is here reversed and blown up to a cosmic scale. Grandville shows the overtaking of the cosmos by industry, the "commodification" of nature on a cosmic scale, by how "the ring of Saturn becomes a cast-iron balcony on which the inhabitants of Saturn take the evening air" (A 18). Similarly, the Milky Way is a bride whose white wedding dress is held by a train of comets, the moon rests on pillows, and the rainbow is the *éventail* (fan) of Iris.

Benjamin further points to a literary counterpart of the commodification of nature, in Alphonse Toussenel's zoology. Here it is primarily through the theme of fashion that "modernization"—that is, the newly produced—invades nature: "His zoology classifies the animal world according to the rule of fashion. He considers woman the intermediary between man and the animals. She is in a sense the decorator of the animal world, which, in exchange places at her feet its plumage and its furs" (A 18). This description of primal nature pervaded by the forever new, fashion, is yet another fundamental ambiguity that belongs to the dream image of the world exhibitions. It might be read at first as a rather benign anthropomorphism of nature, just as the fantasies of Grandville can seem to be nothing more than a humorous extension of man's mastery of nature. But, as with Benjamin's reading of *Elective Affinities*, where cultivation encroaches on elemental nature, here too we begin to sense the signs of fate: repetition, which expresses the indistinguishability of life and death, characterizes the rule of fashion. Far from overtaking nature by means of human categories, identification with the commodity in fashion introduces death into the human world, pairing life with the corpse, making the attraction of the inorganic in fetishism into the vital nerve of fashion.

The theme of fashion gives new meaning to the presence of the earth, the planets, and the cosmic in this section. It is not coupled with charming visions of the fraternity of the human world and animals but rather with dead, inorganic matter. The motto from Leopardi, "Fashion: "Madam Death! Madam Death!," clearly brings out the ambiguous duality Benjamin seeks to reveal in fashion. The relationship between fashion and death proclaims the connection of fashion to the primal world: "For fashion was never anything other than the parody on the motley cadaver, provocation of death through the woman.... And that is why she changes so quickly; she titillates death and is already something different, something new, as he casts about to crush her" (A 63 [B1,4]). Fashion makes death disappear from our sense of time and from the space of our existence—as if fashion can negate death as a limit through its constant transformation.

An epigraph from Balzac opens the convolute on fashion: "Nothing dies; all is transformed." Far from expressing immortality, fashion belongs to "the temporality of hell: to showing how this time does not recognize death." It aims at "eliminating all discontinuities and sudden ends" (A 66 [B2,4]). Indeed, the only way of conceiving of the dimension of immortality (the divine) is through hope. And the space of hope, "divine temporality," can only be opened by recognizing death as caesura.

The introduction of "eternal life" through constant metamorphosis is just the other face of the repetitiveness of the eternal return. Fashion, even when it appears to be ever new, feeds on the primal: "Each time, what sets the tone is without doubt the newest, but only where it emerges in the medium of the oldest, the longest past, the most ingrained. This spectacle, the unique self-construction of the newest in the medium of what has been, makes for the true dialectical theater of fashion" (A 64 [B1a,2]).

With fashion, then, the ritual character of the fetishism of commodities reemerges and its nature becomes more pronounced. It is a ritual in which there is no escape from guilt—that is, in which death permeates life and life denies death: "Grandville extends the authority of fashion to objects of everyday use, as well as to the cosmos. In taking it to an extreme, he reveals its nature. It couples the living body to the inorganic world. To the living, it defends the rights of the corpse. The fetishism which thus succumbs to the sex appeal of the inorganic is its vital nerve" (A 18–19).

"[Death] appears in fashion as ... [having been] 'overcome,' and precisely through the sex appeal of the inorganic, which is something generated by fashion" (A 79 [B 9,2]).[13] The perverse presence of death in life is evident in the features of fashion that "parcel" the human body—for instance, the way in which there are fashion accessories for this or that part of the body. This forms a further connection between fashion and the corpse, and contributes to establishing the baroque as the fore-history of modernity: "The detailing of feminine beauties so dear to the poetry of the Baroque, a process in which each single part is exalted through a trope, secretly links up with the image of the corpse. This parceling out of feminine beauty into its noteworthy constituents resembles a dissection, and the popular comparisons of bodily parts to alabaster, snow, precious stones, or other (mostly inorganic) formations makes the same point. Such dismemberment occurs also in Baudelaire: 'Le Beau Navire'" (A 79–80 [B9,3]).

Through the extension of fashion to nature, everything is incorporated into fashion.[14] The section ends with a quotation from Apollinaire: "Any material from nature's domain can now be introduced into the composition of women's clothes. I saw a charming dress made of corks..." (A 19).

The World as the Totality of Things (Louis-Philippe, or the Interior)

In this section we turn to the dialectic of one of the fundamental dimensions of human experience, the inner and the outer, related as it is to the distinction between mind and matter. Benjamin develops the way in which the interior of the bourgeois house mimics subjective inwardness and becomes the refuge of the individual seeking to retain a hold on their unique existence. Uniqueness, what is most my own, is understood as privacy, reflected in the character of the private dwelling. The phantasmagorical character of the interior emerges in relation to the transformation of the relation between home and workplace. With the development of the bourgeois dwelling place, the strict division between the two is instituted (in earlier forms of life, the home could also be the workplace). Since work touches upon the "realities" of existence and the contradictions inherent in them, the home becomes a locus of avoidance, of defense, of the unwillingness to address these real contradictions.

Attempts at overcoming the contradictions of reality by changing the conditions of private existence without a radical transformation of the conditions of labor are doomed to fail. This is reflected in the ambiguous character of the bourgeois interior, in particular in the attempt to make the home a self-sufficient whole that corresponds to the fantasy of the self-sufficient individual. It is evident in the fantasy of home as the place in which we have "everything"—in other words, the sense of the interior as representing the world itself: "In the interior he brings together remote locales and memories of the past. His living room is a box in the theater of the world" (A 9; translation modified). Instead of Grandville's extension of the commodity to the universe, we get the world concentrated in the living room.

The expression "theater of the world" relates back to the *theatrum mundi*, that is, the conception of the world as a theater in which a divine plan unfolds. In the baroque period, that sense of the world is allied with melancholy, with the contemplative distance correlative with the destructive character of human history. Put differently, the concentration of objects in the interior does not give it the unity of a *living* room but rather that of gathered remains. This becomes clear in the connection that Benjamin forms between the resident of the interior and the collector: "The collector proves to be the true resident of the interior." The collector is not merely the most succinct expression of the phantasmagoria of the interior but at the same time a "true" resident, one who at least points to what the transformation of that condition comes to. In particular, the collector takes up the task of divesting things of their commodity character.

The character of a collection is determined by diverse concrete particulars rather than a systematic or organic unity. Collecting is a materialist practice defined by the accumulation of material objects.[15] Its opposition to idealism is evident in the collector's being thrilled by the discovery of things that are defective in relation to their concept or exemplar (e.g., a stamp that has a printing mistake). The collector occupies a peculiar position with regard to these objects, one that must be distinguished from commodity fetishism. On the one hand, it signifies a possessive relation to objects, and in that sense the collector must be classified together with other practitioners of bourgeois ownership. But the object that fascinates the collector does not acquire its aura as a commodity; in fact, the collector's attitude counters the possessiveness that is associated with the fetishism of commodities that is evident, say, in the rule of fashion. The end of Benjamin's "Unpacking My Library" suggests this transformation or metamorphosis of possession: "For a collector—and I mean a real collector, a collector as he ought to be—ownership is the most intimate relationship that one can have to objects. Not that they come alive in him; it is he who lives in them" (SW 2:492).

Collecting raises the question of what it is to draw significance from our relation to material objects, even the most ordinary objects. We can of course think of collecting in the context of masterpieces (paintings, sculptures, etc.), but there is a sense in which collecting comes into its own precisely when we envisage the possibility of collecting *everything*, including what appears to be worth practically nothing in the context of its use. Thus, for instance, people collect bottle caps or bus tickets. One could say that collecting disregards the division into major and minor.

The second important characteristic that accounts for the difference between an object's value in a collection and its value in terms of its use in life is the object's being taken out of its functional context when placed in a collection. But far from producing identification with the abstract indifference of exchange value, as in the case of the objects in world exhibitions, severing an object from its function in a practical context bestows upon it a singular conspicuousness; through this dissociation from function, even the most banal of objects can be striking. In the collection, the object acquires a secret meaning. It is transformed by being brought into the new order of the collection. One might even say that in being detached from its functional context it undergoes transformations of meaning that point to a deeper historical life of the times in which it was produced. The object comes to figure as a detail in a new order whose meaning is something the collector seeks to reveal.

There seems to be, internal to the passion of collecting, an openness to the lucky or accidental find. This element of contingency also applies to the collector's interest in the history of the object (i.e., its previous ownership). This accidental history then becomes part of the new life of which the object partakes. Collecting is a form of struggle against dispersion and an incorporation of contingency into significance; there is an element of rescue to collecting. Benjamin aligns the collector with the important figure of the allegorist in his book on the baroque: "Perhaps the most deeply hidden motive of the person who collects can be described this way:

He takes up the struggle against dispersion. Right from the start, the great collector is struck by the confusion, by the scatter, in which the things of the world are found. It is the same spectacle that so preoccupied the men of the Baroque: in particular, the world image of the allegorist cannot be explained apart from the passionate distraught concern with this spectacle" (A 211 [H4a,1]). We should note that because the significance of the object now depends so much on the collector, there will also be a dimension of arbitrariness in the ordering of a collection. This reinforces the connection that Benjamin recognizes between the collector and the allegorist of the baroque: "In every collector hides an allegorist, and in every allegorist a collector" (A 211 [H4a,1]).

The lack of a clear distinction between living and nonorganic matter is further elaborated in the second section, where the concept of the interior is related to that of the trace. The dwelling becomes something of a shrine, celebrating the existence of the private individual. In the face of their self-inflicted exclusion from the possibility of making a difference in the public sphere of life, the inhabitant of the interior leaves everywhere in their house the traces of their days on earth. Thus Benjamin writes in "Experience and Poverty": "If you enter a bourgeois room of the 1880s for all the coziness it radiates, the strongest impression you receive may well be, 'You've got no business here.' And in fact you have no business in that room, for there is no spot on which the owner has not left his trace—the ornaments on the mantelpiece, the antimacassars on the armchairs, the transparencies in the windows, the screen in front of the fire" (SW 2:734; translation modified).

The house is not so much the surroundings of living but, as it were, a hardened mold whose shape the life of the inhabitant must take; the interior is like a cast or receptacle of the inhabitant, who fits it just as a mollusk takes the shape of its shell. This is suggested by the fashion for the creation of *étuis* for all objects, that is, making each and every object into something exactly fitting its cover. The fashion for covers is symptomatic of the protective (thus defensive) character of the interior; the interior is similarly the receptacle to which the soul of the living individual is bound (the "*étuis*-man" is Benjamin's name for the inhabitant of the interior).

This description of the "individual touch" makes clear that it is a relation to "what is mine," to possessions. But the objects possessed also possess their owner, by way of the habits they demand in return—habits rendering the inhabitant a slave to the preservation of their habitat, their traces: "The *intérieur* forces the inhabitant to adopt the greatest possible number of habits—habits that do more justice to the interior he is living in than to himself. This is understood by everyone who is familiar with the absurd attitude of the inhabitants of such plush apartments when something broke ... and this affect ... was above all the reaction of a person who felt that someone has obliterated 'the traces of his days on earth'" (SW 2:734).

Possessions are opaque, suggesting that seeing through something is the best way to give up one's hold on it. This establishes from yet another perspective what we have recognized in Benjamin's references to Scheerbart and the utopian character of glass architecture: glass is not only transparent, bringing the exterior into the interior, but it is also a material on which no traces are left.

The trace belongs to the register of the sign (as opposed to the mark). It is imprinted on a background. There is thus in the trace a contrast with what belongs to the "natural" manifestation—for instance, of character in physiognomy (in the medium of the body). In other words, traces must be "deciphered." Understanding the logic of the trace can be related to the emergence of detective fiction in the mid-nineteenth century. There forms in the imagination an antithesis that can be represented by two types: the flâneur, who is attuned to expression, to the physiognomy of the crowd (of the exterior), and the detective, who deciphers traces in things and is the physiognomist of the interior. The full development of this dialectical configuration, however, must await our discussion of the flâneur (in the section on Baudelaire, or the streets of Paris).

Nevertheless, at this point we can identify the difference between the recognition that belongs to the physiognomical understanding of the flâneur and the kind of logic that characterizes the detective. There is a total deductive structure of the world of things in the reading of traces, where the smallest thing can lead to the most distant conclusions. This is opposed to the immediate, intuitive grasp of physiognomy on the part of the flâneur. The flâneur lives outside, whereas the detective could conceivably solve a crime through the sheer logic of the trace without leaving home (Poe). But probably the most salient thing to note is the way the detective thrives in an environment of guilt. Whether there is ultimately an overcoming of the dialectical opposition of flâneur and detective will be discussed later on.

The third part of the section on the interior identifies Jugendstil as the after-history of the interior (and the after-history of Baudelaire as well, in ways that will become clear). Benjamin characterizes Jugendstil as a "liquidation" of the interior, which only brings out its phantasmagorical character. Indeed, "liquidation" does not really mean overcoming or leaving behind; Benjamin uses it here in the context of "sales" (the French term for sales is *liquidation*): the cheap liquidation of what is left over, thus still belonging to the dream world of capitalism.

In the 1935 exposé, written in German, the term used is *Erschütterung*, which is more like a tremor. A tremor does not really awaken; for Benjamin, Jugendstil is the dream that one has awakened: "The first tremors [*Weckreize*] of awakening serve to deepen sleep" (A 391 [K1a,9]). If the true annihilation of the interior is the revolutionary turn to the open, to the communal, in Jugendstil there is only the semblance of awakening, only a languid somnambulistic movement that still belongs to the phantasmagoria of the interior: Jugendstil introduces the technology of iron construction into the house (as opposed to its earlier use only in places of transition). Even though this iron construction is used for the exterior of the house—as ornament, as an addition to the frame of the building—it still belongs to the expression of individual subjectivity and is continuous with the way in which the resident of the interior leaves traces of their existence in the private dwelling. Benjamin writes that "with [the architecture of] van de Velde, the house becomes the plastic expression of the personality" (A 20) and adds that such ornamentalizing is like the signature in a painting.

Elements of iron construction are incorporated into the support or framework by ornamentalizing them. Jugendstil is not an authentic response to the alienation expressed in the character of the interior; rather, it is itself a heightened expression of the solitary soul, which attempts to realize itself and appropriate technology through its inward impetus: "For Jugendstil, the isolation of the individual is typical (see Ibsen)" (A 559 [S9a,3]). This character of Jugendstil is evident in its tendency to stylization: "Jugendstil is the stylizing style par excellence" (A 556 [S8,2]). In one sense, style is the opposite of the art of genre that is characteristic of the interior—that is, whereas genre assumes conventions, what is expressed in Jugendstil is a tendency to overcome limitations. Jugendstil is an outward expression of the aspiration of the isolated soul.

Genre pertains to a certain category of objects, whereas style is a sensibility that pertains to everything. It is manifest in a deformation by elongation, a tendency to linear form. This elongation is the stylistic expression of an open-ended aspiration that fits no form but, as it were, inflects all forms; it is the impossibility of resting content with any form. This is the universal *mal de siècle* that characterizes Jugendstil. Insofar as something like an open-ended inner life is what seeks expression in style, Jugendstil is an aestheticization of existence, which remains within the confines of the impotent isolated soul.

Stylization is a false response to the crisis of "form," to the crisis of tradition. It is a false attempt to find a new meaning for "youth," which has lost its living relation to previous generations. The youthful is taken to be an awakening from the age-old, from the burden of the forms of the past, as it were. But the idea of youth (*Jugend*) that is at work in Jugendstil still lacks force; it is merely an open aspiration that is utterly helpless and impotent. (Such open aspiration has the character of the bad infinity that denies death—or if it incorporates death, it is "death in beauty.")[16]

Variations of the same ornamental motif are potentially endless, the endpoint determined only by the surface to be covered. Ornamental stylization is a linear language in which the twists and turns of the elongated line are an expression of an endless, thus empty, aspiration. It can be traced to vegetal forms, the plant-like, which may also be characterized through their immobility as well as their muteness. The plant-like is thus also evident in the attraction of Jugendstil to silence: "Maeterlinck pushes the unfolding of the auratic to the point of absurdity. The silence of the characters in his plays is one of its manifestations" (A 557 [S8,8]).

This silence or emptiness is also something one could glean from the predominance of the empty (the space) over the full in Jugendstil: "the predominance of the hollow form over the filled form" (A 557 [S8,5]). There is also a peculiar way in which, through the vegetal, the imagination brings together two characteristics of the nervous system, as plant-like branching and as electric current (manifest psychologically as diseased hypersensitivity): "In the typical Jugendstil line—conjoined in fantastic montage—nerve and electrical wire not infrequently meet" (A 558 [S9,3]). It is not an authentic mediation of life and technology.

The flowering of plants is contrasted in Benjamin's discussion of Baudelaire's poetry with bearing fruit; thus the vegetal motifs of Jugendstil are closely associated with infertility. This is also evident in the attraction of Jugendstil to prepubescent youth and the androgynous character of its eroticism. The motif of flowering clearly shows Jugendstil to belong to the after-history of Baudelaire: "The fore-history of Baudelaire, as educed by current scholarship, resides in allegory; his after-history, in Jugendstil" (A 475 [N10,3]). Benjamin cites lines from *Le Spleen de Paris* (The spleen of Paris: Small poems in prose) that are a prefiguration of Jugendstil's dreamy elongation of forms: "A room that is like a dream, a truly *spiritual* room.... Every piece of furniture is of an elongated form, languid and prostrate, and seems to be dreaming—endowed one would say, with somnambular existence, like minerals and plants" (A 553 [S5a,3]). Yet the most obvious connection to be drawn between Jugendstil and Baudelaire lies in the introduction of the flower motif: "In *Les Fleurs du mal*, this Jugendstil emerges for the first time with its characteristic floral motif" (A 560 [S10,1]).

The New and the Typical (Baudelaire, or the Streets of Paris)

The opening of this section provides guidance for understanding the poetry of the city in Baudelaire: "Baudelaire's genius, which feeds on melancholy, is an allegorical genius."[17] Melancholy is not just a subjective characterization of Baudelaire's creative mood, nor is allegory merely a stylistic characterization of his poetry. Allegory, schema, and symbol are distinguished as various ways of thinking of the relation between concept and particular. To put it in the most general terms, whereas the schema mediates between the concept and its particular instantiations, and in the symbol the concept permeates the particular, in allegory the particular is made to stand for an idea or concept. This is not natural expression; instead, allegory involves arbitrariness in the choice of an object that through a number of specific properties serves to indicate what is external to it, other and higher. For this reason, allegory is often understood as the "illustration" of a concept rather than the total interpenetration of the conceptual and the particular found in the symbol.

Allegory can be related to melancholy insofar as we recognize that particulars can be made to mean something higher than themselves when things no longer "speak" for themselves, when they no longer emanate meaning, as when things are severed from the life that imbues them with their own significance. Allegory can grow out of the deadness of things dissociated from their use.[18] Allegory arises from a sense of the dispersion and abandonment of things taken out of their life context. This relationship between allegory, dispersion, and melancholy is internal to Benjamin's interpretation of Dürer's famous engraving *Melancholia*. The angel of melancholy is itself an allegorical expression of melancholy, not an attempt to capture the living expression of someone in that mood. Melancholy conceived of in terms of allegory is a posture of thought, what one might call brooding. Baudelaire is characterized by Benjamin as a brooder.

This further clarifies why melancholy is not just a subjective state of mind. It is a form of thoughtfulness that is attuned to the character of the world. As Benjamin puts it in his *Origin of the German Trauerspiel*: "The theory of mourning... is to be elaborated... only in description of the world that opens under the gaze of the melancholic. For the feelings, however vague they may appear to introspection, respond... to an objective structure of the world" (O 141). For Baudelaire this world is the city.

Baudelaire's poetry of the city is very different from the poetry of soil and homeland. The city appears not as the home of the poet but rather in its alien character. Baudelaire paints a picture of modernity in his poetry of the city; for him, a poetry of modern life is a poetry adapted to the "the experience of giant cities." Baudelaire's dedication of the *Petits poèmes en prose* speaks of the fantasy, the "miracle," of a poetic prose "musical, yet without rhythm and without rhyme, supple and resistant enough to adapt to the lyrical stirrings of the soul, the undulations of reverie, and the sudden leaps of consciousness" (SW 4:320). It is a fantasy because it seeks to mediate an opposition: the continuous undulation of reverie and the "sudden leaps of consciousness." Its obsessive character reflects a problem in the character of experience. It is a symptomatic idealization in the face of an ambiguity "born, above all, from the experience of giant cities, from the intersecting of their myriad relations" (SW 4:41).

The fantasy of wedding the lyrical to sudden leaps of consciousness reflects the contradiction between the continuity of significant experience and the prevalence of shock, the discontinuity in the modern configuration of experience. A multitude of small tremors constantly felt is characteristic of the encounters of the city. One might speak here, as Benjamin does, of the problem of a poetry that belongs and gives expression to the transformation of experience by the omnipresence of shock. This is not a matter of horrifying events but rather the weaving of shock into ordinary experience; shock threatens to reduce the continuity of experience into a mass of isolated impressions.

Correlative with the loss of that weave or continuity of experience we will find the addiction to momentary strong, lively impressions. The person who has lost the capacity to draw significance from experience and is overtaken by boredom and *taedium vitae* craves the impressive, the sensational. The momentary excitement of strong sensations replaces and comes at the expense of experience playing a role in the meaningful appropriation of the world. Whatever the factors that contribute to the poverty of modern experience, Benjamin recognizes its central manifestation as the prevalence of lived experience (*Erlebnis*) over significant or meaningful experience (*Erfahrung*), the latter depending on the appropriation of the past in a medium of tradition.[19]

In "On Some Motifs in Baudelaire," Benjamin explicates the nature of this transformation of experience in terms of the insights of psychoanalysis regarding the mode of response of the psyche to shock. The fundamental defense mechanism that serves to counter shock is to isolate the event from the rest of the psychic apparatus. This is best achieved by giving it clear limits, that is, conscious meaning determinations. The neutralization of shock is achieved by isolating experience and giving it the characteristics of information (a time and place as well as a readily available meaning articulation in, say, a caption). Consciousness is thus primarily identified as a defense mechanism whose role is to parry shock. It follows that in an environment in which shock is prevalent, one will find consciousness to be constantly on the scene. This parrying of shock that turns the environment into a number of conscious isolated experiences would do away with the possibility of drawing from the depth and continuity of involuntary memory. It would "sterilize [it] for poetic experience." These considerations raise with renewed force the question of "how lyric poetry can be grounded in experience [*einer Erfahrung*] for which exposure to shock [*Chockerlebnis*] has become the norm. One would expect such poetry to have a large measure of consciousness; it would suggest that a plan was at work in its composition. This is indeed true of Baudelaire's poetry" (SW 1:318). Allegorical poetry is a highly "conscious" form of poetry.

The duality identified in the task of making lyric poetry out of the experience of shock is reflected in a number of figures of ambiguity. Ambiguity is, as Benjamin puts it, "the imagistic appearance [*die bildliche Erscheinung*] of dialectic, the law of dialectics at a standstill" (A 10). This ambiguity is the manifestation of the contradictions of modernity, "the ambiguity peculiar to the social relations and products of this epoch." It is the modern expression of the ambiguity essential to the manifestation of fate. "Such an image is afforded [presented = *stellt*] by the commodity per se: as fetish. Such an image is presented by the arcades, which are house no less than street. Such an image is present in [*stellt*] the prostitute—seller and sold in one" (A 10). Other types that embody such ambiguity are the flâneur, the gambler, the collector, and the conspirator.

Benjamin focuses in his discussion of Baudelaire on the ambiguous character of the flâneur, the type through whose transformation Benjamin presents the dialectic at the heart of Baudelaire's poetry. The flâneur is the "resident" of the exterior, of the streets of the city. He is apparently the counterfigure to the resident of the interior, yet as will become clear, he ultimately belongs to the same ambiguous logic. The flâneur lives the mirage of the endless interest and beauty of the crowd. It is as though his existence outside has the pace of someone who leisurely considers a variety of beautiful objects (in a salon). In the phantasmagoria of the flâneur the exterior is made into an "interior." This forms an intimate connection between the flâneur and the phenomenon of the arcades. Public space comes to wear the character of an interior. But the beauty he is attracted to is not that of immobile objects but rather of the masses. The flâneur is the explorer of the crowd, who is capable of transforming the masses into an always interesting and lively spectacle.[20]

As a model for this type, Baudelaire chooses Constantin Guys. In "The Painter of Modern Life," Baudelaire describes the inspiration Guys draws from the changing impressions he has of the crowd. He dives into the crowd as into his element and is enlivened by the constantly new and surprising encounters with the types of the modern city. At night he struggles to give form to the visions of the day, urgently capturing images from the onslaught of impressions before they disappear. This activity demands swiftness and agility in translating memory to paper, a mnemonic technique that is deployed to catch passing details of some appearance or other that cannot be absorbed and reworked gradually: "In the daily metamorphosis of external things, there is a rapidity of movement which calls for an equal speed of execution for the artist." What emerges from this struggle with impressions is almost of necessity a beauty of the typical. With this rhythm of committing memory to drawing, there is no way to hold on to the details of a unique individuality. New types such as the military man, the dandy, and the courtesan become the subject matter of art. It is the beauty of changing fashion, the beauty of the carriages that fill the city, of the passing scene of the streets that Guys seeks to capture.

The interest in types is pervasive, encountered in a wide variety of contexts in the first half of the nineteenth century. Thus, for instance, it is reflected in the development of caricature (itself made possible by the development of lithography at the service of the printing press). Caricature is indeed a particularly powerful way of making the typical perceptible by the exaggeration of features. Baudelaire admired Honoré Daumier and Paul Gavarni. The fascination with the typical is also apparent in the flourishing of the literature of types, to which such writers as Honoré de Balzac, Eugène Sue, and Charles Nodier contributed (including such compilations as *Les Français peints par eux-mêmes*, *Le Diable à Paris*, etc.).[21] The flâneur, himself a type frequently described and drawn, is the observer of types; standing apart, as it were, he prides himself on his knowledge of physiognomy.

Baudelaire further identifies the flâneur with the figure of "the man of the crowd," found in Poe's story by that name, a story that Baudelaire translated into French. Benjamin challenges this identification: the man of the crowd is characterized by Poe in terms of his constant emergence from and reabsorption into the crowd. The crowd is for him an environment in which he repeatedly disappears. If for the flâneur the crowd is a veil thrown over the city to bring out its beauty, the man of the crowd veils himself in the crowd. The man of the crowd, in Benjamin's view, is not the flâneur who contemplates the crowd but rather someone who hides in the crowd. This hiding is a sign of guilt: "To Poe, the flâneur was, above all, someone who does not feel comfortable in his own company. This is why he seeks out the crowd.... Poe purposely blurs the difference between the asocial person and the flâneur. The harder a man is to find, the more suspicious he becomes.... The narrator quietly sums up his insight as follows: 'This old man is the embodiment and the spirit of crime.... He refuses to be alone. *He is the man of the crowd*.'"

This transformation of the flâneur can thus be seen to be related to the figure of the detective we encountered in our discussion of the interior, which Baudelaire knew very well from his translations of the tales of Poe. The latter operates in an environment of crime and guilt, in the city in which the guilty person can hide traces of their existence. As opposed to the intuitive cognition of types characteristic of the flâneur, who loves the variety of social types, the detective prides themselves on their implacable logic in reading the almost invisible traces of the asocial person who hides in city.

In Poe's "Man of the Crowd," the crowd is viewed not as an expression of liveliness but rather as taken up by a distinct automatism, as though responses become part of a mechanism that rules the behavior of the inhabitants of the city. The flâneur's eccentricity, the sense of his individuality, is correlative with his capacity to make fine distinctions in his reading of the types of the city. Benjamin suggests that the specter of repetition that threatens this activity is the theme of Baudelaire's "Les sept vieillards," in which, instead of the richness of endlessly interesting variations of the human, the same repulsive figure shows up again and again. The multiplicity of types encountered in the city, far from being the source of a new beauty, becomes a locus of anxiety about the possibility of expressing uniqueness—another expression of the eternal return of the same that overtakes the space of human existence.

For Baudelaire, modern beauty celebrates the new: "By 'modernity' I mean the ephemeral, the fugitive, the contingent, the half of art whose other half is the eternal and the immutable."[22] Novelty is an absolute—it is incomparable, uninterpretable, or unexpected on the basis of the past. Against spleen (melancholy) Baudelaire sets up the passion of the new. Modern beauty is geared to the sense of excitement of the new and is ready to accept its ephemerality as the price to pay for such a transformation of value. In the loss of immortal beauty, of the ideal, one turns to the incomparable value of the new: "*La nouveauté* represents that absolute no longer accessible to any interpretation or comparison. It becomes the ultimate entrenchment of art" (A 22).

The inestimable value of novelty is meant to overcome the repetition that is internal to commodity production. And yet Benjamin argues that the beauty of the new, which is art's last line of resistance, is also the commodity's most advanced line of attack. As we saw in the discussion of fashion, the repetition of the new *is* the logic of the commodity. The excitement of the new is demonic life; it is a mask of repetition, of the presence of the primal past. It is the eternal recurrence of the new that is the logic of the commodity. As Benjamin puts it: "Baudelaire's poetry reveals the new in the ever-selfsame, and the ever-selfsame in the new" (SW 4:175). Benjamin describes Baudelaire not as revealing the temporality of the ephemeral and the movement of the passing but rather raging hopelessly against the "storms of seconds," the repetitive mechanical time that belongs to the indistinguishability of the multitude of impressions.

The new always revealed as repetition makes for a space of experience in which the only radical novelty is death: "For people as they are now, there is only one radical novelty—and always the same one: death" (SW 4:171). The only place in which one can "experience" something that one has never experienced before is death (which is not an experience). This is expressed in the conjunction of voyage (in search of the new) and death in Baudelaire's "Le voyage," the last of the poems in the first edition of *Les Fleurs du Mal*. The voyage in search of the unknown, the new, is one whose captain is death. There is no way to hold on to the idea of modern beauty, and it feeds into spleen (not because it is passing and one cannot hold on to it but because even the new comes to be recognized as assuming the character of eternal return). The new in whose name the poet seeks to withstand despondency, itself bears the stigma—in the highest degree—of the reality he rebels against. The supposed beauty of the passing beauty is seen through; it is semblance, and what is recognized in it is the paralyzing gaze: "The face of modernity itself blasts us with its immemorial gaze. Such was the gaze of Medusa for the Greeks" (A 23).[23]

Straight Lines, Empty Spaces (Haussmann, or the Barricades, and Conclusion)

Why does Benjamin conceive of Haussmann's project as a phantasmagoria (on a par with the arcades, the interior, the streets, or the world exhibitions)? It would seem to be much more a matter of straightforward political despotism, motivated by the problem of barricade fighting, by the aim of driving the proletariat out of the heart of the city, as well as by the contribution of a huge project to the development of "investment capital." And do the barricades similarly belong to the universe of phantasmagoria developed in this section? Are they an expression of the dream character of this environment?

In the introduction to "Paris, Capital of the Nineteenth Century" (1939), Benjamin presents Haussmann as the champion of the "phantasmagoria of civilization itself." This suggests that we are to read the section on Haussmann in relation to the very "reification" of historical time. As he puts it in the introduction, "[The nineteenth-century conception of history] corresponds to a viewpoint according to which the course of the world is an endless series of facts congealed in the form of things. The characteristic residue of this conception is what has been called the 'History of Civilization,' which makes an inventory, point by point, of humanity's life forms and creations" (A 14). This suggests that what is at stake in Haussmann's project is a spatialized and reified sense of history. The destruction of old Paris not only constitutes violence against the "organic" individual cohesion of the city and the specific character of its parts, or quartiers, but it also serves to spatialize the sense of time. In the "aerarium of civilization" the past appears as a series of things, or rather, kinds of things, representing their species: "It has been said of the Ile de la Cité, the cradle of the city, that in the wake of Haussmann only one church, one public building, and one barrack remained" (A 22). All that is needed is "one of each kind." The city comes to express the reification of history in the form of things. With Haussmann, it is as though time itself becomes a petrified landscape and is celebrated with pomp and splendor: "With the Haussmannization of Paris, the phantasmagoria was rendered in stone" (A 24).[24]

This is closely related to the character of the boulevards, the straight lines cutting through the city. The line is the paradigmatic form of the spatialization of time. It is in this context that we should think about the emphasis on the linear in this section: "Haussmann's ideal in city planning consisted of long straight streets opening onto broad perspectives" (A 24). The opening of these linear perspectives is understood as providing a view of the temples of bourgeois society, as it were, one by one, not as integral to the city but as monuments raised on a pedestal. "The perspectives, prior to their inauguration, were screened with canvas draperies and unveiled like monuments; the view would then disclose a church, a train station, an equestrian statue, or some other symbol of civilization" (A 24).

The linear conception of time goes hand in hand with the possibility of a measure of time, and more specifically, in this context, a measure through which history is viewed in terms of a schema of progress. The linear perspectives are the phantasmagoria of the progress of human civilization so characteristic of the nineteenth century. This is closely related to what we may call the "aestheticizing" of the political: "Contemporaries christen the operation 'strategic embellishment'" (SW 3:42). It explains why Benjamin chooses as a motto a statement from Haussmann's memoirs in which he speaks of the veneration of the beautiful. The embellishment of the city is aestheticizing to the extent that it occurs at the expense of truly transforming society. If in the context of the "Work of Art" essay aestheticizing was coupled with fascism, here it is clearly brought together with "dictatorship" and "despotism." Just as with Marinetti we find an apotheosis of destruction, here too Haussmann is proud of his "demolition." He "gives himself the name of 'demolition artist.'" Benjamin ends the section with another statement of the relation between aestheticization and destruction: "The burning of Paris is the worthy conclusion to Baron Haussmann's work of destruction" (A 25).

What are we to make of the barricades? After all, these are also straight lines. Do they belong to the same phantasmagoria? Obviously there are important differences: whereas the boulevards open onto a series of isolated monuments, the barricade is constructed among other things, using a multitude of ordinary object packed together to form a wall. The barricades are constructions in which objects are collected and "repurposed." If the boulevards open an empty linear perspective for the gaze, the barricades are an orthogonal obstruction to it. Yet as with the case of surrealism, one might ask how the energies of revolt can be harnessed to the demands of revolution, as well as, given the ultimate failure of the 1848 revolution, how hope and hopelessness may be conceived of in terms of this space of phantasmagoria. This is the theme of the concluding section of the exposé.

In the 1935 version of the exposé, the section on Haussmann ends with a reference to surrealist practice and the possibility of awakening by cunning—that is, one might say, on a hopeful note. In the 1939 version, Benjamin adds a concluding remark devoted to Louis Auguste Blanqui. It sums up the phantasmagoria of humanity by presenting the image of modernity as a landscape of hell. The formulation of the thought of eternal return in *L'éternité par les astres* is characterized by Benjamin as the "resignation without hope . . . of the great revolutionary" (A 26).

Blanqui presents his vision as a hypothesis of natural science but does not recognize that it is a mirror "of that society which . . . has defeated him." Blanqui's vision "opens the way to merciless speculations that give the lie to the author's revolutionary élan [*inflige a l'élan revolutionnaire de l'auteur un cruel démenti*]" (A 25). While Blanqui presents his vision as a metaphysical interpretation of Being as such, it is a phantasmagoria that is a fitting expression of the form of existence of his times. Indeed, we shouldn't be tempted to take this as the truth of Being: it is a phantasmagoria, a proper summation of the primal history of the nineteenth century. "'Eternal return' is the *fundamental* form of the *urgeschichtlichen*, mythic consciousness" (A 119 [D10,3]). It is the form of humanity suffering under the burden of myth: "The essence of the mythical event is return. Inscribed as a hidden figure in such events is the futility that furrows the brow of some of the heroic personages of the underworld (Tantalus, Sisyphus, the Danaides" (119 [D10a,4]).[25]

It is in this conclusion that one gets the clearest statement of the way in which this space of existence is ruled by the primal, the way in which progress and eternal return belong together. Indeed, we might say that Blanqui's eternal return is the exact complement of Grandville's cosmic fantasy: the commodity taking over the universe, becoming, as it were, the schema of our metaphysical image of the world. This connection is indeed suggested by Benjamin's remark that "the stars in Baudelaire present the rebus image [*Vexierbild*] of the commodity. They are the 'eternal return of the same' in great masses" (A 340 [J62,5]).

Blanqui's vision of eternal return is a phantasmagoria.[26] The hopelessness it expresses is a distorted image of what hope comes to. It corresponds to the distortion of the hope of immortality in seeking it in what is constantly changing, in the eternal life of nature through its infinite metamorphoses. This is also evident if we trace in Benjamin's writings the motif of the stars and its relation to the theme of hope. The stars belong to the dream image of hope. We encountered this theme in our discussion of the end of Benjamin's essay on Goethe's *Elective Affinities*, where the theme of hope is developed in the relation between the shooting star in the novel and Benjamin's figuration of hope through the identity of Venus, the morning and the evening star.

In the essay on Baudelaire, the falling star is similarly an image of the hope inherent in the wish. The stars belong to our sense of the distant; it is that distance that makes the very form of the wish and thus of hope possible: "The earlier in life one makes a wish, the greater one's chances that it will be fulfilled. The further a wish reaches out in time, the greater the hope for its fulfillment. But it is experience that accompanies one to the far reaches of time, that fills and articulates time. Thus, a wish fulfilled is the crowning of experience" (SW 4:331). The layering of experience is precisely what allows us to recognize something as the occasion for a wish made long ago to be fulfilled in an unforeseen way. In other words, it is not as though we merely wait with hope for wish fulfillment; waiting is expectation as it gathers the weight of experience, in turn allowing us to recognize something as an occasion for fulfillment (see our discussion in Chapter 11). In the figure of eternal return, the stars are dissociated from wish, hope, and experience.

The decline of the aura, of intimacy with the distant, parallels the disappearance of the stars from the sky of the city and from Baudelaire's poetry. The illumination of the city by means of gas provided the dreamy atmosphere conducive to noctambulism, but it also made the starry sky disappear from the city. The last lines of Benjamin's Baudelaire essay reflect this predicament: "This poetry appears in the sky of the Second Empire as 'a star without atmosphere.'" This expression is in quotes and was probably taken from part 7 of Nietzsche's "On the Use and Abuse of History for Life": "All living things need an atmosphere around them, a secret circle of darkness. If this veil is taken from them, if people condemn a religion, an art, a genius to orbit like a star without an atmosphere, then we should no longer wonder about their rapid decay and the way they become hard and barren."[27] Thus it is precisely the decline of the aura, that is, of the veil of secrecy, that makes

Baudelaire's poetry a star without atmosphere, a barren and hard landscape from which the stars are excluded (A 116 [D9,1]). It is when stars no longer illuminate the night sky that they appear in the phantasmagorical illumination of the vision of eternal return.

Eternal return is the temporal pendant to the spatialization of time in the phantasmagoria of civilization. The one-of-a-kind in the vision of progress is the very same as the repetition of that which appears in masses. It is the expression of the petrifying melancholy in the face of the new that is just another form of the ever-same primal. "The belief in progress ... and the representation of eternal return are complementary. They are the indissoluble antinomies in the face of which the dialectical conception of historical time must be developed" (A 119 [D10a,5]).

Notes

Introduction: The Natural in the Human

1. I use the expression "nature in the human" in order to distinguish this dimension both from a discussion of human nature as well as from the idea of a natural condition of humanity (say, in the way it would appear in accounts of the state of nature). This locution is used in Benjamin's "Fate and Character" as he brings out the relation of fate and character to life: "Both concern the natural man—or, better, the nature in man [*die Natur im Menschen*]" (SW 1:204). In the same essay Benjamin also speaks of the "the life in man" and "the natural life in man," which are not "the life of man."

Chapter 1: God, Nature, and Man in Language

1. In chapter 5 of his book *The Messianic Reduction: Walter Benjamin and the Shape of Time*, Peter Fenves draws a similar "semantic triangle." But in his account there seems to be no place for human naming to partake in divine creation.

2. The relation between these considerations and the fundamental structure of Rosenzweig's "Star of Redemption" should be developed. The trichotomy World, Man, God is central to part 1 of "Star." The trichotomy creation, revelation, redemption is also at the center of the tripartite division of part 2 of "Star." It is worth noting that Benjamin's essay was written long before the publication of "Star."

3. In this context Humboldt's understanding of the "inner form" of a language is worth considering. See the discussion of this concept in Cassirer's 1923 essay "The Kantian Elements in Wilhelm von Humboldt's Philosophy of Language."

4. One of the interesting recent studies of Benjamin's conception of language is Alexander Stern's *The Fall of Language: Benjamin and Wittgenstein on Meaning*. Stern insightfully relates Benjamin's essay to the expressivist tradition and in par-

ticular to Johann Georg Hamann. He stresses how the understanding of communicability is transformed by making mediality central. A further important feature of the book is the way Stern seeks to bring together Benjamin and Wittgenstein, a conjunction hinted at in Stanley Cavell's "Signals and Affinities" and further developed by Stern. To my mind the distinction between "saying" and "showing" in the *Tractatus* and the progress of that book is equally important and might provide a way to understand Benjamin's relation not only to Russell's paradox (as is brought out by Fenves and Stern) but also to the origin of analytic philosophy more broadly. For an earlier account of the relation of Benjamin's thought on language to Hamann, see Winfried Menninghaus's important book *Walter Benjamins Theorie der Sprachmagie*.

5. As Schopenhauer humorously puts it in a related context, "A serpent can become a dragon only by devouring a serpent" (Schopenhauer, *World as Will and Representation*, 170). He also describes the character of the hierarchical ruling internal to life: "Given the standpoint we have adopted, we will certainly find traces of chemical and physical interactions in the organism but we will never be able to base an explanation of the organism in these interactions; this is because the organism is absolutely not a phenomenon that has arisen through the unified operations of such forces, which is to say accidentally. Rather it comes from a higher Idea that has subjugated all the lower ones through an *overwhelming assimilation*. This is because the *one* will objectifies itself in all Ideas; and in striving for the highest possible objectivation, it now abandons the lower levels of its appearance after a conflict between them, in order to appear on a higher and thus more powerful level. No victory without struggle: since the higher Idea or objectivation of the will can come forward only by overpowering the lower Ideas, it encounters resistance on their part. Even when the lower Ideas are quickly brought into submission, they nonetheless keep striving to express their essence in a complete and self-sufficient manner" (170).

6. Alexander Stern makes a related point as he takes up the notion of God's condescension, drawn from his reading of Benjamin after Hamann, as essential to understanding the possibilities of man's naming nature.

7. If we think about post-Kantian speculative metaphysics, both in Fichte and Schelling, this original ground prior to judgment is identity. Fichte's starting point is with intellectual intuition, or the "I = I," and Schelling's philosophy of identity can suggest a way to characterize the multiplicity in nonsynthesis as belonging to the standpoint of the absolute in identity. Identity similarly has a central place in Benjamin's program for a speculative metaphysics.

Indeed, Benjamin refers to the centrality of identity in the argument of his "Program for the Coming Philosophy": "The fixing of the concept of identity, unknown to Kant, will likely play a great role in the transcendental logic, inasmuch as it does not occur in the table of categories yet presumably constitutes the highest of transcendental logical concepts and is perhaps truly suited to founding the sphere of knowledge autonomously beyond the subject-object terminology" (SW 1:107).

8. Another extremely important source for elaborating the logic of identity is Benjamin's essay "Two Poems by Friedrich Hölderlin" (1915). Identity in the poetic world (as a realization of absolute identity) is the complete interpenetration of the spiritual and the experiential: "The law according to which all apparent elements of sensation and ideas come to light as the embodiments of essential, in principle infinite functions is called the Law of Identity" (SW 1:20). For an analysis of this essay, see my "Retreat of the Poet in Walter Benjamin's 'Two Poems of Friedrich Hölderlin,'" 207–218.

9. Fenves places similar importance on Benjamin's account of identity but traces it to a different context—namely, Benjamin's interest in Russell's paradox and the way in which equation in mathematics becomes "translation" of the register of nature to human language.

10. In this context, see the reinterpretation of the relational categories to leave place for the noncategorial identity in Benjamin's "On the Program of the Coming Philosophy."

11. Fenves recognizes this difference but draws the conclusion that the naming of a person is from the start "improper" (*Messianic Reduction*, 144–145).

12. For a discussion of a similar related moment in Wittgenstein's *Tractatus Logico Philosophicus*, see my "Logic, Ethics and Existence in Wittgenstein's *Tractatus*."

13. There is an absence in the essay on language of traditional ways of thinking of the Fall and original sin in terms of the relation between Adam and Eve, which involves temptation, the emergence of sexuality, and a sense of nakedness and shame. It will be important for us to understand how those elements fit into the picture that Benjamin lays out; they will come into play in our discussion of the essay on Goethe's *Elective Affinities*.

14. This is strangely reminiscent of Kafka's parable "Before the Law": a man comes seeking knowledge of the law, but it is his approach to the law as something external (not immediately belonging to him) that makes him guilty. It is not impossible that Benjamin had this parable in mind while writing: it was first published in the Jewish weekly *Selbstwehr* in 1915, and Benjamin may have become acquainted with it through Scholem.

15. We should note Benjamin's passing reference to the relation between overnaming and tragic precision, as though tragedy exemplifies the way in which ambiguity is characteristic of fallen life, of life as a field of fate. But this ambiguity of fate is the other face of the precision that manifests itself as everything closes in on the hero of tragedy. Ambiguity and tragic precision are not opposites but belong to each other in that field of meaning that is fate.

16. We might speak here of sadness as a fundamental mood (*stimmung*), as Heidegger uses that term. It opens the world in a certain way and reveals to us

through that affective coloring the fundamental condition of being-in-the-world. The primary locus of such an analysis of the world in the mood of mourning is no doubt Benjamin's account of melancholy in his *Origin of the German Trauerspiel*. For an insightful discussion of this aspect of Benjamin's thought, see Ilit Ferber's *Philosophy and Melancholy*.

Chapter 2: Naming Beauty

1. An excellent discussion of the centrality of Benjamin's writings on color to his philosophical views can be found in Howard Caygill's *Walter Benjamin: The Color of Experience* and Peter Fenves's *The Messianic Reduction*, chaps. 2 and 3.

2. The most sustained account of the colors of fantasy and their relation to painting appears in Benjamin's early essays, in particular "Conversation on the Rainbow," a conversation between Margarethe and Georg, as well as the fragment "The Rainbow." My presentation is based mostly on these writings.

3. In the "Conversation on Fantasy," Margarethe reports her "experience" of the colors of fantasy in a dream. I bracket here the broader question where these manifestations are encountered and how pervasive they are at the heart of our experience of the world. Benjamin's discussion of the colors of fantasy is closely related to his writings on childhood. For a discussion of these writings, see my "Learning from the Colors of Fantasy." What will concern us in this chapter is the presence of the colors of fantasy in painting.

4. With a view to establishing parallels to the account of language, this should remind us of Benjamin's characterization of language as a self-communicating medium.

5. In his First Critique, Kant characterizes space as one, an infinite intuitive whole and therefore to be distinguished from the mere given of perception, which is always limited. In space, moreover, there is a primacy of the intuitive whole with respect to its parts, which are always delimitations of the one space. When Kant seeks a formal analogue to the unity of content of the divine, intuitive intellect, he turns to space pure and simple (Kant, *Critique of the Power of Judgment*, 5, 409). The intuitive understanding is for Kant a limit conception in which fundamental divisions internal to the standpoint of finitude are "collapsed." As its very name makes evident, the intuitive intellect stands beyond the division of the finite intellect into intuition and understanding. An intuition is a singular and immediate representation. By calling the infinite intellect intuitive, Kant suggests that for it, what is singular, unique, is primary. It intuitively apprehends the one, the whole, prior to its parts. Such parts, which we would call its internal specifications, are nothing but delimitations of the preexisting whole, and as such, they are merely privations of the highest actuality of the whole. For the intuitive intellect, Spinoza's dictum that every determination is negation holds. In contrast, our finite understanding is discursive and thus mediate. We understand by means of general concepts under

which the particular is subsumed in a judgment. We articulate our understanding of the particular object of knowledge from the characterization of its parts and their behavior by way of concepts.

6. The colors of fantasy in the painting are its soulfulness, the principle of life in it. This relation between genius and soulfulness is neglected in many interpretations of Kant's account of genius.

7. In relation to problematic attempts to treat the colors of fantasy as a model, to introduce colors of fantasy into painting as elements, Benjamin mentions the Italian Renaissance painter Dosso Dossi. He might have in mind Dossi's painting in which Jupiter is painting the patina on the wings of butterflies, with Mercury and virtue behind him.

8. We are receptive to that unity of life only in and through our activity: "What lives can be received only by being generated" (EW 215). It is this balance of activity and receptivity, of what we do and what manifests itself, that we seek to clarify.

9. The relation of the register of beauty to that of life emerges prominently in Kant's construal of the field of the beautiful through subjective purposiveness and of the field of living beings (natural ends) as that of objective purposiveness. These are the two parts of his *Critique of the Power of Judgment*. It is inherent in Kant's understanding of judgment that both of these are lacking in objective reality; they are merely reflective judgments. The challenges to Kant's position in the nineteenth century are numerous (starting with Hegel all the way to Nietzsche).

10. As Schlegel puts it: "But the highest beauty, indeed the highest order, is only that of chaos, namely, of a chaos that waits but for love's touch in order to unfold into a harmonious world" (Schlegel, "Dialogue on Poesy," 183).

11. Think of it in relation to Kant's conception of genius. Kant faces a similar problem with the idea of forming as essential to art, for making or forming involves (as it were analytically) the concept of a principle or law of forming. But if we attribute to the artist knowledge of that law, then it is impossible to distinguish the making of an artifact from that of a work of art. Moreover, the principle of making might then be available to the judge of taste, making the judgment depend on knowledge of the rule—a matter of correctness rather than an aesthetic judgment. Kant therefore argues that genius receives this hidden law of which he is not conscious from nature. Nature is the locus or unconscious ground of forms in art.

This can be also explicated in terms of the understanding of art as an organ of philosophy in Schelling's *System of Transcendental Idealism*. In the "preliminary division of transcendental philosophy" (§3), Schelling establishes an opposition that is constructed from the subjective as the fundamental opposition between the theoretical and the practical. The two fundamental convictions are (1) that there is a world of things independent of us and that our representations are constrained by it, and (2) that there are representations arising in us freely that pass over from thought to the real world and attain objective reality (§§A and B, pp. 10–11). This appears to form a contradiction, for the first demands the dominance of the objective while the second demands the dominance of the subjective. The contradiction can be resolved only if we refer it back to a higher preestablished harmony that must manifest itself in the final stage of the construction. If we call the activity that belongs to the world "nonconscious" and the practical activity of the subject "conscious," then we seek something that is the return to an identity of the conscious and nonconscious. Schelling argues that there is only one activity that produces that identity—namely, art.

12. We have here a prefiguration of the distinction between cult value and exhibition value developed by Benjamin in "The Work of Art in the Age of Its Technological Reproducibility."

13. Compare Schelling: "I define creative imagination in relation to fantasy as that in which the productions of art are received and formed, fantasy as that which intuits them externally, casts them out from within itself, as it were, and to that extent also portrays them. The relationship is the same as that between reason and intellectual intuition. Ideas are formed within reason and, in a sense, from the material of reason; intellectual intuition is that which presents them internally. *Fantasy is thus the intellectual intuition within art*" (Schelling, *Philosophy of Art*, 38; my emphasis).

Chapter 3: The Life and Afterlife of Words

1. Hegel, *Aesthetics: Lectures on Fine Art*, 7. Similarly, in Schelling's *System of Transcendental Philosophy*, we find art to be the organ of philosophy. Art is the indifference between the real and the ideal, between nonconscious nature and the productive activity of the subject.

2. In his "Two Poems by Friedrich Hölderlin" (SW 1:18–36), Benjamin conceives of the intensification of relatedness as the expression of the highest principle, the law of identity. For an elaboration of this difficult issue, see my "Retreat of the Poet in Walter Benjamin's 'Two Poems of Friedrich Hölderlin.'"

3. The relation of the Romantic concept of reflection to Kant's conception of the aesthetic reflective judgment needs to be elaborated beyond this short remark. For Kant, reflection begins from an object in its particularity and is elevated to present through it, its individual purposive form. The Romantics absolutize reflection, making reflection overstep the limitation of form; it is not limited to an object but unfolds in bringing together forms of different objects. This, as will become clear, is the orientation of reflection toward the idea of art. Moreover, reflection is released from its mooring in a psychology of the faculties; its field is the fact of art, its historical existence, in its manifestation over time in a variety of forms, genres, and works. Reflection is expressed in critical acts, through which this multiplicity becomes a systematic unity of thought, the idea of art. For an account of reflective judgment in Kant's aesthetics, see my *Expressions of Judgment*.

4. Friedrich Schlegel, "On Goethe's *Meister*," 59.

5. The work is both the subject and object of reflection, or more precisely, the account of reflection in art must be indifferent to the polarity of subject and object characteristic of representation. Such indifference can be traced, once again, to the mediating character of Kant's conception of reflective judgment, where only through the purposiveness in the movement of the faculties does the purposive form of the object emerge—think of this as the *medial* character of reflection. It is through reflection that a work relates itself to the transcendental medium of its intelligibility. Benjamin suggests the relation to Kant without elaborating on it: "It is difficult to decide whether this formulation contains a reference to Kant's theory of the free play of the mental faculties, in which the object retreats as a nullity in order to form merely the occasion for a self-active, inner attunement of the spirit" (SW 1:150).

6. In this context, see our discussion of the prosaic in Chapter 6. In the early essay on Hölderlin, Benjamin explicitly relates the intensification of relationships to the disappearance of the mythological figuration and thus to a higher prose.

7. One could argue that ultimately these dimensions can be traced to a fundamental opposition—namely, between two limit conceptions through which Kant articulates the infinite intellect: intellectual intuition and intuitive intellect. The first was appropriated by Fichte, the second by Schelling and Goethe. For an important discussion of this bifurcation in post-Kantian thought, see Förster, *Twenty-Five Years of Philosophy*.

8. The language of vectors is meant to suggest a connection to Benjamin's theologico-political fragment, which expresses the same idea by distinguishing the tendency internal to life toward happiness and the vector of messianic fulfillment.

9. As Benjamin notes, his use of "ironically" is meant to relate translation to Romantic critique. For the Romantics, *irony* purifies a work by dissolving what is contingent in it, so as to reveal its essential character. This is not to say that translation has the same character as critique. The latter is "another, if lesser, factor in the continued life of literary works" (SW 1:258).

10. For a discussion of the various possible readings of this figure as well as the problems in translating it from German to English, see Paul de Man, "'Conclusions' on Walter Benjamin's 'The Task of the Translator.'" I find de Man's analysis to unnecessarily complicate the interpretation of the figure.

11. It is significant that this same figure can be found in Schelling's *Philosophical Investigations into the Nature of Human Freedom*. "Selfhood or self-will is, however, only spirit and thus free or above nature by virtue of the fact that it is actually transformed in the primal will (the light) so that it (as self-will) indeed remains in the ground (because there must always be a ground)—just as in a transparent body the matter which has been raised to identity with the light does not for that reason cease to be matter (the dark principle)—yet, it does so merely as a carrier and,

as it were, receptacle of the higher principle of light" (33). Here what is at stake is precisely to conceive of doing away with the particular determinations of a human being so that through their existence they are transparent, or let the medium of the absolute reveal itself through them.

12. I leave it to the reader to draw the connection between this account and our discussion of the presence of the colors of fantasy in painting in Chapter 2.

Chapter 4: The Life of Forms

1. In Schopenhauer, ideas are objectifications of the world-will manifest in appearance as life. It is in beauty and art that we recognize the highest objectification of will in ideas. We should also mention in this context Simmel's understanding of the self-transcendence of life in ideas.

2. Similarly, Benjamin is challenging Croce's rejection of classification in the arts for the sake of the all-important unity of the individual work: "It remains inconceivable that the philosophy of art would ever willingly relinquish its richest ideas, such as that of the tragic or the comic" (O 22). But one should not think of this higher unity as classification, which belongs to the conceptual, but rather through the unity of the idea.

3. In Schopenhauer we find ideas to be the highest objectification of the will. Ideas are not concepts; they are not representations serving the cognition of the world. Ideas are not essences that are "given in advance" but rather must be presented, discovered, or made recognizable by the gathering of what is the variety of their refractions in space and time.

4. To fully develop the analogy, we need to think how ruling grants the existence of the people something like a destiny. Consider how this is expressed in the essay on Hölderlin, where the poet's image is presented as in a mosaic by the extension of the people. For an analysis of this essay, see my "Retreat of the Poet in Walter Benjamin's 'Two Poems of Friedrich Hölderlin.'"

5. The case of languages is important in yet another way: in conceiving of the unity of the idea, it is important to avoid associating its unity with a unity of reflection and consciousness. Benjamin takes the Romantics' account of truth in art as developing out of the character of a reflecting consciousness. The intensification of reflection is the mode of revelation of the medium of the idea. The alternative to this reliance on reflection is what Benjamin characterizes as the reliance on language: "In [the Romantics'] speculation, truth assumed, instead of its linguistic character, the character of a reflecting consciousness" (O 15). Language has a completeness that is objectified (even if dependent on the activity of the speakers). A language is of the world and contains in its own way all that is essential. It gives us a model of how each essence-unity (language) is infinite and all-encompassing and yet all are of one and same world.

6. For an illuminating discussion of the language of hierarchy in Leibniz's monadology, see Ferber's *Philosophy and Melancholy*, chap. 4.

7. For an interpretation of the distinction between *Repräsentation* and *Vorstellung*, see my discussion of the constellation, below.

8. For the source of this concept, see Schelling, *The Grounding of Positive Philosophy*, 171–192.

9. The figure of an obstacle in the flow of a river that forms a whirlpool, that is, a unity, appears in Schelling: "Suppose for illustration, a stream, it is *pure identity*; where it meets resistance a whirlpool is formed; this whirlpool is not an abiding thing, but something that vanishes at every moment, and every moment springs us anew" (Schelling, *First Outline of a System of the Philosophy of Nature*, 206).

10. The relation between imprint and seal is further developed by Benjamin in "Goethe's Elective Affinities" (SW 1:299–300). Note also the recurrence of the figure of the seal in relation to divine violence in the last lines of "Toward the Critique of Violence."

11. Here Benjamin is probably referring to the role played by the visionary in various forms of life-philosophy, where it is modeled on intellectual intuition. In this context the term "intellectual intuition" refers not so much to the standpoint of the absolute but rather to a holistic insight into phenomena that is independent of conceptualization. Benjamin's critique of this position is evident throughout his writings, from the early "Two Poems by Friedrich Hölderlin" to the late "On Some Motifs in Baudelaire."

12. Here the musical is to be understood broadly as what pertains to the ideal as a *discontinuous harmonic multiplicity*, that is, to the highest manifestation of significance. If we look into the various uses of *vernehem*, we find it would be used in speaking of a "hearing" in a court. In the sense of "letting" all sides be heard, we can speak of the balanced proportion of the order of ideas. The French equivalent of *vernehem* would be *entendre*, which similarly stands between the mere hearing of sound and comprehension or understanding (*entendement*). *Entendement* is also related to *entente*, that is, a form of agreement or *attunement* of all sides.

13. Benjamin adds: "In what way and manner do they (ideas) get hold of (*erreichen*) phenomena? And the answer will be: as their [i.e., the phenomena's] representation (*Representation*)" (O 10; translation modified). Benjamin uses the term *Representation* (rather than *Vorstellung*) to express the hold of the idea on phenomena. I take it that what he wants to bring out is the way in which the idea is something like a "representative," or *stands for* the multitude. This is in line with our discussion of the relation of a higher idea to lower ideas, where the figure of the monarch was used to clarify how the harmony of the lower ideas establishes an order in the life of the people, rendering the monarch the representative of this ordered existence.

14. One can find this use of "objectification" in a number of thinkers in the nineteenth century. In particular, for Schopenhauer, the will's complete objectification is in ideas. Ideas are, as it were, the polar correlates of the will, the in-itself of the world. They are the thing-like unity that belongs to the "thing-in-itself" conceived

as will. Closer to Benjamin, this is the relation between life and idea that underlies Georg Simmel's conception (itself informed by Schopenhauer and Nietzsche). See Simmel, "The Turn toward Ideas."

15. See Peter Fenves's discussion of the relation of Cohen's method to Benjamin in *The Messianic Reduction*, chap. 6.

16. Consider, for instance, Kant's famous claim in the preface to the second edition of the First Critique: "Reason, in order to be taught by nature, must approach nature with its principles in one hand, according to which alone the agreement among appearances can count as laws, and in the other hand, the experiments thought out in accordance with these principles—yet in order to be instructed by nature not like a pupil, who has recited to him whatever the teacher wants to say, but like an appointed judge who compels witnesses to answer the questions he puts to them" (Kant, *Critique of Pure Reason*, B xiii).

17. "Only in its multiplicity does the concept of knowledge stand up. Its unity cannot lie in its own sphere; it cannot be a summation, a judgment. If by 'unity' is meant a unity not just of knowings but also as knowledge, then there is no such thing as a unity of knowings" (SW 1:278).

18. This figure relates to that of the funeral pyre through which Benjamin articulates the relation of commentary and critique in the opening of the essay on Goethe's *Elective Affinities*.

Chapter 5: The Guilt and Innocence of Life

1. This understanding of fate would differ, then, from the mythological conception that even the Gods are subject to Moira.

2. The relation between unrealized life and fate is also evident in Benjamin's understanding of the relation between nature and history. This is succinctly expressed by Benjamin in an unpublished essay, titled "Calderón and Hebbel," that was no doubt an offshoot of his work on the book on the German *Trauerspiel*: "We might say, to put it briefly, that the historical drama involves the representation of nature as something that embraces all the vicissitudes of history and triumphs in it. The nature of humanity, or rather the nature of things, is precisely the end result of historical drama. . . . Nature presents the factual reality of historical events as fate. In fate lies concealed the latent resistance of the never-ending flow of historical development. Wherever there is fate, a piece of history has become nature" (SW 1:365).

3. Benjamin stresses that insofar as we can speak of laws of fate, these remain unwritten and appear to provoke and bring about the transgression: "Laws and definite norms remain unwritten in the prehistoric world [*Vorwelt*]. A man can transgress them without suspecting it and then must strive for atonement. But no matter how hard it may hit the unsuspecting, the transgression in the sense of the law is no accident but fate, which appears here in all its ambiguity." He adds: "In a

side-glance at the idea of fate in Antiquity, Hermann Cohen came to a 'conclusion that becomes inescapable': 'The very orders [*Ordnungen*] of fate seem to be what provokes and brings about the misstep'" (SW 2:797; translation modified).

4. For an elaboration of the different model of the presence of fate and its overcoming in Benjamin's analysis of the *Trauerspiel* and its contrast with tragedy, see my *Walter Benjamin: A Philosophical Portrait*, chap. 6, in particular §§3 and 4.

5. Friedrich Nietzsche, *The Birth of Tragedy*, 50.

6. One of the clearest elaborations of the redeeming character of tragedy can be found in Schelling's *Philosophy of Art*. Tragedy overcomes the opposition between freedom and necessity. Schelling calls this state indifference—namely, the two absolutes fulfilled side by side, as it were, beyond the struggle of freedom with necessity and the surrender of self to necessity: "The essence of *tragedy* is thus an actual and objective conflict between freedom in the subject on the one hand, and necessity on the other, a conflict that does not end such that one or the other succumbs, but rather such that both are manifested in perfect indifference as simultaneously victorious and vanquished" (251). Tragedy expresses the highest absolute in which "absolute freedom is absolute necessity" (255).

7. Benjamin's understanding of character should be contrasted with the idea of moral, intelligible character central to Kant's *Religion within the Bounds of Mere Reason*.

8. We can think of the connection between simplicity and a higher sense of nature in terms of Schiller's idea of the naïve. Something working according to its own inner law has a fundamental simplicity to it and is deeply moving.

9. The question of freedom in the univocity and simplicity of the comic character can productively be compared with Bergson's discussion of laughter. The difference between the two is symptomatic of Benjamin's and Bergson's divergent attitudes toward the rule of the technological in modernity.

10. This is to be contrasted with the way Schiller uses the figure of self-absorption (or self-enclosedness), in opposition to the division introduced by reflection, as the fundamental figure for the innocence of the naïve in "On Naïve and Sentimental Poetry."

Chapter 6: Fate, Redemption, and Hope in Love

1. One of the surest signs of an unrealized existence is the false harmony that is suggested in the relation between the pairs. Eduard and Ottilie play music together, but Ottilie has to play out of rhythm and tune to remain attuned to Eduard. A further sign of the space of fate is the power that things come to acquire over human lives. As Benjamin puts it in relation to the manifestation of fate in the *Trauerspiel*: "For once human life has sunk into the bonds of the merely creaturely, the life of seemingly dead or inanimate things gains power over it as well. The efficacy of the thing within the sphere of guilt is a harbinger of death" (O 132).

2. For an illuminating account of demonic ambiguity in the essay as well as in "Fate and Character," see chapter 5 of Kirk Wetters's *Demonic History*, 111–133.

3. Benjamin discusses the prosaic character of truth contents in several writings from "Two Poems by Friedrich Hölderlin" to the epistemo-critical foreword to the *Origin of the German Trauerspiel*. In his "Concept of Criticism" he writes: "The legitimation of criticism ... consists in its prosaic nature. Criticism is the preparation of the prosaic kernel in every work" (SW 1:178).

4. The distinction between approaching something that is external and ever receding and the sense of the inner measure is a central theme of Goethe's fairy tale "The New Melusine," which Benjamin mentions at the end of his discussion of the novella (and on which he wrote a now-lost essay).

5. The massive complications of the novel are purified and concentrated into what is essential in the simplicity of the novella. This simplification is a mark of innocence, as is clear from our discussion of the simplicity of character. We might have to distinguish the anonymity that belongs to a failure of naming, in the figures in the novel, from the authentic dimension of the impersonal in the idea of character. Benjamin speaks of the "genuine anonymity of [the novella's] characters and the partial, undecided anonymity of those of the novel" (SW 1:331).

6. The issue of natural "innocence" comes up in the essay on *Elective Affinities*, in the attempt to determine whether it is possible to speak of the innocence of Ottilie: "It is, after all, in this figure that the novel appears most visibly to grow away from the mythic world. For even though she falls victim to dark powers, it is still precisely her innocence which, in keeping with the ancient requirement that the sacrificial object be irreproachable, forces on her this terrible destiny" (SW 1:334). This formulation brings out the ambiguous character of Ottilie's innocence: innocence is precisely what makes her the object of sacrifice by mythic powers. Benjamin's discussion of the chastity of Ottilie points in the same direction. She is "as unapproachable as someone in a trance" (SW 1:334), and "the untouchableness of that semblance places her out of reach of her lover" (SW 1:336). Her virginity is similarly problematized: the *tableau vivant* in which she portrays the Virgin Mary carrying the baby Christ is paired in real life with her carrying the dead child (in both cases without a husband). For Benjamin, natural innocence can therefore not be accounted for in terms of virginity. The ambiguity of the figure of virginity as a figure of innocence is evident, as "that which is considered the sign of inner purity is precisely what desire most welcomes" (SW 1:335). It cannot be a proper understanding of the innocence of life—it belongs to fate. It is character that is spiritual innocence.

7. In chapter 4 of her *Walter Benjamin: Images, the Creaturely, and the Holy*, Sigrid Weigel lays stress on the nontragic character of Ottilie, as well as on the difficulty this presents for articulating the dimension of the redemptive as internal to the world of the characters of the novel. She does, however, retain something of the

character of the expressionless—namely, as what produces transport to the plane of representation itself. This other plane is identified in the stance of the narrator. Nevertheless, her insightful analysis fails to address the figure of the evening/morning star and thus the dimension of afterlife essential to distinguishing the tragic struggle with myth from the space of hope.

8. There is thus a close connection between the essay and Benjamin's reading of the *Symposium* in the "Epistemo-Critical Foreword" (see my discussion in Chapter 4).

9. In "Walter Benjamin's Variations of Imagelessness," Winfried Menninghaus articulates the inner relation between beauty, life, and semblance as well as the arrest by the sublime shock of that ambiguity characteristic of demonic semblance. He takes the paradigm of the irreducible interplay of the beautiful and the sublime to be Nietzsche's understanding of the Apollonian and the Dionysian. As I argue, part of the difficulty with the elaboration of the temporality of hope in the essay is that it cannot be identified with the tragic model.

10. See my "Appearance of the Ideal of Philosophical Questioning in the Work of Art."

11. We should bear in mind that translation has the capacity to make present this expressionless force. This is particularly important in avoiding misleading pictures of what the sublime "arrest" of expression comes to, and especially of identifying it too closely with the shock of the tragic.

12. There is a similar structure in Kant's analysis of the sublime. Indeed, the sublime is in no way the formless and violent counterpurposive nature; rather, it is what allows the revelation of reason as the *absolute power*. See my *Expressions of Judgment: An Essay on Kant's Aesthetics*, pt. 2. As long as the sublime is the absence or destruction of any form, the sublime and the beautiful will be mere external opposites. But once we recognize that the unfathomability of beauty is the mystery internal to the possibility of its unity as world—that is, that its unity emerges out of chaos—then the possibility of the arrest associated with the moment of the sublime is not the destruction or return into nothing but rather the emergence of truth content, of a fragment of the true world.

13. Benjamin also mentions Hölderlin's hymnic poetry. The reference to Hölderlin can, I take it, be understood in terms of Benjamin's early essay on Hölderlin. Indeed, the opening of a destiny for the living, the relationship between the living and the divine, is correlative with recognizing that the place out of which these relationships emerge and that the poet courageously occupies is death. For a reading of this theme, see my "The Retreat of the Poet in Walter Benjamin's 'Two Poems of Friedrich Hölderlin.'" Also recall that the release of the expressionless force is not just identified in the tragedies but also reinforced in Hölderlin's translations of Sophocles (see SW 1:262).

14. Giorgio Agamben conceives of an exposure that does away with the duality

of the veil and the veiled as what would correspond to the absolute manifestation of pure appearance. This seems to me problematic precisely because the moment of exposure demands the realization of meaning afforded by the "corpse," that is, what is only recognized in the afterlife of meaning. See Agamben, *Nudities*, 84–89.

15. Recall our discussion of the musical character of truth in Chapter 4.

16. Wetters reads this figure as implying that ambiguity, or twilight, is the backdrop of Benjamin's understanding of fidelity. Ambiguity is ever present. "Thus Benjamin does not hope for a utopian solution to the 'problem' of demonic ambiguities. There is nothing that can permanently banish them from the forms of life and society in which they inhere" (Wetters, *Demonic History*, 133).

Chapter 7: Myth, Law, and Life in Common

1. The new critical edition of the essay (Stanford University Press, 2021), and in particular the introduction by Peter Fenves and afterword by Julia Ng, are invaluable in laying out the cultural and philosophical context in which Benjamin wrote and with which he is implicitly and explicitly in conversation.

2. Rousseau sees in that moment the reason why the legislator must appeal to divine or mythical authority: "What the legislator puts into the mouth of the immortals are decisions based on a high-flying reason that is far above the range of the common herd, the aim being to constrain by divine authority those who can't be moved by human prudence. But it's not just anyone who can make the gods speak, or be believed when he claims to be their interpreter. The only miracle that can prove a legislator's mission is his great soul" (Rousseau, *Social Contract*, 87). We will see how for Benjamin it is indeed mythical violence that manifests itself in this ambiguity of law-positing.

3. There has always been a question as to how we are to account for the legitimacy of this transition and what is the force that drives it; it can in no way be identified with the kind of legislation enacted in society.

4. Judith Butler points to this lack of justification or reason in mythical violence, but she interprets it to mean that it is just instituting law "by fiat" (and thereby the necessity to continually reassert it through preserving violence). This does not bring out clearly enough the relation of the mythical to the very character of unrealized life. It makes law itself what determines fate, whereas it is law that serves the orders of fate. See her "Coercion and Sacred Life in Benjamin's 'Critique of Violence.'"

5. Schopenhauer, *World as Will and Representation*, 159.

6. Alison Ross perceptively discusses Benjamin's reconception of the means-ends structure in this essay and to my mind criticizes Hamacher and Fenves correctly for conflating divine violence with the nonviolent sphere of pure means (and thus conceiving of the proletarian general strike as the model for furthering the divine "violence" in human politics). See her "Distinction between Mythic and Divine Violence."

7. Consider for a moment what might be taken as the reverse of destructive divine violence, namely, divine creation. Creation is distinguished from modes of making or a causality that has to do with using means to realize a will. Put differently, creation does not belong to a teleological scheme of nature, nor is something like the argument from design the way to recognize the dimension of the created. Even a more sophisticated version of teleology, such as we find in Kant's account of the highest good as the final end of nature, misses the mark precisely because it does not incorporate the destructive dimension into the scheme of the ethico-theological proof.

8. Compare this to my discussion of Benjamin's account of the revelation of the pure language in translation in Chapter 3. It is only the destruction of the unity of sense that frees a force in language.

9. We do not have here the world of integral actuality to come, but there is a relation to the highest actuality in the total destruction of perverted potentiality, that is, of power for its own sake.

10. It is worth quoting here Fenves and Ng's new translation of this passage: "The release of legal violence stems . . . from the inculpating of mere natural life, which delivers the living, innocent and unfortunate, into the hands of an expiation that 'atones' for this inculpation—and doubtless also de-expiates the guilty, not of guilt to be sure, but of law. For the domination of the law over the living ceases with mere life. Mythic violence is blood-violence over mere life for the sake of violence itself; divine violence is pure violence over all of life for the sake of the living. The former demands sacrifice; the latter assumes it" (CV 58). My translation differs from both the earlier translation and the new one, in particular in regard to their decision to translate *entsühnt* as "de-expiate." I understand the prefix *ent* here to indicate the beginning of an action, as in *entstehen* (to arise)—that is, *entsuhnen* is a coming-to-be-expiated.

11. Agamben's understanding of mere life as what is excluded in establishing law might not fit Benjamin's sense that it is a characterization of a condition in which one may speak of the guilt inherent in life as such, as it remains unrealized by way of the agency of law.

12. This can be compared to Levinas's claim that the commandment "Thou shalt not kill" is not law but the very manifestation of the accusing face of the Other (standing before the deed. as it were): "The Other is the only being that one can be tempted to kill. This temptation to murder and this impossibility of murder constitutes the very vision of the face. To see a face is already to hear 'You shall not kill'" (Levinas, "Ethics and Spirit," 8).

13. As we have seen, this contrast between the elective and the decisive is one of the central themes of Benjamin's essay on Goethe's *Elective Affinities*, written around the same time as "Critique of Violence."

14. The paradigm, the ur-type, of this solitary struggle in which one's faith is

tested in solitude and in which one cannot appeal to any ethical law for securing or justifying the decision to kill, is probably articulated in Kierkegaard's reading of the story of the Akedah (the binding of Isaac) in *Fear and Trembling*.

15. Benjamin, "Notes toward a Work on the Category of Justice" (CV 65).

16. For a commentary on the last paragraphs of this essay, see my "Assuming Violence."

Chapter 8: The Language of the Body and the Body of Language

1. See chapter 4 of my *Walter Benjamin: A Philosophical Portrait* for further discussion of this important essay.

2. Compare this to the discussion of chirality in Kant's *Prolegomena*, where he draws from it the conclusion that space is a form of intuition. Benjamin would argue that my own position in space as a whole is sensed corporeally and grounds the bodily perception of spatial relations.

3. The mythic significance of the horizontal and the vertical is evident in "Painting and the Graphic Arts" and "Signs and Marks" (SW 1:82–86).

4. Benjamin doesn't always separate "body" and "corporeality" through special terminology. As in the present quote, the exact meaning of the term *Leib* has to be identified through the context of the discussion.

5. Benjamin adds: "But this ability finds its limit in the world of color. The human body cannot produce color. It relates to it not creatively but receptively: through the shimmering colors of vision" (SW 1:442; translation modified). We have seen that mimetic behavior in ritual assumes a higher identity through which one partakes in the world of significance. The question therefore arises whether this ground is itself presentable as such. One would surmise that if it is, it would not be as something imitated but rather as what is essentially inimitable but gives the passing character to our mimetic acts. The inimitable is, interestingly enough, already recognizable in the world of the child, which can be seen clearly in Benjamin's discussion of color in the world of the child, and more specifically, of the colors of fantasy. The colors of fantasy are a limit to the mimetic capacity. We cannot imitate color. We are absorbed in color (and ultimately this provides the unity of world in experience). As we have seen, the inimitable as a manifestation of identity that underlies the division in representation of subject and object will also be present in forms of productive mimetism. In every ambitious "imitation"—say, in painting—there is the presence of the inimitable, that is, of the colors of fantasy. A painting draws its force from the balance between the mimetic production through form and the receptivity of fantasy.

6. We could say with Schopenhauer that the mimetic faculty is a form of access to the world as will rather than being a mode of representation. One's own body is the medium to sense the world as will. In Schopenhauer's language, the issue is how my body not only enables the expression of my conscious will but also makes the world-will present through itself.

7. The example of the elk cave paintings suggests that we are considering here a dimension that is essential to the power of art and that this concentration of our relation to a totality into our involvement with an individual object inevitably involves semblance. Compare the gestures of the healer in the "Work of Art" essay.

8. See my discussion of reading in Benjamin's "Berlin Childhood" in my "Learning from the Colors of Fantasy," esp. 128–131.

9. We have discussed in Chapter 5 how concepts such as fate and character similarly problematize the separation of inner world and outer world.

10. Translation, one might say, brings out the nonsensuous similarity between languages. Recall that translation is not based on identifying common elements to the two languages, nor is it dependent on similarity in sense.

11. The magical nature of the sign is evident in practices that fall under "word-magic."

12. Compare this to the characterization of the moment of the expressionless discussed in Chapters 3 and 5.

Chapter 9: Acting Naturally

1. An earlier version of some parts of this chapter appeared in my discussion of Hent de Vries's conception of the tradition of spiritual exercises and the way it can bear on modern existence. See Dika and Shuster, *Reason in Religion: Metaphysics, Ethics, and Politics in Hent de Vries.*

2. Here an introductory remark concerning the scope of the account is in order. On a number of occasions, Benjamin asserts that moral judgment falls only on the actions of individuals. This is often raised in the context of criticizing attempts to pass moral judgment on figures in a literary work. Benjamin stresses that one does not judge moral character, qualities of the individual, or the life of a person: "As moral philosophy is obliged to demonstrate, only actions and never qualities can be of moral importance" (SW 1:205). In particular, in his earlier "Program for the Coming Philosophy" Benjamin challenges the relation between morality and freedom established in Kant. Nor is Benjamin following Kant in construing an opposition between the natural and the moral: "The impact of nature falls not on people's actions but on their lives, which alone are subject to fate. It is here, not in the realm of action, that freedom has its home" (SW 1:398).

In this regard, see the claim made concerning moral judgments and fictional characters in "Goethe's Elective Affinities": "It remains for moral philosophy to prove in rigorous fashion that the fictional character is always too poor and too rich to come under ethical judgment. Such a judgment can be executed only upon real human beings. Characters in a novel are distinguished from them by being entirely rooted in nature" (SW 1:304). See also the important discussion of fictional character and moral judgment (O 104–105).

3. This is why a decisive moral action will have to go beyond the expressive sphere of character. It is why Benjamin speaks of the expressionless character of morality.

4. Nor, for that matter, does it mean that character is wholly there at a particular point in time. Moreover, it is not to be seen as given at birth.

5. "It is a deeply rooted prejudice that will is the key to success. This would be true enough if success concerned only the individual—if it were not also an expression of the fact that the individual's life intervenes in the structure of the world as a whole" (SW 2:589).

6. This last figure receives some further elaboration in Benjamin's writing. He makes evident how a special nobility of character has to do with fortunate fit. Chaplin is a figure of fortunate existence in that he can fit in the world, come what may. Benjamin thus remarks that "[Chaplin's] clothes are impermeable to every blow of fate. He looks like a man who hasn't taken his clothes off for a month. . . . Wet through, sweaty, in clothes far too small for him, Chaplin is the living embodiment of Goethe's *aperçu*: 'Man would not be the noblest creature on earth if he were not too noble for it'" (SW 2:199). Chaplin is consistent mismatched with any *specific* circle of existence in which he happens to find himself, but following the logic of Goethe's aphorism, he therefore embodies a nobility of spirit, a deeper fit to the world as such. To fit the world is to be at odds with any partial social world, to be essentially odd.

7. Compare this to Kant's understanding of the purity of action dissociated from all ends. For Kant, this would be acting from the form of the will as such; Benjamin suggests that it is possible to also conceive of a purity in willing only means, without ends.

8. This description bears on the dialectic of allegory that Benjamin discusses in the last pages of his book on the *Trauerspiel*. The allegorist exhibits the arrogance of subjectivity in the mastery of objects whose secret they take themselves to uncover. In the final moment they recognize the empty endlessness of subjectivity that is mirrored precisely in this sphere of dead objects—emptied out into it, as it were, and revealed as coming to nothing.

9. For a thoughtful analysis of "Practice" in relation to the first thesis of Benjamin's "On the Concept of History," see de Vries, *Le miracle au coeur de l'ordinaire*. De Vries brings out how the consideration of practice belongs to a long tradition of spiritual exercises.

10. In the essay "Analogy and Relationship," Benjamin argues that "the type of person who is defined by [the] confusions between relationship and analogy is the sentimentalist" (SW 1:209). The sentimentalist seeks to grasp by way of metaphor what can only be revealed in the convergence of relationships.

11. Think here of the way something similar is described in "The image of Proust": "Proust has brought off the tremendous feat of letting the whole world age by a lifetime in an instant. But this very concentration in which things that normally just fade and slumber consume themselves in a flash [*Blizhaft*] is called rejuvenation. *A la Recherche du temps perdu* is the constant attempt to charge an entire lifetime with the utmost awareness. Proust's method is actualization, not reflection. He is filled

with the insight that none of us has time to live in the true dramas of the life that we are destined for. This is what ages us—this and nothing else" (SW 2:244). (Note that this is a reinterpretation of the *mémoire involontaire*, and that the theme of actualization is central.) Importantly, this is a model of the self-consuming image that is related to actualization, to integral actuality. It is not a further action "in life" but rather an awakening (rejuvenation), which is correlative with the concentration and consuming in a flash all that slumbers and is unrealized (forgotten). This is why, in the essay on surrealism, Benjamin calls the space of the image opened "the world of universal and integral actualities" (SW 2:217).

12. We might wonder, What is an image that is not recognized in vision? But recall that what is at issue is image *space*, and in image space, there is precisely no figure to contemplate, only relationships. We have seen something similar in Benjamin's discussion of the constellation (see Chapter 4).

13. Consider in this context the claim made by Benjamin in the *Arcades Project* to the effect that one of the two articles of his politics is "the idea of the 'cracking open of natural teleology'" (631 [W7,4]).

14. In her *Body and Image Space*, Sigrid Weigel mentions the analysis of the distinction between body and corporeality in Benjamin's "Outline of the Psychophysical Problem" but argues that this distinction becomes far less important to Benjamin later on (including in the essay on surrealism). It's my contention that, while Benjamin does not use the terminology as he did in the "Outline of the Psychophysical Problem," the distinction itself is just as important in his later writings. For a thoughtful account of body and corporeality and their bearing on Benjamin's conception of the collective, see Barbisan, "Eccentric Bodies: From Phenomenology to Marxism."

15. As we will see, the significance of film is as follows: "Hence, the presentation of reality in film is incomparably the more significant for people today, since it provides the equipment-free aspect of reality they are entitled to demand from a work of art, and does so precisely on the basis of the most intensive *interpenetration* of reality with equipment" (SW 2:116; my emphasis). I will pursue these considerations in Chapter 12 through reading the "Work of Art" essay, which shows precisely how this division of the functional body is afforded by the new photographic technology.

16. In *Body and Image Space*, Sigrid Weigel relates the closing image of the essay to its opening, the image of the gradient through which even a weak stream at its source that can generate great energy in the valley. She takes Benjamin's essay as performing something of this energetic conversion of the French sources of surrealism.

Chapter 10: "From the Pagan Context of Nature ... into the Jewish Context of History"

1. Marx, *The German Ideology*, 26.
2. Goethe, *Scientific Studies*, 156.

3. The fore-history of the baroque *Trauerspiel* includes Socrates' trial and its contrast with tragedy; its after-history includes Baudelaire and expressionism. Benjamin gives a further example in the *Arcades Project*: "Thus, for example, the fore-history of Baudelaire as it presents itself in this current research resides in allegory [i.e., presumably in the baroque]; his after-history in Jugendstil" (A 475 [N10,3]; translation modified).

4. Recall in this context our discussion in Chapter 2 of the differential in relation to the register of fantasy, as well as the destruction of the particular in revealing the higher unity of the constellation of elements.

5. Goethe, *Scientific Studies*, 75.

6. Benjamin draws together the considerations of translation and history in "Paralipomena to 'On the Concept of History'": "The idea of universal history stands and falls with the idea of a universal language. As long as the latter had a basis—whether in theology, as in the Middle Ages, or in logic, as more recently in Leibniz—universal history was not wholly inconceivable. By contrast, universal history as practiced since the nineteenth century can never have been more than a kind of Esperanto)" (SW 4:406).

7. Goethe himself was concerned with the danger of the idea of metamorphosis: "The idea of metamorphosis deserves great reverence, but it is also a most dangerous gift from above. It leads to formlessness, it destroys knowledge, dissolves it. It is like *vis centrifuga* and would be lost in the infinite if it had no counterweight; here I mean the drive for specific character, the stubborn persistence of things which have finally attained reality" (Goethe, *Scientific Studies*, 43).

8. Recall how this denial of mortality is the other side of the adulation of nature that Benjamin attributes to Goethe in his essay on *Elective Affinities*: "Just as the idea of immortality belonging to myth was shown to be an 'incapacity to die,' so, too, in Goethe's thought, immortality is not the journey of the soul to its homeland but rather a flight from one boundlessness into another" (SW 1:317).

9. The relation between phantasmagoria and phantasy is striking: they both emerge as deformation; they form the polarity of the utopian and the mythical.

Chapter 11: Matters of Memory

1. Benjamin accuses this philosophy of life of forgetting death; in his view, in Bergson's conception of *durée* he has become estranged from history: "Bergson the metaphysician suppresses death." The fact that death has been eliminated from Bergson's *durée* isolates it effectively from a historical (as well as prehistorical) order. Bergson's concept of *action* is in keeping with this. The "sound common sense" that distinguishes the "practical man . . . is its godfather. The *durée* from which death has been eliminated has the bad infinity of an ornament" (SW 4:336). The sentence quoted above is from Max Horkheimer's "Zu Bergsons Metaphysik der Zeit." Benjamin's remark is particularly striking given its similarities to the critique of

Goethe's adulation of nature in the essay on *Elective Affinities*. (See also the significance of ornament and arabesque in the conjured figure of Ottilie [Chap. 5] as well as in Jugendstil [Chap. 13].)

2. Bergson adopts a dualism of mind and body. Dualism, as he puts it, is the intuitive view of common sense, for which he provides the metaphysical grounding. Yet Bergson's dualism is very different from its better-known versions in the philosophical tradition, such as Descartes's duality of the extensive and the thinking substance. In particular, the character of Bergson's dualism is going to turn on the elaboration of the duality of space and time, or better, matter and memory; the title of the work thus presents us with the fundamental terms of the dualism. The appeal to matter is not new, but the term "memory" is surprising. It is memory and not thought, memory and not consciousness, that is central to the essence of the mind.

3. Here is the central passage in Bergson: "The characteristic of the man of action is the promptitude with which he summons to the help of a given situation all the memories which have reference to it; yet it is also the insurmountable barrier which encounters, when they present themselves on the threshold of his consciousness, memories that are useless or indifferent. To live only in the present, to respond to a stimulus by the immediate reaction which prolongs it, is the mark of the lower animals: the man who proceeds in this way is a man of impulse. But he who lives in the past for the mere pleasure of living there, and in whom recollections emerge into the light of consciousness without any advantage for the present situation, is hardly better fitted for action: here we have no man of impulse, but a dreamer. Between these two extremes lives the happy disposition of memory docile enough to follow with precision all the outlines of the present situation, but energetic enough to resist all other appeal. Good sense, or practical sense, is probably nothing but this" (Bergson, *Matter and Memory*, 153).

4. In that sense, someone who "acts crazy" has not brought their memories into line with the necessities of lived action. They as it were behave out of the deep and singular stratum of memory.

5. There is a similar moment in Benjamin's "Berlin Childhood around 1900." Benjamin clarifies how he does not seek to express his early life narratively, in terms of biographical events and persons, but rather seeks to do away with the continuity of contingent biographical experience for what he calls the depth of experience, where he encounters the impersonal and collective: "This has meant that certain biographical features, which stand out more readily in the continuity of experience than in its depths, altogether recede in the present undertaking. And with them go the physiognomies—those of my family and comrades alike" (SW 3:388).

6. For a more systematic account of the difference between various forms of similarity, see my discussion of Benjamin's fragment "Analogy and Relationship" in Chapter 9.

7. Bergson, *Time and Free Will*, 172.

8. For a discussion of Benjamin's writing on childhood, see my "Learning from the Colors of Fantasy" and "A Mood of Childhood in Benjamin," as well as *Walter Benjamin: A Philosophical Portrait*, 103–111.

9. In her *Revolution and History in Walter Benjamin*, Alison Ross builds a complex argument that leads from a highly specific context, Benjamin's construal of the world of childhood, to the very broad context of the idea of revolution in history. In this careful construction, a number of important stages that allow the "mediation" between those two extremes can be singled out. In particular, Ross is well aware that it is not possible to take up the figure of the child unproblematically in order to account for the revolutionary tendencies of the collective in history. A central piece of her conceptual analysis is directed to the understanding of the structure of wish and wish fulfillment in Benjamin's account of childhood, as well as the problems of its transfer to the context of the collective and of history.

10. As we have already seen in the discussion of "Ibizan Sequence" in Chapter 9, when we are dreaming, it is precisely the ordinary that has escaped us in the lived moment to which we become attentive: "Everyday experiences, hackneyed expressions, the vestiges that remain in a glance, the pulsating of one's own blood—all this, hitherto unnoticed and in a distorted and overly sharp form, makes up the stuff of dreams" (SW 2:592).

11. The relation of the dream to ordinariness and afterlife is suggested in Benjamin's essay "Dream Kitsch." The dream is to be found not in the "Blue Flower" of Romanticism but in the gray, the ordinary, or rather in the dust of age that things acquire in their afterlife: "No longer does the dream reveal a blue horizon. The dream has grown gray. The gray coating of dust on things is its best part. Dreams are now a shortcut to banality" (SW 2:3).

12. Just as we can speak of the relation of the dream to remembering, we can similarly conceive of it in terms of forgetting. Through the dream, remembering and forgetting are related dialectically rather than being merely opposed. In the context of the individual, as Freud articulates it, the dream is the image of the fulfillment of a wish, and as such it presents, in a distorted form, what is repressed. A similar relation must be established in the context of history between forgetting and the distortion of the dream. The distortions and deformations inherent in the dream configuration of the past are the manifestation of the forgotten. It is through what the self-image of the victorious present has left behind in constituting itself that the past appears distorted. The relation between distortion and forgetting is evident in a number of places in Benjamin's writing, perhaps most succinctly in the figure of the hunchback who takes their share of experience into oblivion. In the distortion characteristic of dream material, we recognize the forgotten as that which holds in it the secret of awakening, that which has within it signs of the force of the currents of nature: "Every current of fashion or of worldview derives its force from what is forgotten" (A 393 [K2a,3]).

13. It is far from straightforward to recognize opportunities for the fulfillment of a wish. See the passage in Benjamin's "Berlin Childhood" titled "Winter Morning" that opens with: "The fairy in whose presence we are granted a wish is there for each of us. But few of us know how to remember the wish we have made; and so, few of us recognize its fulfillment later in our lives" (SW 3:357).

14. The child as it were transforms what lies "in the darkness of the lived moment" into something that is revealed as significant in memory. This darkness, a kind of amorphous materiality, is clearly expressed in the following passage: "What the child (and through faint reminiscence, the man) discovers in the pleats of the old dress to which it clings while trailing at its mother's skirts—that's what these pages should contain" (A 391 [K2,2]; translation modified). This figure is suggestive in a number of ways. First, it is a figure for the material (*Stoff*), the contact with the lived present, but second, it also suggests that it is in considering such things as a dress (fashion) that we can open to this dream configuration of the past: "The eternal is far more a ruffle on a dress than some idea" (A 463 [N3,2]). The figure of the pleats in the dress is particularly interesting: the material has a fold (the pleats), and its unfolding is what is given to the adult in recalling the dream.

15. We also find this identity of the new and the return to the primal in Benjamin's formulation of Proust's dreams of happiness: "There is a dual will to happiness, a dialectics of happiness: a hymnic form as well as an elegiac form. The one is the unheard of, the unprecedented, the height of bliss; the other, the eternal repetition, the eternal restoration of the original, first happiness—it could also be called the Eleatic—which for Proust transforms existence into a preserve of memory" (SW 2:239).

16. Richard Eldridge's *Images of History* presents a forceful and philosophically rigorous recent interpretation of the concept of the image in Benjamin and brings it together with an analysis of the function of the "moral image of the world" in Kant. This transformation of the role of the idea in Kant requires drawing it out of the historically contingent material without losing its unconditioned character. His analysis shows that there is no way to establish ideals through speculation on general human characteristics; rather, it is always necessary to conceive of them as arising from and in response to the historically concrete, and conversely, of conceiving of the historically concrete as recognizable only out of the projection of such ideals. What is striking in Benjamin is that the image comes to us not from the future but from the past, so that its actualization is a transformation of our present.

17. Image is archetype—in other words, it is an image in the order of being, not an image as the product of thinking or imagining. This ontological dimension must be understood in relation to the highest actuality, whereby we understand how what is conceived of as becoming in time acquires the character of being. This is what is implied by introducing arrest into the dialectical movement of thinking. The critical moment is to be conceived of in relation to the arrest of the movement

of thinking in an image. Arrest is a category of thought that has its parallel in the striking recognition of the highest actuality of being. Viewed in terms of the discussion of origin, it is the moment of being in becoming: "To root out any trace of 'development' from the image of history and to represent becoming... as a constellation in being: that is no less the tendency of this project" ("First Sketches," A 845 [Ho,16]; note how close this is to the formulation of origin as the establishment of being in becoming).

18. Bergson, *Time and Free Will*, 172.

Chapter 12: First and Second Nature in Art

1. The example of unmanned aircrafts could be a reference to Scheerbart's "*The Development of Aerial Militarism and the Demobilization of European Ground Force, Fortresses, and Naval Fleets.*" The wit of this text also suggests, beyond the destructive use of the technology for war, its utopian horizon.

2. It takes new forms in the metamorphosis of love that Benjamin analyzes, for instance, in the short essay "On Love and Related Matters."

3. For an insightful analysis of this distinction in the context of comparing Benjamin and Heidegger on the question of technology, see Beatrice Hanssen, "Benjamin or Heidegger: Aesthetics and Politics in an Age of Technology," esp. 82–83. Hanssen draws a fascinating picture of this philosophical and political juncture. While suggesting affinities between Benjamin's and Heidegger's understanding of the relations among art, technology, and politics, she develops a forceful critique of Heidegger's appropriation of Ernst Junger's idea of total mobilization.

4. Indeed, Benjamin presents Goethe as the modern artist for which the fascination with semblance was at its highest: "Goethe's work is still entirely imbued with beautiful semblance as an auratic reality. Mignon, Ottilie, and Helena partake of that reality" (SW 3:127).

5. The second nature is determined through the interrelation of humanity with social and technological forces. It is essentially relational and therefore must be understood in terms of Benjamin's account of the body (*Leib*). The first nature is the elemental vitality of corporeality: "In addition to the totality of all its living members, humanity is able to partly draw nature, the nonliving, plant, and animal, into this life of the body of mankind.... It can do this by virtue of the technology in which the unity of its life is formed. Ultimately, everything that subserves humanity's happiness may be counted part of its life, its limbs" (SW 1:395). See my reading of "The Outline of the Psychophysical Problem" in Chapter 8.

6. The initial contrast and relation between the two is articulated as follows: "The more widely the development of humanity ramifies, the more openly utopias based on the first nature (and especially the human body) will give place to those relations to society and technology. That this regression is provisional can be taken for granted" (SW 3:134).

7. For an insightful analysis of this moment, see David Ferris's "The Shortness of History, or Photography in Nuce," esp. 19–23.

8. See Cavell, *The World Viewed*, 24.

9. For a rich and layered reading of Benjamin's treatment of Atget, see Gelley, *Benjamin's Passages*, 87–101.

10. See, in particular, Hegel, *Aesthetics: Lectures on Fine Art*, 153.

11. Here, as in many other moments in the essay, Chaplin is something like a paradigm. He fully incorporates the discontinuity inherent in assembly and montage into his bodily presence: "Concerning [discontinuity's] significance we have at least one very important pointer. It is the fact that Chaplin's films have met with the greatest success of all up to now. The reason is quite evident. Chaplin's way of moving [*Gestus*] is not really that of an actor. He could not have made an impact on the stage. His unique significance lies in the fact that, in his work, the human being is integrated into the film image by way of his gestures—that is, his bodily and spiritual [*geistiges*] posture. The innovation of Chaplin's gestures is that he dissects the expressive movements of human beings into a series of minute innervations. Each single movement he makes is composed of a succession of staccato bits of movement. Whether it is his walk, the way he handles his cane, or the way he raises his hat—always the same jerky sequence of tiny movements applies the law of the cinematic image sequence to human motorial functions. Now, what is it about this behavior that is distinctly comic?" (SW 3:94; translation modified). Relating Chaplin to the assembly line might seem to us obvious, but note that the fragment was written in 1935 and *Modern Times* came out in 1936.

12. See Cavell, *The World Viewed*, chap. 5.

13. In this regard, see my "Wittgenstein, Benjamin and Pure Realism."

14. Let me illustrate this other presence of nature, or the presence of another nature than the one that speaks to the eye, with a short discussion of Benjamin's account of Blossfeldt's photography. In his "Small History of Photography," Benjamin relates the Goethean method and its delicate empiricism to certain photographic practices. In his discussion of August Sander's serial photography of types, Benjamin characterizes that photographer's mode of observation in the spirit of Goethe's remark: "There is a delicate empiricism which so intimately involves itself with the object that it becomes true theory." In his review of Blossfeldt's book *Urformen der Kunst*, which self-consciously points back to Goethe's investigation of the *ur*-phenomenon, Benjamin suggests an emendation to Blossfeldt's characterization of his achievement: "*Originary Forms of Art*, certainly," Benjamin writes. "What can this mean, though, but originary forms of nature? Forms, that is, which were never a mere model for art but which were, from the beginning, at work as originary forms in all that was created" (SW 2:156). In other words, Benjamin suggests that the primal images resting in nature can be revealed, or better, realized, in art, and particularly in that art which has internalized technology, namely, photography.

Benjamin writes that in the enlarged plants we encounter vegetal "Forms of Style." This last expression, put by Benjamin in scare quotes, refers most probably back to Alois Riegl's *Questions of Style*, which unfolds the history of the vegetal motif in ornament. Riegl does not argue for a simple realism that takes nature as a model but for a more fundamental account of the presence of nature as archetype in ornament. This natural origin of art is what Riegl identifies as the *Kunstwollen*, or the will at work in art (see the discussion in Chapter 4). Style then would be misunderstood if seen merely as a framework of conventions of a period or, alternatively, in terms of the characteristic personality of the artist. Style, here, would point to the unity of nature that is at work in art, a kind of unity that only a whole environment of manifestations, methodically inventoried and ordered, can make evident. It is this more fundamental relation of art to nature that Benjamin recognizes in the medium of similarity mirrored in Blossfeldt's photographs. They afford us a sense of creative nature at work in the human world.

15. See my discussion of "Berlin Childhood" in *Walter Benjamin: A Philosophical Portrait*, 103–111.

16. If anything, this aestheticization of the political is a distortion of the sublime rather than the beautiful. See my essay "Some Thoughts on Kitsch."

Chapter 13: Distorted Life

1. Among the few attempts so far to encompass the *Arcades Project* as a whole, probably the most sustained and thorough is still Susan Buck-Morss's *The Dialectics of Seeing: Walter Benjamin and the Arcades Project*.

2. Benjamin uses the term "phantasmagoria" to characterize these dreams. Literally, phantasmagoria was used to describe theater shows involving the projection with a magic lantern of images having a frightening character (ghosts, demons, etc.). In Benjamin's use of the term, we might characterize these as the dream images materialized in the form of existence of the nineteenth century.

3. Compare this to the peculiar alteration of the material content in time as it is formulated in the opening of the essay on *Elective Affinities*.

4. The discussion of Fourier is thus in line with various themes that Benjamin suggests inform later artists such as Klee (see "Experience and Poverty" and the engineering thought that characterizes the new painting), as well as his sense of the importance of Chaplin's mechanical character.

5. Benjamin suggests a parallel between his idea of the innervation of the collective and the idea of propagation by explosion: "Fourier's conception of the propagation of the phalansteries through 'explosions' may be compared to two articles of my 'politics': the idea of revolutions as an innervation of the technical organs of the collective (analogy with the child who learns to grasp by trying to get hold of the moon), and the idea of the 'cracking open of natural teleology'" (A 631 [W7,4]).

On the connection between fantasy and utopia, see Benjamin's remark on Fourier and Mickey Mouse: "For the purpose of elucidating the Fourierist extravagances, we may adduce the figure of Mickey Mouse, in which we find carried out, entirely in the spirit of Fourier's conceptions, the moral mobilization of nature. Humor, here, puts politics to the test. Mickey Mouse shows how right Marx was to see in Fourier, above all else, a great humorist. The cracking open of natural teleology proceeds in accordance with the plan of humor" (A 635 [W8a,5]).

6. Benjamin returns to this theme in the "Theses on History": "According to Fourier, cooperative labor would increase efficiency to such an extent that four moons would illuminate the sky at night, the polar ice caps would recede, seawater would no longer taste salty and beasts of prey would do man's bidding. All this illustrates a kind of labor which, far from exploiting nature, would help her give birth to the creations that now lie dormant in her womb" (SW 4:394).

7. This emphasis on movement and speed recalls the way in which Benjamin describes the "indefatigable assistants" in Kafka's world. They are those who exist to assist—that is, in the sphere of pure means—or have escaped from the guilt that burdens the creatures of that world.

8. Scheerbart and Taut, *Glass Architecture*, 41.

9. In convolute G, Benjamin lists a number of such exhibitions, the first of which took place in 1798 at the Champ de Mars in Paris (see A 178 [G4,4]).

10. Cf. "Capitalism as Religion" (SW 1:288). In this fragment, Benjamin characterizes the religion of capitalism as involving ritual only; it is a religion without dogma or theology.

11. Note a similar point in part 2 of Nietzsche's *On the Genealogy of Morality*. The origin of guilt in the relation between creditor and debtor intensifies to the point of becoming the infinite guilt of humanity that Christ takes upon himself.

12. The idea of compactness is to be contrasted with the "airiness" or "well ventilated" character of Scheerbart's fantasies. Compactness is a concept that Benjamin uses in characterizing the relation of fascism to the masses. See, in particular, SW 3:129.

13. Similarly, Benjamin suggests how the other moment of "discontinuity"—namely, birth—is "overcome" in fashion: "The natural engendering of life [is] 'overcome' by novelty in the realm of fashion" (A 79 [B9,2]).

14. The analysis of fashion is closely connected to an understanding of how primal time manifests itself in the space of life. The rhythm of fashion and its relation to time seem initially to be determined by its premonition of trends, which allies it with soothsaying, the reading of fate. But with fashion, just as much as with the soothsayer, the capacity to sense the future is a matter of relating to the presence of the primal past and its peculiar manifestation in the rhythm of life: "The unique self-construction of the newest in the medium of what has been[ ] makes for the true dialectical theater of fashion" (A 64 [B1a,2]). The power of fashion, its life, draws on what is destroyed and forgotten: "Every current of fashion or of worldview derives

its force from what is forgotten" (A 393 [K2a,3]). "Fashions are a collective medicament for the ravages of oblivion. The more short-lived a period, the more susceptible to fashion" (A 80 [B9a,1]).

15. In the essay "Eduard Fuchs, Collector and Historian," Benjamin explicitly opposes the materialist practice of collecting to a history of ideas.

16. In Jugendstil the relation between youth and death is introduced in an utterly distorted way, by wedding death or decline to beauty: "The bourgeoisie senses that its days are numbered; all the more it wishes to stay young. Thus, it deludes itself with the prospect of a longer life or, at least, a death in beauty" (A 559 [S9a,4]). In an early essay, "Stefan George in Retrospect" (SW 2:706), Benjamin speaks of the "tortured ornamentation that was typical of the furniture and facades of the day."

17. Note how the epigraph "Everything for me becomes allegory" (A 21) is from Baudelaire's poem "Le cygne," which in the duality of its title (*cygne / signe*) brings out the transformation of the living being into a sign, an allegory.

18. As Benjamin writes in his *Origin of the German Trauerspiel*: "If the object becomes allegorical under the gaze of melancholy, if melancholy causes life to flow out of it and it remains behind dead, but eternally secure, then it is exposed to the allegorist, it is unconditionally in his power. That is to say it is now quite incapable of emanating any meaning or significance of its own; such significance as it has, it acquires from the allegorist" (O 183–184).

19. This prevalence of lived experience is diagnosed by Benjamin in different domains, from the development of "news" in newspapers to the structure of gambling (to take only two examples). The dissociation of meaning from a higher unity is the fundamental form of the newspaper page: the sensation replaces coherence with the force of the new. Similarly, gambling is such that each bet is essentially disconnected from past ones; nothing can be learned from previous occurrences. Thus its structure is essentially distinct from an experience in which the past bears on and informs the way we open onto the present. The simple yes/no, winning or losing, with its value polarity and its drastic consequences, has the immediacy of shock. Benjamin notes that a move in a game of chance is called a *coup*, which also means something that strikes or hits. But furthermore, we can see that this is correlative with the reduction of significance to information. As sensation becomes sensational, meaning, one might say, is reduced to mere number.

20. It would be instructive to compare and contrast the *promeneur* in nature (e.g., Rousseau) to the flâneur in the city. The latter is experiencing the diversity of "natural" life in the city through the beauty of the human plurality of types

21. Benjamin characterizes the crowd as a veil that covers the city. The suggestion implied in this figure is that the new beauty found in the crowd of the city is also semblance, covering a violence that pertains to its presence.

22. Baudelaire, *The Painter of Modern Life*, 13.

23. The relation between allegorical poetry and the petrifying gaze is a theme

of the second part of Benjamin's *Origin of the German Trauerspiel*: "[In] allegory there lies before the eyes of the observer the *facies hippocratica* of history as petrified primal landscape. History, in everything untimely, sorrowful, and miscarried that belongs to it from the beginning, is inscribed in a face—no, in a death's head" (O 174).

24. Compare the phantasmagoria in stone and the end of the section on Baudelaire, where Benjamin writes about the petrifying Medusa gaze. The relation between Baudelaire and Haussmann becomes particularly clear if one thinks about the destruction brought about by the construction of the boulevards, the destruction of old Paris. Indeed, the transition from Baudelaire to Haussmann is from the streets of Paris to their destruction. It is as though the victors establish their monumental history at the expense of another sense of the past in the city, which is destroyed in the construction of the boulevard. The attempt to hold on to that other past as it is in the process of disappearing has several champions: "Maxime du Camp's monumental work *Paris* owes its existence to this dawning awareness. The etchings of Meryon (around 1850) constitute the death mask of Paris" (A 23). Baudelaire's allegorical genius feeds precisely on the ruins of old Paris.

25. For an excellent presentation of the theme of mythical guilt and eternal return in the exposés, see Lefebvre, "Things Temporal Exposé: Passages from Benjamin."

26. This has important implications for thinking Benjamin's relation to Nietzsche. Indeed, it implies that Nietzsche's abyssal thought is itself a phantasmagoria: "Thinking once again the thought of eternal recurrence in the nineteenth century makes Nietzsche the figure in whom a mythic fatality is realized anew" (A 119 [D10a,4]).

27. Nietzsche, *Untimely Meditations*, 97.

Bibliography

Throughout this work I refer to Benjamin's writings immediately following the quotations by way of the following abbreviations:

  A *The Arcades Project*. Translated by H. Eiland and K. McLaughlin. Cambridge, MA: Belknap Press of Harvard University Press, 1999.
  C *The Correspondence of Walter Benjamin, 1910–1940*. Translated by Manfred R. Jacobson and Evelyn M. Jacobson. Chicago: University of Chicago Press, 1994.
CAB *Theodor W. Adorno and Walter Benjamin: The Complete Correspondence, 1928–1940*. Edited by Henri Lonitz; translated by Nicholas Walker. Cambridge, MA: Harvard University Press, 1999.
CBS *The Correspondence of Walter Benjamin and Gershom Scholem, 1932–1940*. Edited by Gershom Scholem; translated by Gary Smith and Andre LeFevere. Cambridge, MA: Harvard University Press, 1989.
  C *Toward the Critique of Violence: A Critical Edition*. Edited by Peter Fenves and Julia Ng. Stanford, CA: Stanford University Press, 2021.
 EW *Early Writings 1910–1917*. Translated by Howard Eiland. Cambridge, MA: Harvard University Press, 2011.
 GS *Gesammelte Schriften*. Edited by Rolf Tiedemann and Hermann Schweppenhaüser. Rev. paperback ed. 14 vols. Frankfurt am Main: Suhrkamp, 1991.
  O *Origin of the German Trauerspiel*. Translated by Howard Eiland. Cambridge, MA: Harvard University Press, 2019.
 SW *Selected Writings of Walter Benjamin*. Edited by Marcus Bullock and Michael W. Jennings. 4 vols. Cambridge, MA: Belknap Press of Harvard University Press, 1996–2003.

Agamben, Giorgio. *Nudities*. Translated by David Kishik. Stanford, CA: Stanford University Press, 2009.
Barbisan, Léa. "Eccentric Bodies: From Phenomenology to Marxism—Walter Benjamin's Reflections on Embodiment." Special issue, *Anthropology and Materialism: A Journal of Social Research*, no. 1 (2017).
Baudelaire, Charles. *The Painter of Modern Life and Other Essays*. Translated and edited by Jonathan Mayne. New York: Phaidon Press, 1964.
Bergson, Henri. *Matter and Memory*. Translated by N. M. Paul and W. S. Palmer. New York: Zone Books, 1988.
———. *Time and Free Will: An Essay on the Immediate Data of Consciousness*. Translated by F. L. Pogson. New York: Dover, 2001.
Buck-Morss, Susan. *The Dialectics of Seeing: Walter Benjamin and the Arcades Project*. Cambridge, MA: MIT Press, 1989.
Butler, Judith. "Coercion and Sacred Life in Benjamin's 'Critique of Violence.'" In *Political Theologies: Public Religions in a Post-secular World*, ed. Hent de Vries, 201–219. New York: Fordham University Press, 2006.
Cassirer, Ernst. "The Kantian Elements in Wilhelm von Humboldt's Philosophy of Language." In *The Warburg Years (1919–1933)*, trans. S. G. Lofts, 101–129. New Haven, CT: Yale University Press, 2013.
Cavell, Stanley. "Benjamin and Wittgenstein: Signals and Affinities." *Critical Inquiry* 25, no. 2 (1999): 235–246.
———. *The World Viewed: Reflections on the Ontology of Film*. Cambridge, MA: Harvard University Press, 1979.
Caygill, Howard. *Walter Benjamin: The Color of Experience*. London: Routledge, 1998.
de Man, Paul. "'Conclusions' on Walter Benjamin's 'The Task of the Translator.'" *Yale French Studies* 97 (2000): 10–35.
De Vries, Hent. *Le miracle au coeur de l'ordinaire*. Paris: Encre Marine, 2019.
Dika, T. R., and M. Shuster, eds. *Reason in Religion: Metaphysics, Ethics, and Politics in Hent de Vries*. London: Routledge, 2022.
Eldridge, Richard. *Images of History: Kant, Benjamin, Freedom, and the Human Sciences*. Oxford: Oxford University Press, 2017.
Fenves, Peter. *The Messianic Reduction: Walter Benjamin and the Shape of Time*. Stanford, CA: Stanford University Press, 2010.
Ferber, Ilit. *Philosophy and Melancholy: Benjamin's Early Reflections on Theater and Language*. Stanford, CA: Stanford University Press, 2013.
Ferris, David. "The Shortness of History, or Photography in Nuce: Benjamin's Attenuation of the Negative." In *Walter Benjamin and History*, ed. Andrew Benjamin, 19–37. London: Continuum, 2005.
Förster, Eckart. *The Twenty-Five Years of Philosophy: A Systematic Reconstruction*. Translated by Brady Bowman. Cambridge, MA: Harvard University Press, 2017.

Friedlander, Eli. "The Appearance of the Ideal of Philosophical Questioning in the Work of Art." *Yearbook of Comparative Literature* 57 (2011): 103–116.

———. "Assuming Violence: A Commentary on Benjamin's 'Critique of Violence.'" *boundary 2* 42, no. 4 (2015): 159–185.

———. *Expressions of Judgment: An Essay on Kant's Aesthetics*. Cambridge, MA: Harvard University Press, 2015.

———. "Learning from the Colors of Fantasy." *boundary 2* 45, no. 2 (2018): 11–137.

———. "Logic, Ethics and Existence in Wittgenstein's *Tractatus*." In *Wittgenstein's Moral Thought*, ed. Edmund Dain and Reshef Agam-Segal, 97–132. New York: Routledge, 2017.

———. "A Mood of Childhood in Benjamin." In H. Kenaan and I. Ferber, *Philosophy's Moods: The Affective Grounds of Thinking*, 39–50. Berlin: Springer, 2011.

———. "The Retreat of the Poet in Walter Benjamin's 'Two Poems of Friedrich Hölderlin.'" In *Tsimtsum and Modernity: Lurianic Heritage in Modern Philosophy & Theology*, ed. Agata Bielik-Robson and Daniel H. Weiss, 207–218. Berlin: de Gruyter, 2021.

———. "Some Thoughts on Kitsch." *History and Memory* 9, no. 1/2 (Fall 1997): 376–392.

———. *Walter Benjamin: A Philosophical Portrait*. Cambridge, MA: Harvard University Press, 2011.

———. "Wittgenstein, Benjamin and Pure Realism." In *Wittgenstein and Modernism*, ed. Michael LeMahieu and Karen Zumhagen-Yekplé, 114–129. Chicago: University of Chicago Press, 2017.

Gelley, Alexander. *Benjamin's Passages: Dreaming, Awakening*. New York: Fordham University Press, 2015.

Goethe, Johan Wolfgang von. *Scientific Studies*. Vol. 12 of *The Collected Works*, ed. and trans. Douglas Miller. Princeton, NJ: Princeton University Press, 1995.

Hanssen, Beatrice. "Benjamin or Heidegger: Aesthetics and Politics in an Age of Technology." In *Walter Benjamin and Art*, ed. A. Benjamin, 73–92. London: Continuum, 2005.

Hegel, G. W. F. *Aesthetics: Lectures on Fine Art*. Vol. 1. Translated by T. M. Knox. New York: Oxford University Press, 1975.

Horkheimer, Max. "Zu Bergsons Metaphysik der Zeit." *Zeitschrift für Sozialforschung* 3, no. 3 (1934).

Kant, Immanuel. *Critique of Pure Reason*. Edited and translated by P. Guyer and A. Wood. Cambridge: Cambridge University Press, 1999.

———. *Critique of the Power of Judgment*. Edited and translated by Paul Guyer and Eric Matthews. Cambridge: Cambridge University Press, 2000.

———. *Religion within the Bounds of Mere Reason*. Edited and translated by A. Wood and G. di Giovanni. Cambridge: Cambridge University Press, 1998.

Lefebvre, Alexandre. "Things Temporal Exposé: Passages from Benjamin." *Journal of Cultural Research* 7, no. 1 (2003): 47–60.

Levinas, Emmanuel. "Ethics and Spirit." In *Difficult Freedom: Essays on Judaism*, trans. Sean Hand, 3–10. Baltimore: Johns Hopkins University Press, 1990.

Marx, Karl. "The German Ideology." In *Karl Marx: A Reader*, ed. John Elster, 23–28. Cambridge: Cambridge University Press, 1986.

Menninghaus, Winfried. *Walter Benjamins Theorie der Sprachmagie*. Frankfurt am Main: Suhrkamp, 1995.

———. "Walter Benjamin's Variations of Imagelessness." *Critical Horizons: A Journal of Philosophy and Social Theory* 14 (2013): 407–428.

Nietzsche, Friedrich. *The Birth of Tragedy and Other Writings*. Edited by R. Geuss and R. Speirs; translated by R. Speirs. Cambridge: Cambridge University Press, 1999.

———. *On the Genealogy of Morality*. Edited by Keith Ansell Pearson; translated by Carol Diethe. Cambridge: Cambridge University Press, 2006.

———. *Untimely Meditations*. Edited by Daniel Breazeale; translated by John Hollingdale. Cambridge: Cambridge University Press, 1997.

Rosenzweig, Franz. *The Star of Redemption*. Translated by Barbara E. Galli. Madison: University of Wisconsin Press, 2005.

Ross, Alison. "The Distinction between Mythic and Divine Violence: Walter Benjamin's 'Critique of Violence' from the perspective of Goethe's 'Elective Affinities.'" *New German Critique*, no. 121 (Winter 2014): 93–120.

———. *Revolution and History in Walter Benjamin: A Conceptual Analysis*. London: Routledge, 2018.

Rousseau, Jean-Jacques. *The Social Contract*. Translated by Maurice Cranston. London: Penguin, 1968.

Scheerbart, Paul. *The Development of Aerial Militarism and the Demobilization of European Ground Force, Fortresses, and Naval Fleets*. Translated by M. Kasper. Brooklyn, NY: Ugly Duckling Press, 2007.

Scheerbart, Paul, and Bruno Taut. *Glass Architecture*. Edited by Dennis Sharp. New York: Praeger, 1972.

Schelling, Wilhelm F. J. *First Outline of a System of the Philosophy of Nature*. Translated with an introduction by Keith R. Peterson. Albany: SUNY Press, 2004.

———. *The Grounding of Positive Philosophy*. Translated with an introduction by Bruce Matthews. Albany: SUNY Press, 2008.

———. *Philosophical Investigations into the Nature of Human Freedom*. Translated with an introduction by Jeff Love and Johannes Schmidt. Albany: SUNY Press, 2006.

———. *The Philosophy of Art*. Edited and translated with an introduction by Douglas W. Stott; foreword by David Simpson. Minneapolis: University of Minnesota Press, 1989.

———. *The System of Transcendental Idealism*. Translated by Peter Heath; introduction by Michael Vater. Charlottesville: University of Virginia Press, 1978.

Schiller, Friedrich. *On Naïve and Sentimental Poetry and On the Sublime: Two Essays*. Translated by Julius A. Elias. New York: F. Ungar, 1964.

Schlegel, Friedrich. "Dialogue on Poesy." In *Theory as Practice: A Critical Anthology of Early German Romantic Writings*, trans. and ed. J. Schulte-Sasse, 180–193. Minneapolis: University of Minnesota Press, 1997.

———. "On Goethe's *Meister*." In *German Aesthetics and Literary Criticism*, ed. Kathleen M. Wheeler, 59–72. Cambridge: Cambridge University Press, 1984.

Schopenhauer, Arthur. *The World as Will and Representation*. Vol. 1. Edited and translated by Judith Norman, Alistair Welchman, and Christopher Janaway; introduction by Christopher Janaway. Cambridge: Cambridge University Press, 2010.

Simmel, Georg. "The Turn toward Ideas." In *The View of Life: Four Metaphysical Essays with Journal Aphorisms*, trans. John A. Y. Andrews and Donald N. Levine, 19–62. Chicago: University of Chicago Press, 2010.

Stern, Alexander. *The Fall of Language: Benjamin and Wittgenstein on Meaning*. Cambridge, MA: Harvard University Press, 2019.

Weigel, Sigrid. *Walter Benjamin: Images, the Creaturely, and the Holy*. Translated by Chadwick Truscott Smith. Stanford, CA: Stanford University Press, 2013.

Wetters, Kirk. *Demonic History: From Goethe to the Present*. Evanston, IL: Northwestern University Press, 2014.

Index

absolute, 45, 70, 123, 125, 132, 166, 241, 274, 289n11; form, 49; identity, 38, 53, 166, 282n7, 283n8, 291n6, 294n14; revelation of, 23–26, 288n11, 293n12

accumulation, 216, 221, 231, 262; of the past 207, 210–211; of similarities 163

action(s), Chapter 9 passim; and image space; and memory, 209–215, 226–227, 300n1, 301n3; and nonaction, 121, 126; and playacting, 152, 174–175, 233, 242; 177–183; in tragedy, 91–93, 94–95

actuality: higher(est) 28–29, 52, 75, 78, 133–134, 166, 174, 177, 200–201, 210, 216, 224, 284n5, 295n9; integral, 224, 295n9, 299n11

actualization: of meaning, 14, 23, 25, 29, 32, 57, 118, 140; of the past (history), 195, 197, 200, 201, 212, 215, 222–227, 298–299n11, 303–304n17; and the unactualized, 149, 203, 225

aestheticization, 82, 247, 267, 276, 306n16

affinity: and kinship, 57–58, 112, 159–160; in memory, 211, 213; as relationship, 16, 37, 47, 77, 178–180, 192, 200, 251, 287n6, 298n10, 299n12

allegory, 263–264, 268–269, 298n8, 300n3, 308n17, 309n23

ambiguity: arrest of, 44, 83, 93–94, 96, 114–115, 293n9, 293nn11–12; of fate (myth), 91–96, 98, 100, 103–108, 115, 202, 283n15, 290n3, 292n2, 292n6, 294n16; of legal violence, 123–125, 128, 130, 132–133, 138–141, 294n2; in modern life, 256, 258–260, 262, 269, 271; in reflection, 47

Apollo, 53, 127–128, 293n9

apparatus, 180–181, 228, 240–247, 270

arcades, 191–192, 198, 201–202, 204, 214, 217–218, 251–255, 271, 275

archetype: as image, 195–198; not model, 39–40, 54, 104, 285n7; true nature as, 40–43, 51–55, 104, 195, 305–306n14

assumption, 134, 136, 201; of power, 128, 133

318 *Index*

Atget, Eugene, 237–238, 305n9
attention (attentiveness), 55, 73, 168, 175–176, 196, 199, 204, 246
attunement, 38, 265, 287n5; harmony as 53, 64, 71–72, 289n12; to the world 166, 269
aura, 229, 232, 262, 267, 304n4; decay of 234, 237, 240, 278
authenticity, 68, 99, 167, 232; authentic time, 97, 188, 202, 204, 225
awakening, 182, 213, 238, 277, 299n11; and dialectical reversal, 216, 223; dream and, 180, 205, 219–221, 225, 302n12; Jugendstil as semblance of, 266–267; and memory, 208, 215–216

Balzac, Honoré de, 202, 260, 272
Baudelaire, Charles, 261, 265–266, 268–275, 277–279, 309n24
Beauty, Chapter 2 passim; as enigmatic (secret in), 42, 54, 82, 108–112, 125, 293n12; life and, 44, 108, 118, 285n9, 293n9; love and, 81–83, 101, 108, 111, 113–114, 118; modern, 271–274, 308. *See also* beautiful semblance; truth and beauty
behavior, 172, 204, 239–240, 245, 253, 305n11; habitual, 168, 209, 246, 273. *See also* mimetic behavior
being. *See* linguistic being; spiritual being; essential being
Benjamin (works): *Arcades project*, 7–8, 168, 187–188, 196, 204, 213, 221, 251, 299n13, 300n3, 306n1; "Berlin Childhood around 1900", 155, 216, 297, 300–301, 313; "The Concept of Criticism in German Romanticism", 45–54, 116, 292n3; "Epistemo-Critical Foreword", 3, 53, Chapter 4 passim, 149, 292n3, 293n8;

"Experience and Poverty", 238, 256, 264, 306n4; "Fate and Character", 5, Chapter 5 passim, 119, 124, 136, 149, 165, 203, 281n1, 292n2; "Franz Kafka, On the Tenth Anniversary of his death", 173–175, 204, 307; "Goethe's *Elective Affinities*", 4–5, 52, 74, 83, 98, Chapter 6 passim, 138, 140, 145, 198, 201, 205, 233–234, 259, 278, 283n13, 289n10, 290n18, 292n6, 295n13, 297n2, 300n8, 301n1, 306n3; "Ibizan Sequence", 165–171; "On the Image of Proust", 179, 208–212, 298n11; "On Language as Such and on the Language of Man", Chapter 1 passim, 48, 70; "On the Mimetic Faculty", 6, 145, Chapter 8 passim (151–163); "On Some Motifs in Baudelaire" 206–208,, 289n11, 300n3, 308n17, 308n22; *Origin of German Trauerspiel*, 3–4, 7, Chapter 4 passim, 93, 187–188, 191, 194, 196, 200, 269, 284n16, 290n2, 291n4, 291n1, 292nn2–3, 298n8, 300n3, 308n18; "Paris Capital of the Nineteenth Century Chapter", Chapter 13 passim; "Surrealism: The Last Snapshot of the European Intelligentsia", 175–183, 224, 225, 299n11; "The Task of the Translator", 56–64; "Two Poems of Friedrich Hölderlin", 145, 178, 283n8, 286n2, 287n6, 288n4, 289n11, 292n3, 293n13; "The Work of Art in the Age of its Technological Reproducibility", Chapter 12 passim, 257, 297n7, 299n15
Bergson, Henri, 7, 206–213, 215, 219, 224, 226, 291n9, 300–301nn1–3
Blanqui, Auguste, 251, 277
Blossfeldt, Karl, 305–306n14

body, 99, 273, 298n6; collective, 181, 182, 218, 304n5; as functional, 146–147, 149–151, 169, 181, 218, 220, 299nn14–15; and mimetic behavior, 151–154, 161, 233, 296n5; and mind 146–147, 170, 172, 301n2. *See also* corporeality

boundaries, 66, 103–104, 130, 132, 134, 175

boundlessness, 105, 132, 300n8

Breton, André, 176

capitalism, 205, 222, 235, 246, 248, 254, 266; as manifestation of nature, 222, 235; as religion, 257, 307n10

Cassirer, Ernst, 189, 281n3

catastrophe, 93, 102–103, 105, 137, 227

causality, 26, 89, 131, 164, 187, 191, 198, 295n7

chance, 93, 171–172, 198, 208, 215, 278, 308n19

chaos, 41–44, 80, 104–5, 114, 109, 285n10, 293n12

Chaplin, Charlie, 9, 166, 239, 298n6, 305n11, 306n4

character, 87–92, 98–100, 164–166, 239, 242, 298n4, 298n6; intelligible, 291n7; morality and character, 297n2–3; simplicity of, 98–100, 291n7, 292n5–6; and world 90, 100

childhood, 208, 236, 303n14; collective, 213–215, 219; memory of 208, 213, 219; play of 152, 157, 296n5; task of 221–222

choice, 30, 102, 164–165, 169, 171, 212, 268; vs. decision, 107, 138

cognition, 27–28, 33, 43, 47–48, 223, 273, 288n3. *See also* knowledge

Cohen, Hermann, 73, 290n15, 291n3

collecting, 9, 262–264, 308n15

color(s), 15, 19, 34–42, 63, 284n1, 296n5; of fantasy, 34–42, 284nn2–3, 285nn6–7, 288n12, 296n5; as primal phenomenon, 189–193

comedy, 5, 9, 87, 98–100, 166, 291n9, 305n11

commodity, 271, 274, 277; fetishism of, 256, 260, 262; identification with, 257–259, 263

communication, and language, 15–18, 59–64, 76, 113, 158; of nature 18–22, 24, 33–34; and the non-communicable, 60–61

completeness, 66, 74–75, 126, 135, 137, 283n8, 288n5

concentration: and distraction, 245–246; of fate, 93–95, 107; of form, 40, 43; of a lifetime, 212, 224, 226, 298–299n11; novella as, 106–107, 116; of relationships, 163, 178–180

concept(s), 34, 193, 211, 262, 282–283n7, 285n11, 289n11; and allegory 268–269; and ideas 52, 54, 67–69, 77–82, 288nn2–3; and judgment 28–29, 48; subsumption under, 22, 29, 68–69, 189; unity through 36–37, 284–285n5; will as causality from 164

concreteness, 29–30, 196, 224–225, 251; concretization, 52, 103, 106, 110, 112, 115, 203, 217, 225; in concreto, 8, 52

conflict(s), 24, 106, 120, 125–127, 131, 167, 282n5, 291n6

consciousness: conscious will (intention), 17, 164, 169–172, 210, 286n11, 296n6; as defense, 243–244, 270; unity of, 80, 82, 181 17, 94, 124, 181 203, 210, 216, 219, 225, 270–271, 285–286n11; nonconscious, 169, 219, 286n11, 286n1; reflecting, 46–50, 56; self-consciousness, 17, 35, 46–47, 66, 99, 172, 223; unconscious, 47, 164, 169, 181, 207, 210, 216–217, 219, 233, 243–244

320 *Index*

constellation, 65, 76–78, 156, 162, 196, 300n4, 304n17
construction(s): in art, 40–42; constructive principle, 197, 253; of history, 197, 199, 203, 226; iron construction, 176, 214, 253–254, 266; in painting, 39–41
consummation, 6, 173–174, 179, 225, 299n11
contemplation, 69, 71, 79, 180–182, 245–246, 262
content(s): a priori of, 51–52; essential, 45, 69, 74, 106, 120, 149; material, 54–56, 66–67, 74–75, 81, 101, 103, 106, 112, 116, 149, 151, 191–194, 196–201, 203–204, 217, 220, 223, 251, 253, 306n3; pure, 53–55, 116; truth, 44, 54–56, 74–76, 78, 81–82, 106, 112, 115–116, 201, 251, 292n3, 293n12
continuity, 49, 200, 202, 211, 224, 270, 301n5
contraction: in memory 212; of the past, 212, 226–227;
corporeality, 145–151; and action, 170–171, 180–182; and the collective, 218–219, 255; and mimetic faculty, 153- 156, 161
cosmos, 154, 259–260, 277; macrocosm, 150–151, 154, 218; microcosm, 150–151, 154
creation, 13–15, 151, 281nn1–2, 295n7; and conjuration 113–114; and creature, 41, 68, 155, 307n7; by the (divine) word, 14, 22, 61, 64, 76, 114; vs forming in art 41–44; reading of creation in Genesis 25–28
critique, 44–45, 103–104, 118, 203; and commentary, 52, 55–56, 82, 112 ,198, 201, 290n18; critical (moment), 51, 120, 163, 200, 204, 226–227, 286n3, 303n17; impossibility (rejection) of, 51–52, 103; as mortification (destruction) of beauty, 46, 56–57, 81–83, 111–112, 115; Romantic, 46–50, 54, 287n9
crowd, 206, 256, 258, 265, 271–273, 308n21
culture, 217, 234, 247, 256, 294n1; cultivation, 102, 109, 233, 259; economy and culture, 190–191; material, 204–205; and nature 102, 188, 190

death: fashion and 259–261; first nature and, 101, 231, 233; indistinction of life and death, 103–105, 110, 259, 308n16
decisiveness, 95, 105, 107–108, 109–110, 113–114, 138–140, 182, 226–227, 295n13, 296n14, 297n3
decline, 110, 123, 187, 308n16; of aura (beautiful semblance) 229, 239, 278; periods of, 67, 194, 200–201
destiny: of the past, 219, 225; of the people (living), 69, 288n4, 293n13; seizing, 293n13
destruction, 109, 112, 140, 220, 293n12; and construction, 74, 199–201; vs. deformation, 38; destructive critique, 81, 83, 112; divine violence and, 119, 131–134, 137–138, 295nn8–9; of old Paris, 275–276, 309n24; of unity, 57,75
detail(s), 105, 158, 197, 211, 252, 263, 272; camera accentuation of, 237, 244; and monadological presentation, 72–73, 192; in work of translation (commentary), 55, 62, 66 82, 112
dialectics. *See* dialectical image
discontinuity(ies), 260, 270, 307n13; in film, 240, 305n11; of order ideas, 51, 53, 71, 78, 289n12
dispersion, 37; allegory and, 269; collecting as struggle against, 263–

264; in contingent, 66, 75–76; of intention in translation, 59–60
dissolution: of conflict, 126–127, 167; in fantasy 37–38; in irony 49–50, 56, 287n9; by relationships, 200
distortion, 37, 97, 104, 257, 219–220, 278; of dream, 210–211, 302n12; and forgetting, 203–204; of life, 251–253; by similarity, 179, 199
distraction, 168, 244–246, 252, 258
divine. *See* divine violence
Don Quixote, 166, 174
dream: as configuration of the collective, 205, 214–221, 224, 25–253, 238, 303n14, 306n2; and everyday, 175–176, 179–180, 216–218, 302nn10–11; and memory 209–216, 301n3, 302n12. *See also* dream image

echo, 59–60, 62, 69, 130, 160, 177, 201
economy, 164, 191, 204, 248, 253–254
empirical, 43, 49, 69, 71–78, 80, 89, 187; empiricism, 3, 73, 305n14
end(s): endless, 106, 135, 146, 192, 198, 232, 239, 254–255, 267, 271, 275, 298n8; just, 120, 131, 139; legal, 121, 128, 139; natural, 120–122, 285n9. *See also* means
energy(ies), 104, 171–172, 175–176, 178, 212, 221, 247, 276, 299n16
ephemeral: colors as, 38, 189; modern beauty as, 273–274
essence(s), 25, 75, 158, 191, 194; vs. appearance 112, 191; essence-multiplicity, 68–70, 71–73, 76–77; essence-unity, 68–70, 72, 77, 288n5; essential being, 16, 18–20, 25, 27–28, 45, 82, 194–195; expression (communication) of 16, 18–22, 25, 57, 282n5; man has no, 27, 33, 148. *See also* essential content(s)

eternal recurrence (return), 141, 162, 219, 252, 260, 274, 277–279, 309n25
everyday, 210, 243, 260; dream character of, 168, 214, 216–217, 302n10; and exception 182–183; and habitual, 168, 176; illumination of 176, 179–181. *See also* ordinary
evil, 28, 30–31, 102, 137–138, 178
exercise(s), 164, 169–170, 181, 297n1, 298n9
exhibition. *See* exhibition value; world exhibitions
existence: and corporeality, 146–149; and life, 139–140; as non-categorial 42–43, 67, 80, 111, 166, 174
experience: constancy of, 90–91; lived, 55–56, 107, 199, 201, 206, 258, 270, 308n19; object of, 36–38, 147, 245; shock, 243–245, 270–271; 308n19; significant, 107, 207, 270–271
experiment, 48, 189, 215, 231, 239–240, 290n16
exposure, 101, 113, 115, 237, 240, 271, 293–294n14
expression: of character, 90, 165; of economy in culture, 191, 205; expressionless, 44, 61, 94, 113–115, 293n7, 293n11, 293n13, 297n3; of identity, 16, 21, 26, 28; inexpressible, 24, 60, 113; of nature (essential being) 14–20, 24–25, 31–33, 45, 189; of subjectivity (soul), 66, 266–267
exterior, 90, 217, 238, 256, 265–266, 271
external world, 33, 88–90, 129, 153, 208, 211, 212, 219

Fall, the, 28–32, 70, 113, 283n13
fantasy: vs. imagination, 35, 37–38, 286n13; and utopia, 254–256, 259, 306n5; 262, 269–270, 277. *See also* colors of fantasy

fashion, 259–261, 272, 274, 302n12, 303n14, 307–308nn13–14
fate, Chapter 5 passim; 100–107, 139, 141, 164, 172–173, 201, 234, 247, 252, 271, 281n1, 283n15, 290nn1–2, 291n4; and capitalism, 248, 257; and law, 95–96, 119, 124, 127–8, 130–131, 135–136, 290–291n3, 294n4; and life, 87, 92, 94, 96, 102, 136, 149, 203, 257, 281, 283, 290, 297n2; reading of, 88–89, 97, 156, 162, 307n14; and repetition, 105, 117, 162, 259; time of, 97, 162
Fichte, Johann Gottlieb, 26, 46–47, 51, 282n7, 287n7
fidelity: in love, 107, 109, 294n16; in translation, 62–64
figure, 83, 156, 177–178, 278, 287n6; of hope, 116–118; human, 34, 66, 182, 238, 241
film, 8, 181, 229–230, 232, 234, 238–247, 299n15; actor, 231, 238–242; audience in, 231, 239–241, 246; camera in, 239–240, 242–244; cinematic technology, 230–-232, 239–241, 247, 305n11; montage in, 232, 239, 305n11; performance (screen) test in, 238–241; as training ground, 241, 244–246
finite: being, 27, 147, 170, 203; finitude and mortality, 103, 105, 203; products of language, 61, 64, 114; thinking (intellect), 25, 27–28, 43, 47, 284n5
fit, 53, 59–60, 239, 264, 298n6; as harmony, 62, 71, 165–168; not achievement, 90, 147, 149, 165–168, 170, 177, 247
flâneur, 221, 251, 265–266, 271–273, 308n20

flash: of awakening, 223; consummation in a, 212, 226, 298–299n11; of similarity, 163; of wit, 180
force(s): divine, 131, 133; expressionless, 113, 293n11, 293n13, 295n8; in history, 192–193, 195, 204; in love, 108–109; mythical, 102–103, 105, 235; revolutionary, 124, 131; ruling the order of ideas, 68–79; social-technological, 236, 247–248, 304n5. *See also* violence
forgetting, 49, 170–171, 195, 300n1, 302n12; the forgotten, 171, 204, 299n11, 302n12, 307n14; oblivion and, 102, 204, 302n12, 308n14
form(s): continuum of, 49, 51, 53; deformation, 37–38, 40, 42, 44, 204, 253, 267, 300n9; formal, 40, 44, 49, 52, 121, 146–148, 150, 193, 284n5; forming (in art), 34, 40–42, 44–45, 54, 114, 285n11; forming vs. conjuration, 114–115; formless 105, 155, 209, 300n7; literary (poetic), 50, 65–66, 93, 116; order (hierarchy of), 22–23, 282n5; presentational, 49–50; 301n1. *See also* form of life
fortune, 92, 165–166, 168, 298, 171–172, 174; misfortune, 93–96, 130, 134, 136, 295n10
Fourier, Charles, 251, 253–256, 306–307nn4–6
fragment, 66; fragmentation of bodily presence, 239–240; Romantic 48, 180; of the true world, 112, 293n12; of vessel, 62
freedom: freedom in character, 99–100, 226, 291n9; freedom from nature, 233; freedom and necessity, 291n6; freedom of play, 241, 244, 287n5; freeing of language 27, 64, 71, 76,

113–114, 295n8; no freedom in choice, 102, 107, 212; radical (anarchic), 175; in translation, 62, 64, 113
Freud, Sigmund, 243, 302n12
fulfillment, 133, 165, 202; in afterlife, 117–118; of corporeality, 148–149, 151, 170; of creaturely nature, 44; of love, 109, 116,; of meaning, 23, 32, 57, 106–107; unfulfillment of life, 32, 87, 89, 212; of wish, 172–173, 278, 302n9, 302–303nn12–13; of work in criticism, 48, 51. *See also* actualization; completeness

gambling, 171–172, 182, 308n19
gaze, 40, 107, 253, 276; divine 112; historical 140, 204, 253; of medusa 274, 308–309nn23–24; of melancholy 269, 308n18; and passion, 108 ,110
gesture(s), 88, 153–155, 161, 231, 297n7, 305n11
glass, 129, 214, 253, 256, 265; architecture, 256, 265–266
God, Chapter 1 passim, 64, 95, 131, 166, 170, 237, 281n2; gods, 53, 66, 91–92, 95, 127–128, 130, 178, 290n1, 294n2; as highest actuality, 52, 80, 133, 139; opposed to myth 132
Goethe, Johann Wolfgang von, 7, 20, 42, 46, 51, 53–54, 77, Chapter 6 passim, 140, Chapter 10 passim, 222, 287n7, 292n4, 298n6, 300nn7–8, 304n4; *Farbenlehre* 72, 104, 189, 191
good: choice between good and evil, 30–31, 102; desiring the semblance of the good, 118; goods, 126, 167, 258; in naming, 26–28, 30, 43;
Grandville, Jean-Ignace-Isidore, 251, 256, 259–260, 262, 277
guilt. *See* guilt of life, mythical guilt

habit(s), 257, 265; and attention, 168; and corporeality 169, 180–181, 246; and distraction 244–246; illumination of 176, 216–217; memory and 209
happiness, 166, 221, 236, 252; vs. bliss 43, 303n15; and fortune 92, 172; humanity's dreams of, 181, 236, 252, 304n5, 287n8; risking, 107
harmony: out of chaos, 42–44, 285n10; of languages, 58, 61–62, 64; of mind and body, 169–170; pre-established, 70, 72, 78–79, 286n11; of truth contents (ideas), 53, 69–72, 76–77, 80–81, 289nn12–13
Haussmann, Georges-Eugène, 251, 275–277, 309n24
Hegel, Georg Wilhelm Friedrich, 45, 66, 73, 196, 220, 285n9
Heidegger, Martin, 283n16, 304n3
hierarchy, 22–23, 32–33, 68, 76, 87, 104, 116, 149, 282n5, 288n6
history, chapter 10 passim, chapter 11 passim; after-history, 193–195, 203, 266, 268, 300n3; fore-history, 193–195, 203, 261, 268, 300n3; historical materialism, 119, 175–176, 189, 196, 198, 199, 201, 213, 224; historical process, 121, 134, 146; as inward, 74, 194; natural, 2, 4, 7, 74, 188, 194–195; object of, 193–195, 197, 199, 200, 203, 226–227; primal history, 15, 148, 154, 188, 192, 197, 202–204, 222, 277; reification of, 226, 252, 275
Hölderlin, Friedrich, 64, 114–115, 293n13
hope, 105, 107–108, 116–118, 128, 140, 177, 260, 276–278, 293n7, 293n9, 294n16; hopeless, 117, 140, 274, 277; of immortality, 38, 105, 260, 278

Idea(s): abbreviation of world of ideas, 72–73, 192, 252; of art, 8, 47–56, 286n3; vs. concept, ,52, 67–69, 77–79, 288n3; configuration of, 73, 75–78; higher (ruling), 69, 72, 77, 81, 282n5, 289n13; ideas (essences), 53, 71, 77–78; idea-unity, 73; ideal, 34, 49, 51–55, 66–67, 73, 75, 78, 111–112, 116, 182, 195, 236, 273, 276, 286n1, 289n12, 303n16; independence of order of, 72–73, 75, 289; as regulative, 13, 52, 107. *See also* presentation of ideas

identity: a-identical, 25; of linguistic and spiritual being, 16, 20–24; non-categorial, 80, 111, 283n10; not reversible, 25; self-identical, 24–25, 42, 61, 112, 211; standpoint of absolute, 25–26, 28, 30, 36–38, 40, 42–43, 53, 61, 70, 80, 96–97, 111, 145–146, 149, 282–283nn7–10, 286n2, 286n11, 287n11, 289n9, 296n5

illumination, 100, 168, 180–182, 257; of material contents, 204, 253–254; profane, 156, 168, 176, 181–182

Image(s), 254–255, 257; cinematic (photographic), 185, 232, 237–239, 244–245; dialectical image, 10, 163, 193, 197, 199, 203, 205, 225–226, 271; dream image, 178–179, 212, 218, 251, 259, 278, 306n2, 302n12; image of the past, 204, 215, 219, 222, 224, 226–227; image space, 177–183, 298–299nn11–12; image of the world, 72, 264, 277; mirror image, 36, 42; primal image, 43, 52, 197, 305n14; wish image, 173–175, 203, 253. *See also* archetype

incorporation, 160, 192, 200–201, 244, 263; in ideas, 78, 80–81; of lower language, 22; of novella in novel 105–106; of technology, 181–182, 214, 253, 255

indifference: and higher identity of opposites, 38, 40, 89–90, 165–166, 286n1, 287n, 291n6,

indirect, 44, 57, 126, 141, 167, 169, 220

infinite, 36–37, 47, 267, 278, 283n8, 288n5; of art in Romanticism 51–53, 56; bad 267, 300n1; infinite task 107, 178; intellect 284n5, 287n7

inner: bourgeois interior, 238, 251, 256, 261–262, 264–267, 271, 273, 275; inner world, 88–90, 92–94, 99, 153, 165, 181, 239, 261, 297n9; interiority, 98, 238–239; interior of the collective, 218–219; internalized, 244, 305n14; problematization of distinction inner and outer, 88–90, 92–93, 165, 239, 261, 297n9

innervation, 171–172, 182, 213, 221, 236, 305n11, 306n5

innocence, 87, 91–92, 95, 291n10, 295n10; of character, 98, 136, 165, 292nn5–6

instrument, 31, 92, 96, 130, 136, 150–153, 164, 241, 254; instrumental, 17, 95, 182, 232

intellect, 27, 43; intellectual intuition, 43, 47, 76, 282n7, 286n13, 287n7, 289n11; intelligence, 6, 46, 164, 168–169, 182, 208; intelligible, 48–49, 73, 77, 291n7; intuitive intellect, 284n5, 287n7

intensification, 56, 110, 114, 178, 192–193, 229, 247, 286n2, 287n6, 288n5

Intensive: concentration, 47, 163; in memory, 207, 209–211; presentation, 53, 57–58, 189–192, 199; scale (hierarchy), 32–33, 149; universality 21–22

interest, 45, 161, 172, 192, 225, 234, 241, 263, 271–272

Index 325

interpenetration, 140, 182, 195, 209, 211, 243, 254, 269, 283n8, 299n15
intuition, 27, 36, 43, 46, 52, 63, 75–76, 78, 104, 133, 284n5, 296n2; intuitive, 5, 15, 37, 161, 168, 176–177, 188, 196, 265, 273. *See also* intellectual intuition; intuitive intellect
irony, 31, 47, 49–50, 56, 93, 287n9
isolation, 3, 49, 71, 191, 243, 266, 270

judgment, 98, 166, 234, 241, 245, 290n17, 297n2; colors of fantasy vs. 35–36, 38; identity not 25–26, 282n7; Last Judgment, 115, 135; and law 95–96, 138–139, 285n11; vs. naming 21, 29; reflection and 46, 48–49, 234, 245, 285n9, 286n3, 287n5; sense and 59, 63; and value 30–31
Jugendstil: dream character of 266–268, 300n3, 308n16
Jung, Carl, 203, 207
justice, 9, 80, 83, 112, 122, 126, 139, 181, 225, 265
justification, 64, 69, 88, 120, 124, 132, 294n4

Kafka, Franz, 9, 165, 167, 171, 173–174, 204, 283, 307
Kant, Immanuel, 43, 120, 220, 255, 282n7, 290n16, 291n7, 296n2, 297n2; aesthetics in, 35, 46, 234, 245–246, 285n6, 285n9, 285n11, 286n3, 287n5, 293n12; Copernican revolution, 222–223, 225; ideas in, 13, 52; ; infinite intellect in, 284n5, 287n7; teleology in, 197, 295n7; unconditioned action, 132, 138, 298n7;
Kierkegaard, Søren, 30, 296n14
Klages, Ludwig, 188, 207, 228
Klee, Paul, 238, 306n4

knowledge: beauty resisting 81–82, 111; conceptual 68, 76, 78–80; Copernican revolution of 223–224; divine (absolute), 25–28, 52, 283n7; of good and evil, 30–31, 102; intuitive, 196, 201, 221, 285n5; philological 55–56, 112

Language(s), chapter 1 passim; 58–64, 70–71, 114, 159–160, 288n5, 297n10; as such, 3–4, 14,20, 27, 32, 45, 57–64, 76, 160; higher, 22–24, 118; kinship of, 57–58, 70–71, 160; linguistic being 16–21, 23–25; of nature, 19–25, 30, 32; pure language, 4, 32, 58, 61–64, 70–71, 76, 113–114, 160, 295n8
law(s), 102, Chapter 7 passim; 189, 196, 235, 285n11; law and fate, 91, 95–96, 127–131, 290n3, 294n4; legislation, 121, 123–125, 235 294n2; mythic origin of, 31, 102, 283n14; of nature, 18–19, 78, 129, 189, 196, 290n16; positive, 120–121, 123; transgression of, 128, 130, 231, 290n3
Leibniz, Gottfried Wilhelm, 72–73, 300n6
Life: afterlife, 4, 46, 55–57, 115–116, 118, 135–137, 140, 198–201, 217, 220, 293n7, 294n14, 302n11; bare, 124, 149, 235; creaturely, 41, 44, 115; enlivening, 4, 42, 46, 56, 112, 114; form of, 2, 7, 20–21, 23, 33, 57, 65, 67, 69, 71, 73, 75, 77, 79, 81, 83, 87, 94, 119, 146, 190, 213, 218, 220, 238, 251, 255, 261, 294n16; guilt of, 31, 87, 91–92, 94, 96–98, 108, 113, 135–136, 139–140; higher, 33, 44–46, 57,74, 89, 189, 192–194, 200–201; inner, 18, 42, 44, 56–57, 61, 66, 99, 191, 195, 267; life-forms, 2, 65, 204; life-philosophy, 206–207, 289n11,

Life (*cont.*)
300n1; lifetime, 212, 298; lifeworld, 55, 74, 217; lived experience, 55–56, 107, 199, 206, 216, 258, 270, 308; lived moment, 216, 218, 302n10, 303n14; the living, 136–137, 149, 293n13, 295n10; living nature, 20, 33, 188–189; mere, 5, 42, 91, 96, 101, 113, 136, 139, 203, 295nn10–11; as vitality, 4–5, 45, 56, 65–66, 149–151, 194, 202–203, 206, 235, 260–261, 304n5

light, 50, 63–64, 106, 110, 117, 189–190, 193, 256, 287–288n11

line, 39, 88, 178, 267–268, 274; linear, 267, 276; linear perspective, 40, 276; straight, 275–276

love: and affection, 108–110, 116; and emotion, 108–110; and erotic ascent, 81–83, 101, 108–110, 116; and first nature, 232–233, 236; as passion, 104, 107–110, 113, 116;

mark(s), 39–41, 152, 265

Marx, Karl, 7, 189–191, 195, 205, 255–256, 307n5

Marxism, 195–196, 202, 205, 256

masses, 176, 206–207, 229, 241, 244–248, 256–258, 279, 307n12

mastery, 167, 259; of first nature 101, 232–233, 235–236, 247–248; through habit 180, 246; through practice 169;

material: basis, 27, 218, 223; material conditions 15, 176; object, 63, 208, 215, 262–263. *See also* material content

materialism, *See* historical materialism

matter: physical, 19, 23, 27, 190, 260–261, 264, 287n11, 301n2

meaning: meaningfulness (significance), 15, 20–21, 23, 30, 100–101, 161, 202, 218, 270; meaningless, 161; way of meaning, 59–60, 62, 160;

means: for an end, 120–121, 127–128, 131–132, 252–255; pure (without end), 120, 125–126, 164, 167, 169–170, 188, 254, 294n6, 298n7, 307n7

mechanism, 198, 231, 243, 255, 270, 273; machines, 228, 252–255

medium: artistic, 28, 33–34, 229, 242, 244; color as, 36–37, 39–41,193; language as, 14–15, 18, 20–22, 27, 61, 63–64, 76,156–158, 284n4; memory as, 208, 211–214, 216–217; of reflection, 47, 49–51, 53–54, 56, 287n5, 288n11

melancholy, 238, 262, 268–269, 273–274, 279, 284n16, 308n18

memory, 75, 118, 179, Chapter 11 passim, 262, 270, 272, 301nn2–4, 303nn14–15; involuntary memory, 7, 208–209, 215, 270, 299n11; pure, 208, 210–212; strata of, 22, 61, 114, 207–210, 212, 214, 301n4; remembrance, 75–76, 206, 208–210, 214–216, 218, 302–303

metamorphosis, in *Elective Affinities*, 103–104; Goethe's conception of, 197–199, 300n7; and historical time 198–199, 202–204; of material contents, 223, 253; eternal life and 260, 278

metaphysics, 3, 8, 13, 33, 282n7, 300n1

method: dialectical, 216, 225; Goethe's scientific, 19, 188, 190, 196, 200, 298n11, 305–306n14; of knowledge, 81–82; presentation as, 80; reflection as, 46–47, 52

mimetism: and magic, 154, 156–157, 160–161, 163; mimetic identification, 54, 145, 151–162, 230–231, 233, 239, 257–258, 261, 296n5; and ritual 152–155;

mind, 168, 172, 174, 182, 221; mindful, 168–172; mindless, 168. *See also* spirit; presence of mind
miniature, 50, 58, 107, 154, 192
mirror, 36, 42–43, 50, 72, 129, 277
modern: beauty, 273–274; modernity, 202, 206–207, 214, 222, 243, 246, 261, 269–271, 274, 277; modernization 206, 231, 259; view of fate, 87–90, 97–98
monad, 53, 58, 65, 72, 190–191, 199, 252
mourning, 32, 108, 117, 269, 284n16
multiplicity: of essences (pure contents), 53, 68, 71–73, 78, 80, 282n7, 289n12; of languages, 31–32, 70; of phenomena, 191, 196–197
music, 71, 97, 116, 169, 291n1
mystery, 176, 229, 236–237; in beauty, 42, 44, 54, 62, 80–82, 112, 293n12; of hope 116, 118
myth: in *Elective Affinities*, 101–107, 113, 117–118; mythical guilt, 31, 102, 203, 231, 238, 256- 257, 283n14, 291n1, 307n7, 309n25; mythical sacrifice, 102, 136, 231, 233, 235, 238, 247, 292, 295n10; mythology, 5, 53, 127, 178, 203, 287n6, 290n1; presence in history, 202–204, 219, 222, 252–253; and struggle with elemental nature, 233–235, 247–248, 277. . *See also* mythical violence; primal history

nakedness, 111–115, 283n13
name, 8, 21, 27–31, 69, 94, 103, 110, 145, 148, 167; nameless; 30; naming, 3, 20–21, 23, 25–35, 39–41, 69, 76, 103, 158, 259, 281n1, 282n6, 283n11, 283n15, 292n5; proper, 28–29, 91, 94, 103
natural history. *See* History
nature: creaturely, 25, 41, 44; currents of 149–150, 153, 156, 218–219, 302n12;

elemental, 101–102, 232–233, 235–236, 259; first, 232–233, 236, 247, 257, 304nn5–6; primal, 102–104, 150, 188, 190, 202, 219, 221–222, 233–235, 259; scale of, 21–23, 32; second 228, 232–233, 235–236, 304n5
nearness, 148, 179–181, 229
negation, 24, 31, 38, 48, 78, 82, 92, 114, 193, 260, 284n5
Nietzsche, Friedrich, 90, 94, 278, 285n9, 290n14, 293n9, 307n11, 309n26
night, 110, 116–118, 210, 217, 272, 279, 307n6
nothing, 24, 30, 173–174, 180, 204, 293n12, 298n8; nothingness, 42, 114
novelty (the new), 221–222, 259–260, 272–274, 307n14, 308n19, 308n21
nuances, 37–38, 62–63, 73, 198

objectification: in ideas 67, 72, 74, 76, 78–79, 282n5, 288n1, 288n3, 289n14
objective, 37, 49, 56, 80, 111, 151, 158, 162, 214, 216, 256, 269, 285n9, 285–286n11; image, 219, 224; interpretation, 72, 78
occasion: awakening as 216, 220–221; for manifestations of character, 90, 99; for the manifestation of fate, 93–94; recognizing, 165, 168, 170, 182, 278; of violence, 129–130
oneness, 36–38, 42, 77, 79, 111, 129, 150, 154
ontology, 22, 130, 303n17
opaqueness, 36, 193, 211, 265
opportunity, 168, 195, 215, 239, 246; to exhibit art 236–237; missed, 172, 227; waiting and 219–221. *See also* occasion
optical, 172, 176, 180–181, 246; unconscious, 243–244

ordering: of (contingent) phenomena, 8, 19, 23, 75, 77–78, 189–192, 196, 199–200, 251, 306n14

ordinary, 254, 263, 270, 276; film's revelation of 242–244; illumination of, 176, 302n10. *See also* everyday

organ(s), 149, 169–170, 181–182, 189, 218–219, 248; of the collective, 306n5; organic form, 40, 43, 56–57, 262; organism, 57, 65, 157, 200, 282n5

origin: concept of, 73–75, 187–189, 304n17; mythical origin of law, 31, 124; presentation of, 19, 191–194, 197–199

original: vs. translation, 56–60, 62–64, 160, 201

ornament, 264, 266, 300–301n1, 306n14, 308n16

pain: as indicator of corporeality, 147–148, 150, 161; painless 38. *See also* pleasure

painting: cave, 154–155, 229–230, 306n4; color in 34–35, 39–42, 284nn2–3, 285nn6–7 296n5; vs. photography 237

passing, 10, 21, 38, 110, 203, 218, 226, 238, 272, 274, 296n5. *See also* ephemeral

passivity, 108–109, 114, 162, 173, 219

perception: apperception, 244–246; and body (corporeality), 146–148, 296n2; empirical, 29, 35–36, 43, 243; new forms of, 180, 243, 346; perceptibility, 42–43, 191, 272, 253; utopian (higher), 42–44, 54

perfection, 34, 42–43, 50, 60, 110, 114

permeation, 31, 44, 66, 168, 182, 209, 212

perverse, 102, 121, 124–125, 128, 130, 132, 134, 141, 261, 295n9

petrification, 44, 110, 252, 279, 308–309nn23–24

phantasmagoria, 204, 253–254, 271, 277, 300n9, 306n2, 309n24; of civilization, 252, 275–276, 279; of interior, 261–262, 266

phenomena: and ideas, 67–69, 71–75, 77–78, 80–81, 289n13; primal (ur) phenomenon, 54, 77, 104–105, 156, 187–194, 196, 199–204, 221, 305n14

photography, 8, 176, 229–230, 234, 237–239, 305n14

plants, 7, 20, 87, 104, 148, 187, 189–190, 202, 268, 304n5, 306n14

Plato, 52, 66, 69, 75, 78, 80, 118; *Symposium,* 81–82, 293n3

play: of colors, 37; interplay, 228–230, 232–233, 235–236, 244–245, 293n9; mimetic behavior and, 151–152; of the mind, 46, 246, 287n5; second nature and 232–236; semblance and, 233–234, 239. *See also* playacting

pleasure: indifference of pain and 38, 43; and pain as indicators of corporeality 147–148, 150, 161

plurality, 31, 50, 52–53, 62, 66–67, 69, 73, 78–79, 189, 308n20

Poe, Edgar Allan, 265, 272–273

polarity: of cult value and exhibition value 228–229, 231, 234, 257–258; of form and chaos, 42; of good and evil, 29–30; in history 194–195, 203, 252; of judgment, 49; in nature 192–193; of pleasure and pain 147; of positive and negative, 38; of potentiality and actuality, 133; of semblance and play, 233–234; of sexuality and spirit, 150

political: and film (photography), 228–229, 235, 238, 247–248; and history, 219, 223, 225; and image space, 177–178, 181–182

potential, 25, 93, 134, 138, 172, 204, 229, 239, 254, 267
power: arrogation of, 127–135, 133–134, 137–138, 141, 295n9; creative, 27–28; expressive, 3, 192, 199; mythic, 104, 118, 222, 292; sovereign (ruling), 70, 75–76
practical, 6, 27, 47, 169, 212, 218, 263, 285–286n11, 300n1, 301n3
practice. *See* exercise
presence of mind, 168, 172, 174, 182, 221
presentation: dialectical, 193, 195, 252; of ideas, 4, 8, 54–55, 66–80, 251; intensive, 53, 57–58, 190–192, 199; presentational form, 49–50;
primal. *See* primal history; primal nature; primal image; primal phenomenon
progress, 177–178, 224, 252, 256, 276–277, 279; progression, 97, 130
prohibition, 31, 257; on killing, 138–139, 221, 295n12, 296n14
prose, 50, 106, 268–269, 287n6; prosaic, 50, 106, 287n6, 292n3
Proust, Marcel, 7, 9, 179, 208, 210–216, 219, 226, 298n11, 303n15
punishment: divine violence not, 132–133; in education, 121, 137; and fate, 91, 94, 96, 290n3; mythical violence not, 127–128, 130, 135; and threat, 123, 130
purpose, 6, 17, 57, 121, 127, 149, 164–165, 169, 171–172, 175, 179, 198, 220, 224; counterpurposive, 113–114, 201, 293n12; purposive, 3, 35, 57, 113, 132, 157, 169, 197–198, 201, 220–221, 285n9, 286n3, 287n5

radiance, 40, 43, 100, 110, 264
reaction, 88, 150, 172, 207, 212, 265, 301n3; reactivity, 150, 209–210

reading, 176, 198, 265, 273; fate, 88–89, 97, 307n14; mimetism in, 151, 155–156, 162–163; the real, 154–156, 198, 217, 220
reality: distinct from existence, 146; empirical (contingent), 69, 72–73, 75, 80, 215, 217, 224; highest, 24, 52, 75, 78, 80, 111, 133, 139; of the past, 198, 207, 215, 217, 223, 224; presentation in film, 237, 242–243, 299n15; reading the real, 154–156, 198; realism, 51, 54, 177, 306n14
realization: of (the language) of nature, 19–21, 23, 26, 305n14; of mimetic capacity, 151, 157–158, 160; in translation, 58, 61–62; unrealized life, 25–26, 87, 92–93, 96, 290n2, 291n1, 294n4, 295n11, 299n11; of the work in criticism, 48–52;
reason, 82, 100, 104, 129, 134, 169, 202, 220, 232, 286n13, 290n16, 293n12; principle of sufficient reason, 89, 147
reception, 180, 246; receptive absorption, 155, 162–163, 179, 245–246, 296n5; receptivity, 20, 22, 31, 34–37, 39–40, 153, 155–156, 162–163, 285n8, 296n5; tactile, 36, 180–181, 245–246
reconciliation, 108–109, 116–118, 140; opposed to conciliation 109, 116
reflection: vs. expression 205; in Kant and Romantic aesthetics, 45–56, 285n9, 286n3, 287n5, 288n5; impossible in film, 244–246; lacking in character, 98–99; reflective, 35, 234; vs. refraction, 51, 53, 58
relational: beauty as, 81; mind-bodily as, 146–148, 304n5; truth as nonrelational, 82
release. *See* freeing
religion, 8, 23–24, 45, 91, 176, 214, 235, 257, 278, 307n10

remains, 210, 212, 217–218, 237–238, 262

repetition, 47, 73, 103, 105, 117, 141, 168–169, 252, 259–260, 273–274, 279, 303n15

representation: idea as 68, 72, 289n13; image not, 179, 195; representative, 95, 231, 275

reproduction, 35, 59, 62–63, 175, 230, 235, 237, 253

rescue, 105, 107, 115, 118, 206, 227, 263

resemblance, 43, 54, 152, 179, 211–212, 226. *See also* similarity

resolution: of antinomy, 131, 286n11; nonviolent, 125–127, 167; of problems of second nature, 235

rest, 28, 72, 164, 170, 259; restfulness, 40; restless, 167

revelation (divine), 8, 14–15, 23–26, 33, 60, 76, 78–79, 81, 113, 132–134, 281n2, 295n8; flow of, 22, 45, 63–64, 76, 149, 160, 207, 289n9

reversal: dialectical, 107, 216, 220, 223, 240–241; mythical, 31, 102, 128

revolution, 175–176, 222–225, 276, 302n9, 306n5; revolutionize 181, 236

rhythm, 26, 50, 134–135, 163, 269, 272, 291n1, 307n14

Riegl, Alois, 67, 306m14

ritual, 229–233, 235–237, 247, 256–258, 260, 296n5, 307n10

Romanticism, 46–54, 103, 286n3, 287n9, 288n5, 302n11

Rosenzweig, Franz, 281n2

Rousseau, Jean-Jacques, 124, 294n2, 308n20

sacrifice. *See* mythical sacrifice

sadness, 32, 109–110, 125, 173, 212, 238, 283n16

Scheerbart, Paul, 255–256, 265, 304n1, 307n12

Schelling, Friedrich Wilhelm Joseph, 3, 9, 15, 26, 42–43, 53, 239, 282n7, 285–286n11, 286n13, 286n1, 287n7, 287n11, 289n9, 291n6

Schiller, Friedrich, 50, 234, 246, 291n8, 291n10

Schlegel, Friedrich, 48–50, 285n10

Schopenhauer, Arthur, 129, 147, 161, 252, 282n5, 288n1, 288n3, 289–290n14, 296n6

science, 19, 72, 78, 191, 195–196, 206–207, 277

secret. *See* mystery

semblance: in beauty, 42, 44, 80, 108–118, 239, 292n6; critique of 54–55, 81, 83, 112; life and 205; mere semblance, 5, 112, 114–115; and play, 233–234

sense, 31, 76; common (good) sense, 300–301nn1–3; of the corporeal, 147–151, 153, 155–157, 161–162, 296n2, 296n6; nonsense, 30, 58; as obstacle, 63, 114, 295n8; sensoria, 157, 219; translation not reproducing, 58–59, 61–64

sensuous, 35, 43, 46, 66, 147, 158–159, 284n5

sexuality, 5, 8, 98, 150, 283n13

shame, 109, 113–114, 283n13; shamelessness, 114

shock, 110–111, 243–245, 270–271, 293n9, 293n11, 308n19

sign, 156, 172, 204, 292n6, 297n11, 302n12, 308n17; of fate, 89, 97, 102, 104–105, 259, 273, 291n1; vs. mark, 39, 265; and symbol, 27, 160–162

significance, 55, 105, 148, 197, 213, 243, 251, 253–254, 296n3, 296n5, 303n14; being in, 28, 30, 161–162; experience of, 154, 167–168, 270; expression of 30, 57, 194, 197, 201, 289n12; in film

238–241; loss of, 30, 161, 258, 263–264, 269–270, 308nn18–19; opening (recognition) of, 21, 30, 44, 152, 156, 161, 230; of world, 19–21

similarity, 37, 103, 189, 193, 197, 306n14; as analogy, 70, 159–160, 177–178, 182, 200, 301n6, 298n10, 306n5; in dream 179, 211, 252; in memory, 209, 211; nonsensuous similarities, 151, 157–160, 162–163; production of 145, 151–154, 233; in translation, 22, 62, 70, 297n10

Simmel, Georg, 188, 288n1, 290n14

simplicity, 77, 98–100, 166, 256, 227, 291nn8–9, 292n5; simplification, 100, 227, 292n5

sin, 30, 91–92, 94–95, 131, 283n13

sleep, 168, 170, 174, 210, 216–217, 222, 266

society, 96, 138, 205, 253–254, 271, 298n6, 304n6; order (organization) of, 91, 124, 214, 222, 228, 235, 245, 255; social apparatus, 181, 241, 246–247; social contract, 124; social forces, 236, 248, 304n5; social practices, 218; transformation of, 177–178, 248, 276

Socrates, 81–82, 300n3

solitude, 252, 266; before God 109, 113, 139–140, 295–296n14

space, 36, 129, 207, 209, 284n5, 288n3, 296n2; pictorial, 40; spatialization, 224, 275. *See also* image space

speculative, 9, 67, 73, 282n7

speed, 163, 174, 247, 255, 272, 307n7

spell, 105, 109, 162; spellbound, 44, 108, 115

Spengler, Oswald, 188, 200

Spinoza, Baruch, 13, 43, 51, 284n5

spirit: and body (corporeality), 66, 145–148, 150, 182, 305n11; character as spiritual, 98, 292n6; spiritual being, 16–18, 20–21, 23–25, 27; spiritual character of color, 35–37, 40

spontaneity, 20, 22, 35, 60, 78–79, 82

standard, 51–53, 104, 139, 197, 200

stars, 100, 256; in astrology, 156, 162–163; in constellation, 71, 77; and image of hope, 116–118, 277–279, 293n7

strike, 132, 308n19; proletarian general strike, 121–123, 126–127, 294n6

struggle, 99, 222, 255, 272, 291n6, 295n14; to act decisively 108, 138; against dispersion, 263–264; in love, 108–109; with myth, 101, 103, 105, 118, 128, 131, 202, 204, 232–233, 293n7; for the presentation of ideas 72–73

style, 177, 254, 266–268, 306n14

subject: independence of ideas from 78–79; in reflection, 46–48, 51, 55, 285n9, 287n5; subject of cognition, 223, 283n7, 286n11

subjectivity, 79, 196, 244, 256, 258; arrogance of, 298n8; and inwardness, 29, 234, 238, 256, 261, 266; dream configuration not subjective, 217, 219, 225; melancholy not subjective, 268–269; subjective form, 46; virtues, 126, 167

sublime, 94, 99, 111, 113, 115, 293n9, 293nn11–12, 306n16;

substance, 13; category of 25–26, 36–37; corporeal 113, 145–151, 153–155, 158, 161, 170; thinking and extensive 301n2

success, 90, 149, 165–168, 171–172, 239, 298n5; indifference to success or failure, 96, 99, 165–166, 173, 177, 276, 292n5

symbol, 155, 162, 203, 228, 268–269, 276; symbolization, 61

332 Index

synthesis: conceptual 22, 26, 35–36, 79–80, 223; higher, 101, 108, 148, 196–197; non-synthesis, 282n7

system, 80, 236, 247, 267; of classification (concepts) 26, 68, 196; legal, 120–123, 126, 128, 130, 135; of signs 97, 161, 189, 196; systematic relations, 43, 47–48, 52, 79; systematic unity, 262, 286n3

technology, 175, 206; first technology, 230–233, 235–236; immature 214, 222; incorporation of 181–182, 255–256, 266, 268; and nature, 181, 222, 228–229; photographic (cinematic) 240–247, 299n15, 305n14; second technology, 230–233, 235–237, 241, 304nn5–6; and war 247–248, 304n1

teleology, 194, 197, 295n7; cracking open of natural, 255, 299n13, 306–307n5; of the dream, 216, 219–220, 225–226; external, 189

time: of hope, 260, 293n9; nowtime (the Now), 14, 134, 195, 215–217, 219, 224–227; temporality of mythic violence, 134–135; temporal order, 97, 162–163, 194; time-differential, 198; timeless, 90; timing, 170–171

trace, 171, 203, 217, 237; interior and 264–265; of violence 133

tradition, 92, 98, 178; in experience, 207, 214, 230, 267, 270

tragedy, 49, 135, 233, 288n6, 293n13; and the caesura, 114; as expressing contradictions, 94–95; fate in, 87, 93–98, 128; hero(ine) of, 93–96 108, 111, 114, 118, 128, 283n15; necessity and freedom in, 291n5–6; nontragic, 292n7; silence of tragic hero, 94–95; trauerspiel and, 93, 291n4, 300n3

transcendental, 46, 282n7, 285n11, 287n5; transcendent, 107; transcending, 41, 136, 182;

transience, 38, 42, 110, 158, 189

transition, 115, 215, 294n3; in color, 37–38; emotion as, 110–111; places of 254–255, 266

translation, 56–64, 70–71, 113–114, 287n9, 293n11, 297n10, 300n6; and non-sensuous similarity 160; and ontology, 22–23, 30–33, 283n9; as supplementation, 58, 62, 201

transparency, 36, 39, 63–64, 190, 265, 287–288n11

truth: not a correlate of thinking (intention), 26, 32, 75, 77; musical character of truth, 64, 71, 76, 97, 294n15; true language, 60–61, 70; true world, 293n12; truth and beauty, 44, 80–83, 101, 111–115, 234; truthfulness, 40, 80, 108, 111, 234; unquestionable (unapproachable), 79–80, 82, 111–112, 129

type(s), 166, 172, 198, 209–210, 221, 298n10; beauty of, 271–273, 308n16, 308n20; character and, 99; flâneur as observer of, 265, 272–273; modern 251, 271–272; photography (film) and, 242, 305n14

unconditioned, 124, 132–134, 303n16

universality, 21–22, 67, 81, 96, 138–139, 150, 191, 224, 257–258, 267; universal history, 252, 300n6; universe and commodity, 259, 262, 275, 277

use: everyday, 260, 263, 269; of force (violence), 121–122, 128; of human beings, 230–231; of nature, 232; of technology, 231–232, 241, 246–248, 255, 304n17. *See also* use value utopia, 203, 236, 252–255, 304n1, 304n6, 306n5

value: cult, 155, 228–230, 232, 234, 236, 238, 247, 257–258, 286n12; exchange value, 256–258, 263; exhibition value, 228–229, 234, 236, 239, 257, 286n12; knowledge and, 28, 30–31; use value, 256–258; value-neutral, 30
veil, 83, 110, 112, 115, 221, 272, 278, 294n14, 308n21; veil-less, 113
violence, 231, 238, 275, 308n21; divine violence, 119, 131–138, 140, 201, 289n10, 294–295nn6–7, 295n10; immediate, 127–132; law-positing violence, 122–30, 140–141, 294n2; law-preserving violence, 124–125, 127, 130, 140–141; monopoly of violence, 121–125, 128, 130; mythic violence, 31, 97, 101–107, 116, 119, 124, 127–136, 141, 167, 178, 202–204, 219, 222, 233, 235, 238, 247–248, 277, 292n2, 294n4, 295n10; nonviolent, 120, 125–127, 167, 294n6; pure violence, 130–131, 133–134, 136–137, 295n10; spectral character of law preserving, 125, 140–141; threat of, 123, 130, 132–134, 140

vision, 243, 277, 279, 295n12; image not object of 75–76; invisible, 43, 54–55, 100, 273; and passion, 108–109; pure vision, 35–37, 39, 40, 296n5; visibility, 30, 54–55, 63, 89–90, 92–93, 95–96, 100, 153; visual, 34, 36, 162, 245

waiting, 59, 170, 176, 219–221, 278,
wakefulness, 168, 211; awakening, 182, 205, 210, 215–216, 218- 225
wish, 116, 172–174, 180–181, 203, 253, 278, 302n9, 302–303nn12–13
Wittgenstein, Ludwig, 9, 29, 282n4, 283n12
work, 54, 112, 121, 169, 231, 234, 240, 257–258, 261; and division of labor, 232, 240; workers 121–122, 127, 256
world: being in the world, 32, 69, 90–92, 154, 161, 239, 284n16; fit with the world 90, 165–166 168,177; world exhibitions, 9, 251, 256–259, 263, 275, 307n9; world-soul, 154, 256, 258; worldview, 5, 88, 90, 97, 204, 302n12, 307n14; world-will, 154, 252, 288n1, 288n3, 296n6

youth, 113, 213–214, 267–268, 308n16

Cultural Memory in the Present

Helmut Puff, *The Antechamber: Toward a History of Waiting*
Raúl E. Zegarra, *A Revolutionary Faith: Liberation Theology
    Between Public Religion and Public Reason*
David Simpson, *Engaging Violence: Civility and the Reach of Literature*
Michael Steinberg, *The Afterlife of Moses: Exile, Democracy, Renewal*
Alain Badiou, *Badiou by Badiou*, translated by Bruno Bosteels
Eric Song, *Love against Substitution: Seventeenth-Century
    English Literature and the Meaning of Marriage*
Niklaus Largier, *Figures of Possibility: Aesthetic Experience,
    Mysticism, and the Play of the Senses*
Mihaela Mihai, *Political Memory and the Aesthetics of Care:
    The Art of Complicity and Resistance*
Ethan Kleinberg, *Emmanuel Levinas's Talmudic Turn: Philosophy and Jewish Thought*
Willemien Otten, *Thinking Nature and the Nature of Thinking: From Eriugena to Emerson*
Michael Rothberg, *The Implicated Subject: Beyond Victims and Perpetrators*
Hans Ruin, *Being with the Dead: Burial, Ancestral Politics,
    and the Roots of Historical Consciousness*
Eric Oberle, *Theodor Adorno and the Century of Negative Identity*
David Marriott, *Whither Fanon? Studies in the Blackness of Being*
Reinhart Koselleck, *Sediments of Time: On Possible Histories*, translated
    and edited by Sean Franzel and Stefan-Ludwig Hoffmann
Devin Singh, *Divine Currency: The Theological Power of Money in the West*
Stefanos Geroulanos, *Transparency in Postwar France: A Critical History of the Present*
Sari Nusseibeh, *The Story of Reason in Islam*
Olivia C. Harrison, *Transcolonial Maghreb: Imagining
    Palestine in the Era of Decolonialization*
Barbara Vinken, *Flaubert Postsecular: Modernity Crossed Out*
Aishwary Kumar, *Radical Equality: Ambedkar, Gandhi, and the Problem of Democracy*
Simona Forti, *New Demons: Rethinking Power and Evil Today*
Joseph Vogl, *The Specter of Capital*
Hans Joas, *Faith as an Option*
Michael Gubser, *The Far Reaches: Ethics, Phenomenology, and the Call
    for Social Renewal in Twentieth-Century Central Europe*
Françoise Davoine, *Mother Folly: A Tale*
Knox Peden, *Spinoza Contra Phenomenology: French Rationalism from Cavaillès to Deleuze*
Elizabeth A. Pritchard, *Locke's Political Theology: Public Religion and Sacred Rights*

Ankhi Mukherjee, *What Is a Classic? Postcolonial Rewriting and Invention of the Canon*
Jean-Pierre Dupuy, *The Mark of the Sacred*
Henri Atlan, *Fraud: The World of Ona'ah*
Niklas Luhmann, *Theory of Society, Volume 2*
Ilit Ferber, *Philosophy and Melancholy: Benjamin's Early
    Reflections on Theater and Language*
Alexandre Lefebvre, *Human Rights as a Way of Life: On Bergson's Political Philosophy*
Theodore W. Jennings, Jr., *Outlaw Justice: The Messianic Politics of Paul*
Alexander Etkind, *Warped Mourning: Stories of the Undead in the Land of the Unburied*
Denis Guénoun, *About Europe: Philosophical Hypotheses*
Maria Boletsi, *Barbarism and Its Discontents*
Sigrid Weigel, *Walter Benjamin: Images, the Creaturely, and the Holy*
Roberto Esposito, *Living Thought: The Origins and Actuality of Italian Philosophy*
Henri Atlan, *The Sparks of Randomness, Volume 2: The Atheism of Scripture*
Rüdiger Campe, *The Game of Probability: Literature and Calculation from Pascal to Kleist*
Niklas Luhmann, *A Systems Theory of Religion*
Jean-Luc Marion, *In the Self's Place: The Approach of Saint Augustine*
Rodolphe Gasché, *Georges Bataille: Phenomenology and Phantasmatology*
Niklas Luhmann, *Theory of Society, Volume 1*
Alessia Ricciardi, *After La Dolce Vita: A Cultural Prehistory of Berlusconi's Italy*
Daniel Innerarity, *The Future and Its Enemies: In Defense of Political Hope*
Patricia Pisters, *The Neuro-Image: A Deleuzian Film-Philosophy of Digital Screen Culture*
François-David Sebbah, *Testing the Limit: Derrida, Henry,
    Levinas, and the Phenomenological Tradition*
Erik Peterson, *Theological Tractates*, edited by Michael J. Hollerich
Feisal G. Mohamed, *Milton and the Post-Secular Present: Ethics, Politics, Terrorism*
Pierre Hadot, *The Present Alone Is Our Happiness, Second Edition:
    Conversations with Jeannie Carlier and Arnold I. Davidson*
Yasco Horsman, *Theaters of Justice: Judging, Staging, and
    Working Through in Arendt, Brecht, and Delbo*
Jacques Derrida, *Parages*, edited by John P. Leavey
Henri Atlan, *The Sparks of Randomness, Volume 1: Spermatic Knowledge*
Rebecca Comay, *Mourning Sickness: Hegel and the French Revolution*
Djelal Kadir, *Memos from the Besieged City: Lifelines for Cultural Sustainability*
Stanley Cavell, *Little Did I Know: Excerpts from Memory*
Jeffrey Mehlman, *Adventures in the French Trade: Fragments Toward a Life*
Jacob Rogozinski, *The Ego and the Flesh: An Introduction to Egoanalysis*
Marcel Hénaff, *The Price of Truth: Gift, Money, and Philosophy*

*For a complete listing of titles in this series, visit the
Stanford University Press website, www.sup.org.*

The authorized representative in the EU for product safety and compliance is:
Mare Nostrum Group
B.V Doelen 72
4831 GR Breda
The Netherlands

www.ingramcontent.com/pod-product-compliance
Lightning Source LLC
Chambersburg PA
CBHW031754220426
43662CB00007B/402